Planning Under Pressure

DEDICATION

to MARI (Friend) and JUDITH (Hickling)

whose tolerance, inspiration and support have been so important to us over all the years while we have been working on successive editions of this book.

They too have had to plan under pressure in managing the work/life balances of their own creative careers, and in meeting the ever-changing demands of our growing families while we have so often been absent or preoccupied.

John Friend
Allen Hickling

Planning Under Pressure
The Strategic Choice Approach

Third edition

John Friend
Sheffield, UK

Allen Hickling
Warwickshire, UK

Plus a new chapter containing invited contributions
from 21 users

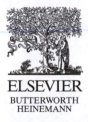

ELSEVIER
BUTTERWORTH
HEINEMANN

AMSTERDAM • BOSTON • HEIDELBERG • LONDON • NEW YORK • OXFORD
PARIS • SAN DIEGO • SAN FRANCISCO • SINGAPORE • SYDNEY • TOKYO

Elsevier Butterworth-Heinemann
Linacre House, Jordan Hill, Oxford OX2 8DP
30 Corporate Drive, Burlington, MA 01803

First published 1987
Second edition 1997
Third edition 2005

British Library Cataloguing in Publication Data
A catalogue record for this book is available from the British Library

Library of Congress Cataloguing in Publication Data
A catalogue record for this book is available from the Library of Congress

ISBN   0 7506 63731

For information on all Elsevier Butterworth-Heinemann publications
visit our website at http://books.elsevier.com

Typeset by Integra Software Services Pvt. Ltd, Pondicherry, India
www.integra-india.com
Printed and bound in Great Britain

Working together to grow
libraries in developing countries

www.elsevier.com | www.bookaid.org | www.sabre.org

ELSEVIER   BOOK AID International   Sabre Foundation

Contents

List of Contributors to Chapter 13

Authors' preface to the third edition

In 1996, when we drafted our authors' preface to the second edition of this book, we would have been very surprised by any suggestion that we might find ourselves again invited to come together to produce a third edition in the early years of the twenty-first century.

We are, of course, delighted that interest in the strategic choice approach and its applications has continued to grow, spreading to new parts of the world and new generations as fresh areas of application continue to emerge. So we welcome the opportunity to add some new content, and to review the way in which we had presented our concepts and methods in earlier editions. Both of us have now passed normal retiring age, and have started to limit our commitments accordingly. So the question arose: were we ourselves necessarily the ones who should be writing about these new developments? Or should we now invite others to join us in presenting the learning points arising from their recent experiences, and speculating about what further developments the next few decades will bring?

CONTRIBUTIONS FROM OTHERS

Finally we agreed to invite several of our more recent associates, and also some whom we have known for many years, to make short contributions to a new chapter, entitled *Learning from Others*. Fifteen contributions in all are brought together in our new Chapter 13. They present the views of twenty-one authors and co-authors, about half of them from our own country and half from other parts of the world. Among the key points that come through are the following:

- It is both possible and worthwhile to be **inventive** in combining the methods presented in this book with complementary methods of interactive working from other toolboxes – and to reflect deeply on the outcomes so that lessons from these experiences can be widely shared;
- The guidelines to the management of extensive projects offered in Chapter 11 offer new and practical solutions to the development of agreed positions in important fields of national and indeed trans-national **policy**. This has been demonstrated not least in the important and complex domain of environmental policy, which different stakeholders tend to approach from opposing and sometimes deeply entrenched positions;
- In parallel, the potential has now been widely demonstrated for introducing the principles and methods of the Strategic Choice Approach quickly and informally into more informal and **localised arenas** of decision-making such as community development, urban regeneration and rural capacity-building, where manifold external policy influences can impinge in intricate and unpredictable ways;
- It is a matter for celebration rather than concern that several people who have found the Strategic Choice Approach helpful in their own worlds of decision-making have introduced **interpretations and transformations** of their own, to increase its acceptability in the various decision-making cultures in which they work.

OTHER CHANGES

To pave the way for the new multi-authored Chapter 13, we have made some adaptations to the coverage of the two newer Chapters 10 and 11 that we added in our second edition. Chapter 10 reflects the experiences of John Friend in developing software to support strategic choice since the first edition appeared, while Chapter 11 reflects Allen Hickling's experiences in adapting the approach to the management of extensive projects. Also, we have inserted a linking chapter – Chapter 12 – in which we take stock of the variety of changes in presentation and terminology that have been introduced by other people – and sometimes by ourselves. Each chapter from 11 onwards begins with a synopsis in bold typeface, to highlight its contribution to this edition.

After the introduction of the twenty-one new voices in Chapter 13, we return in our closing Chapter 14 to look afresh at the developmental challenge that was posed in the final chapter of our second edition – recognising that the world around us continues to change in ways to which we and our successors must learn to fashion responses in practical yet creative ways.

In general, the additions in this new edition have been more concerned with developments in practice than in theory. Co-incidentally, however, the international journal *Planning Theory* is publishing a special issue (Volume 3, No. 3, November 2004; Mandelbaum, ed.) just as our new edition appears, in which four sets of invited contributors from Europe and North America present appreciations of the contributions of our work to the development of planning theory. All these papers emphasise our uniquely close link with planning practice, and the issue ends with an invited response from John Friend.

A COMPANION WEBSITE

Advances in technology, since our second edition appeared, now offer a new solution to the familiar challenge of keeping the content of any book such as this one up to date. The companion website that our publishers have made available for *Planning under Pressure* has been designed not only for use by students, but also as a forum in which a broader dialogue with users, researchers and consultants can be allowed to develop in a flexible, spontaneous and sustainable way. We shall have to see how this new channel develops; all we can do now is to do our best to give it a flying start. The web reference is **http://books.elsevier.com/companions/0750663731**.

A NEW FOREWORD

We could think of nobody more appropriate to invite to write a short foreword for this third edition than Arnold de Jong, our long-standing Dutch associate who has worked alongside us on many assignments in Europe and who, through his extensive facilitation practice, has demonstrated repeatedly how the skills and methods presented in this book can generate additional confidence and wider support for important development decisions at local, regional, national and international levels. Our hope is that his example will be followed by many talented and inventive younger people as our new twenty-first century unfolds.

John Friend
Allen Hickling
April 2004

Foreword to the third edition

Throughout my 45-year working life, which spanned successive careers as an agricultural engineer, a corporate information manager, a senior local politician and a decision process consultant, I have had an ever-increasing concern for interactive participation processes. In spite of widespread criticism that they are not effective, it has always been my belief – backed by my experience – that, skilfully managed and facilitated, the opposite is true.

Over my last two decades as a consultant, facilitator and trainer, Strategic Choice has played a central and indeed a guiding role. So I can confirm from long experience that not only does it offer a fresh and relevant approach to complex management and planning tasks in theory; it also delivers in practice. It does so at many levels from that of enhancing democratic action in local communities to that of consensual policy development in the European Union. It has no parallel in building agreement between seemingly opposed stakeholder groups across national and disciplinary frontiers, and across those between the government, business and voluntary sectors. In the mid-1970s, I was becoming drawn into the intricacies of local politics from my position as Alderman of the municipality of Arnhem in The Netherlands, with the portfolio of Town Planning and Urban Renewal. Issues of participation and democratic process in planning were then coming strongly to the fore, and we were looking for new ideas to help us turn them into reality. In 1976, I led a visiting team from Arnhem on a visit to the offices of the Institute for Operational Research in Coventry, having heard of their innovatory approach and the influence it was starting to have on public planning in the UK.

This first meeting with John Friend and his colleagues of the 'IOR School' was to mark a turning point in my professional career. Then, from 1980, through the 1980s and 1990s, I had the privilege of working closely with Allen Hickling. We became immersed, jointly and separately, in a succession of demanding projects to tackle daunting issues of environmental, economic and social policy, in each case working interactively with as many of the stakeholders as possible. Evidence of what has now been achieved will be found scattered throughout the pages of this book. In particular it will be found in the new Chapter 13 which brings together contributions from people in many countries who have recently been extending the frontiers of Strategic Choice in new and promising directions. From my twenty-first century retirement home in Athens, I look back on more than two decades in which the philosophy and methods of the Strategic Choice approach have provided the central thread of my consulting career, helping to turn the ideals of democratic planning into reality.

Planning under Pressure is not a theoretical study. From my 20 years working as a facilitator using the concepts of strategic choice, I can witness to the practical value of this book. The fact that it now appears in a third edition, with many new contributions, holds much promise for the decades ahead.

Arnold de Jong
Decision Process Consultant and Facilitator
April 2004

Authors' preface to the second edition

NEW DIRECTIONS

Our original intention had been to keep our preface to this new edition short. For the first edition included an invited foreword and a lengthy preface, both of which we wished to retain; and, in the reader's interest, we wished to avoid a surfeit of introductory material. Yet, once we came to draft the additional chapters for this edition, we recognised that there were many things we wished to say which fitted better here in a new preface than in the body of the book.

Over the decade since our first edition went to press, both of us have been developing the ideas presented in *Planning under Pressure* in new directions, while continuing to work as independent consultants with different clienteles. So, inevitably, there have been divergences in the directions in which the two of us have been moving. Yet, whenever we meet to compare experiences, we discover intriguing opportunities for synthesis and it is these that have guided us in drafting the additional chapters for this edition.

In brief, we have agreed that we need make only minor changes in the first nine chapters. However, it was clear to us that the final Chapter 10 of our first edition, concerned with horizons for future development as we saw them in the mid-1980s, had now become quite out of date. What we have therefore done is to replace that chapter by three new chapters which, taken together, reflect our experiences over the last decade, and the consequent shifts in our view of opportunities for future development.

The new Chapter 10 – The electronic resource – discusses what we have learnt from our recent experiences in developing computer software for strategic choice, and in introducing this as an additional resource both for decision-makers and for teachers and students of management and planning.

Then the new Chapter 11 – Extensions in process management – reviews a complementary set of experiences in adapting the participatory style of planning discussed in Chapter 9 to ever more demanding challenges; challenges in which the groups involved have tended to become larger and more diverse, in terms of both their cultural backgrounds and the interests which they represent. Here, the concern has been to develop practical ways of helping people to work creatively with each other, as much as with the complexities of the issues that they face.

In the new Chapter 12 – The developmental challenge – we stand back and review the wider implications of these two directions of development – one leading towards smaller-scale explorations using more tightly structured problem-centred methods, the other towards larger-scale interactions using more loosely structured people-focused methods. How widely, we ask, should the boundaries of the strategic choice approach, as presented in this book, now be drawn? And how does our approach relate to other recent developments in decision support and participatory planning throughout the world?

OUR CONTRASTING EXPERIENCES

Chapter 10 is based largely on the experiences of John Friend over the last decade, while Chapter 11 is based largely on those of Allen Hickling. It does not seem appropriate for us to dwell on issues of historical development in those two chapters themselves, so it is important that we should say at least a little here in this preface about the principal influences at work.

For John Friend, the development of computer software for strategic choice has been a major programmatic concern since this was identified as a priority in the final chapter of our first edition. Meanwhile, he has continued to be involved – more intermittently than Allen Hickling – in various facilitation and consultancy projects in which the computer has played little or no role. The decision to start developing software for strategic choice was triggered in 1987 when John Friend found that he shared this interest with his former Tavistock colleague John Stringer, then living not far away, and they worked together on this in the early stages. The development work has subsequently been sustained through close collaboration between John Friend and his son Dave, working for him in a software development role.

Originally, the software – which has been named Strategic Adviser, or STRAD for short – was seen as primarily a means of making the philosophy of the strategic choice approach more accessible to individuals and to small informal meetings, where the organisational arrangements involved in setting up a workshop with expert facilitation cannot readily be justified. However, the software development project has also turned out to have wider implications for the development of the strategic choice approach.

On the one hand, it has led to some significant extensions and refinements of the specific problem structuring methods introduced in this book; on the other hand, it has helped to spread awareness of the strategic choice approach within other domains of policy in which we ourselves had had little direct facilitation experience at the time when our first edition appeared – not least, within the domains of industry and commerce, as opposed to the world of public policy.

While Allen Hickling's work as a facilitator has also taken him into a diverse range of contexts, the main thrust of his work has been the development and co-ordination of major programmes of work in important fields of environmental policy, in local, national and – increasingly – international settings. These programmes had their roots in his earlier work in facilitating policy-making in the Netherlands in such areas as management of toxic wastes, estuarial pollution and transport and storage of hazardous petrochemical feedstocks – work which is reflected in several of the illustrations from practice that appear in Chapters 5, 6, 7 and 8.

Since the publication of our first edition, this programmatic interest has led him first into process management roles in the shaping of the first National Environmental Policy Plan for the Netherlands, then into an ambitious programme of projects in which representatives of government, industry and community interests from different nations of the European Union have come together to harmonise their policies for various types of environmentally sensitive waste. These experiences have in turn led to work with a similar orientation in the Baltic states and other eastern European countries.

Meanwhile, in Britain, a developing relationship with the Environment Council – a national organisation concerned with promotion of environmental awareness and co-operation – has drawn Hickling into facilitation and mediation roles in the management of more acute issues of environmental conflict resolution, in which the stakeholders often set out from deeply opposed positions. In the process, he has worked alongside other consultants with expertise in such fields as negotiation, mediation and consensus-building.

EXPANDING NETWORKS

Over the last decade, the range of people who have become exposed to the principles and methods of the strategic choice approach has been expanding in several directions. This has come about not only through direct collaboration with one or other of us in project work but also through publications – and significantly through the publication of the first edition of this book. We find it particularly encouraging when we come across consultants, planners, managers and academics with whom we, as authors, have had little or no personal contact, yet who have developed enough interest in the methods, and enough confidence in their ability to use them, to start applying them to situations in their own contexts without any reference to ourselves. The result is that, in our extended Guide to further reading,[1] we are able to point to a number of published applications of strategic choice methods by other people working in such varied fields as third world development, local community action and information systems strategy in commercial enterprises.

Although some of their accounts are tantalisingly brief, others are more extensive. Taken together, they indicate not only that strategic choice methods have now been successfully used in a growing range of contexts – but also, significantly, that many users have sought to explore the scope for combining them with other approaches to participatory planning or problem structuring that have already demonstrated their value in their respective fields.

In discussing this trend towards synthesis with the work of others, our new concluding chapter speculates about the potential for recognising a new generic field of developmental decision science, differing in its orientation from the broad field of systems science with its various schools – but potentially of comparable significance for coping with complexity in human affairs. This leads to a review of future prospects and opportunities in terms of eight interlocking themes – research, methodology, facilitation, communication, technology, sponsorship, application and education. Among the opportunities we review here is that of developing computer software for use in what is sometimes called a 'groupware environment' – with use of the fast-expanding capabilities of the Internet to overcome constraints of space and time. Although much of the initial momentum here has so far been technology-driven, the scope is now becoming clear for introducing a more process-oriented approach.

Our concluding review leads us – as in the concluding section of our first edition – to the educational challenge, now seen as part of a broader developmental challenge. How can learning of the type presented in our book be made as accessible as possible to new generations of decision-makers, so that they can build on it in their own ways? Here, both of us can draw on recent training experiences of our own – in the case of Hickling, in running facilitation courses for the Environment Council and other clients, and in the case of Friend in contributing to courses in the management of sustainable development, in his capacity as honorary professor with the Centre for Development Planning Studies at the University of Sheffield.

We both recognise the scale of the longer-term challenge for facilitation skills are not easy to develop in students whose life experience is so far limited; yet academic staff will only be able to help develop such skills to the extent that they can draw upon a reservoir of first-hand facilitation experience in their own cultural context. We are aware of scattered successes in meeting this kind of challenge in many parts of the world. One of our wider aspirations is to help in building a broader cross-cultural momentum in this direction – not only through this book but also through an intensifying web of collaborative projects covering research, development and exchange of experiences on a global scale.

---

1 Now transferred to the companion *Planning under Pressure* website.

The authors' preface to our first edition – reprinted here – contains a long list of acknowledgements to people from whom we had drawn inspiration at that time. We could now extend that list considerably. However, we shall refrain from doing so here, because many of the newer names will be found in our revised Guide to further reading or in our expanded section on Points of contact.[2]

If the last 10 years provide any guide, we can look forward to a continuing expansion and diversification of these global networks, through electronic and other channels, into the start of the new millennium and well beyond.

John Friend
Allen Hickling
1996

---

2 Both now on the companion *Planning under Pressure* website.

Authors' preface to the first edition

HISTORICAL PERSPECTIVE

Twelve years have passed between the conception and completion of this book. For a book concerned with *Planning under Pressure*, that may seem a surprisingly long time. But the 12 years of gestation have seen much in the way of development both in the practice and the theory of the general approach to planning about which we write. Over this period, we have found ourselves collaborating with users in many kinds of organisations, public and private, throughout the world. So several thousands of managers, planners and policy-makers have now become exposed to the strategic choice approach; and there are hundreds of these who have played a part alongside us in its development. There have been many interim publications too; some of them reporting on particular research and application projects, others emanating from training programmes designed to introduce the essentials of the approach to prospective users in particular countries.

The origins of the approach – and of this book – are to be found in the work of IOR – the Institute for Operational Research. IOR was formed in 1963, as a unit of the Tavistock Institute of Human Relations in London, as the result of a joint initiative on the part of the Councils of the Tavistock Institute and the national Operational Research Society. Its dual aims were to extend the realm of application of operational research towards broader policy issues, and to build stronger links between OR and the social sciences. These are aims that have remained to the fore through many subsequent organisational changes, with the impetus now being maintained through an extensive network of individuals and groups in several parts of the world.

The first book on the strategic choice approach was published in 1969 (Friend and Jessop, 1969/77), followed tragically soon by the death of its co-author Neil Jessop, the first director of IOR. The first experimental applications of the approach to practical planning problems were conducted in 1970, in collaboration with six teams of British local government officers; and the first training courses for managers were launched in 1971 at a Coventry hotel. Many other colleagues from the IOR Coventry and London offices had become involved in these early experiences. Then, in 1973 we were also joined in Coventry by Ray Bunker – the contributor of our foreword – who was revisiting the county of his birth on sabbatical leave from the University of Sydney in Australia. As a professional planner, he readily agreed to make it his task to visit as many as possible of the planners and other professionals who had taken part in our experiment in application 3 years earlier, in order to discover what influence, if any, the experience had had on the organisations and individuals taking part.

At that stage, it appeared that the impact on individuals had been generally more substantial than that on organisations. But the extent of that impact was both variable and elusive; and if dissemination was to proceed further, an obvious next aim was for us to produce a readable, accessible 'how to do it' guide to the approach. So, the understanding at the end of 1973 was that the three of us would work on this task together. Soon, however, the time came for Bunker to return to Australia – sailing by the long sea route, with prospects of plenty of writing time on the voyage. Then time scales became extended and, gradually, the idea of Bunker remaining a co-author became a less practical one – to be replaced by the idea of his providing some introductory remarks from his varied experiences as planning practitioner, consultant, teacher and researcher. Meanwhile, another prospective co-author had emerged: Alan Sutton, an IOR colleague who became closely involved with the two of us in developing training programmes in Canada, and subsequently in a major government-financed project in Britain to apply strategic choice methods to the exploration of policy alternatives in County Council Structure Plans. But then Sutton too receded as a prospective co-author when, in 1977, he moved to a new base in Western Canada; so, the responsibilities of authorship reverted to the two of us.

SHIFTING PRESSURES

Work on this book continued during the later 1970s – but in a sporadic way as we were both working under high pressure on IOR consulting and research projects for clients in Britain and overseas. For one of us, Hickling, the thrust continued to be on practical applications of the strategic choice approach; but for the other, Friend, it shifted towards research on the organisational and inter-organisational dimensions of complex planning processes, bringing a contrasting perspective to our training activities and our continuing work on the manuscript of this book.

The late 1970s were, for both of us, a difficult time in terms of continuity of our project work. In 1980, Hickling set up as an independent consultant; Friend continued to work part-time at the Institute while also taking up an Honorary Senior Visiting Fellowship at the Management Centre of the University of Bradford. Around this time we were both becoming immersed in quite different ventures as well. Hickling, having recently relinquished the management of the village stores and post office adjoining his home, launched a company called Endless Games, through which to enter the burgeoning market of fantasy role-playing games. Meanwhile, Friend, from a new home location in West Yorkshire, found himself working in partnership with his wife to set up a countryside interpretive centre, as an initiative in environmental education run on small business lines.

For both of us, the involvement in work on planning processes continued; and with it our efforts to bring the book to completion. The members of Pergamon's advisory committee for the Urban and Regional Planning Series – of which Friend was a long-standing member – offered a judicious blend of encouragement and exhortation, supported by the editorial staff. We met together whenever we could, usually at least once a month, to progress the writing work. These meetings took place in all kinds of locations – not only in offices but in hotels and restaurants, at motorway service stations, in airport lounges and railway buffets. We met often at our respective homes; indeed, we have photographs of our working one sunny day in an English country garden, with flip charts hung among the greenery climbing up the walls of the cottage behind. Meanwhile, our children grew up and started to go their separate ways; and our wives continued to tolerate our joint writing endeavours with surprising good humour, while developing their own careers in their respective fields of creative art.

The breakthrough finally came in the latter half of 1985. By this time, we had both disposed of most of our other entrepreneurial interests and Friend was again working full time from the Tavistock Centre in London. Hickling was now fully stretched in some challenging applications of the strategic choice approach for Dutch governmental agencies, while Friend was becoming drawn into running strategic choice workshops in new fields ranging from community health planning to information technology strategy within the firm. A high point came during the new year break in January 1986, when a conjunction of circumstances allowed a brief reunion, at Hickling's home, of key people who had been associated with the earlier stages of preparation of the book including both Ray Bunker and Alan Sutton, who was now resident again in Europe. This was not only a convivial occasion, it also saw a significant step forward in the consolidation of our ideas about technology, organisation, process and product, as presented in Chapter 4. There were still to be six agonising months of meetings, long telephone calls and redraftings before we were finally able to commit our finished text to the publishers. It was far from easy, but the sense of relief was overwhelming.

COMPLEMENTARITIES

Our different experiences and work patterns over the 12 years, along with different and complementary personal skills, have led us to recognise differences and complementarities in our respective contributions to the writing process. For much of the time, the main load of drafting and co-ordination has fallen on one of us, Friend, as and when pauses in the pressures to maintain a continuing flow of project work have allowed. Yet the endeavour has been a joint one, which neither of us could have brought to fruition without the other. For Hickling's immersion over this period in practical applications of the strategic choice approach provided an all-important base of experience against which to judge the realism of the advice we wished to offer and the most practical way of presenting it; and the interdependence of our contributions became more and more apparent during the final nine-month period of intensive collaboration in the writing process.

We found during this period that some significant differences had developed between us on matters of emphasis and terminology; and we had to work long and hard at these before reaching agreement on simple, practical ways in which they could be overcome. We recognised too that there were differences in our styles of presentation – written, verbal, graphical – but we agreed that these stylistic differences could be a source of strength rather than weakness, if only we could achieve a creative synthesis between them. Some clues to the complementarities between our perspectives can be found in our respective biographical notes. Among the many facets of his early work experience, Hickling admits to operating as a semi-professional magician; Friend, meanwhile, admits to having graduated in the abstract discipline of mathematics before embarking on his early career in industrial operational research. So, a background of magic comes together with a background in logic; a contrast which, at first sight, seems to sum up neatly enough the main differences in our backgrounds and their influence on our respective styles. But the potential for creative collaboration would not have existed had we not been capable of meeting each other at least half way. For, in the late 1960s, when Friend was struggling to adapt his ingrained belief in rationality, quantification and logical rigour to the untidy social and political realities of decision-making on Coventry City Council, Hickling was taking his postgraduate degrees at the University of Pennsylvania, to become both Master of Architecture and Master of City Planning. It was here that he became exposed to the influence of Ackoff and others in the field of operational research; and it was through the convergence of this experience with Friend's searing experiences of decision-making in Coventry – together with a shared inclination towards use of graphics in expressing ideas and their relationships – that the basis for a productive collaboration was forged.

The logic/magic tensions surfaced repeatedly when Friend's writing tended to become laboured, in the attempt to pin down more formally aspects of the strategic choice approach which had hitherto developed in quite an intuitive way. Sometimes, this led to proposed changes in terminology or technique which did not fit well with Hickling's evolving base of experience in the field; so we found we had to make many fine adjustments: a little more magic here, a little more logic there. In retrospect, the opportunity which the writing task has provided for us to consolidate, review and modify the concepts and methods of the strategic choice approach has been an important one for both of us. The hope now must be that the fruits of this labour will be of as much value to our readers, whether they be practitioners, students, teachers or researchers. The demand for an authoritative, practical guide to the strategic choice approach has been expressed to us often enough since 1973 and, indeed, earlier.

Our hope now is that this volume will succeed in meeting the demand and thereby help in sustaining the momentum of application, teaching and development of ideas. If the past is any guide, the practice of strategic choice is likely to continue to evolve in different ways in different places in response to different demands and pressures. So, we hope that this book can provide a significant milestone in maintaining the wide-ranging collaborative endeavour on which the advance of the strategic choice approach has been built over the last 12 years.

ACKNOWLEDGEMENTS

There have been enough references to other people already in this preface for us to have gone some way towards the important and congenial task of acknowledging the contributions by others in this work. The contribution of the late Neil Jessop was seminal and has been acknowledged more fully in the second edition of Local Government and Strategic Choice (Friend and Jessop, 1969/77). The far-reaching contributions of Raymond Bunker and Alan Sutton over the 12-year writing period have already been mentioned in earlier sections. Another major contribution to be acknowledged is that of Andreas Faludi who, from his Chair in Planning at the University of Amsterdam, has persistently sought to encourage development of the comparatively neglected academic perspectives of the strategic choice approach, and the study of its relatedness to other bodies of planning theory.

Others who have contributed to the development of the approach over the years include many past and present members of IOR and Tavistock Institute staff – Eric Trist, Hugh Murray, Paul Spencer, John Stringer, John Luckman, Don Bryant, James Morgan, Michael Luck, Chris Yewlett, Ken Carter, Hadley Hunter, John Pollard, Brian Quarterman, Gloria Overton, Martin Elton, David Millen, Peter Spink, Michael Floyd and Michael Norris – the last of whom has contributed many incisive comments in recent years. Other significant collaborators and sources of ideas in Britain and elsewhere have included Russell Ackoff, Felix Wedgwood-Oppenheim, Jonathan Rosenhead, Peter Fishburn, John Power, Fritz Scharpf, Bill Ogden, Harry Lash, Robin Fried, Arnold de Jong, Luc Wilkin, Fernand Debreyne, Hans Mastop, Angela de Melo, Robert Glass, Nathaniel Lichfield, Morris Hill, Martin Payne, Doug Spencer, Don Miller, Obbo Hazewinkel, Bram Breure, Paul de Jongh, Fernando Galvão, Maximino Losehiavo de Barros, Moacyr Parahyba, Ken Bowen, Peter Bennett, Colin Eden, Sue Jones, Stephen Cropper, Christine Huxham, Jim Bryant and Tsunekazu Toda. But even to list the academic, international and other affiliations of these and other individuals would take up too much space – let alone to describe the rich and varied nature of their contributions.

Contributors to the typing of successive chapter drafts have also been numerous over the 12 years since this book was conceived – but special acknowledgement must go to Betty Fox, for long the key resource person in IOR's Coventry office; to Ann Jamieson at the Tavistock Centre; and to Jayne Moore who, working from her home, was finally able to commit the text to disk in a way that we could scarcely have conceived in the dim and distant days of 1973.

Foreword to the first edition

When Neil Jessop's and John Friend's seminal work Local Government and Strategic Choice appeared in 1969, I was teaching in the Department of Town and Country Planning at the University of Sydney. I was so impressed that I reviewed it for the then Journal of the Australian Institute of Planners, and it has had a marked influence on my work since.

I had the profit and pleasure of spending a sabbatical year with John Friend, Allen Hickling and their colleagues in 1973. This book appears many years afterwards, and it is enlightening to turn back to my impressions of the strategic choice approach at that time. These impressions followed not only from extensive discussions with the authors of this present book, but also from a programme of visits to most of the planners, managers and others who had then begun to use the approach. We generally agreed that the process of strategic choice would benefit from being presented as more cyclic rather than linear and sequential, should be extended to address policy questions of major significance, and could be applied and used in fields of activity other than urban and regional development. This present book shows how much developmental work has taken place in these directions since the early 1970s.

It would be a pity if the comprehensiveness and thoroughness of this book led to the neglect of opportunities to use the strategic choice approach in partial or informal ways. This is particularly important in working situations where it is difficult to use the approach deliberately and deliberatively, because policies and problems have to be shaped and addressed through a diffuse process of negotiation with many different people and groups. One major example of this style of working was the joint Commonwealth-States study of soil conservation in Australia which I co-ordinated as a Commonwealth public servant in the mid-1970s.

This study had become static and rigidly programmatic. It was dominated by the current technology of soil conservation and by construction of capital works to arrest land degradation with little consideration of any national interests or priorities. The study had been in progress for 2 or 3 years and, in the circumstances of that time, it was not feasible for me to introduce strategic choice explicitly to all the various groups of inter-governmental officers who were involved in different ways. But the study was able to conclude with a principal recommendation, agreed to by all parties, about the need for mutual commitments to raise the level of soil conservation effort. This, of course, was supported by a series of statements about what that meant in terms of substance and priorities. These conclusions were then supported by a series of subsidiary recommendations which defined the principles of resource allocation needed to support an enhanced soil conservation effort; the organisational requirements of this expanded programme; and the dynamics of its continued development and modification. Inter-governmental relations were a particularly important part of this operation, and the recommendations were structured to express these.

In effect, the study was changed from one dominated by the heavily structured characteristics of traditional planning, towards an emphasis on the qualities of the strategic choice approach as expressed in this book. This soil conservation study accordingly represents an example of the approach being introduced informally but effectively to address the crucial aspects of process and organisation in policy-making and programme/project development and operation.

In an educational context, the strategic choice approach can be used in quite comprehensive and explicit ways. At the most ambitious level, I believe that it can be used as the major structuring element in the design of courses in town and country planning. More pragmatically, I have used it both as a means of illuminating different philosophies of planning, and as a vehicle for problem-solving in planning exercises. Either it can be taught carefully and comprehensively along the lines shown in this book; or students can be thrown into the deep end in dealing with a planning situation, after only a brief introduction to strategic choice. In a recent exercise of this latter kind, at the South Australian Institute of Technology, I defined the broad attributes of a planning situation, divided students into three groups and asked them to develop different solutions. Each group acted as a professional planning group advising the local council and taking the problem through a series of progressive decisions over three or four months. To encourage their imagination and to save time on the laborious collection of data and information, I asked them to write up the exercise as three different short stories, inventing information along the way which was supportive of, and consistent with, the progressive series of decisions of different kinds. The three answers showed the leading importance, respectively, of cash flow to the development agency; of an opportunity to accommodate a major metropolitan showground facing relocation; and of the resolution of land use conflicts with adjoining activities. Along the way the students learned a lot about the roles and relationships of decision-makers and decision-takers.

The way strategic choice is used in teaching depends on the educational environment. In the example cited above, the students were in the third year of an undergraduate course: But ideally the students should be introduced to the concepts of strategic choice in the first year, and the approach built up throughout the course.

Finally, I believe the stage of development of strategic choice in this book is not the final one. One of its greatest contributions has been to break down the rigidities attending planning, problem-solving and policy-making. I feel that too many people see implementation of plans and policies as simply the routine carrying out of decisions. Yet, I am convinced that aspects and instruments of implementation often need to be shaped, adapted, or accepted as given, right from the beginning of addressing a problem. Otherwise, we will continue to have too many ineffective policies and too many pigeonholed plans.

Raymond Bunker

A quick access guide

How should you start reading *Planning under Pressure*? Your choice will depend on the nature of your interests; the time at your disposal; and the extent of any prior familiarity you may have with the strategic choice approach.

The purpose of this quick access guide is to help you in making your decisions about selective reading. It does so first by outlining the principles on which the book is designed, then by making some suggestions to help you establish your priorities.

THE FIGURES

One of the first things you will notice on flicking through the pages of this book is the number and positioning of the illustrations. There are 102 full-page figures, all boldly numbered. Some figures are professionally drawn, while others are drawn freehand – deliberately so, in order to stress the spontaneous way in which the methods are usually used in practice. Other figures again take the form of photographs, illustrating the approach in use in a workshop setting.

Above and below most of the figures will be found various key words and symbols. These are designed to help the reader in making rapid cross-references within the text. Their meaning will be explained in the next section.

THE STRUCTURE OF THE BOOK

Three of the fourteen chapters – Chapters 1, 4 and 9 – present the main characteristics of the strategic choice approach at a general level:

Chapter 1 describes its Foundations, which are based on first-hand experience of the challenges facing decision-makers in group situations; Chapter 4 draws out the general Orientations and shifts of attitude which are central to this approach; Chapter 9 discusses the Practicalities of applying the approach in practice, based on cumulative experience over more than 30 years.

Both Chapters 4 and 9 are organised with reference to a general view of four complementary aspects through which any approach to planning can be described and compared to others. These four aspects, expressed through the mnemonic **A-TOPP**, are as follows:

> *Approach*: *Technology*
> *Organisation*
> *Process*
> *Product*

In most of the figures of these two chapters, you will see that the aspect of the approach which is currently in the foreground is highlighted in the lower left-hand corner.

The intervening chapters are grouped into two sets:

1. **Chapters 2 and 3**, which together introduce the basic concepts and methods of the strategic choice approach;
2. **Chapters 5, 6, 7 and 8**, which expand on these basic concepts and methods, emphasising the practical skills involved in applying them to the complexities of decision-making in practice.

The structure of these six chapters reflects a general view of four complementary modes of decision-making. This view is presented in diagrammatic form in Figure 8. The four basic modes are:

Shaping   Designing   Comparing   Choosing

In these six chapters, a small motif of four circles, based on the framework of Figure 8, appears in the corner of each figure to identify the mode which is currently in the foreground. Throughout these chapters the concepts, methods and skills are introduced gradually through the development of a case example – the South Side story – in which they are applied to a semi-fictitious yet realistic situation of *Planning under Pressure* in the public domain.

In this third edition, the main sequence of Chapters 1–9 is followed by five further chapters presenting significant developments since the first edition was published.

Chapter 10 describes briefly – with illustrations – progress in developing computer software as an additional form of support in applying the approach in practice, making it more accessible to individuals and small informal management groups. Chapter 11 describes some important extensions in process management, which have helped in adapting the approach to large and challenging projects.

Whereas Chapters 10 and 11 revise chapters that were first presented in our second edition of 1997, the final three chapters are new to this edition. In Chapter 12 we describe some of the many ways in which other people have interpreted and sometimes transformed the toolbox for strategic choice to fit different contexts of decision-making. Then Chapter 13 brings together twenty-one invited contributors in reporting their experiences and the lessons that they draw from them. Finally, Chapter 14 reviews the altered horizons of future development as they appear at the time this edition goes to press.

READING PRIORITIES

The guidelines that follow are organised according to the results you may reasonably expect to obtain from different reading strategies. They are presented broadly in terms of increasing levels of comprehensiveness.

For a first *quick appreciation of the approach*, we recommend a fast reading of Chapter 1, then a skim through the figures of the next two chapters – glancing at the definitions of key concepts that appear below the figures in Chapters 2 and 3. This can be followed by reading through the review of the main orientations of the approach, as summarised at the end of Chapter 4.

For a *grasp of the main principles, concepts and methods*, we recommend a fuller reading of the first four chapters. To reinforce your understanding, you then have the option of trying out the short exercises which appear at the end of Chapters 2 and 3. If you are interested in a clearer understanding of the challenges of applying the approach in practice, you can then skim through Chapter 9; and, if you are interested in using the computer as a tool, you can then browse through Chapter 10.

For a *more thorough appreciation of how you can apply the approach*, we recommend first a familiarisation with the concepts introduced in Chapters 2 and 3, then a browse through Chapters 5, 6, 7 and 8, using Chapter 4 as your point of departure. Having developed a feel from these chapters of the kinds of skill which are involved in applying the approach in practice, we suggest you now read Chapter 9 – especially the section on selectivity and adaptiveness. Then you can either proceed to Chapter 10 or to Chapters 11 and 12, for a fuller appreciation of different contexts of application; alternatively you can return to work through Chapters 5–8 in more depth.

For a *fuller feel of the realities of using the strategic choice approach in practice*, we recommend selective reading of the fifteen contributions from other people that are brought together in Chapter 13, together with some of the snapshots of people at work that appear towards the end of Chapters 5, 6, 7, 8 and 12; then a study of the four management checklists relating to technology, organisation, process and practice which are presented in Figures 83, 85, 86 and 88 of Chapter 9, and the further developments in process management described in Chapter 11.

LEARNING BY DOING

As with any other approach to planning, one cannot expect to prepare oneself for all the challenges one may encounter in practice through reading books alone.

Our hope is that you will feel encouraged by what you read to try putting the principles, concepts and methods of the strategic choice approach into practice in your own decision-making and planning, whether you already carry significant responsibilities for decisions that impinge on other people, or whether you a student on the threshold of your career.

THE WEBSITE

Rather than end up with a *Guide to Further Reading* as in our earlier editions, it seems more appropriate in this electronic era to transfer most of this information to the companion website to this book, where it can be continuously revised and extended as further experiences continue to accumulate, and as the lessons from those experiences continue to be shared. The companion website will be found at **http://books.elsevier.com/companions/0750663731**.

1 Foundations

A PHILOSOPHY OF PLANNING

There are many ways in which it is possible to approach the challenge of planning in an uncertain world.

The approach to be introduced in this chapter is one in which planning is viewed as a continuous process: a process of choosing strategically through time. This view of planning as a process of strategic choice is, however, not presented as a set of beliefs which the reader is expected to embrace uncritically at this stage. That would be too much to expect – especially of an introductory chapter, which is intended merely to open the door for the more specific concepts, methods and guidelines to be offered in those that follow. People involved in any kind of planning activity of course build up their own sets of beliefs about the practice of planning in the course of their working lives: beliefs which they will not wish to set aside lightly. Yet experience in applying the approach offered here has shown that its fundamentals can usually be accepted without much difficulty by those planners or managers whose working philosophy draws more on their own practice than on taught beliefs. This is because, in essence, the approach sets out to do no more than to articulate, as clearly as possible, the kinds of dilemma that experienced decision-makers repeatedly face in the course of their work, and the often intuitive judgements they make in choosing how to respond.

In practice, such judgements may sometimes be accompanied by a sense of discomfort or even guilt. For the decision-makers may feel they are departing from certain principles of rational behaviour which they have been taught to respect. Indeed, the view of planning as strategic choice is found to offer more of a challenge to such idealised principles of rationality than it does to the intuitive judgements and compromises that seem characteristic of planning practice. If this point can be accepted, the reader should be able to relax in following the ideas put forward in this chapter and view them as offering perspectives that can help make sense of current practice – without necessarily demanding any revolutionary change in familiar ways of working.

THE CRAFT OF CHOOSING STRATEGICALLY

It is important to emphasise that the view of strategic choice presented here is essentially about choosing in a strategic *way* rather than at a strategic *level*. For the idea of choosing at a strategic level implies a prior view of some hierarchy of levels of importance in decision-making; while the concept of strategic choice that will be developed here is more about the connectedness of one decision with another than about the level of importance to be attached to one decision relative to others.

It is not too surprising that these two senses of the word strategic have tended to fuse together in common usage. For it is often the more weighty and broader decisions which are most obviously seen to be linked to other decisions, if only because of the range of their implications and the long time horizons over which their effects are expected to be felt. This, in turn, can lead to a view that any process of strategic decision-making should aspire to be comprehensive in its vision and long range

FIGURE
1

Planning Under Pressure: A View of the Realities

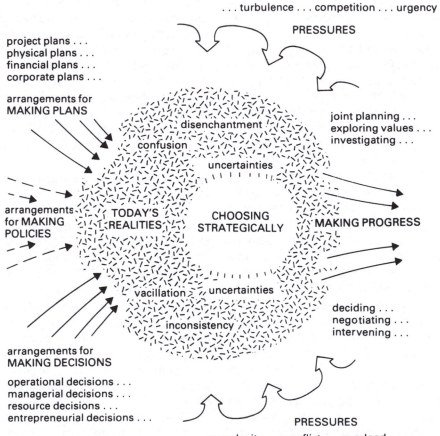

... turbulence ... competition ... urgency

PRESSURES

project plans ...
physical plans ...
financial plans ...
corporate plans ...

arrangements for
MAKING PLANS

disenchantment

confusion

uncertainties

joint planning ...
exploring values ...
investigating ...

arrangements
for MAKING
POLICIES

TODAY'S
REALITIES

CHOOSING
STRATEGICALLY

MAKING PROGRESS

vacillation   uncertainties

inconsistency

deciding ...
negotiating ...
intervening ...

arrangements for
MAKING DECISIONS

operational decisions ...
managerial decisions ...
resource decisions ...
entrepreneurial decisions ...

PRESSURES

... complexity ... conflict ... overload

in its time horizon, if it is to be worthy of its name.

But such a view of strategic choice can become a restrictive one in practice; for it is all too rarely that such idealistic aspirations can be achieved. The approach to strategic choice to be built up in this chapter is not only about making decisions at a supposedly strategic level. It goes beyond this in addressing the making of any decisions in the light of their links to other decisions, whether they be at a broader policy level or a more specific action level; whether they be more immediate or longer term in their time horizons; and no matter who may be responsible for them. This concept of strategic choice indicates no more than a readiness to look for patterns of connectedness between decisions in a manner that is selective and judgemental – it is *not* intended to convey the more idealistic notion that everything should be seen as inextricably connected to everything else.

So this view of planning as a process of strategic choice implies that planning can be seen as a much more *universal* activity than is sometimes recognised by those who see it as a specialist function associated with the preparation of particular sorts of plans. At the same time, it allows planning to be seen as a craft, full of subtlety and challenge; a craft through which people can develop their capacity to think and act creatively in coping with the complexities and uncertainties that beset them in practice.

ORGANISATIONAL CONTEXTS OF STRATEGIC CHOICE

This relatively modest interpretation of the word *strategic* means that the view of planning as strategic choice is one that can be applied not only to decision-making in formal organisational settings, but to the choices and uncertainties which people face in their personal, family and community lives. For example, any of us might find ourselves involved in a process of strategic choice in addressing the problem of where and when to go on a holiday next year, or how to sell an unwanted vehicle,

or how to deal with a difficult request from a relative or friend. Of course, the craft of choosing strategically becomes more complicated where it involves elements of collective choice – of negotiation with others who view problems and possibilities in different ways. Indeed, most of the more demanding problems to which the strategic choice approach has been applied have involved challenges of collective decision-making, either in organisational or inter-organisational settings; and this can have the effect of blurring many of the familiar distinctions of task and discipline around which organisational structures are usually designed. For the skill of choosing strategically through time is one that can become just as essential to the manager or executive as to those in more formal planning roles. This point is illustrated schematically in Figure 1, through which is presented a view of planning under the practical pressures of organisational life. It is a view in which an organisation's arrangements for making plans and those for making day-to-day decisions, tend to merge together into a less clearly bounded process through which progress is sustained. This is a process of choosing strategically in coping with difficult problems, amidst all the complex realities – or perceptions of reality – which contribute to organisational life.

The larger and more complex the organisation, the more it is to be expected that decision-making responsibilities will have become differentiated according to a multitude of operational, managerial or entrepreneurial roles. The more likely it is too that specialised plan-making functions will have been developed in an effort to maintain a co-ordinated, longer-term view isolated from everyday management pressures. However, no plan-making activity will remain valued within an organisation unless it can provide support for the more difficult and important of the decisions people face; and it is a common experience that carefully prepared plans can quickly lose their relevance under the pressures of day-to-day events. The combined pressures of urgency, competition for resources and turbulence in the world outside can soon lead to disenchantment and confusion in the arrangements for making plans; while the pressures of complexity, conflict and overload can lead to vacillation and inconsistency in the making of day-to-day decisions. To counter the resulting personal and organisational stresses, those responsible for organisational guidance sometimes look towards some over-arching framework of policies or aims. But, in practice, such policy guidelines can often be difficult to agree – especially when working in inter-organisational settings – and their contributions towards sorting out the predicaments of day-to-day management can be disappointingly small.

The making of generalised policies is therefore given its place in Figure 1; but it is not given pride of place. Instead, the emphasis is on the more subtle process of making progress through time by choosing strategically; and on the creative management of multiple uncertainties as a crucial means towards this end. And progress through time can itself take many forms. Immediate progress can take the form of intervening, or negotiating with others, as well as taking decisions on matters where direct action is possible. Meanwhile, progress in building a base for later decisions can also take different forms – not only investigations but also clarification of values and cultivation of working relationships with other decision-makers.

So the term 'planning' will be used in this book to refer generally to this more loosely defined process of choosing strategically, in which the activities of making plans, decisions and policies can come together in quite subtle and dynamic ways. But with a wide variety of ways of making progress to be considered, the process can soon begin to appear as one not so much of planning but of scheming – to introduce a term which has a similar literal meaning but which carries very different undertones in its everyday usage. Whereas the notion of planning may invoke a sense of idealism and

detachment, the notion of scheming tends to suggest working for sectional advantage in an often devious way. So there is a case to be made that people involved in planning must learn to become effective schemers; and furthermore that it is possible to exercise scheming skills in a responsible way. Those who are troubled about social responsibility in planning – including both the authors of this book – may wonder whether there must always be a divide between responsible planners and irresponsible schemers; and, if so, whether it must always be the latter who will win. The concept of *responsible scheming* need not be considered a contradiction in terms. Indeed, it is towards the search for a theory and a practice of responsible scheming that the strategic choice view of planning can be said to be addressed.

It is, however, one thing for an individual to embrace a philosophy of planning as strategic choice; and quite another thing for a group of people working together to share such a philosophy as an unequivocal foundation for their work. Experience has shown that there are some settings where a sense of shared philosophy can indeed emerge – either where a set of close colleagues have learnt to work together as a coherent team, or where they discover that a common professional background allows them to proceed on shared assumptions as to how decisions should be made. Yet those whose work involves cutting across organisational boundaries must expect often to find themselves working alongside people with whom they do not share a philosophical base. So it is important to think of the philosophy presented in this chapter as a helpful frame of reference in making use of the more specific concepts and methods to be introduced in this book, rather than as a necessary foundation from which to build.

Indeed, it is a common enough experience, when working with strategic choice concepts, that people of quite diverse backgrounds can make solid progress towards decisions based on shared understandings, with little or no explicit agreement at a more philosophical level. Often it is only through the experience of working together on specific and immediate problems that they find they are beginning to break through some of the philosophical barriers which may have inhibited collaboration in the past.

DILEMMAS OF PRACTICE

The view of strategic choice presented in this book gained its original impetus from the experience of a particular research project, which offered unusually extensive opportunities to observe the kinds of organisational processes indicated in Figure 1.

The setting of this research was the municipal council of a major English city – Coventry – which, between 1963 and 1967, agreed to act as host to a wide-ranging project on the processes of policy-making and planning in local government, viewed as a microcosm of government as a whole. This seminal research was supported by a grant from the Nuffield Foundation, and has been more fully reported elsewhere (Friend and Jessop, 1969/77). Over the 4-year period, the research team was able to follow a wide range of difficult issues including the review of the city's first development plan; the redesign of its urban road network; the reorganisation of its school system; the renewal of its housing stock; the finance of public transport; and the scheduling of capital works. The researchers were able to hold many discussions with the various politicians, administrators, planners and professional experts involved, and to observe the processes of collective decision-making in which they came together – not only in the departmental offices and the formal meetings of Council and its committees, but also in the smoke-filled rooms of the opposing political groups.

Through these experiences, some impressions of the persistent dilemmas of decision-making in such complex circumstances gradually came to the fore. Among the clearest impressions were:

- that people held different and continually shifting views about the **shape** of the issues they faced and, not least, about how closely or widely the boundaries of their concern should be drawn;
- that there were persistent pressures for them to arrive at commitments to action in an **incremental** or piecemeal way, however committed they might be in theory to the idea of taking a broader, more comprehensive view of the issues before them;
- that there was a continuing dilemma of balancing **urgency** against **uncertainty** in decision-making through time; and
- that there were persistent difficulties in distinguishing the **technical** from the **political** aspects of the decision process, even though the entire organisational structure was built around the maintenance of distinctions of this kind.

These impressions of the practical difficulties of choosing strategically in organisations facing complex problems have been strengthened and extended by many other experiences since the conclusion of the Coventry project – not only in the world of local government but in other public sector organisations, in industry and commerce, in voluntary organisations, and in the increasingly wide range of problem situations where these different domains of decision-making tend to converge. On the strength of this broader experience, a view is presented in Figure 2 of the five broad dimensions in which difficult choices of *balance* tend to arise in the management of a continuing process of strategic choice. There is a choice between:

1. a more **focused** and a more **synoptic** treatment of problem *scope*;
2. a more **simplifying** and a more **elaborating** treatment of *complexity*;
3. a more **reactive** and a more **interactive** treatment of *conflict*;
4. a more **reducing** and a more **accommodating** treatment of *uncertainty*;
5. and a more **exploratory** and a more **decisive** treatment of *progress* through time.

FIGURE
2

Judgements of Balance in Strategic Choice

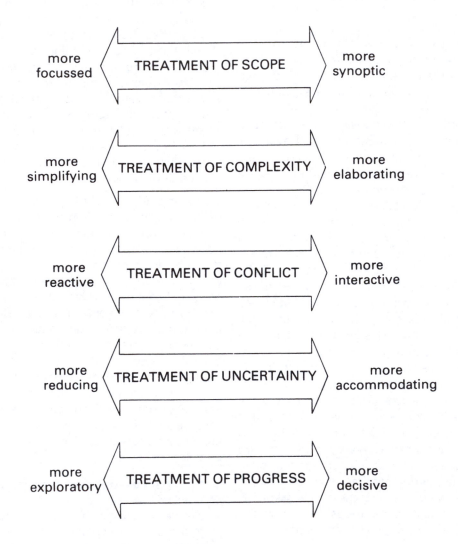

more
focussed ⟨ **TREATMENT OF SCOPE** ⟩ more
synoptic

more
simplifying ⟨ **TREATMENT OF COMPLEXITY** ⟩ more
elaborating

more
reactive ⟨ **TREATMENT OF CONFLICT** ⟩ more
interactive

more
reducing ⟨ **TREATMENT OF UNCERTAINTY** ⟩ more
accommodating

more
exploratory ⟨ **TREATMENT OF PROGRESS** ⟩ more
decisive

The practical task of choosing a position in each of these five dimensions is not one of making a firm and lasting commitment to one extreme or the other. It is more a task of maintaining an appropriate balance in continually changing circumstances, shifting from time to time in one direction or another, according to the – often intuitive – judgements of those involved. In the chapters that follow, the picture presented in Figure 2 will be used as a point of reference in building more structured frameworks of ideas through which to expand further on the view of planning as a process of strategic choice. These frameworks will give deeper significance to the various contrasts which, at this stage, can only be indicated in outline terms.

In later chapters, fuller interpretations will be offered of other related aspects of the dilemmas of practice observed in Coventry and elsewhere, which are not brought out so clearly in the comparatively broad set of balances presented in Figure 2. In particular, later chapters will have more to say about the issues of urgency and incrementality, and about the relationship of the political arena to the technical domain. This is a dichotomy which, in Coventry City Council, could be seen as the fundamental organising principle on which the formal structures of accountability were designed; but it is a relationship with far wider implications for decision-making, even in contexts where such distinctions may become more blurred.

RESPONDING TO DIFFICULTY IN MAKING DECISIONS

The view of planning as a process of strategic choice is, above all, a dynamic one. However, in building up a view of the way this process works, it is useful to begin with a more static picture. This picture, which is quite simple yet also quite general in its application, has as its focus any situation in which one or more decision-makers are experiencing *difficulty* in choosing how they should act in response to some particular *decision problem* with which they are currently concerned. A snapshot view of such a decision situation is presented in Figure 3. The decision problem itself is depicted as a cloud to indicate that its shape will often be in some degree obscure. However, what makes it problematic to the decision-makers is that they are experiencing some pressure to arrive at a decision, yet it is not clear to them what course of action they should choose.

Where a group of people find themselves collectively in such a situation, then it is often found that different members of the group will advocate different ways of responding; so some degree of conflict of opinion may emerge. Three types of response which are repeatedly offered in practice are indicated by the three different 'bubbles' shown emerging from the central cloud in Figure 3.

Very often, people will see the way out of their present difficulties in terms of explorations of a more or less technical nature. The suggestions offered typically include various forms of costing or forecasting exercises, surveys, technical analyses, research studies; or, in some circumstances, proposals for investment in more ambitious forms of mathematical or economic modelling. Whatever the form of investigation, however, the purpose is to reduce the difficulties of making decisions by investing in a process of *exploration* into particular aspects of the decision-makers' working environment about which it is felt that too little is currently known. Other people, meanwhile, may see the way out of the difficulty in terms of other, less technical, kinds of exploration designed to establish more clearly what policy values should guide their choice of action. Typically, they may call for investment in activities designed to clarify goals, objectives, aims or policy guidelines, whether through formal or informal channels. In some situations, this may mean simply consulting decision-takers who bear more direct responsibility for organisational policy; in others it could mean deliberately seeking fuller involvement in the process by a range of affected interest groups or their representatives.

FIGURE

3

Three Types of Uncertainty in Decision-Making

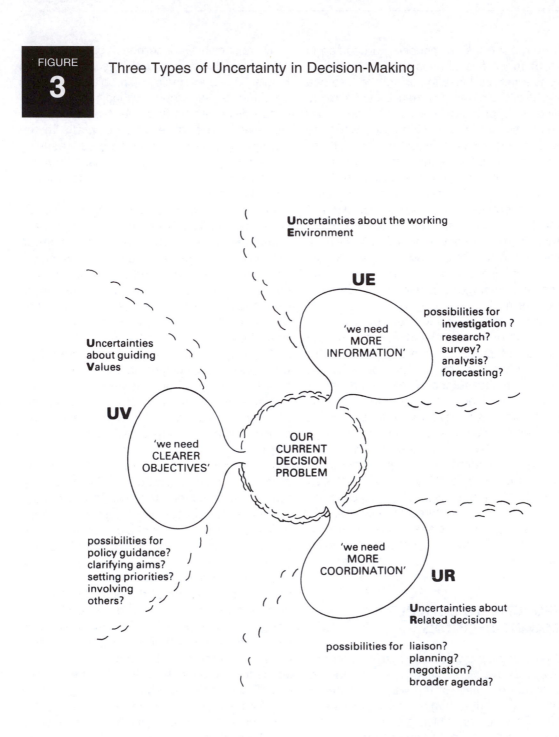

Uncertainties about the working **E**nvironment

UE

'we need MORE INFORMATION'

possibilities for investigation ? research? survey? analysis? forecasting?

Uncertainties about guiding **V**alues

UV

'we need CLEARER OBJECTIVES'

OUR CURRENT DECISION PROBLEM

possibilities for policy guidance? clarifying aims? setting priorities? involving others?

'we need MORE COORDINATION'

UR

Uncertainties about **R**elated decisions

possibilities for liaison? planning? negotiation? broader agenda?

A third response is to seek the way out of the difficulty by moves to extend the current agenda of decision-making concern. People advocating this response will often argue that the decision problem currently in view is one that cannot realistically be addressed in isolation, because it is connected to one or more other decision problems which lie ahead. So the demand here is likely to be for some form of co-ordination, negotiation or planning exercise that will allow the current decision problem to be explored alongside others within a broader, more synoptic problem focus. Each of the three kinds of demands – most typically expressed as demands for *more information*, for *clearer objectives* and for *more co-ordination* – can be regarded as a different kind of attempt to manage the current state of uncertainty over what should be done about the current decision situation. Indeed, it is possible to go on to identify three general categories of uncertainty along the lines indicated below, which are distinguished by the different forms of response that can be made. These three types of uncertainty play an important part in the philosophy of planning as a process of strategic choice; they can be formally described as follows:

1. Uncertainties about the working Environment: **UE** for short;
2. Uncertainties about guiding Values: **UV** for short;
3. Uncertainties about Related decisions: **UR** for short.

It is important to stress that the idea of uncertainty in strategic choice is normally viewed in relative rather than absolute terms. It is treated as an attribute of particular situations and people rather than something with an objective reality of its own. In practice it is often far from easy for people to agree which of the three kinds of uncertainty are most crucial in a particular decision situation; and, therefore, how much attention should be given to each possible form of response. For instance, members of a city planning team, considering whether to recommend approval of an application to build a new hotel, might see possibilities either for calling for deeper investigation of its traffic implications; or for seeking clearer guidance on the Council's policies in relation to this particular kind of development; or for initiating a wider review of tourism possibilities within the city as a whole. They might of course want to move in all three directions more or less at the same time; however, this is not always possible where there are pressures to make a speedy decision. Nor will it necessarily be desirable to invest resources in all possible ways of responding to uncertainty – especially if some of them are expected to be less effective than others, in terms of reducing the feelings of uncertainty among the decision-makers involved.

MANAGING UNCERTAINTY: A DYNAMIC VIEW

So, in practice, it may be far from easy to judge how uncertainty is to be managed at any moment, even in situations where the sources of that uncertainty have been clearly identified.

To consider further the possible ways of managing uncertainty through time, it becomes necessary to move to a more *dynamic* view. Such a view is presented in Figure 4, which builds on the 'snapshot' picture of Figure 3 by introducing the reality that any form of investigative, policy clarifying or co-ordinating initiative must take some time to carry through. Indeed, explorations in some of these directions may, in practice, take longer to carry out than others. However, the intended consequence of pursuing any chosen exploratory path is to make the decision situation less difficult to deal with once the outcome of the exploration is known – in other words, to lessen the feelings of uncertainty being experienced by the decision-makers, and thus to increase the level of *confidence* with which they can act. In practice, however, it will not often be realistic to expect that the feelings of uncertainty surrounding a difficult

FIGURE

4

Opportunities for Managing Uncertainty through Time

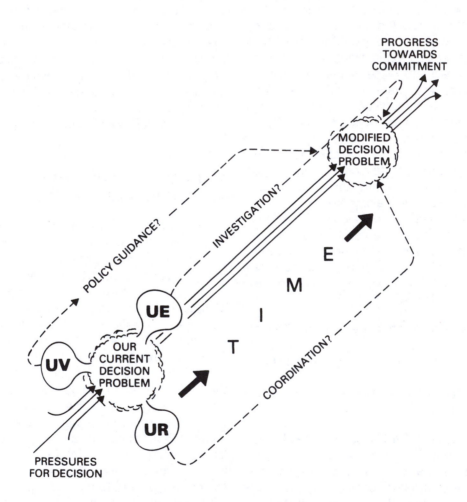

decision problem can be made to vanish altogether; however much effort may be invested in exploratory activities. In terms of the symbolism used here, the process can be pictured as one whereby the original cloud becomes smaller in its dimensions and, by implication, less obscure.

Sometimes, of course, feelings of uncertainty may be reduced through time without any conscious action on the part of the decision-makers. Expected events may or may not unfold; trends may become more apparent; the intentions of other parties may be revealed; policy positions may become more clear cut. In general, however, uncertainty can only be reduced at a cost – whether this be merely the cost of delay when there may be urgent issues to be settled, or whether it also includes more direct costs in terms of money, skills or other scarce resources. So the management of uncertainty through time is rarely simple in the types of judgement it entails. It is the raising of these judgements to a more conscious level that is one of the most distinctive characteristics of the strategic choice approach.

INTERCONNECTED AGENDAS OF DECISION-MAKING

Of the three exploratory routes indicated in Figure 4, it is the co-ordinative (UR) route which is of most far reaching significance in developing the idea of planning as strategic choice. The demand to move in this direction arises when there is a sense that the present agenda of decision-making is too restricted – that the decision problem currently in view is significantly influenced by uncertainties to do with intended actions in other fields of choice. Such a concern for a wider view will often lead to an extension in the time frame as well, because the pressures for decision may be less immediate in some of these related areas. The concern for co-ordination may also shift the process in the direction of some form of liaison or joint working with other sections or departments, and sometimes, also, with

other decision-makers quite outside the organisational framework within which the current problem is being addressed.

The concern for co-ordination in dealing with related fields of choice does not, however, inevitably mean transcending organisational boundaries in this way. At a more modest level, it may simply be a matter of the same decision-maker recognising that an issue to be dealt with today should be considered in relation to some other issue to be dealt with next week. In the case of the hotel development mentioned earlier, for instance, it could be that a proposal to develop an indoor leisure centre is known to be pending on a neighbouring site, suggesting that either proposal could affect the other.

In general, the pursuit of the co-ordinative (UR) route implies forging a relationship between one decision process or planning process and others, in the manner indicated in Figure 5. The dynamic view here is taken a step further than in Figure 4, by showing the fuller implications of a shift from a more limited to a broader decision focus. The investment in 'more co-ordination' can be seen as shifting the focus, temporarily at least, from the original decision problem to a broader and more complex problem within which it is contained.

INCREMENTAL PROGRESS IN PLANNING

One of the most important points about this shift to a broader problem focus is that it does not automatically mean that those involved should be aiming for early decision in respect of all the related choices now brought into view. It is perfectly possible that the shift to a broader focus will help to reduce uncertainty in the original decision problem and so enable firm commitment to be agreed, without leading to simultaneous commitments in any or all of the other related areas. Indeed, the issue of balance between exploratory and decisive progress has already been highlighted (Figure 2) as one of the main areas of judgement in strategic choice; and it is a balance of critical importance in managing uncertainty through time.

FIGURE
5

Extending the Problem Focus

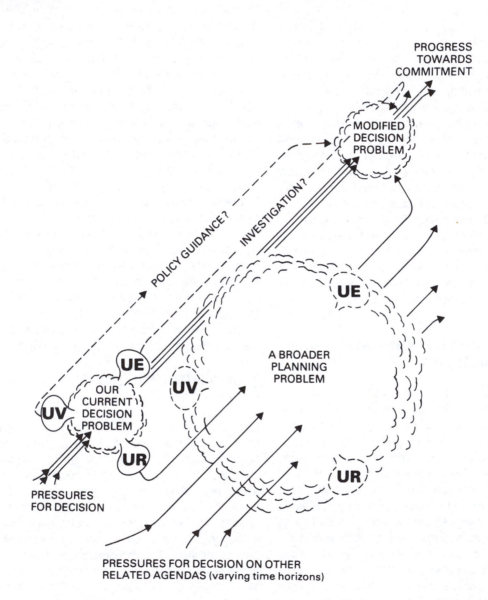

PROGRESS
TOWARDS
COMMITMENT

MODIFIED
DECISION
PROBLEM

POLICY GUIDANCE?

INVESTIGATION?

UE

A BROADER
PLANNING
PROBLEM

UV

UE

OUR
CURRENT
DECISION
PROBLEM

UV

UR

UR

PRESSURES
FOR DECISION

PRESSURES FOR DECISION ON OTHER
RELATED AGENDAS (varying time horizons)

The broader the focus of the problem within the larger cloud in Figure 5, the more it is likely to be thought of not simply as a decision problem but as a *planning problem* because it contains elements of both immediate and longer-term decision. But the distinction is not so much an absolute one as one of degree. This point is made in Figure 5 by showing the three kinds of uncertainty surfacing again at the broader level of the more complex planning problem. Indeed, if uncertainties of type UR again appear important at this level, this may trigger off concerns to move to an even broader level of concern, and to begin to explore the shape of an even larger and more obscure cloud. But this process of continually enlarging the scope of the problem will always have its limits in practice; and, if useful pointers to action are to emerge, then the focus of concern must be kept within manageable bounds.

It is not hard to see how planning procedures conceived with ambitions towards comprehensiveness can develop their own internal momentum. Such tendencies can be found in corporate planning procedures for the guidance of large and diffuse commercial enterprises, and also in exercises in the production of land-use plans or economic planning frameworks, through which public agencies endeavour to set a context for the actions of other parties. The danger is always that such activities will become separated from other management processes and so cease to exercise any real influence on the more immediate decisions they were designed to inform. This risk of disengagement between arrangements for planning and for management has already been suggested in the keynote diagram (Figure 1); it is a risk that can be confronted directly from the perspective of planning as a process of strategic choice.

HUMAN SETTINGS FOR DECISION-MAKING

The shift from a 'snapshot' view of decision-making (Figure 3) to a more dynamic, multi-level picture (Figures 4 and 5) implies that the imagery of the cloud should itself be conceived in more realistic, multi-dimensional terms. To extend the metaphor, clouds in reality are not flat: they have length, depth and breadth; their edges may be blurred; they progress across the sky, changing shape as time passes; they dissolve, they merge, they break up; and, in so doing, they assume new and often unpredictable forms.

With such a picture in mind, it is possible to look more closely at some different kinds of human context for decision, as a step towards a closer examination of the processes of thought and communication which go on 'within the cloud', Figure 6 begins by looking at an organisational context of the most simple and restricted kind – in a pre-computer office environment: An individual sits on a chair (symbolising a defined organisational role), with successive matters for decision arriving in an 'in' tray on a table (symbolising an agenda). The matters are dealt with in sequence, agreed rules are applied, and decisions are then transferred to the 'out' tray one at a time.

If the rules are unambiguous in their bearing on the issue currently being dealt with, then the cloud representing the thought process of the decision-maker is a small one and quickly evaporates to be replaced by the next. Indeed, the symbolism of the cloud can be replaced by the more mechanistic image of the black box – and the decision-maker at the table is at risk of being superseded by an electronic counterpart. Of course, the cloud may sometimes become larger, when a more complex case arrives. The decision-maker now experiences uncertainty and, as in the case of the public official dealing with the application to build a new hotel, this uncertainty may be in part due to awareness of links to other related cases – as symbolised perhaps by some matters marked for further attention in a 'pending' tray.

Figure 6 then demonstrates another context of sequential decision-making, by contrasting the situation of a single decision-maker sitting at his or her small table with that of a collective decision-making body – a committee or management board – grouped around a larger table.

FIGURE
6

Two Contexts for Sequential Decision-Making

Such a group will often have a pre-circulated agenda, presenting an ordered list of issues to discuss and where possible resolve, corresponding to the 'in' tray of the single decision-maker. Among the occupants of the roles symbolised by the chairs around the larger table, there will usually be someone in a 'chairing' role, responsible for ensuring that the business is dealt with in an orderly and expeditious way. In place of the 'out' tray, there will usually be a running record of decisions kept by a committee secretary or clerk; while the occupants of at least some of the other chairs around the table will sometimes be recognised as having different representative or expert roles to play.

The decision-making process is now not purely one of cogitation within an individual's head; it embraces processes of communication, verbal and nonverbal, among the members of the group. For the observer of the process, the elongated cloud above the large table in Figure 6 takes on additional substance, in that it becomes possible to follow the dynamics of information sharing, negotiation and – if decisions are to be reached – compromise between conflicting views. For instance, if the issue of permission to build a new hotel has been brought up on the planning committee's agenda, there may be a variety of financial, aesthetic, engineering and commercial considerations to be exposed and shared. Further, there may be various conflicts of interest to be managed; for instance, there could be conflicts between the committee's responsibilities to the local community and the relationships of some members with the developer, who could perhaps be a well-known and influential local figure.

However, many decision processes in practice fail to conform to either of these tidy, sequential models. If the issues are complex and their boundaries unclear, then organisational responsibilities too are likely to be diffuse and probably confused. Communications may take place not just around tables but on the telephone, in corridors, in small backrooms. The inputs and outputs can no longer be seen as falling into any clear sequence, and

the image of the single cloud may have to be replaced by one of several separate clouds which continually come together, drift apart, coalesce or disappear. For instance, the hotel developer, in making his or her own investment decisions, may have a series of meetings with planners and other public officials, as well as finance houses, landowners and other commercial interests. The developer as well as the committee members will have uncertainties to manage in some or all of the three categories of UE, UV and UR; and the extent to which the different planning processes can be linked may begin to raise a host of difficult administrative, political, ethical and legal issues.

MODES OF DECISION-MAKING

In developing further the view of planning as a process of strategic choice, it is helpful to see the process within any 'cloud' as continually shifting between different and complementary 'modes' of decision-making activity. In the simple situation of sequential decision-making, where the nature of the problem inputs and the expected decision outputs is well defined, this movement can be seen in terms of only two complementary modes: the one concerned with *designing* possible courses of action, and the other with *comparing* them in the light of some view of what their consequences might be. This relatively simple view is indicated in Figure 7. The process may not in practice be strictly linear because a comparison of the consequences of any pair of alternatives – for instance a straight 'yes' or 'no' to the application to build a hotel – may reveal that either response could have undesirable consequences and so trigger off a search for some other compromise solution. So it becomes necessary to allow for the possibility of a feedback loop returning from the comparing to the designing mode. So, in Figure 7 the single 'cloud' is shown as tending to change shape into two smaller clouds which may still not be clearly separable in practice, insofar as the interplay between designing and comparing may become rapid and difficult to trace.

FIGURE
7

A Process of Simple Choice

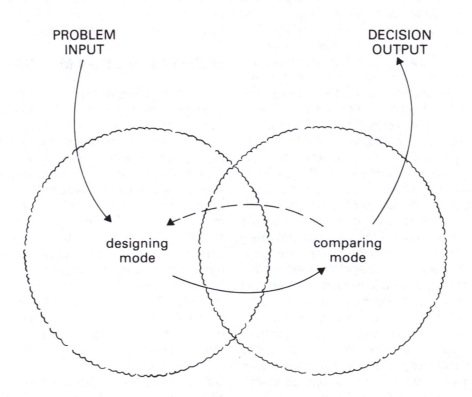

PROBLEM
INPUT

DECISION
OUTPUT

designing
mode

comparing
mode

This picture has much in common with other, more orthodox models of decision-making processes, which tend to present stages or activities in logical sequence, having a beginning and an end, while allowing for elements of feedback or recycling in between. However, the more diffuse, continuous kind of process which is characteristic of the making of complex decisions in practice involves coping with multiple problem inputs and multiple decision outputs, with no clear sequential relationships between the two. To represent this kind of process, it is necessary to move to a rather more elaborate picture of the process within the cloud, introducing two additional modes as shown in Figure 8.

The two further modes of decision-making activity which make their appearance in Figure 8 are both of a more subtle and political kind. One of these is concerned with the *shaping* of problems; a mode within which judgements about the possible connections between one field of choice and another can have a crucial role to play. The other, referred to as the *choosing* mode, is concerned with the formation of proposed commitments to action progressively through time. Here it has to be kept in mind that the more complex the shape of the problem, the wider the choices that have to be faced. There will be choices, not only about what courses of action are preferred, but also about what degree of commitment is appropriate at this stage; which decisions should be deferred until later; and what explorations could be set in train in response to different types of uncertainty. So instead of two partially overlapping foci within the cloud, there now appear four, with a variety of possible directions of movement between one mode and another. The most orthodox progression might appear to be from shaping problems, through designing possibilities, to comparing their consequences and then on to a final choosing of actions. However, such a progression is likely to be neither straightforward nor realistic, insofar as the process is to be seen as a continuous and incremental one, with no clear beginning and no single end. For the choice of actions

to deal with some parts of the problem situation will leave other choices open for the future, creating opportunities for future reshaping of problems as unexpected events occur and new connections begin to appear.

CHALLENGES TO MANAGEMENT AND PLANNING NORMS

Already, the ideas presented here can be seen to pose some direct challenges to long-established management and planning norms: norms which have indeed been under sustained challenge from other sources, yet remain extremely persistent in the design of formal management and planning procedures – often for reasons of organisational stability and accountability which cannot be lightly criticised. Among the more deeply established norms in any management system are those of *linearity*, *objectivity*, *certainty* and *comprehensiveness*. These can be summarised as follows:

- *Aim for linearity* – 'Tackle one thing at a time';
- *Aim for objectivity* – 'Avoid personal or sectional bias';
- *Aim for certainty* – 'Establish the full facts of the situation';
- *Aim for comprehensiveness* – 'Don't do things by halves'.

Such norms may be adequate for the functionary sitting at a desk, working to highly constrained terms of reference. However, even here the system of rules can rarely be exhaustive in representing the situations that could arise; so feelings of uncertainty about how to act will sometimes surface and with them will arise difficulties in conforming to the norms of linearity and objectivity in their pristine forms. When a shift is made from decision-making to plan-making, the same four norms tend to show a remarkable persistence, even though the language may change. Yet the experience of working on difficult and complex planning problems is that the norms of linearity, objectivity, certainty and comprehensiveness keep on breaking down. So, in this book, they

FIGURE

8

A Process of Strategic Choice

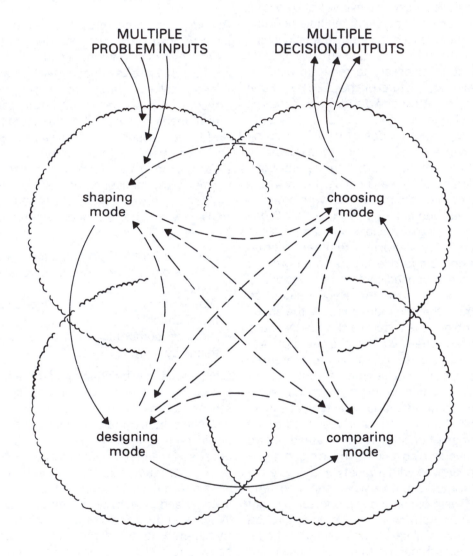

MULTIPLE
PROBLEM INPUTS

MULTIPLE
DECISION OUTPUTS

shaping
mode

choosing
mode

designing
mode

comparing
mode

will be replaced by less simple prescriptions of the following form:

- *Don't aim for linearity* – learn to work with cyclicity;
- *Don't aim for objectivity* – learn to work with subjectivity;
- *Don't aim for certainty* – learn to work with uncertainty;
- *Don't aim for comprehensiveness* – learn to work with selectivity.

These alternative prescriptions may appear to be less straightforward to interpret in practice than the more familiar norms. But experience demonstrates that they offer a much more effective guide for people in attempting to choose strategically in practice. What is more, once they are stated and developed more fully, they can help people cope constructively with any sense of residual guilt they may feel in failing to apply simple management and planning norms when they encounter problems of a more complex kind.

IMPLICATIONS FOR A TECHNOLOGY OF STRATEGIC CHOICE

There are many forms of management and planning technique which have been devised to help people deal with difficult decision problems. Indeed, systematic methods of designing courses of action, and comparing their likely consequences, have reached a considerable level of sophistication in some professional fields. For instance, systematic methods have been developed for assessing investment proposals in the light of predictions of not only their economic but also their social and environmental implications, while there are various computer-aided methods which can help generate a range of alternatives within some of the better understood fields of technological design. Meanwhile, mathematical programming techniques can allow analysts to conduct a systematic search for better solutions within a complex, multi-dimensional field, provided certain stringent assumptions

about the structure of the problem can be met.

As yet, however, there has been much less investment in the development of techniques to support the two modes of decision-making which appear in the upper part of Figure 8 – even though these two modes take on special significance in confronting decision problems of a less clearly structured kind, where it becomes necessary to cope with multiple inputs and outputs in a highly flexible, cyclic and, necessarily, subjective way.

Just as a distinction can be drawn between the two lower, more technical, modes in Figure 8 and the upper, more political modes, so can another kind of distinction be drawn between the two modes to the left of the diagram and the two modes to the right. Whereas the former two modes are primarily addressed towards the task of opening up the field of choice facing the decision-makers, the latter two modes can be seen as addressed towards the complementary task of narrowing that field down again in order to work towards agreement on action.

This distinction will be used as a basis for the organisation of the next two chapters. These will introduce and illustrate a series of basic concepts and techniques which have been developed, tested and modified progressively through repeated application to a range of applied planning problems. Together, these concepts and techniques can be seen as constituting an *appropriate technology* for strategic choice: appropriate in the sense that it is not intended as an advanced technology for use primarily by the expert. Rather the technology is designed to support the interactive work of groups of people who have different perspectives to contribute to a problem; who face quite daunting challenges in communicating with each other; yet who may appreciate the importance of working quickly and informally under the pressures of day-to-day events. So, the concepts to be introduced in the next two chapters will only occasionally be worth applying with a high level of analytical sophistication by specialists in a backroom setting.

FIGURE

9

A Structure for Subsequent Chapters

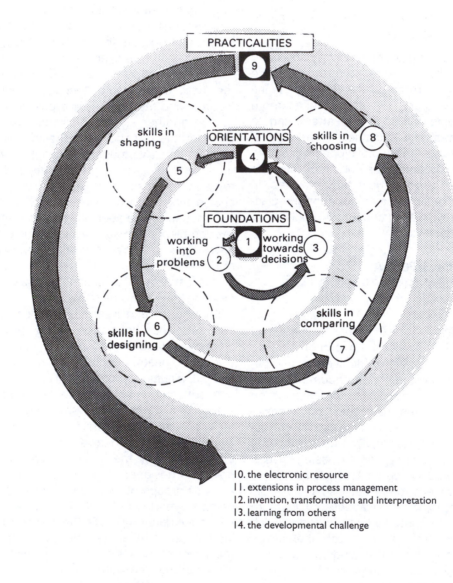

10. the electronic resource
11. extensions in process management
12. invention, transformation and interpretation
13. learning from others
14. the developmental challenge

Indeed, the more complex and unclear become the issues and their relationships, the more problematic become the more political modes of shaping problems and choosing actions, and the more vital it becomes that any technology of strategic choice be capable of use in a flexible and relatively non-technical way.

IMPLICATIONS FOR CHAPTER STRUCTURE

The emphasis in the chapters that follow will therefore be on quite simple and *transparent* concepts and techniques – most of them involving graphical forms of representation. These are intended to aid the processes of communication between people whose perspectives, attitudes and experiences may differ, as much as to help individuals in structuring their own personal thought processes. Working on these principles, Figure 9 presents a preview of the way in which the content of the nine chapters that follow will relate to the four modes of strategic choice which were distinguished in Figure 8. This picture can be used in conjunction with the 'Quick access guide' at the beginning, by the reader who wishes to

refer at any moment to the principles of structure on which this book has been designed.

Chapter 2, which is concerned with concepts and techniques for working into complex problems, will begin with the shaping mode, and will introduce some simple concepts which can help in structuring areas of choice and the interconnections between them. It will then move down to the designing mode, to introduce some further ideas to help in organising views about the options available and the patterns of compatibility or incompatibility between them. Chapter 3 is concerned with the complementary process of working towards decisions; it will begin with some concepts intended to help in comparing the foreseeable consequences of alternative courses of action, taking uncertainty explicitly into account. It then moves on to introduce further concepts addressed to the explicit management of uncertainty and the choice of incremental actions through time, drawing on the UE/UV/UR framework which has already been introduced. Together, the two chapters provide a foundation for the discussion, in later chapters, of the many different ways in which the basic concepts and methods can be brought into play in practice.

2 Working into problems

INTRODUCTION

The aim of this chapter is to introduce a set of basic concepts and methods which, taken together, offer a means of helping people to structure complex decision problems in terms of interrelated elements of choice. These concepts and techniques are addressed in particular to the work of the shaping and designing modes as set out on the left-hand side of the general process diagram (Figure 8). This means that they are concerned both with the shaping of problems and with the designing or formulation of possible courses of action in response to those problems. A further set of concepts and techniques for comparing those possible courses of action and for choosing between them will then be described in Chapter 3, to complete this introduction to a basic 'technology' for strategic choice.

The basic concepts to be introduced in this chapter will include those of the decision area; the option within a decision area; and the decision scheme, consisting of a set of mutually consistent options drawn from a set of interconnected decision areas. These and other concepts will be introduced in turn, illustrated by example and more formally defined. Taken together, they offer a quite general and flexible basis for the formulation of complex decision problems; and, more specifically, for the use of an analytical method known as Analysis of Interconnected Decision Areas – AIDA for short. The essentials of the AIDA method will be explained in this chapter, but some of the more important variations on it will be deferred for discussion in later chapters.

The approach to structuring of complex problems to be introduced here is quite simple in its essence. Yet, because it involves trying to express complex realities in simple and comprehensible terms, it can demand subtle and shrewd judgements of those participating in the process; judgements of a kind which are often made intuitively by individuals, yet are rarely exposed to argument in the normal course of debate. The nature of these judgements will become more apparent as this chapter unfolds.

For the purpose of introducing the basic ideas as simply and clearly as possible, this chapter will begin to develop a case example to be known as the *South Side Story*. It is a story of a group of decision-makers faced with a set of linked investment and locational decisions which impinge on a residential community of around 7000 people, living on the fringe of a larger urban area long dominated by heavy industry, but now in a state of economic and environmental decline.[1] The story is one which will be developed gradually in this and later chapters, as further concepts are introduced, and the skills and judgements involved in applying them in practice are discussed. For purposes of exposition, the various concepts and techniques will at this stage be introduced sequentially and in an orderly way. However, it has to be kept in mind throughout that in practice the process of strategic choice is normally much more flexible and adaptive. The process can shift rapidly from one mode to another, with a continued readiness to 'recycle' through earlier stages of analysis

---

1 The South Side Problem as presented here is closely – though by no means exactly – modelled on one of the first successful experiences in applying strategic choice methods to urban development problems.

FIGURE
10

SOUTH SIDE
EXAMPLE

The Concept of a Decision Area

DECISION AREA	LABEL
which route to choose to take the new arterial road across South Side?	ROAD LINE?
where to locate the local shopping centre for South Side?	SHOP LOC'N?
whether or not to declare West Street a housing improvement area?	WEST ST?
what land use to specify for the area of cleared housing in the centre of South Side	CENT'L SITE?
what level of investment to indicate for the continued life of South Side as a residential area?	DIST LIFE?
what land use to specify for the disused gasworks site?	GAS SITE?
when to schedule the closure of Griffin Road school?	GRIFF SCHL?

SHAPING

CONCEPTS

A DECISION AREA is an opportunity for choice in which two or more different courses of action can be considered.

as new insights emerge and the level of understanding grows.

THE CONCEPT OF THE DECISION AREA

The concept of a **decision area** provides the most fundamental element in the approach to problem structuring to be described in this chapter.

In essence, this concept offers no more than a means of describing and labelling any problem situation where people see an opportunity to choose between different courses of action. To begin with a simple example, you, the reader, may even now be thinking about a choice as to whether to read the remainder of this chapter or to skip ahead to the next. Or a person lying in bed may be conscious – even if only dimly – of a choice about what to do when a bedside alarm sounds: whether to get up, to ignore it, or to silence it by whatever means may be available. On a less personal note, a bank manager may encounter a decision area when judging what level of interest to charge a particular client for a loan; while the local authority planners mentioned in the last chapter found themselves faced with a decision area as to whether or not to approve the proposal for a new hotel. Meanwhile, the developer in question might face a range of decision problems, to do with timing, choice between alternative locations, scale, design, financial backing and other important commercial matters. These could either be expressed as a single, rather complex decision area or – as would be more usual when using strategic choice methods – as a set of different decision areas, the mutual relationships of which would have to be explored.

Implicit in each of these situations is an opportunity for decision-makers, whether alone or in association with others, to act in at least two alternative ways.[2] Also implicit in each situation is some sense of pressure or

concern to arrive at a commitment to some preferred course of action amongst those believed to be available even though it is only to be expected that some decision areas will carry a greater sense of urgency to act than others. It is this sense of pressure to act that creates a *decision problem* for those concerned – it being useful to distinguish the idea of a decision problem from that of other types of problem or puzzle which may be picked up and worked on casually as a diversion by anyone looking for interesting ways of passing their time.

To illustrate the concept of the decision area through the example of the South Side story, it is now necessary to set the scene a little more fully, by describing how the pressures to act have arisen in this case. At this stage, the context will be taken as one in which South Side comes within the administrative boundaries of a large urban municipality – the city of Dockport, serving around a quarter of a million people in all. South Side itself is an old-established neighbourhood with a strong sense of community among the residents – though they have been steadily declining in number as older housing has been cleared and local employment opportunities have dwindled.

This population base is likely to be reduced further over the next few years by the impending closure of the local steelworks, which has been a source of many jobs – but also of severe local air pollution that has lessened the attraction of South Side as a residential area. Although many of the older houses which remain in South Side are scheduled to be demolished in the next 2 or 3 years, others could have a prolonged life if designated for improvement, with financial aid from governmental grant aid programmes.

Suddenly, however, a new note of urgency has arisen for the municipality in considering

---

2 Purists sometimes point out that the word 'alternative' applies logically to an 'either/or' situation, so it is not

strictly correct to talk of a set of more than two different courses of action as 'alternatives'. However, this need not be treated as a serious source of difficulty here, as in the chapters that follow the comparison of alternatives will usually be treated as essentially a pair-wise process.

FIGURE

11

SOUTH SIDE
EXAMPLE

The Concept of a Decision Link

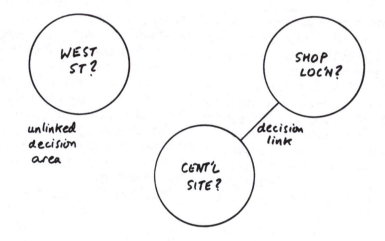

SHAPING

CONCEPTS

A DECISION LINK is a relationship between two decision areas expressing a belief that it could make a difference to consider them jointly instead of separately.

what to do about South Side – and, in particular, in addressing the problem of how far to invest in its continued viability as a residential community. For a proposal has just been published by a transportation agency to route a new arterial highway carrying industrial and other traffic directly through the neighbourhood. As might be expected, this heightens the sense of anxiety about the future among the local residents and traders. In response, the municipality calls for an early report on the problem from a specially formed internal working party of planners, engineers, accountants, and legal and valuation experts. From their initial discussions, it will be supposed that a list of seven potentially important decision areas emerge, as indicated in Figure 10.

In this list, it will be noticed that each decision area has not only been described with some care, but also given a brief label for purposes of future reference. The question marks – though they can be treated as optional in practice – are here added as a reminder that each decision area is supposed to represent an *opportunity* for choice rather than any particular *outcome* of the decision process. This is a point that is also stressed in the more formal definition accompanying Figure 10.

As the example shows, any list of decision areas can be quite diverse in the types of opportunity for choice which it contains. The first decision area in the list concerns choice of alignment for a road; the second concerns choice of location for a proposed local facility; two others concern choice of land use for particular sites; while the last in the list concerns a choice of timing.

There can also be variations between decision areas in the level of generality at which they are expressed. Whereas the fifth decision area concerns choice of policy stance in relation to investment in South Side as a whole, the third concerns a much more specific choice of action in relation to one particular street. It is one of the inherent strengths of the decision area concept that it allows different types and levels of choice to be considered together within a common analytical framework.

LINKS BETWEEN DECISION AREAS

As soon as a set of opportunities for choice has been formulated as a list of decision areas – even if only in a tentative way – it will usually begin to become apparent that some of them at least can be viewed as *interconnected*, in the sense that there is a case for considering them jointly rather than attempting to come to decisions taking each of them one at a time.

For example, an appreciation of the local geography of South Side might make it apparent that it could be unwise to consider the choice of use for the central site without any reference to the choice of location for the future local shopping centre. This implies a belief that the choices made if the two decision areas were considered together could *differ* from those that might emerge if each were looked at in isolation, on separate 'agendas' of decision-making. This might be the case if the choice of particular uses for the central site made some conceivable locations for the shopping centre physically impossible, or vice versa; it could also be the case if certain choices in either decision area seemed likely to make some choices in the other less attractive in terms of costs, implications for local residents or other consequences with which the working party could be concerned. More obviously, there could be an interconnection between the two decision areas if one of the possible locations for the shopping centre were the central site itself.

However, not every pair of decision areas in a list is likely to be directly linked in any of these ways. For instance, there may be no direct reason for supposing that the choice as to whether or not to improve West Street cannot be arrived at independently from the choice of location for the shopping centre, or the choice of use for the central site.

Using labelled circles to represent the decision areas and connecting lines to represent the presence or absence of direct links between them, a picture of mutual relationships can be built up graphically as shown in Figure 11. Here the connecting line, or

FIGURE

12

SOUTH SIDE
EXAMPLE

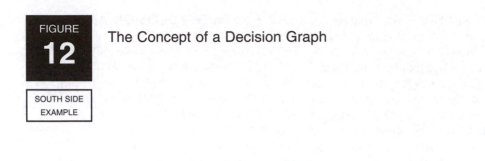

The Concept of a Decision Graph

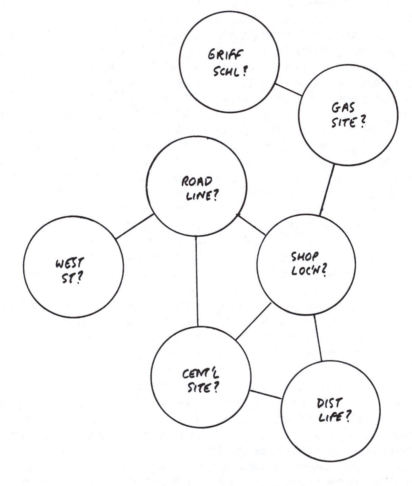

SHAPING

A DECISION GRAPH is a diagrammatic representation of a set of decision areas and the relationships between them expressed as decision links.

CONCEPTS

decision link, represents no more than a working assumption that, at least at the present stage of understanding of the problem, it makes sense to look into the mutual relationships between the two decision areas CENT'L SITE? and SHOP LOCN? Meanwhile, the absence of a link between WEST ST? and either of the other decision areas represents a working assumption that this choice can be dealt with independently from the other two.

The idea of a decision link forms a second 'core' concept in the strategic choice vocabulary, and is more formally defined in a statement appearing below Figure 11. The term *decision link* is usually abbreviated simply to *link* for working purposes, because it is usually clear from the context that the word is being used in this special sense. It is important to note at this stage that the concept of a decision link implies no particular view about the *sequence* in which the linked decisions should be taken, or about possible causal relationships. People who may be versed in other approaches to the mapping of relationships among decisions or systems are sometimes tempted to add arrowheads to decision links, to suggest directions of influence or precedence between one choice and another. However, it has not been found helpful to introduce such conventions into the approach being discussed here, which is purely concerned with the logic of mutual connectedness between one decision area and another.

Another caution concerns the tendency to interpret the concepts of decision area and decision link too narrowly in terms of familiar forms of relationships. In dealing with land use or locational problems in particular, there is a tendency for planners to focus on spatially defined decision areas and to look for links in terms of geographical adjacency or similar relationships. But decision areas and relationships between them can be used to reflect all kinds of non-spatial considerations as well, as the further unfolding of the South Side story will make clear. For this reason, no physical map of South Side is introduced at this stage: but any reader who may find it helpful to form some view of the geographical layout of South Side may like to glance briefly at the sketch map at the end of this chapter (Figure 18).

THE DECISION GRAPH AS A REPRESENTATION OF PROBLEM STRUCTURE

In any situation where a complex problem can be expressed in terms of a set of several decision areas, some but by no means all of which may be directly connected by decision links, it is possible to use the graphical connections introduced in Figure 11 to build up a wider view of the structure of that problem in the form of what is called a **decision graph**.[3]

A decision graph is, in effect, no more than a two-dimensional 'map' showing a set of decision areas and a set of links which connect some pairs but not others. Figure 12 gives an example of a decision graph for the set of seven decision areas so far identified within the South Side decision problem. This indicates that there are eight decision links in all, out of the total of 21 which would be theoretically possible if each of the seven had been directly linked to each of the other six.

This particular decision graph reflects an agreed view, among people who can be supposed to have specific knowledge of the realities of the South Side situation, that some decision areas are more directly interconnected than others. For instance, it shows several links connecting the four decision areas concerned with ROAD LINE?, SHOP LOCN?, CENT'L SITE? and DIST LIFE? – even though ROAD LINE? and DIST LIFE? are only linked indirectly through the other two. The WEST ST? and GRIFF SCHL? decision areas, in contrast, are comparative outliers, each being directly connected to only one of the other decision areas. Indeed, had it not been for the sudden introduction of a choice to be made about the road line, as a result of a highway

---

3   In some earlier writings this was referred to as a *strategy graph*.

FIGURE

13

SOUTH SIDE
EXAMPLE

The Concept of a Problem Focus

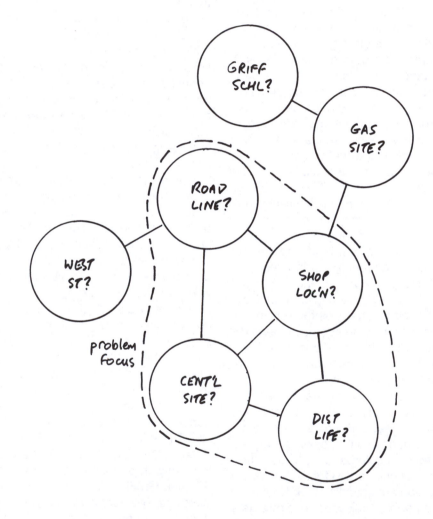

A PROBLEM FOCUS is any subset of the decision areas in a decision graph which is selected for closer examination.

planning exercise over a wider area, the WEST ST? decision area would have been completely disconnected from the SHOP LOC'N? and CENT'L SITE? decision areas, as was earlier suggested (Figure 11). This is a relatively simple example of a common occurrence not only in urban planning but in other fields, where the introduction of new decision areas can introduce additional complexity into a hitherto much simpler pattern of decision links.

Where a decision graph includes a larger number of decision areas than the example of Figure 12, it may be quite important to explore ways of rearranging it to bring out its underlying structure more clearly. It is important to note that there is no set rule to guide the positioning of each decision area on the graph: the map is a *topological* one, the meaning of which would not be changed if the relative positions of the decision areas were altered. The essential information conveyed by Figure 12 would be exactly the same if the WEST ST? decision area was shifted from the left to the right of the picture. However, it might then show some awkward crossovers between decision links, unless other decision areas were to be repositioned at the same time. The value of any decision graph lies essentially in the picture it presents about the structure of relationships between elements of a complex problem; a picture which can be modified through time and challenged wherever there is disagreement between participants in the process. In this way the participants can proceed, through as many iterations as need be, towards deeper examination of possibilities for action and their consequences, either within the graph as a whole or within selected decision areas or clusters within its structure.

THE CHOICE OF A PROBLEM FOCUS

The possibility of focusing on a selected cluster of decision areas within a larger decision graph offers an important field of judgement in a process of strategic choice. Indeed, it can mark a critical point of transition from the work of the shaping mode to that of the designing mode – especially where the decision graph is so large and complex in its structure that it is difficult to think of designing possible ways forward while keeping the full set of interconnected decision areas in view.

Any focus for the examination of possible ways forward which has been deliberately selected to include some but not all the decision areas in a decision graph can be referred to as a **problem focus**. It is important to note here that the scope of this problem focus can be changed, repeatedly if so desired, as work on the problem proceeds. There are many different considerations that can be taken into account in choosing a problem focus, and these will be discussed more fully in Chapter 5. At this stage it is the general concept of the problem focus that is important, as a means of managing the transition from the shaping to the designing mode.

In Figure 13, one possible problem focus has been selected for the South Side problem, by exercising a degree of selectivity within the decision graph of Figure 12. The comparatively isolated WEST ST?, GAS SITE? and GRIFF SCHL? decision areas have here been excluded, and a boundary indicating the limits of the resulting problem focus has been drawn around the other four. In the case of a decision graph of comparatively simple structure such as this, the step of choosing to concentrate on these four may seem a somewhat obvious one to take, working on the basis of the structural information alone (Figure 12). But it is not hard to see that the judgement could become more difficult if there were many more decision areas and connections to consider, and if it was thought important to take into account other reasons for focusing – such as the relative urgency and importance of different decision areas.

Even in this simple example there are several other choices of focus that could have been made. It could have been decided to focus only on the triangular cluster of ROAD LINE?, CENT'L SITE? and SHOP LOC'N? decision areas, on the grounds that each has at least

FIGURE

14

SOUTH SIDE
EXAMPLE

The Concept of a Decision Option

DECISION AREA	OPTIONS	OPTION LABEL
ROAD LINE ?	– northern route	– NORTH
	– southern route	– SOUTH
SHOP LOC'N ?	– Main Street	– MAIN
	– King Square	– KING
	– gasworks site	– GAS
CENT'L SITE ?	– industry	– IND
	– housing	– HOUS
	– open space	– OPEN
DIST LIFE ?	– 10 year horizon	– 10 YR
	– 20 year horizon	– 20 YR
	– 40 year horizon	– 40 YR

options in further decision areas excluded from problem focus :

WEST ST ?	– improve West Street	– YES
	– no action	– NO
GAS SITE ?	– shopping	– SHOP
	– open space	– OPEN
	– housing	– HOUS
	– industry	– IND
GRIFF SCHL ?	– schedule for early closure	– EARLY
	– keep open a few more years	– LATER

DESIGNING

CONCEPTS

A (DECISION) OPTION is any one of the mutually exclusive courses of action that can be considered within a decision area.

three decision links joining it to other decision areas, whereas DIST LIFE? has only two. It could also have been decided deliberately to keep all seven decision areas within the problem focus, or even to restrict it to only one decision area in the first instance – SHOP LOC'N? being one possible candidate because of its pivotal position on the graph. The narrower the focus, the less work there will be to do in the designing mode, especially if the alternatives within the decision area or areas concerned can be considered clear cut. So the more rapid can be the progress forward into the comparing mode. However, this is not to suggest that the case for choosing a broader focus will not re-emerge later, once the uncertainties involved in working within the narrow focus have taken clearer shape.

OPTIONS WITHIN DECISION AREAS

Despite all the information about the structure of a decision problem that may be contained within a decision graph, or even within a particular problem focus within a decision graph, this form of problem representation does nothing in itself to indicate what range of possible actions is likely to be open to the decision-makers. To make progress in this direction, it is necessary to move into the more technical domain of the designing mode, which takes its place in the bottom left-hand corner of the general process diagram (Figure 8). This is where the analytical method of *Analysis of Interconnected Decision Areas (AIDA)* begins to have an important part to play.[4]

The term **decision option** – usually referred to in practice simply as an option – will be introduced at this point to describe any one course of action within a decision area, out of whatever range of possibilities may be seen as

available. In the South Side case it will be supposed, for the sake of example, that the members of the local working party are able to agree that the range of choice in each of the seven decision areas can be represented by a set of two or more possible options, as indicated in Figure 14.

In practice, of course, it may sometimes be necessary to list more options than indicated in this example if a fully representative picture of the range of possibilities within a decision area is to be presented. Indeed, there may be a good deal of debate about these options among participants who may have different appreciations of the problems before them. During such a debate, different perceptions could well emerge not only about the number of options in each decision area, but also about the terms in which they should be expressed. For instance, it could be asked why the set of options for public investment in the continued life of South Side as a residential district should be limited to the range of 10-year, 20-year and 40-year horizons. Why not 5 years, or 15, or 100? And why express the range of possibilities in terms of time horizons at all? Could not the alternative policies perhaps be expressed in some broader, more flexible but still meaningful way, such as a choice of short-, medium- and long-term strategies?

It is also important to check that the options within a decision area are *mutually exclusive*. For instance, if industrial use of the central site did not necessarily rule out the possibility of housing or open space on part of the site, then mixed use options might have to be introduced; or perhaps the decision area itself could be reformulated in some way, to enable the options available to be expressed in a different form. Questions about whether the options within a decision area can be considered both representative and mutually exclusive can be well worth discussing if they help to focus critical attention on what is meant by the decision area in question and to suggest possibilities for reformulation of the problem in more realistic ways.

---

4 The AIDA method was first developed in the course of a seminal IOR/Tavistock Institute project on communications in the building industry, conducted in parallel with the Coventry local government study. See in particular Luckman (1967).

FIGURE
15

SOUTH SIDE
EXAMPLE

The Concept of an Option Bar

COMPATIBILITY TABLE FOR OPTIONS FROM
FIRST TWO DECISION AREAS - ROAD LINE?
& SHOP LOC'N?

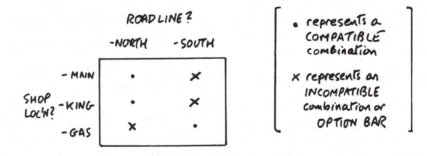

ROAD LINE?

	-NORTH	-SOUTH
- MAIN	•	✗
-KING	•	✗
- GAS	✗	•

SHOP LOC'N?

[
• represents a COMPATIBLE combination

✗ represents an INCOMPATIBLE combination or OPTION BAR
]

EXTENSION TO INCLUDE A THIRD
DECISION AREA - CENT'L SITE?

	ROAD LINE?		SHOP LOC'N?		
	-NORTH	-SOUTH	-MAIN	-KING	-GAS
-IND	•	✗	•	✗	•
-HOUS	•	✗	•	•	•
-OPEN	•	•	•	•	•

CENT'L SITE?

An OPTION BAR is a representation of an assumption that two options from different decision areas are incompatible with each other.

Once the set of options within a decision area is agreed to be adequate as a base for further analysis, it can be a useful practical step to give them short labels, as in Figure 14. So long as these labels do not suppress too much of the information contained in their full descriptions, they can save a great deal of time and space when it comes to examining combinations of options from different decision areas.

COMPATIBILITY OF OPTIONS IN INTERCONNECTED DECISION AREAS

Once options have been identified, the question arises of what possibilities for choice are to be found, not merely within each decision area taken separately, but within linked pairs or sets of decision areas within the selected problem focus. It therefore becomes necessary to introduce assumptions about how far options from different decision areas can be combined. For instance, the ROAD LINE? decision area in South Side contains two options while the SHOP LOCN? decision area contains three; if each option in the first decision area could be freely combined with each option in the second, this would give a total of $2 \times 3 = 6$ possible combinations from which to choose. In practice, however, the range of possibilities may be more restricted, because of various kinds of constraint which may be encountered in trying to combine particular options in one decision area with particular options in other decision areas. For example, a knowledge of local geography in South Side might make it sensible to assume that the choice of the southern road line would rule out the choice of both the Main Street and the King Square shopping locations, because either would mean that the majority of residents would be cut off from their neighbourhood shopping centre. Such a combination could be seen as violating what might be recognised as an important design principle – if not altogether destroying the centre's economic viability. A similar check on other combinations of options from these two decision areas, followed by a check of

options in the CENT'L SITE? decision area against those in each of the previous decision areas, might generate further assumptions on incompatibilities as shown in Figure 15.

Such a table is sometimes known as a *compatibility matrix*. When other decision areas are added, it can be extended further in a stepwise fashion to form a triangular array, until each pair of the decision areas within the present problem focus is covered. Each relationship of incompatibility between a pair of options from different decision areas, as indicated by a cross in any particular cell of the table, is known as an **option bar**. In the South Side example, there are altogether three option bars connecting the ROAD LINE? and SHOP LOCN? decision areas, which rule out three of the six conceivable combinations of options; then there are a further three option bars ruling out certain further combinations once the CENT'L SITE? decision area is added.

As in the identification of options within a decision area, it is quite normal for different participants to hold different views as to which combinations of options are feasible and which are not. Again, such differences can be used as a point of departure in working towards a clearer shared view of the structure of the specific decision problem which the decision-makers face.

BUILDING UP AN OPTION GRAPH

Where there are many decision areas and options to consider, and so the number of possible combinations is large, it can become a correspondingly laborious matter to check each option in each decision area for compatibility with each option in every other decision area in a systematic way. This itself is one good argument for choosing a limited problem focus of no more than four or five decision areas within a complex decision graph. However, in building up a series of two-way tables such as those in Figure 15, it is usually found that crosses representing option bars appear in only a minority of the cells. This can greatly

FIGURE
16

SOUTH SIDE
EXAMPLE

The Concept of an Option Graph

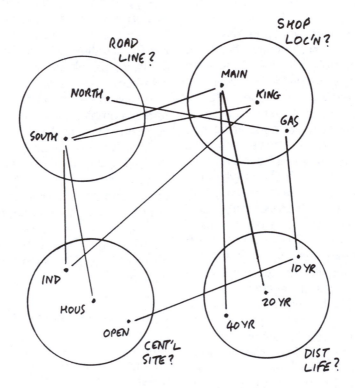

An OPTION GRAPH is a diagrammatic representation of the compatibilities and incompatibilities of options within a problem focus.

simplify the analysis of which combinations are possible and which are not.

The same kind of information can be built up by graphical methods, through an extension of the kinds of conventions used to develop the decision graph. This involves constructing what is known as an **option graph**, in which decision areas are represented by circles, as in the decision graph, but the set of options available within each decision area is specified within each circle as in the example of Figure 16. This allows the structure of relationships between specific options to be represented by drawing in connecting lines between those pairs of options from different decision areas where option bars have been identified.

It can avoid clutter in the option graph to use abbreviated labels for the options within each decision area and also to write the name of the decision area itself outside, rather than inside, the circle. The pattern of option bars can then be built up gradually, scanning the whole graph for possible incompatibilities rather than working logically through the combinations one at a time – and concentrating on pairs of decision areas which are directly connected through decision links. This kind of approach can provide a more open means of building up a picture of incompatibilities than the matrix approach – especially where there are several participants with different kinds of insight to offer.

Although the picture of Figure 16 may look quite complex and hard to interpret at a glance, it is worth noting that it includes only 10 option bars in all, as compared to the much larger number of combinations of pairs of options from different decision areas – in this example, 35 – which remain feasible. This observation helps to explain the convention of using connecting lines in an option graph to represent *incompatible* combinations rather than compatible ones. When first encountered, this convention can be found surprising and counter-intuitive. Nevertheless, a little experience soon shows that it is normally far more economical to use links between options

to represent the few incompatible pairs of options than the many compatible pairs. Not only does this make the picture of criss-crossing lines less impenetrable to the eye; more importantly, it allows new option bars to be introduced gradually as new reasons for incompatibility suggest themselves, and makes it much easier to keep track of the logic within the option graph.

It is only to be expected that the pattern of option bars in an option graph will bear some resemblance to the pattern of decision links within the corresponding part of the decision graph – if only because one obvious way in which a pair of decision areas can be interconnected is through some restriction on the extent to which options within them can be combined. However, the correspondence will not necessarily be precise: for instance, a pair of decision areas may be seen as linked on the decision graph not because there are any combinations of options which are incompatible, but because there are some combinations which appear to bring particular advantages or disadvantages in terms of costs or other consequences. So decision links do not necessarily imply option bars. Nor is it inconceivable that option bars will be identified to connect pairs of options from decision areas which were not thought to have been linked when the decision graph was first drawn; it is always possible that deeper reflection will bring insights into the problem structure which were not apparent at first sight.

GENERATING FEASIBLE DECISION SCHEMES

At this point the core concept of a **decision scheme** will be introduced to describe any combination of options, one drawn from each of the decision areas within a problem focus, which is feasible in the sense that it does not violate any of the option bars included in the current formulation of the decision problem. Even where the number of option bars in an option graph is quite limited, it can be far from easy to see what range of possible decision

FIGURE

17

SOUTH SIDE
EXAMPLE

The Concept of a Decision Scheme

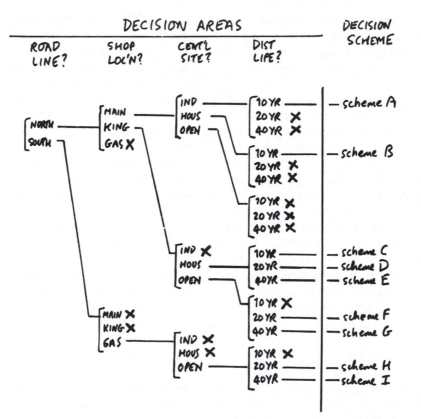

A DECISION SCHEME is any feasible combination of options containing one from each of the decision areas within a problem focus.

schemes is available simply by looking at the option graph itself. Instead, it is necessary to embark on a logical procedure for testing the feasibility of different combinations of options from the decision areas, considered not just two at a time but in sets of three or more taken together.

This means first arranging the decision areas within the current problem focus according to some chosen sequence, and then proceeding logically through that sequence in the manner illustrated in Figure 17. Here the various feasible combinations of options from the four selected decision areas for South Side are built up by proceeding through a systematic branching process. The combinations are presented in the form of a tree-like display somewhat similar in format to the 'decision tree' used in classical decision analysis. However, the aim here is not to provide a framework for analysing contingencies and probabilities, but simply to display all available decision schemes for further examination. To emphasise this difference, the alternative phrase **option tree** will be adopted here.

In Figure 17, for example, the path through the tree which combines the NORTH road line with the GAS shop location is eliminated at an early branching point, because of an option bar linking these two options directly. At a later stage, the NORTH-KING-IND route is terminated because there is an option bar between the KING and IND options, while further on again, the NORTH-MAIN-IND-20YR route is ruled out because of an incompatibility between a 20-year district life and the Main Street shop location. So, in progressing along each branch of the tree, it is necessary to check the compatibility of each new option not only with the option in the immediately preceding decision area, but also with all the others further back. In this example, indeed, the entire branch which begins NORTH-MAIN-OPEN is eliminated, not because of incompatibilities involving any pair of these three options, but because of two different types of option bar which are encountered once the final DIST LIFE? decision area is added.

In this example, the systematic development of the tree shows that there are, in all, nine feasible decision schemes, each of which has been given an alphabetic label for reference purposes. Sometimes there will be only a few feasible decision schemes, or even none at all; on other occasions, there may be so many that they become difficult to compare at all without some further filtering process.

The process of working systematically through the branches of a tree can provide important opportunities for learning. It can, of course, become time-consuming if the number of decision areas and options is much larger than in this example. In such circumstances, computer methods can sometimes be helpful, both as a check on the logic of the process and a means of testing rapidly the effect of different assumptions on options and option bars. There are various alternative ways of setting out the kind of information contained in Figure 17. In this example, the closed branches are included and terminated by a cross to help demonstrate the logic of the process; they could however, have been omitted, so allowing the range of available choices to be presented in a more compressed form. If desired, the set of feasible schemes could have been presented as a straight list rather than in the form of a tree; the advantage of the branching format is essentially in the structural information it conveys. Also, the arrangement of the set of decision schemes could be changed, either by working through the decision areas in a different sequence or by introducing comparative considerations to bring to the fore those schemes which might be considered more desirable. But this latter possibility means moving on to the perspective of the comparing mode, and will be left for further consideration in Chapter 3.

ANALYSING INTERCONNECTED DECISION AREAS: CONCLUDING REVIEW

This chapter has introduced a set of basic concepts which provide a foundation for the general method of problem structuring that has become known as Analysis of Interconnected Decision Areas, or AIDA for short. The most fundamental concepts of the AIDA method – those of the decision area, the option and the option bar – together form the basic elements required as input to build an option graph as a representation of the structure of choices within a problem or part of a problem; and, from this, to find out what range of possible 'solutions' or decision schemes is available. Among the other ideas introduced in the earlier sections of this chapter were those of the decision link, the decision graph and the problem focus – all of these being intended to help people in debating the overall shape of the problem before the more specific AIDA methods are brought into play.

The AIDA method of problem structuring does, of course, have its limitations in representing complexity of certain kinds; and these limitations will be discussed further in later chapters. In particular, it is not always easy to adapt the method to decision problems which are most naturally expressed in terms of adjustments to the levels of a set of more or less continuous control variables. However, decision problems can only be seen in terms of this kind of 'control model' in comparatively stable operating contexts, where the overall shape of the problem can be seen as more or less invariable through time. In such a case, it may be possible to use more sophisticated and specialised forms of analysis concerned with the systemic relationships among the decision variables particular to that operational setting. Nevertheless, even such 'well-structured' problems can often be embedded in wider problem settings with a more volatile structure, to which a more open-ended approach to problem structuring, of the kind described in this chapter, can usefully be applied. For the strategic choice approach has no claims to be a 'systems approach' in the commonly accepted sense: rather, it is a *process* approach in which the elements are choices which are normally supposed to be of a transient nature, and the relationships between elements are not therefore expected to assume any systemic form.

Relating the concepts and methods introduced in this chapter to the five basic dimensions of balance in strategic choice (Figure 2), the first of them – to do with the treatment of scope – has begun to be addressed by the concepts introduced to guide the work of the shaping mode: the decision area, the decision link, the decision graph and the problem focus. The second dimension of balance – to do with the treatment of complexity – has begun to be addressed by the general concepts of the decision option, the option bar, the option graph and the decision scheme, introduced to guide the work of the designing mode. But there is more to be discussed about the treatment of scope and of complexity in strategic choice in later chapters. Meanwhile, the treatment of conflict, uncertainty and progress – while touched upon in some places in this chapter and Chapter 1 – has scarcely begun to be discussed in terms of basic concepts and techniques. It is the introduction of such concepts and techniques that will be the purpose of Chapter 3.

SOME EXERCISES

At this stage, some readers may be glad of an opportunity to test their ability to make use of the concepts introduced in this chapter. To this end, the chapter concludes with a short set of exercises, all of them based on simple variations in the formulation of the decision problem faced in the South Side story as described so far.

1. If every pair of decision areas in Figure 12 which is not shown as directly interconnected were to be connected up, how many additional decision links would there be?
2. Suppose in Figure 12 that two additional decision links were added, one to connect ROAD LINE? to DIST LIFE? and the other to connect WEST ST? to SHOP LOC'N?, could the positions of the various decision areas be altered to make the structure of the decision graph clearer, in particular by avoiding any crossovers between the connecting links?

3. How many different ways can you see of choosing a problem focus within the decision graph as modified in Question 2, so as to include three fully interlinked decision areas?

4. Suppose the 40YR option for DIST LIFE? were to be eliminated as no longer available for some reason, how many of the nine feasible decision schemes in Figure 17 would this remove?

5. If an extra option bar were to be added to Figure 16, to rule out the combination of the 40YR option in the DIST LIFE? decision area with the OPEN option in the CENT'L SITE? decision area, how many of the nine feasible decision schemes in Figure 17 would have to be ruled out as not feasible?

6. Which of the decision schemes in Figure 17 – beyond those eliminated by Question 5 above – would be cut out if option bars were to be added between the NORTH option in the ROAD LINE? decision area and both the 10YR and 20YR options in the DIST LIFE? decision areas?

7. How many additional decision schemes would be added to the list of nine in Figure 17 if the option bar ruling out the SOUTH option in the ROAD LINE? decision area in combination with the IND option in the CENT'L SITE? decision area were to be removed?

Answers to the above questions will be found on the *Planning under Pressure* companion website.

Finally, we offer two more open-ended questions which, unlike those above, have no one answer. First, examine Figure 18, which shows the spatial relationships between the locations and alignments assumed in the formulation of decision areas and options in this chapter.

8. Do the spatial relationships shown in this map lead you to question the reasoning behind any of the decision links shown in Figure 12, or to suggest that any new ones should be included?

9. Do these same spatial relationships suggest that there could be a case for questioning the arguments behind any of the option bars shown in Figure 16 or for adding any further option bars?

FIGURE
18

SOUTH SIDE
EXAMPLE

South Side: Some Local Orientation

PROPOSED NEW ARTERIAL ROAD

north line

south line

→

from
Dockport
central area
5 km

West Street
housing

Main Street

to steelworks
and river

CENTRAL
SITE
(cleared)

King
Square

to the
sea

MAIN BLOCK OF
OLDER HOUSING
STREETS (what life?)

NEWER
HOUSING
ESTATE

possible sites
for future
South Side
local shopping
centre

Griffin Road
School

gasworks
site

to Eastwell 2km

←——— I kilometre ———→

3 Working towards decisions

INTRODUCTION

The aim of this chapter will be to complement Chapter 2 by introducing a further set of basic concepts and methods, designed to guide work within the comparing and choosing modes. Taken together, the various core concepts introduced in the two chapters will form a skeleton for an *appropriate technology* of strategic choice: a skeleton which will be built upon further in Chapters 5–8, where a range of variations on these concepts and methods will be discussed. The transition from the last chapter to this one involves a shift of focus; a shift from a concern with designing possible courses of action to a concern with discriminating among those possibilities in order to make progress towards decisions. As in Chapter 2, the intention will be to introduce a limited set of core concepts in as simple and basic a form as possible. However, they are concepts which address evaluative issues more directly than the concepts introduced to guide the work of the shaping and designing nodes; and these evaluative issues can become quite subtle and complex.

The first three concepts to be introduced are those of the comparison area, the relative assessment and the advantage comparison. All of these terms have their counterparts in everyday use; but they are expressed here in language which is designed to encourage a more explicit consideration of uncertainty than is found in some other approaches to evaluation. These concepts apply generally to any situation where there are different courses of action to be compared, whether there be only two alternatives to consider or a much wider range of possibilities to be scanned. Also, the

concepts are designed to apply whether or not there are numerical or other acceptable scales of measurement in view – recognising that consequences can often be subtle and far-reaching in their impact, so that an attempt to reduce assessments to a single unambiguous scale may not always be an appropriate way of dealing with the complexities and uncertainties encountered in practice.

The fourth concept to be introduced – that of the working shortlist – does however mean introducing more simplified scales of assessment to narrow down the range of possible alternatives. This is especially useful when working with several linked decision areas, generating a wide range of feasible combinations of options to be compared. So it is at this point of the chapter that the basic concepts about comparing come together with those about designing feasible decision schemes through AIDA, which were introduced towards the end of Chapter 2. In the second half of Chapter 3, four further basic concepts will be introduced, designed to guide the work of the choosing mode: these are the concepts of the uncertainty area, the exploratory option, the action scheme and the commitment package. It is in introducing these later concepts that the emphasis on management of uncertainty through time will come directly to the fore, in the spirit of the view of planning as a continuous process of strategic choice which was presented in Chapter 1.

FORMULATING A SET OF COMPARISON AREAS

The task of comparing any pair of alternative courses of action necessarily involves forming

FIGURE

19

SOUTH SIDE
EXAMPLE

The Concept of a Comparison Area

COMPARISON AREA   LABEL

differences in capital outlay
on construction works and
property acquisition :   CAPITAL :

differences in net flows of
income to this authority :   INCOME :

differences in local
employment opportunities :   JOBS :

differences in confidence
and quality of life for
South Side residents :   RESIDENTS :

COMPARING

CONCEPTS

A COMPARISON AREA is a description of any field of concern in which it is desired to compare the
consequences of alternative courses of action.

some view of what the consequences, effects or implications might be if either course of action were to be pursued rather than the other. It is possible to conceive of circumstances in which it may be sufficient to consider implications in relation to only one dominant area of concern. For example, a person choosing a painting to hang on a bedroom wall might be content to compare and choose solely on the basis of personal aesthetic judgement – at least in circumstances where that person lived alone and the set of alternative paintings available were all offered at the same price, with the same physical dimensions. Or a developer comparing competitive tenders for a building project might conceivably be content to compare on the grounds of quoted cost alone – but only in the somewhat artificial circumstances that all tenders met the brief in an identical way and no other comparative information was available with which to discriminate between contractors in terms of their reputations for reliability or quality of work.

These two examples indicate how rarely in practice it is realistic to restrict attention to a single dimension of comparison taken on its own. Indeed, the more far-reaching the implications of a decision problem, the wider the set of participants likely to become involved. So the less practicable it can become to reduce their concerns to a single basis for comparison, whether this be expressed in monetary or other terms.

The approach to comparison to be developed here can therefore be described as essentially a *multi-criteria* approach – to adopt a phrase which has now become fashionable in relation to more specific mathematical methods of comparison. The concept of a *criterion* is of course familiar enough, not only to decision scientists but also to many practising planners and managers. However, the word is one which can convey subtly different meanings to different people – for instance, it conveys to many people an expectation of a defined scale of measurement, even though dictionary definitions tend to suggest the idea of comparison with some pre-set standard or norm.

For this reason, the concept of criterion will here be replaced by a more general concept of a **comparison area**, which will be more carefully defined within the context of the strategic choice approach.

In essence, a comparison area can be seen as simply a description of some area of concern to the participants in a decision process, within which they may wish to consider what the consequences of alternative courses of action might be. Figure 19 illustrates this concept by presenting descriptions of four different comparison areas which could be seen as important in addressing the decisions facing the South Side Working Party, in the planning situation that was outlined in Chapter 2. As in the earlier listing of decision areas, each of these comparison areas is specified in terms of both a brief label, for quick reference, and a fuller and more careful description of what it embraces. By convention, the brief label is followed by a colon (:), so as to distinguish a comparison area from a decision area, the label of which is followed by a question mark (?). The fuller description can serve an important practical purpose, as a means of checking that the same comparison area is being interpreted in a similar way by different participants; and it can of course always be modified later as understanding grows.

It is often helpful to include, within the fuller description of a comparison area, not only an indication of the *types* of effects or consequences that it covers, but also some indication of their *incidence* in terms of community sectors or interest groups, or perhaps over different time horizons. This can be especially significant where the participants see themselves as accountable to more than one 'constituency' of affected interests. Indeed, different participants in a decision process will sometimes be recognised as representing different sectors or groups. Questions of incidence and perceived equity can sometimes become quite crucial to the politics of comparing and choosing; and they can indeed emerge as major sources of uncertainty in the UV category, the management of which can become

FIGURE

20

SOUTH SIDE
EXAMPLE

The Concept of a Relative Assessment

DECISION AREAS				DECISION SCHEME	COMPARISONS	
ROAD LINE?	SHOP LOC'N?	CENT'L SITE?	DIST LIFE?		COMPARISON AREA	RELATIVE ASSESSMENT

NORTH — MAIN — IND — 10YR | scheme A — A = baseline for comparison

1st comparison: B vs A

↓

NORTH — MAIN — HOUS — 10YR | scheme B

assessments of B relative to A:

CAPITAL: about 250k* *less*

INCOME: 10k–30k* *less* per year

JOBS: 100-200 local jobs *fewer*

RESIDENTS: probably *more* confidence

2nd comparison: H vs A

↓   ↓   ↓   ↓

SOUTH — GAS — OPEN — 20YR | scheme H

assessments of H relative to A:

CAPITAL: 200k* *less* to 400k* *more*

INCOME: 40k-100k* *less* per year

JOBS: 40-160 local jobs *fewer*

RESIDENTS: much *less* confidence

[↓ indicates change of option
relative to scheme A]

[* k = 1000 units of this national
currency - e.g. £, $, Fr....]

COMPARING

○○
○●

CONCEPTS

A RELATIVE ASSESSMENT is a name for any statement about the consequences within a comparison
area of pursuing one course of action instead of another.

critical to the guidance of the overall decision process. In order to keep the number of comparison areas manageable, they can if desired be formulated so as to bring together several different elements under a single more general heading. For instance, in Figure 19, the familiar heading of CAPITAL: is used to bring together expenditures on both construction works and property acquisition. In other situations, however, there might also be compensating capital receipts to consider, from the disposal of surplus land or buildings which, according to accounting convention, might be considered either within the CAPITAL: or the INCOME: comparison area.

Sometimes, also, different comparison areas can be combined. For example, it might be agreed that for working purposes the CAPITAL: and INCOME: comparison areas in Figure 19 should be combined into a broader comparison area simply called FINANCE:. These examples merely serve to demonstrate the general point that there may be much scope for choice in the way a set of comparison areas is formulated. Indeed, where there are several participants, it can be valuable to encourage open debate over this choice, leading to elaboration or simplification of the set of comparison areas as work proceeds and the level of shared understanding grows.

ASSESSING CONSEQUENCES WITHIN COMPARISON AREAS

Once a set of comparison areas has been chosen, it can be put to use as a framework for comparing alternative courses of action in the light of people's assessments of what their differing consequences might be. The idea of a **relative assessment** will be treated as another core concept in the strategic choice vocabulary; but it will often be abbreviated to the single word *assessment* so long as the context is clear. The idea of a relative assessment is intended to cover not only any consequences or implications of a direct and immediately foreseeable kind, but also any consequences or implications which may be more gradual, indirect and hard to pin down in any tangible way.

There are two important qualities to bear in mind in making a prior assessment of the consequences of some proposed future course of action, as opposed to a retrospective assessment of the consequences of some course of action already carried through. Firstly, any assessment of future consequences will always be to some degree *conjectural*, in that it will involve elements of speculation or guesswork as to what might follow if that course of action were to be set in train. Secondly, such an assessment will be essentially *comparative* in the sense that, whether explicitly or otherwise, it involves contrasting the consequences of pursuing that course of action with those that might follow from choosing some other course instead. This point applies even if that other course were to take a passive stance and aim to preserve the status quo – which is a common baseline for many kinds of assessment in practice.

Figure 20 presents some examples of relative assessments within each of the four comparison areas for South Side. Two different examples of relative assessments are presented here, both from within the range of nine possible decision schemes which was developed earlier (Figure 17). First, Scheme B is assessed relative to Scheme A – the difference between these two alternatives being only in the choice of option for use of the Central Site. Then, Scheme H is assessed also in relation to the same baseline of Scheme A, recognising that the comparison in this case is likely to be rather less straightforward because Schemes H and A differ in the options selected in each of the four decision areas.

It will be noticed in this example that the forms in which the relative assessments are presented differ from one comparison area to another. Even though the capital and income assessments are both expressed in monetary units, the capital assessments are expressed as lump sums and the income assessments as annual flows, in keeping with familiar accounting conventions. Differences in jobs

FIGURE

21

SOUTH SIDE
EXAMPLE

The Concept of an Advantage Comparison

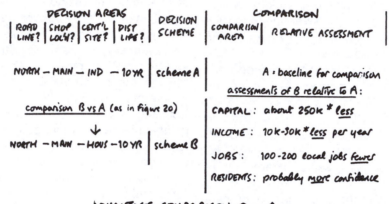

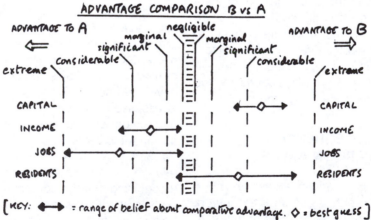

[KEY: ⟷ = range of belief about comparative advantage. ◇ = best guess]

COMPARING

○○
○●

CONCEPTS

An ADVANTAGE COMPARISON is a name for any statement of belief about the balance of advantage between alternatives in one or more comparison areas.

are also expressed in numerical terms, but this time expressed in non-monetary units of the net number of local jobs created. However, the assessments of the consequences for the South Side residents are expressed here purely in terms of words – illustrating a very common situation in practice where there is no accepted numerical scale to which to refer.

The example of Figure 20 also illustrates some of the different ways in which feelings of *uncertainty* can be expressed. In one case – the assessment of capital outlay for Scheme B relative to Scheme A – a single estimate only is presented; but the word 'about' is inserted to convey the information that there is felt to be at least some uncertainty over the extent of the difference. In other places, a range of figures is presented; this conveys additional information about the degree of uncertainty experienced – which may well differ between one relative assessment and another. By moving to a more elaborate format of presentation than that in Figure 20, it would be possible to go into these feelings of uncertainty in more depth, distinguishing between different contributory factors, spelling out underlying assumptions and indicating contingencies which could have a significant effect on the levels of assessment presented. These possibilities will be discussed further in Chapter 7; for the time being, it is enough to stress that there is a wide field of choice in the level of elaboration or simplification employed in presenting relative assessments in practice.

JUDGING COMPARATIVE ADVANTAGE BETWEEN ALTERNATIVES

Because the set of comparison areas is designed to reflect fields of direct concern to decision-makers, any statement that one alternative differs from another within a particular comparison area will usually convey a sense of positive or negative value in the current decision situation; it will be seen as either good or bad, nice or nasty. For example, from the comparison of Scheme B with Scheme A in Figure 20, it will almost certainly count as an *advantage* to B that it should incur about 250 thousand monetary units less than A in capital outlay, but a *disadvantage* that it should yield less income. Again, it is likely to be considered a disadvantage to Scheme B that it should create fewer jobs, but an advantage that it should generate more confidence among the residents of South Side.

Sometimes, there may be some conflict of opinion as to whether a relative assessment should be viewed in a positive or a negative light; and often, there will be some doubt as to whether advantages in some comparison areas should be seen as outweighing disadvantages in others. Such a state of doubt appears to surround the comparison of Schemes A and B for South Side, because the overall balance of advantage across the four comparison areas is by no means clear. However, Scheme H appears to offer no advantages compared to A in any of the four comparison areas, if the same sense of positive and negative values is applied – unless perhaps further investigation of the uncertainty about the CAPITAL: assessment could reveal that H has indeed an advantage over A in this one comparison area.

Various methods of economic analysis have been developed which allow assessments in different comparison areas to be brought together by being expressed in commensurate terms. For instance, annual flows of income can be converted to capital equivalents by forms of discounted cash flow analysis which reflect market rates of return. Some economists have also developed methods for computing monetary values for other quantitative indicators, such as numbers of jobs created. But such conversions can have the effect of suppressing underlying uncertainties of value judgement which, from a strategic choice perspective, may be important to expose to debate.

It is more in keeping with the philosophy of strategic choice to turn to an openly judgemental scale of comparison, in which uncertainties of value judgement can be exposed alongside any other uncertainties that have arisen in assessing the nature or magnitude of the consequences in the various comparison areas. Such an approach is illustrated in Figure 21, which introduces a non-numerical scale of **advantage comparison** as a basis for translating relative assessments within diverse comparison areas into a common framework. The adjectives 'negligible', 'marginal', 'significant', 'considerable' and 'extreme' are intended to represent an ascending scale of advantage to the decision-makers in either direction. However, the way in which these words should be interpreted – and indeed the judgement as to what the relative widths of the various bands of the scale should be – can be left open to the discretion of the users in the particular organisational and political context in which they are working.

For example, Figure 21 interprets the assessment that Scheme B will involve about 250 000 monetary units less capital outlay than Scheme A as representing somewhere between a significant and a considerable advantage to B in relation to the decision situation currently faced in South Side. In another context, the judgement made might be quite different: for example a central government setting a national budget might well regard such a difference as negligible, while a small business, or an individual managing a family budget, would probably consider it extreme. In each row of Figure 21, the convention is adopted of representing the range of uncertainty over where the advantage lies by a pair of arrowheads, with the current 'best guess' marked in between – frequently, but not necessarily, positioned at the mid-point of the range. As the example suggests, this range of uncertainty can vary considerably from one comparison area to another.

It is important to recognise that the range is intended to embrace uncertainties encountered both in assessing alternatives within each separate comparison area and also in judging how these assessments should be transferred to the common advantage comparison scale. For instance, in the South Side case, there may be considerable uncertainty not only over how large the difference in local jobs created might be, but also over how much weight should be attached to any such difference in policy terms. Turning to the impact on South Side residents, uncertainty arises partly because there is no clear numerical yardstick for assessment of different levels of confidence in the future of the area, and partly because some decision-makers may place a higher policy value on residents' confidence than others.

The value of a common judgemental scale, however crude, is that it provides a framework within which assessments in different comparison areas can be balanced and merged. For example, taking the four 'best guess' points in Figure 21, it can be argued that a considerable advantage to Scheme B in terms of capital should outweigh a (merely) significant advantage to A in terms of income; and that the advantage of B to local residents should roughly balance out the advantage to A in terms of jobs, leaving a slight overall advantage to B when all four comparison areas are viewed together.

However, this overall balance of advantage can become more difficult to judge when notice is taken of the uncertainties that surround the various placings on the advantage comparison scale. In the illustration presented in Figure 21, the combined effect of these uncertainties is to make it by no means clear to which alternative the overall balance of advantage for the decision-makers will lie. Some approaches to the more careful analysis of how such uncertainties affect the balance of advantage will be discussed in Chapter 7. However, the most important point about the particular format of advantage comparison illustrated here is that it allows many different sources of uncertainty to be brought together in a common perspective: a perspective which is designed to reflect the political realities of the situation within which the alternatives in question have to be compared. This kind of advantage comparison between specific alternatives will therefore form an important point of reference when it comes to considering methods of working in the choosing mode.

RESTRICTING THE FOCUS FOR COMPARISONS AMONG DECISION SCHEMES

Where there are only a few alternative courses of action to consider, it may not be difficult to compare each with every other, using the same kind of methodical approach to pair-wise comparison which was illustrated in Figures 20 and 21. This is usually feasible enough when comparing a set of three or four options within a single decision area, or when the focus of comparison is limited to only a few feasible decision schemes.

However, this pair-wise approach to comparison can become much more time-consuming where there are many possible combinations of options available. For example, there are 36 possible pair comparisons that might be made among the nine decision schemes for South Side (Figure 17), because each of the nine can be compared with each of the eight others – the resulting number of comparisons being reduced from 72 to 36 when it is remembered that pair-wise comparison is a two-way process. If the number of possible schemes was doubled to 18, the number of possible comparisons would increase more than four-fold, to 153. In general, the longer a list of schemes grows, the more essential it becomes to choose some more manageable set of schemes within the list – in everyday terms, a shortlist – before attempting to compare alternatives more thoroughly in a pair-wise manner. The term **working shortlist** will be added to the basic strategic choice vocabulary to describe any shortlist formed for such a purpose. In effect, it serves the same kind of simplifying purpose when people are working towards decisions as does the idea of problem focus when they are working into complex problems.

One way in which a long list of decision schemes can be reduced is to focus only on those which come within acceptable limits in terms of one or more chosen dimensions of evaluation which the decision-makers see as of particular importance. So it might be decided to place a constraint on the maximum level of capital cost – if capital is regarded as a scarce resource – or the minimum level of income to be generated by a scheme. Or it might be agreed, in the South Side case, to exclude any schemes involving a net loss rather than a gain of local job opportunities compared to the status quo.

Introducing such a constraint normally means resorting to a simplified scale of assessment, on which each scheme can be represented by a single point, with all information about uncertainty set aside for this purpose. This then allows the set of schemes to be rearranged, or ranked, in an unambiguous order of preference so far as that particular scale is concerned, allowing all schemes above or below the agreed threshold to be set aside. Often the chosen scale will be a numerical one, but this is not essential: for instance, a non-numerical scale with seven points labelled 'very high', 'high', 'fairly high', 'medium', 'fairly low', 'low' and 'very low' provides quite an acceptable scale for ranking purposes, because it is quite clear which assessment comes before which other in the sequence.

A simplified scale for purposes of ranking or shortlisting can be defined either within a single comparison area, or to span more than one comparison area where there is some common scale through which they can be linked. For example, a monetary scale can be used to span both capital and recurrent costs, provided there is some agreed convention for converting running costs into capital equivalents or vice versa. In general, however, the use of any such composite scale as a shortlisting device can mean a considerable sacrifice of information in the interests of simplification. Indeed, any approach to shortlisting can mean sacrificing much information about uncertainty which could be important later on. For instance, potentially significant

FIGURE
22

SOUTH SIDE
EXAMPLE

The Concept of a Working Shortlist

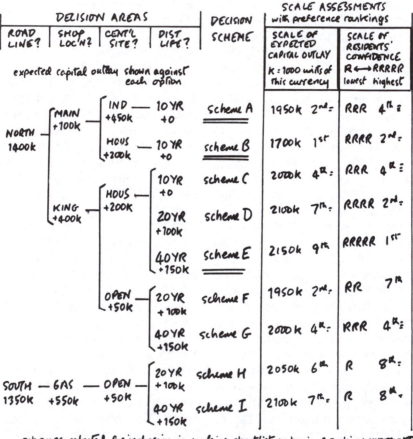

DECISION AREAS				DECISION SCHEME	SCALE ASSESSMENTS with preference rankings	
ROAD LINE?	SHOP LOC'N?	CENT'L SITE?	DIST LIFE?		SCALE OF EXPECTED CAPITAL OUTLAY k = 1000 units of this currency	SCALE OF RESIDENTS' CONFIDENCE R ←→ RRRRR lowest highest

expected capital outlay shown against each option

NORTH 1400k — MAIN +100k — IND +450k — 10 YR +0 — scheme A — 1950k 2nd= — RRR 4th=

HOUS +200k — 10 YR +0 — scheme B — 1700k 1st — RRRR 2nd=

KING +400k — HOUS +200k — 10 YR +0 — scheme C — 2000k 4th= — RRR 4th=

20 YR +100k — scheme D — 2100k 7th= — RRRR 2nd=

40 YR +150k — scheme E — 2150k 9th — RRRRR 1st

OPEN +50k — 20 YR +100k — scheme F — 1950k 2nd= — RR 7th

40 YR +150k — scheme G — 2000k 4th= — RRR 4th=

SOUTH 1350k — GAS +550k — OPEN +50k — 20 YR +100k — scheme H — 2050k 6th — R 8th=

40 YR +150k — scheme I — 2100k 7th= — R 8th=

schemes selected for inclusion in working shortlist on basis of rankings UNDERLINED

COMPARING

CONCEPTS

A WORKING SHORTLIST is any subset of a set of decision schemes in which it is intended to compare alternatives more closely.

information about South Side was presented earlier (Figure 20) through the use of qualifying words such as 'probably' and through using lower and upper limits in place of single-point estimates. Any shortlisting process can also mean loss of much information about the multi-dimensional nature of consequences both within and between the chosen comparison areas. Such losses of information can be quite justifiable as a means of focusing the process of comparison where there are many schemes to consider; but only so long as the possibility is not forgotten of reintroducing that information at a later stage in the decision process.

The use of simplified scales in forming a working shortlist is illustrated in Figure 22. This example introduces two contrasting scales for the purpose of choosing a more limited focus for comparison within the set of nine schemes already generated for South Side. In this example, the scale of expected capital cost is expressed in standard monetary units, defined as in Figure 20. The assessment for each of the nine schemes has here been built up by a straightforward addition of capital estimates for each option, each measured against the same baseline which supposes there to be no capital investment at all. An alternative approach would, of course, have been to make a separate estimate for each of the nine schemes seen as a composite entity. Indeed, this might have been judged preferable if there were believed to be significant capital savings or costs associated with particular *combinations* of options from different decision areas.

The second scale, relating to confidence among local residents, is developed in a different way. The lowest score is awarded to the scheme or schemes judged to have the most negative effect on residents' confidence – in this case Schemes H and I – while the highest score is awarded to the scheme or schemes judged to have the most positive effect – in this case Scheme E. Then intermediate numbers of points are awarded to each of the other possible schemes. Of course, these scores

too could have been built up cumulatively by options, in the same way as the numerical scale of capital cost – but it has been supposed here that the scoring of each scheme viewed as a whole offers a more realistic alternative in the particular circumstances of South Side. Figure 22 shows not only the scores of the nine schemes on each of the two scales, but also the two sets of *rankings* obtained in this way, with tied rankings in some cases. Inspecting this information, it appears that Scheme B shows particular promise, having a high ranking in terms of both indices. In choosing a working shortlist for closer comparison, other apparently promising schemes might also be included, such as Scheme A and Scheme E – which is the most promising in terms of residents' confidence, even if the least promising in terms of capital outlay. Another candidate could be Scheme C, which is moderately well placed in both respects. But a fuller comparison of B with A, C or E might throw up disadvantages in other comparison areas, which might suggest that the focus of comparison should be shifted yet again. Furthermore, some schemes which are apparently poorly placed according to the scales of Figure 22 might well be brought back into consideration later because of the types of advantage excluded from the shortlisting process at this stage.

EXPLORING AREAS OF UNCERTAINTY

All the time comparisons of alternatives are being made, the participants will usually also be subject to practical pressures, political and administrative, to move in the direction of decisions: or, in terms of the general process model (Figure 8), to shift upwards from the comparing into the choosing mode. At such times, attention will shift from the comparison of alternatives under uncertainty to the conscious management of that uncertainty from a decision-making perspective. So it is at this point that the concept of an **uncertainty area** will be introduced. This will be regarded as

FIGURE
23

SOUTH SIDE
EXAMPLE

The Concept of an Uncertainty Area

UNCERTAINTY AREA	LABEL	TYPE	
? attractiveness of central site to employment-intensive industries	?SITEJOBS	UE	identified as major influences on advantage comparison of A and B in relation to JOBS: comparison area
? policy value to us of job creation	? VALJOB	UV	
? decision on future use of steelworks site	?STEELSITE	UR	identified as major influences on advantage comparison of A and B in relation to RESIDENTS: comparison area
? policy value to us of meeting residents concerns	?VALRES.	UV	
? decision on density of new housing developments	?HOUDENS	UR	
? future trends in regional housing market	?HOUMKT	UE	identified as influencing comparison of A and B in relation to INCOME:
? policy decision on level of infrastructure provision on new industrial sites	? INDINFR	UR	identified as influencing comparison of A and B in relation to both INCOME: and CAPITAL:

CHOOSING

An UNCERTAINTY AREA is a description of any source of uncertainty which is causing difficulty in the consideration of a decision problem.

CONCEPTS

another core concept in the strategic choice vocabulary; similar, in some respects, to the concepts of decision area and comparison area as already introduced. All three concepts can be seen as expressing areas of concern to the participants in a planning process, and as offering wide scope for discretion and judgement in the way they are formulated. Indeed, circumstances often arise where what was at first expressed as an area of concern of one type may with advantage be reformulated in terms of any one of the other types.

An uncertainty area can be formulated at any moment in a process of strategic choice where doubts arise over the choice of assumptions on which the designing or comparing of alternatives should proceed. Such assumptions can be of many kinds, but they can be grouped broadly according to the three categories of uncertainty that were introduced in general terms in Chapter 1: **UE** for **U**ncertainties about the working **E**nvironment; **UV** for **U**ncertainties about guiding **V**alues; and **UR** for **U**ncertainties about **R**elated decisions (Figure 3).

In the UE direction, participants in a process of strategic choice may experience personal doubts, or may differ among themselves, as to the assumptions they should make about external circumstances or trends. In the UV direction, they may experience doubts or disagreements as to the values that should influence them, especially when they are seeking to compare alternatives across different comparison areas which reflect the concerns of diverse interest groups. In the UR direction, they may have difficulties agreeing what assumptions to make about the choices that are expected to be made in future in other decision areas outside the current scope of the problem on which they are working: decision areas over which they might conceivably have some influence, even if that influence may be quite limited or indirect.

In Figure 23, the concept of the uncertainty area is illustrated through seven examples which reflect various doubts and disagreements seen as relevant by members of the South Side Working Party, at a moment

when they are trying to judge the balance of advantage between the two decision schemes labelled A and B. This list of uncertainty areas might be part of a considerably longer list built up at successive stages of the process. Here, however, those listed are all seen as having relevance to the particular task of judging whether the overall balance of advantage lies to A or B. This is a judgement that can be approached by focusing on the information about uncertainty that was presented in the advantage comparison analysis of Figure 21 – though that analysis on its own gives no information about what the main sources of uncertainty are.

As in the listing of decision areas, and indeed also of comparison areas, the convention is here adopted of giving each uncertainty area both a fuller description and a briefer label for quick reference. The convention of placing the question mark before rather than after the label is intended merely as a means of distinguishing uncertainty areas from decision areas. Indeed, it allows either kind of area to be quickly transformed into the other whenever it seems sensible to do so.

The list in Figure 23 begins by identifying five uncertainty areas which are seen as between them creating difficulty in judging the balance of advantage between Schemes A and B in the JOBS: and RESIDENTS: comparison areas. These two comparison areas are examined first because they appear (Figure 21) to hold the widest range of doubt when all the four assessments are translated into terms of the advantage comparison scale.

Looking first at the JOBS: assessment, the range of 100–200 local jobs fewer for Scheme B relative to Scheme A may reflect in the main a feeling of uncertainty about the attractiveness of the Central Site to employment-intensive industries – which can be expressed as an uncertainty area of type UE. However, once the attempt is made to translate this assessment into terms of comparative advantage, a substantial degree of doubt may also arise as to what weight the participants should give

FIGURE
24

SOUTH SIDE
EXAMPLE

The Concept of an Exploratory Option

UNCERTAINTY AREA	EXPLORATORY OPTION	COMPARISON OF EXPLORATORY OPTIONS	
		COMPARISON AREA	RELATIVE *ASSESSMENT
? SITEJOBS (UE)	Commission consultants to do market survey	CONFIDENCE:	slightly more confidence in advantage comparison A:B
		RESOURCES:	estimated fee 20k
		DELAY:	allow 3 months from commissioning to reporting
? VALJOB (UV)	informal soundings with leading members of policy group	CONFIDENCE:	much more confidence in advantage comparison A:B
		RESOURCES:	some demands on time of busy policy-makers
		DELAY:	allow 1-2 weeks to contact and discuss
? STEELSITE (UR)	liaison with joint steelworks site planning team	CONFIDENCE:	more confidence in advantage comparison A:B
		RESOURCES:	perhaps ½ day spent in meeting; also preparation time
		DELAY:	allow 1 month

* relative to option of taking no exploratory action i.e. null option

CHOOSING

CONCEPTS

An EXPLORATORY OPTION is any course of action conceived as a means of reducing current feelings of uncertainty within some uncertainty area.

to the creation of new jobs in this locality, relative to other consequences of the choice before them; so this is a doubt that can be expressed as an uncertainty area of type UV.

Turning to the RESIDENTS: comparison, Figure 23 again shows a substantial area of uncertainty of type UV, concerned with the policy value that the municipality should attach to meeting the concerns of local residents. However, the main uncertainties in assessing the actual impact on local residents of choosing Scheme B rather than A can in this case be seen as of type UR rather than UE, because they are to do with two related areas of decision outside the current problem focus. One of these is concerned with the future use of a nearby site, which is expected to be vacated soon by a major steel-making corporation. Some residents of South Side have been campaigning for redevelopment of this site for light industry rather than other purposes; if this case is conceded, it is thought their concern about the use of the Central Site will be less acute than if the site is put to any alternative use. The other uncertainty area relates to the recommendations of the municipality's own housing planning team over density of any future housing development on the Central Site itself. If the density is high enough and the cost low enough to make homes on this site available to local people, then it is judged that residents' confidence in the future of their community would be increased.

Finally, the list of Figure 23 includes two further uncertainty areas which impinge on the INCOME: and CAPITAL: assessments – in one case impinging on them both. However, a glance back to Figure 21 suggests that these uncertainty areas will not be so critical to the overall comparison of Schemes A and B as those affecting the JOBS: and RESIDENTS: assessments. So no attempt need be made at this stage to look for further uncertainty areas which affect these two financial dimensions of the overall evaluation frame.

IDENTIFYING EXPLORATORY OPTIONS

Once a list of uncertainty areas has been developed, the question arises of what, if anything, should be done about them. For each uncertainty area that seems to be relevant to a particular comparison of alternatives, there is always the possibility of *accepting* the current level of uncertainty over what assumptions to adopt, and looking for ways in which it can be accommodated. However, there may also be a possibility of initiating some kind of *exploratory action* which offers a hope that any current feelings of uncertainty can be significantly reduced before decisions have to be made.

Any course of action designed to alter the current state of doubt within an uncertainty area can be called an **exploratory option**. The idea of an exploratory option is of central significance to the work of the choosing mode; so it will be considered as another core concept in the strategic choice vocabulary. In effect, the identification of any exploratory options that could be adopted in response to a particular uncertainty area can be seen as extending the problem formulation by introducing an additional decision area; a decision area concerned with whether or not any investment should be made in the reduction of current levels of doubt within the uncertainty area concerned.

This point is illustrated in Figure 24, which gives examples of exploratory options relating to each of the first three uncertainty areas from the list in Figure 23 – supposing these to be judged the most important at the present moment in the decision process. In each case, one possible exploratory option is identified and is compared with the 'null option' of taking no exploratory action in relation to the uncertainty area in question. The nature of any exploratory action to be considered will tend to vary with the type of uncertainty area addressed. As originally suggested (Figure 3), uncertainty areas of type UE will suggest possibilities for exploration in the form of research, surveys, analytical work or forecasting exercises. Uncertainty areas of type UV

FIGURE
25

SOUTH SIDE
EXAMPLE

The Concept of an Action Scheme

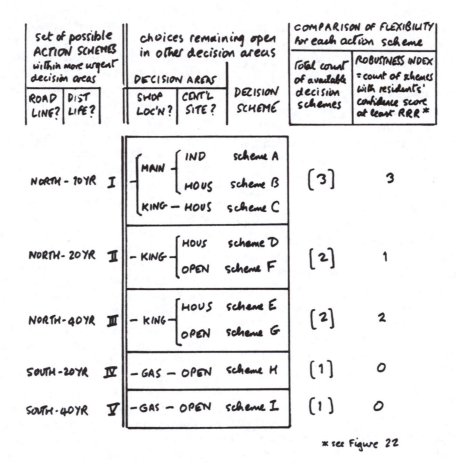

set of possible ACTION SCHEMES within more urgent decision areas		choices remaining open in other decision areas			COMPARISON OF FLEXIBILITY for each action scheme	
		DECISION AREAS			Total count of available decision schemes	ROBUSTNESS INDEX = count of schemes with residents' confidence score at least RRR *
ROAD LINE?	DIST LIFE?	SHOP LOC'N?	CENT'L SITE?	DECISION SCHEME		
NORTH - 10YR I		MAIN — IND, HOUS KING — HOUS		scheme A, scheme B, scheme C	[3]	3
NORTH- 20YR II		— KING — HOUS, OPEN		scheme D, scheme F	[2]	1
NORTH-40YR III		— KING — HOUS, OPEN		scheme E, scheme G	[2]	2
SOUTH-20YR IV		— GAS — OPEN		scheme H	[1]	0
SOUTH-40YR V		— GAS — OPEN		scheme I	[1]	0

* see Figure 22

CHOOSING

CONCEPTS

An ACTION SCHEME is a course of action involving commitments within only some of the more urgent decision areas within a problem focus.

will suggest possibilities for exploration in the form of policy soundings or exercises designed to clarify objectives or goals; while uncertainty areas of type UR will suggest possibilities for exploration in the form of liaison, negotiation, joint planning or co-ordinating initiatives to deal with relationships between the decisions currently in view and others relating to different agendas and decision-making powers.

Sometimes, it is not initially clear which of the categories UE, UV or UR describes a particular uncertainty area best. The step of considering possible exploratory options may itself help to make this classification clearer. However, there may be cases where two or more quite different kinds of exploratory options seem to be available. This may sometimes lead to the possibility of splitting the uncertainty area into two or more separate elements, which will be discussed further in Chapter 8.

In assessing the consequences that might flow from pursuing any exploratory option, there are in general three dimensions of evaluation which will be of importance to the decision-makers. Firstly, they will be concerned with assessing any changes in the level of *confidence* with which decisions can be made, arising from a reduction in the state of uncertainty surrounding key assumptions. Secondly, they will be concerned with assessing any *resources* which may be used up in pursuing that exploratory option; such an assessment might cover not only such tangible resources as money and scarce skills, but also less tangible resources such as personal energy and goodwill, which may also be in short supply. Lastly, they will be concerned with questions of the *delay* involved in pursuing any exploratory option; this may be a critical consideration where there are pressures for early action to be taken into account.

These three dimensions of evaluation can be viewed as different kinds of comparison area within which relative assessments of the impacts of different exploratory options can be made – the aim being to judge whether or not to invest any exploratory effort towards the reduction of doubts within any of the uncertainty areas currently in view. For example, the information presented in Figure 24 suggests that the proposed informal soundings among policy-makers, directed towards the UV-type uncertainty area ?VALJOB, could yield better returns in terms of confidence, for a lesser cost, than the commissioning of a market survey directed towards the UE-type uncertainty area ?SITEJOBS – and furthermore that they could do so with less serious consequences in terms of delay to the decision-making process.

CHOICES IN THE TIMING OF DECISIONS

Because exploratory actions invariably take at least some time to carry through – ranging perhaps from a few minutes in the case of a quick telephone call, to several years in the case of a major research study – the consideration of how to manage uncertainty also means confronting difficult choices about the *timing* of commitments within a continuous planning process. For there is little point in taking actions to improve the confidence with which decisions can be made unless those decisions are deferred until the outcomes of those explorations are known.

However, if the problem involves consideration of choices in several interrelated decision areas, it does not necessarily follow that commitments to decisive action must be deferred in *all* those decision areas until any agreed exploratory actions have been followed through. There may be some decision areas in which the participants' preferred course of action will be little affected, if at all, by the outcomes of these explorations; and, furthermore, there may be some decision areas in which the external pressures for early commitment are much more intense than in others. So, in practice, a choice arises in relation to each decision area within the current problem focus, not merely as to which option should be pursued, but also as to whether commitment in that decision area should be made now, or should be deferred until some later time.

This means that the *extent of commitment* within the present problem focus has itself become a matter of choice for the participants. So at this point they must strike a balance between a more exploratory and a more decisive approach to progress through time (Figure 2). This is a type of judgement which is often confronted in practice by decision-makers, even though it has as yet received comparatively little attention in the development of planning methods.

As a means of dealing with this element of choice in the timing of decisions, the core concept of an **action scheme** will now be introduced.[1] This term will be used to describe any course of proposed action in which commitment to a specific option is indicated in one or more of a set of decision areas, while commitment in others is explicitly deferred until later in the process. An illustration of the way in which this concept can be applied to the South Side problem situation appears in Figure 25.

In this illustration, five possible action schemes for South Side are compared. Each is based on a different combination of options in the ROAD LINE? and DIST LIFE? decision areas — it being supposed that these are the areas of choice in which pressure for commitment is currently most intense. The patterns of subsequent choice associated with each action scheme are displayed by a straightforward rearrangement of the branching sequence through which the original set of nine decision schemes was developed. So the same set of nine decision schemes appears as in the original array (Figure 17), but this time in a slightly modified order because the DIST LIFE? decision area has been brought further forward.

Of the five action schemes, there are two which, in effect, leave no flexibility of future choice at all, because of the structure of option bars. The choice of either of these action schemes implies commitment in each of the remaining three decision areas as well; however, each of the other three action schemes leaves open a future choice of between two and three of the original nine decision schemes.

This illustrates the important general point that action schemes which embody the same level of intended commitment in the more pressing decision areas can differ from each other in terms of the *flexibility* of future choice which is retained. Such flexibility may be of considerable practical value to the participants, especially where they are beset with doubts about what course of action will be the most advantageous in the longer term. One simple, yet practical, means of comparing action schemes for flexibility involves the use of what is called a *robustness* index; a 'robust' action being seen as one which is preferable to others in that it leaves open a wider range of acceptable paths for the future. The underlying assumption is that the more paths are left open which meet some specified level of acceptability, as viewed under current circumstances, the better equipped the decision-makers will be to respond to unexpected circumstances, should they arise in future.

This idea of robustness is not a difficult one in its essentials, but its interpretation in practice can sometimes call for a considerable degree of care. This is firstly because the threshold of acceptability may not be easy to define and, secondly, because flexibility in some decision areas may be valued more highly than flexibility in others. These points can be illustrated with reference to Figure 25, where the five action schemes are compared in terms of two different indices of flexibility. The first is based on a straightforward count of all schemes still left open, while the second is based on a count of only those schemes which pass above a particular threshold of acceptability in terms of residents' confidence (Figure 22). Both these indices assume that flexibility in the SHOP LOCN? and CENT'L SITE? decision areas are valued equally highly; an assumption which could, however, be modified by giving them different weightings if that was felt to be more realistic.

---

1 I The term 'action set' was used in the same sense in earlier writings on strategic choice.

DEVELOPING A COMMITMENT PACKAGE

To conclude this discussion of work within the choosing mode, a final core concept will be introduced, bringing together the various dimensions of the choices people face in considering how to move forward at any moment in a continuous planning process. This is the concept of the **commitment package** – conceived as a balanced assemblage of proposed steps forward which may embrace a set of proposed immediate actions; a set of explorations to deal with important areas of uncertainty; and a set of understandings about the ways in which any deferred choices should be addressed. Any commitment package will, therefore, contain a considered set of proposals as to how to move progressively towards commitment through time: a set of proposals which can be compared against other alternative sets of proposals and, if agreed, can be adopted as a basis for incremental progress in a continuous planning process.[2]

Figure 26 presents an example of one possible commitment package that might be considered as a basis for making progress in the South Side problem situation. It takes into account not only the analysis so far presented in this chapter, but also the political realities of the situation in which the South Side Working Party is currently operating. The basic format that is used here – some variations and extensions of which will be discussed in Chapter 8 – involves dividing the overall tableau into rows corresponding to the various decision areas, and also into columns corresponding to the different types of proposal that could be included in relation to each.

In the format of Figure 26, the heading of 'Immediate Decisions' is used to register not only the set of substantive actions to which commitment is now proposed – in other words, the proposed action scheme – but also any explorations which it is proposed should now be set in train to create an improved basis for future choice. Such proposals for exploration reflect a deliberate choice of exploratory options to deal with some but not necessarily all of the more important uncertainty areas which have been identified. So the set of immediate decisions is in effect conceived as an incremental step forward, not just in relation to the substantive decision problem, but also in relation to the associated problem of how to manage uncertainty through time.

Under the second main heading of 'Future Decision Space', the format of Figure 26 allows not only for an indication of which options in which decision areas are to remain open, but also for any further proposals relating to the arrangements by which future decisions should be made. In relation to these deferred choices, proposals may be made as to the future time horizons at which decisions should be made – proposals which may reflect not only the time scales involved in undertaking relevant exploratory actions but also any procedural considerations arising from the particular administrative and political context in which the participants are working. In South Side, for example, the proposed informal soundings and liaison activities, designed to cope with uncertainty in deciding a use for the Central Site, might be expected to take no more than a month, but it might be two months before the next scheduled meeting of the decision-making group at which a formal decision on this matter could be taken.

The practicalities of the organisational context in which decisions are to be taken can also play an important part in the second subdivision of future decision space, concerned with what is here called *contingency planning*. This heading recognises that it will often be important to prepare in some way for particular contingencies of a foreseeable kind,

---

2 In recent practice, the term *progress package* is frequently substituted for *commitment package*, as it emphasises the incremental nature of the output and leaves open the possibility that, in some circumstances, the plan of action it represents may be more of a recommendation to others than a firm commitment on the part of those who have put it together. Some of the implications of this will be discussed in later chapters.

FIGURE

26

SOUTH SIDE
EXAMPLE

The Concept of a Commitment Package

COMMITMENT PACKAGE

DECISION AREAS	IMMEDIATE DECISIONS		FUTURE DECISION SPACE	
	ACTIONS	EXPLORATIONS	DEFERRED CHOICES	CONTINGENCY PLANNING
ROAD LINE?	NORTH	—	—	IF recommendations not accepted, THEN appeal
DISTRICT LIFE?	10 YEARS	—	—	IF a major developer appears, THEN be ready to extend life
SHOP LOCATION?	MAIN STREET	—	—	—
CENTRAL SITE?	—	informal soundings with leading members of policy group AND liaison with joint steelworks site planning team	in 2 months: decide use of central site [industry OR housing]	—
WEST STREET?	—	investigate designs and costs for possible improvement scheme	in 6 months: decide whether to improve West Street [yes OR no]	—

CHOOSING

○ ○ ●
○ ○

CONCEPTS

A COMMITMENT PACKAGE is a combination of actions, explorations and arrangements for future choice designed as a means of making progress in a planning process.

which could have a crucial effect on future decisions – including possibilities that particular assumptions which seem to offer a firm basis for proceeding in present circumstances might be overturned by subsequent events.

In considering what proposals to enter in the last two columns, it may become necessary to probe certain basic assumptions relating to the terms in which decision areas were formulated for purposes of analysis. For example, in South Side it could be important to realise that even a firm commitment now to the northern road line may be more in the nature of a recommendation to an autonomous highway authority than a matter to be decided on the authority of the municipality of Dockport alone; so some preparation might be advisable for the contingency of that recommendation being turned down. Also, it might be important to recognise that the option of declaring a 10-year commitment to the continued life of South Side as a residential community does not imply an irrevocable commitment to the demise of that community 10 years hence; there might be the possibility of an extension in that life at some later time, given certain conditions which might be anticipated now, even if only in general terms.

It will be noticed that the example of an action scheme incorporated in Figure 26 differs from the examples compared earlier (Figure 25) in that it proposes current commitment in three rather than two decision areas. The scope for future choice within the problem focus is in this case reduced to the two Schemes A and B; so the proposals for exploratory action in this commitment package are focused on the comparison of these two schemes, drawing on the earlier analysis of uncertainty areas and exploratory options (Figures 23 and 24).

A final point illustrated by Figure 26 is that the design of a commitment package offers a point at which aspects of a decision problem that were deliberately omitted from a problem focus or a working shortlist can be brought back into view. In the South Side case, it will be noticed that the West Street decision

area has now resurfaced, even though it had been deliberately left out of the problem focus chosen for most of the designing and comparing work. Despite the judgement that this decision area can be treated in an isolated way, the same judgements about immediate or deferred choice arise in this case; and the same general ideas about management of uncertainty apply.

CHOOSING INCREMENTALLY UNDER UNCERTAINTY

Summarising at this point, this chapter has followed the same principles as Chapter 2 in presenting a set of core concepts and methods – this time designed to help when working in the comparing and choosing modes. As before, the aim has been to introduce these concepts and methods at as simple a level as possible, So the chapter began by introducing some core concepts about comparing alternatives, starting with the concept of the comparison area and then introducing those of the relative assessment, the advantage comparison and the working shortlist, before turning to other concepts to assist work in the choosing mode. These later concepts were those of the uncertainty area, the exploratory option, the action scheme and the commitment package, the last of these offering a general framework within which to build commitments incrementally through time.

As may already be appreciated, these ideas cannot always be applied in practice in such a straightforward way as in the South Side case example as presented here. But the difficulties encountered in practice lie not so much in the concepts themselves as in the realities of the situations to which they are applied; and these difficulties remain to be addressed whatever methods of working it may be decided to apply.

In principle, there is nothing in the concepts introduced here which should make them incompatible with more formalised methods of technical, economic or environmental evaluation of the kind sometimes employed on problems which are seen as of enough importance to justify the investment involved. The key point emerging from the strategic choice philosophy is that there are always choices open to participants in the way in which the processes of comparing and choosing are to be addressed. Referring to the five dimensions of balance that were presented in Figure 2, choices of scope arise in agreeing the range of comparison areas to be included; choices in the treatment of complexity arise in judging how much elaboration or simplification there should be in the assessment of consequences; choices in the treatment of uncertainty arise in judging how far to invest in exploratory actions; and choices in the treatment of progress arise in the design of a commitment package. Choices in the treatment of conflict arise too, in deciding how far people should work on these issues in an interactive, as opposed to a reactive, way; and this raises issues which will be discussed further in Chapter 4.

It is important to emphasise that these various balances need not remain unchanging through time within a continuously evolving process of strategic choice. It is found in practice that this means approaching the work of the comparing and choosing modes in a spirit of *dynamic comparison*, within which attention is continually fluctuating between comparison of many alternatives at quite a rough and ready level, taking little explicit account of uncertainty, and deeper comparison of a selected few alternatives within which issues of managing uncertainty can be more consciously addressed. The broader level of comparison leads to restricted shortlists of alternatives to be examined more closely at the deeper level: while the deeper level in turn affords opportunities to examine critically the simplifying assumptions introduced in any such shortlisting process.

In Chapters 7 and 8, the skills appropriate to management of such a process of dynamic comparison, and the conscious management of uncertainty within that process, will be examined more closely in the light of working experience in a range of different contexts. In particular, the concept of the commitment

package will be developed more fully, with reference to organisational contexts where the participants cannot always be considered as a cohesive team, and the politics of incremental action can therefore become subtle and complex. For simplicity of presentation in this chapter, the participants in a process of strategic choice have been assumed to share a common framework of accountability and a common view of the task they face. Yet the more difficult and far-reaching become the problems to be addressed, the wider and more diffuse the interests on which they are likely to impinge; and the more unrealistic it may become to think of those involved in the process as having the same level of internal cohesion as has been assumed in the case of the South Side Working Party. Therefore, the more it is to be expected that the choices to be made about the treatment of conflict will involve skilled judgements as to how the politics of organisational and inter-organisational relationships should be addressed.

SOME EXERCISES

This chapter – like Chapter 2 – will conclude with a few simple exercises based on variations of the South Side story. These are designed to help the reader begin to develop a working familiarity with the basic concepts and methods introduced here, so most of the questions are of a quite specific and sharply focused form. However, some of them do call for elements of inventiveness as well as interpretation, in that the information about South Side presented in the text and the diagrams will not always be enough to give the required answer. This merely means that the reader will be faced with some realistic problems of managing uncertainty in addressing even some of the simpler of the exercises which appear below.

1. Working solely on the information presented in Figure 19, which of the four comparison areas might be broken down into more narrow comparison areas covering different sub-categories of consequences within the general headings as defined?

2. Working from information in Figure 20, what set of relative assessments could you make for Scheme H if you used Scheme B rather than Scheme A as a baseline? (Where you are not sure how to express this assessment in any comparison area, try to find some way of expressing the uncertainty you feel.)

3. Suppose that the relative assessments for income and jobs were at the same levels as shown in Figure 20, but in favour of Scheme B rather than A, could there then be any grounds for hesitation in expressing an overall preference between A and B? If so, what would these grounds be?

4. Turning from Figure 20 to Figure 21, could the value judgements implied in converting the four relative assessments to a common advantage comparison scale lead you to modify your response to Question 3?

5. Does the advantage comparison of Figure 21 suggest that either scheme is likely to be preferable to the other in terms of a strictly financial evaluation covering both capital and income assessments?

6. Suppose in Figure 22 that the expected capital cost index were + 200 k rather than + 400 k for the King Street shop location, and 1200 k rather than 1350 k for the south road line, how might this modify your choice of working shortlist?

7. Can you infer anything from Figure 22 about the way in which residents' confidence is expected to be influenced by choice of the location for the shopping centre?

8. Would you judge that any of the three exploratory options compared in Figure 24 has a clear advantage over any one of the others as a response to the difficulty of judging comparative advantage between Schemes B and A? If so, on what assumptions does your judgement depend?

9. In Figure 25, suppose the most urgent decision areas are now DIST LIFE? and CENT'L SITE? Which combination of options in these two decision areas leaves open the widest range of choice of schemes, first in total and second when the constraint of at least RRR on the residents' confidence index is applied?

10. Can you modify the commitment package of Figure 26 to reflect the proposal that choice should be left open in the SHOP LOC'N? as well as the CENT'L SITE? decision areas, as in the first action scheme listed in Figure 25? Referring if you wish to the sketch map of Figure 18, can you make a guess as to the sorts of explorations that might be recommended to prepare for this deferred decision?

11. In Figure 27 overleaf, some further information is introduced about the numbers of people, dwellings and traders affected by decisions on the South Side problem. In what ways might this extra information help you in answering any of the questions posed above? What further types of information might you look for if you were a member of the South Side Working Party, assuming time is short and pressures of decision are intense?

Answers and comments relating to these questions will be found on the *Planning under Pressure* companion website.

FIGURE

27

SOUTH SIDE
EXAMPLE

South Side: Some Considerations of Scale

administrative boundary

MUNICIPALITY

OF

DOCKPORT

Total
population
230,000

WEST STREET
HOUSING AREA
160 dwellings
c. 500 residents

MAIN STREET SHOPPING AREA
17 existing traders within area
identified in Figure 18 as a
possible future shopping centre *

MAIN BLOCK OF
OLDER HOUSING STREETS

800 dwellings
c. 2800 residents

NEWER
HOUSING
ESTATE

650 dwellings

c. 2400
residents

SOUTH SIDE NEIGHBOURHOOD AREA
– about 7,400 residents and 28 traders in all

EASTWELL NEIGHBOURHOOD AREA
about 18,500 residents and 70 traders in all

* profitability of several South Side
traders known to be in decline

4 Orientations

BUILDING ON THE FOUNDATIONS

Taken together, the first three chapters present a set of foundations for the approach to planning under pressure which has become known as the strategic choice approach. Chapter 1 presented a view of the realities that people face when attempting to choose strategically under the manifold pressures of organisational life. It was argued that the key to a realistic approach lay in the idea of conscious management of uncertainty through time; an idea which was seen as posing a fundamental challenge to the familiar, if sometimes implicit, norms of linearity, objectivity, certainty and comprehensiveness which have traditionally been valued in the design of formal management and planning systems. In Chapters 2 and 3, this approach was extended by introducing a set of core concepts which could be seen as laying foundations for a technology of strategic choice, with reference to a view of *process* in which four complementary modes of working – shaping, designing, comparing and choosing – were seen as interrelated in a dynamic way.

The aim of this chapter will be to pause and take stock of what has been covered so far. It will do this within a general framework for reviewing alternative approaches to decision-making and planning, in which the considerations of *organisation* and of *product* are given due weight alongside those of *technology* and *process* which were the main focus of concern in the introductory chapters. This will provide a broad base from which more pragmatic advice on the use of the strategic choice approach will be developed in Chapters 5–9.

So, in essence, this chapter offers a philosophical bridge between the three introductory chapters and the five that follow.

REVIEW OF THE CORE CONCEPTS

Before addressing this main task, it will be useful briefly to take an overall view of the set of sixteen core concepts which have been introduced in the last two chapters. Figure 28 brings these concepts together and shows how they relate to the four complementary modes of shaping, designing, comparing and choosing presented earlier (Figure 8).

Because the essence of the process of strategic choice is that work should proceed in an adaptive and exploratory fashion rather than in a rigid sequence, there is no fixed order in which the sixteen core concepts should be applied in practice. The particular sequence in which they were introduced in Chapters 2 and 3 was chosen merely for ease of exposition, recognising that some linear sequence has to be followed when introducing any set of ideas for the first time.

Starting with the *shaping mode*, a complex and possibly ill-defined decision problem can be structured in terms of a set of **decision areas**, some pairs of which are directly interconnected through **decision links**. This leads to a picture of a network of relationships among decision areas, referred to as a **decision graph**, within which a choice of **problem focus** can be made.

Turning to the *designing mode*, a representative set of **decision options** is identified within each decision area, and **option bars** are specified wherever it is assumed that pairs of options drawn from different decision

FIGURE
28

A Vocabulary of Strategic Choice

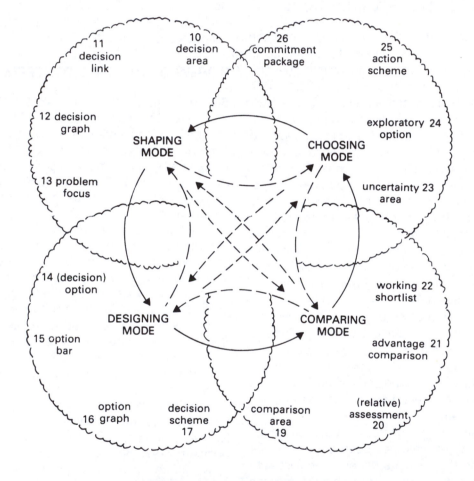

NUMBERS refer to earlier Figures in which
definitional statements and examples appear.

areas are mutually incompatible. The result-ing **option graph** can be seen as a form of map, indicating which combinations of pairs of options are available within the current prob-lem focus. The corresponding set of feasible **decision schemes** can now be developed by arranging the decision areas in some chosen sequence and then moving systematically through all possible branches in the resulting tree-like pattern.

Moving on to the *comparing mode*, **com-parison areas** are formulated for comparing alternative options or schemes, and within these **relative assessments** are made, representing judgements as to what their consequences might be. Such assessments can be balanced against each other through **advantage comparisons** between pairs of selected alternatives, allowing value judgements and feelings of uncertainty to be expressed in a common decision-centred framework. Wherever there are many schemes available, the use of simplified numerical or other scales within some com-parison areas becomes important as a means of choosing a limited **working shortlist**.

In the work of the *choosing mode*, sources of doubt are expressed in the form of **uncer-tainty areas**, leading towards the identifica-tion of **exploratory options** whereby some of these doubts might be addressed. Timing considerations are now introduced, leading to the consideration of **action schemes** which may contain proposals for early action in some, but not necessarily all, decision areas. Such proposals can be brought together with explor-ations in response to uncertainty, and arrange-ments relating to deferred decisions, within the framework of a **commitment package**, designed as an incremental step in a continu-ing process of decision-making through time.

In distilling the essentials of a technology of strategic choice into this basic vocabulary of sixteen core concepts, the guiding principle has been to avoid specialised and esoteric words. Instead, words in common usage are linked together in pairs in such a way as to give them a heightened meaning. Formal defin-itions have already been recorded underneath the appropriate illustrations (Figures 10–17 and 19–26) – so the figure references attached to the sixteen core concepts in Figure 28 can be used as a quick cross-reference whenever clarification is required.

TECHNOLOGY, ORGANISATION, PROCESS AND PRODUCT

In any approach to the challenge of addressing complex decision problems, people and their judgements become involved. In general, the wider the scope of the problem, the wider is likely to be the range of participants and of possible relationships between them. So the more it is to be expected that questions of appropriate organisation will come to the fore. Furthermore, if the process is to be effective for the participants and those to whom they are accountable, judgements will arise as to what the most appropriate forms of its product might be. These judgements too are likely to increase in complexity as the scope of a prob-lem widens.

The four headings of **Technology**, **Organ-isation**, **Process** and **Product** together provide a useful framework through which to summarise at this stage the general ori-entations of the strategic choice approach. This will be done by contrasting them with the emphases of more traditional approaches to management and planning; approaches which still have a persistent influence on thinking in both commercial and govern-mental organisations. The mnemonic **A-TOPP** (Approach – Technology, Organisation, Pro-cess and Product) will be used here in referring to this framework for comparison, with the overall concept on an **Approach** seen as covering all the other four elements.[1] It is

---

1 This framework evolved from one first developed by Hickling; it was later applied to the comparative analysis of approaches in a study of methodologies of regional planning by a joint Birmingham University/Tavistock Institute research team (Hart, Hickling, Norris and Skelcher, 1980)

FIGURE
29

Orientations and Guidelines in Strategic Choice

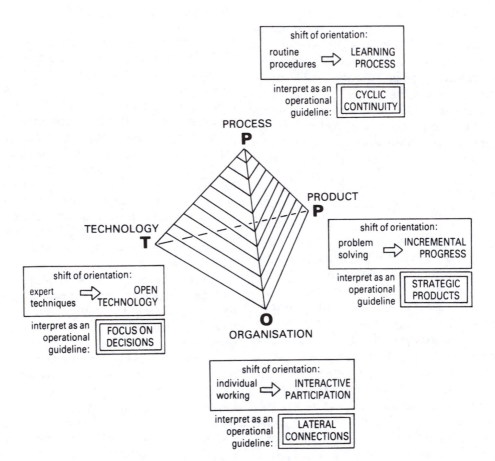

shift of orientation:

routine procedures ⇒ LEARNING PROCESS

interpret as an operational guideline: | CYCLIC CONTINUITY |

PROCESS
P

PRODUCT
P

TECHNOLOGY
T

shift of orientation:

problem solving ⇒ INCREMENTAL PROGRESS

interpret as an operational guideline | STRATEGIC PRODUCTS |

shift of orientation:

expert techniques ⇒ OPEN TECHNOLOGY

interpret as an operational guideline: | FOCUS ON DECISIONS |

O
ORGANISATION

shift of orientation:

individual working ⇒ INTERACTIVE PARTICIPATION

interpret as an operational guideline: | LATERAL CONNECTIONS |

APPROACH

A-TOPP

| ORIENTATIONS |

not only the strategic choice approach that can be examined in terms of the four elements of technology, organisation, process and product; so too can any other approach, whether it is one which has been consciously designed with reference to particular principles or beliefs – such as the norms of linearity, objectivity, certainty and comprehensiveness described in Chapter 1 – or whether it has evolved pragmatically in response to particular local circumstances and constraints.

ORIENTATIONS OF THE STRATEGIC CHOICE APPROACH

The four elements within the A-TOPP framework – Technology, Organisation, Process and Product – are represented in Figure 29 as the four vertices of a tetrahedron. The solid structure of the tetrahedron itself is intended to represent the idea of an overall approach viewed in a relatively complete, multi-dimensional way. The picture as a whole is intended to convey the message that each aspect of the approach can be selected in turn as the focus of attention – yet none of them can ever be viewed entirely in isolation from the other three. In Figure 29, the tetrahedron has been positioned so that the process vertex appears on top. But the whole structure stands on the base formed by the other three vertices, and the tetrahedron could just as easily be tipped over to bring any other vertex to the top, resting firmly on the base provided by the other three.

In Figure 29, the emphases which are characteristic of the strategic choice approach in each of the four 'corners' of the A-TOPP framework are first expressed in terms of general statements of *orientation*. This is to bring out the essential contrasts with more conventional approaches which tend to be well entrenched in decision-making arrangements set up to deal with comparatively clearly structured, bounded problems. There is no intention here to suggest that these well-tried methods should be abandoned altogether; it is more a case of advocating a shift of emphasis, so that a more appropriate balance can be struck.

In terms of *technology*, the strategic choice approach involves a shift away from a reliance on the kinds of *expert techniques* of solution-finding and evaluation which are characteristic of more routine decision-making arrangements. Rather, the orientation is towards what can be described as an **open technology** intended to be freely accessible to participants who have differing and complementary contributions to make. In situations where the very shape of a problem may be obscure and, indeed, a matter of possible controversy, the relevance of what may be called 'black box' technologies becomes considerably reduced. It is no longer enough to produce outputs of advice through the application of well-established methods, the nature of which need not be disclosed because they are considered so well validated by past exercises of a similar kind. Such 'black box' methods may still have their place; but it will be a place of limited significance in the wider process. For in problems of complex and ill-defined shape, it is likely that many different types of choice will become inter-meshed – for instance, choices about finance, about timing, about location, about technological or marketing matters, about people and their roles, and about contractual or procedural considerations. Such matters are, in turn, likely to cut across the preserves of many different experts; and it is only through an emphasis on open technology – a technology to support communication and interaction across these boundaries – that any momentum of joint working on complex problems can be sustained.

In terms of *organisation*, an orientation towards interactive participation is indicated as being characteristic of the strategic choice approach. This is in contrast to the emphasis on *individual working* on assigned tasks which is characteristic of organisational arrangements for working on more clearly structured, recurrent problems. There is, of course, a direct link between the emphasis on participative forms of organisation and that on open technology. Both stress the idea of people working together in an exploratory way, so as to transcend established boundaries of responsibility and specialist expertise. Again, the shift of emphasis is not intended to suggest that the clear assignment of tasks to specific individuals or organisational units no longer has its place. For this latter emphasis remains appropriate in situations where predictable types of issues have to be processed in a consistent and efficient way. So the question is not whether such organisational arrangements should be replaced, but how they can be complemented in circumstances where more challenging situations of strategic choice arise.

In terms of *process*, the shift of emphasis is from reliance on *routine procedures* for dealing with issues which fall into clearly recognisable categories, towards an acceptance that people should be engaged in a **learning process** about issues which no one person can claim to understand in full. Again, the emphasis on a learning process has a clear alignment with the emphasis on open technology and on interactive participation. For, in responding to complex decision problems, people must be prepared to learn from each other, recognising that there may be a variety of complementary sources of insight and experience upon which to draw. Again the emphasis on a learning process is not intended to suggest that routine procedures no longer have a part to play; it is simply that they become less appropriate to the more complex challenges of a process of strategic choice.

Finally, in terms of *products*, the emphasis is shifted from the conventional idea of *problem-solving*, towards an orientation to **incremental progress** through time. Where problems are of a bounded nature, it is reasonable to look for equally clear and definitive 'solutions'. But there will always be some instances where it is not such a straightforward matter to decide what should be done. Action must sometimes be postponed, referred elsewhere, or entered into in a partial or qualified way. In a process of strategic choice, this kind of progressive commitment becomes more the rule than the exception.

INTERPRETING THE ORIENTATIONS INTO MORE SPECIFIC GUIDELINES

None of the four phrases used to describe the general orientations of the strategic choice approach – open technology, interactive participation, learning process, incremental progress – can be considered as exclusive to the strategic choice approach as presented in this book. Other people – practitioners as well as consultants and scholars – have argued for the adoption of these or similar orientations in responding to complex problems. So, as general prescriptions, such statements now have quite a familiar ring. In particular, the virtues of participative forms of organisation have been widely proclaimed, both in industry and the public sector, while the idea of public planning as a learning process has now almost passed into the realm of accepted conventional wisdom.

However, it has proved far from easy for people to give effect to such changes of orientation in practice. They can all too easily remain as pious exhortations, which evoke a cynical response from those who consider themselves to be realists in the art of decision-making under the practical pressures of organisational life. So the challenge is to find ways of interpreting the four broad orientations into more concrete operational terms. This is a challenge which is rarely faced in relation to technology, organisation, process and product considered in combination; however, it is the challenge to which the strategic choice approach is explicitly addressed.

In Figure 29, the first step in this direction is taken by interpreting each statement of preferred orientation into a more specific **operational guideline** which reflects more directly the philosophy of planning as a process of strategic choice. So the orientation towards an open technology is interpreted in terms of a *focus on decisions*; the orientation towards interactive participation is interpreted in terms of an emphasis on *lateral connections*; the orientation towards a learning process is interpreted in terms of *cyclic continuity*; and the orientation towards incremental progress is interpreted in terms of a guideline of *strategic products*.

Each of these guidelines calls for further explanation. This is done in the next four sections of this chapter, drawing on particular aspects of the philosophy of strategic choice as already presented. However, the value of these guidelines does not rest merely on their philosophical content. They are intended to give the statements of orientation a more practical slant; and they serve to draw attention to practical issues that arise in the management of the strategic choice approach, as applied to complex planning situations. So the next four sections will not only offer more precise meanings for the operational guidelines offered here under the four headings of technology, organisation, process and product; they will also indicate the nature of the practical management choices which they imply.

GUIDANCE IN TECHNOLOGICAL CHOICE

If any technology of strategic choice is to be truly open, then it must offer a means of bridging the differences in perception that can exist between participants who view the world from different professional, organisational or cultural perspectives. The adoption of a **focus on decisions** offers one pragmatic means of drawing the attention of participants towards matters which, individually or collectively, they feel to be important in their current planning task. It is only to be expected that they will frequently see the decisions before them in very different terms. They may disagree about the importance of one decision relative to another, or they may have differing views about the level of specificity or generality at which matters for decision should be expressed. Indeed, they can have different views about many aspects of decision-making; but such differences can provide a constructive focus for debate with appropriate guidance – and thus help the participants in moving towards a more realistic sharing of views.

The centrality of the decision perspective is reflected in the focus on a current decision problem which was originally adopted as a starting point in developing a view of planning as a process of conscious management of uncertainty through time (Figure 3). In the subsequent diagrams of Chapter 1, the symbolic shape of the 'cloud' representing this decision problem was variously expanded, pulled apart and examined from a range of contrasting perspectives. Then, in Chapter 2, the decision perspective was given more concrete expression by adopting the decision area as the fundamental unit of analysis, accepting that it could be used to represent choices about many different kinds of things – investment, location, alignment of roads, to mention only a few of the types of choice which were introduced in the telling of the South Side story. It is by the clearer articulation of such choices and their relationships that the form of the cloud representing a current decision problem can be made less obscure. So the adoption of a decision perspective offers one important means – now widely tested and adopted in practice – by which the orientation towards an open technology can be given practical expression, and the transparency of complex planning problems thereby increased.

It has to be recognised, however, that the focus on decisions is not the only possible emphasis that can be adopted in introducing an open technology. Other writers and practitioners have embraced with equal conviction the idea of a *systems perspective* as a key to a more effective approach to complexity in planning. However, in its more traditional forms, the adoption of a systems approach can be criticised as focusing attention on some forms of structural relationships at the expense of others, thus working against the spirit of an open technology. Such a comment would apply, for example, to the modelling of corporate planning problems in terms of systems of financial relationships only, or the modelling of cities in terms of systems of land-use/transport interactions alone.

FIGURE
30

Technological Choice: Settings and Equipment

Meanwhile, some advocates of systems thinking have moved towards what is sometimes called a *soft systems* approach. This recognises that complex phenomena can be examined from many different perspectives, and that much can be learned by subjecting different views of the purposes, boundaries and inter-relationships of systems to structured analysis and debate.[2] So the adoption of a 'soft' systems approach offers an alternative means of giving expression to the emphasis of an open technology. It does, however, focus attention on relationships of a comparatively stable, enduring form, as opposed to the ever-changing relationships between decisions – expressed at various levels and carrying varying degrees of urgency – which provide the primary focus for the strategic choice approach. The approach developed in this book is, above all, intended as an instrument to help people plan under the pressures of the continuously evolving circumstances that they face; which is not to say they cannot also benefit from standing back occasionally to reach out for a broader, more systemic view.

In pursuing the particular expression of an open technology presented here, it is important to see the scope of an *appropriate* technology for strategic choice as embracing not only a set of basic concepts and analytical methods, but also the choice of the physical settings in which people work, the equipment they use and the media through which they communicate with each other. In the more conventional settings of sequential decision-making (Figure 6) – the clerk sitting at a desk, the committee sitting around a long table – such aspects of technology are well established by convention and therefore rarely considered in a conscious way. Background information is presented verbally or in documentary form; while working on a problem, pens and paper may be used by individuals so that notes can be taken and action points recorded. In the case of

the individual decision-maker, dealing with relatively bounded and recurrent issues, the electronic work station has brought changes in this familiar pattern. On the other hand, most *collective* decision processes continue to rely on the simplest of technological equipment; and there are good arguments for this, in so far as full rein can be given to people's capacities to interact with each other through verbal discourse and debate – freely augmented by those nonverbal signals through which a wider range of reactions and emotions can be expressed.

However, there are alternatives available to the technology conventionally used to support the processes of communication and of interaction; and some of these have been found to give fuller expression to the orientation towards an open technology of strategic choice. One alternative setting which has been found to be particularly effective is reflected in the main sketch of Figure 30. This shows a group of people relating to each other not by sitting facing each other from fixed positions around a table, but in an alternative setting which allows them to communicate and interact in a more flexible way. The basic technology in this kind of setting consists of:

- large sheets of paper that can be arranged around the walls of a room, which has to be spacious enough to enable people to move around freely;
- a simple, non-permanent means of sticking paper to walls;
- a liberal supply of wedge-tipped pens of several contrasting colours.

These materials are not, in themselves, very sophisticated; but many decision-makers are unaccustomed to their use, other than in relatively formal presentations. Used together, they have been found to play an important part in encouraging interactive working in groups. More specifically, they can encourage flexibility in use of the various graphical methods for expression of decision problems and their implications which have been introduced in

---

2 See in particular Checkland (1981) and Ackoff (1974).

earlier chapters. It has to be recognised, however, that successful group interaction is not automatically assured merely by creating an appropriate setting, and providing appropriate equipment and tools. It is always possible that one or two members of a group will tend to dominate the process, with others reacting by becoming alienated or withdrawn. Therefore, among the variations in strategic choice technology that will be offered in the next five chapters, some suggestions will be offered for helping members of a group to become more fully involved. For example, this can be done by creating opportunities for people to draw up individual lists of decision areas or uncertainty areas, before attempting to merge these into a shared picture on larger sheets of paper ranged around the walls of the room.

Figure 30 includes a reminder that it is not exclusively when they are working in groups that people can draw on the basic concepts and methods of the strategic choice approach. As several experienced decision-makers have found, ideas such as the UE/UV/UR classification of uncertainty can also be helpful to them when they are reflecting alone on difficult problems – as in the symbolic armchair – or when engaged in informal discussions with one or two colleagues who share an awareness of the basic language and ideas. It is in such individual and small group settings too that the computer can most readily play a role in augmenting the technology of communication and interaction; for, as will be demonstrated in Chapter 10, it can then be used as a facilitation tool in guiding decision-makers through the various paths which are open to them in an exploratory yet disciplined way.

However, within the overall technology of the strategic choice approach, it is important to regard the computer as no more than an optional resource. Even at the time this third edition goes to press, very many of the recorded applications of the approach have made little or no use of computer methods. Yet as the technologies of human-machine interaction and telecommunications continue their

rapid advance, new opportunities will inevitably continue to arise for harnessing electronic resources to the support of strategic decision processes; not least, where those processes involve collaboration or negotiation through global communication networks.

The state of progress so far in developing software for strategic choice will be reviewed in Chapter 10, along with the longer-term opportunities for development. What has to be emphasised at this point is that computer methods should in no way be regarded as an *essential* element in the technology of the strategic choice approach.

In pursuing the emphasis on an open technology, the general rule is to aim continually for simplification rather than elaboration, so that high levels of effective communication and interaction can be sustained. However, it is important to remember that there are always choices of balance to be made in this and other dimensions of the approach (Figure 2). It is only realistic that the appropriate point of balance at any moment should be judged in the light of the participants' local appreciation of their own present problem situation, and the pressures within which they must work.

GUIDANCE IN ORGANISATIONAL CHOICE

Turning at this point to the organisational dimension of the A-TOPP framework, the recommended orientation towards **interactive participation** is by no means as straightforward to interpret in practice as might at first appear. For the wider the scope of the problem being addressed, the broader the range of organisational and other interests likely to have a stake in that problem. Then the harder it becomes to reconcile the desire that all these interests should be adequately *represented* with the desire to encourage interactive working. For the larger and more diverse the group, the more difficult it becomes for all to feel involved, and for progress to be sustained.

In addressing the choice of organisational arrangements to deal with complex planning problems, the conventional approach is to focus attention on the design of comparatively stable, clearly structured frameworks of hierarchical guidance. These usually incorporate elements of conscious forecasting and direction-setting as well as managerial control, and are shaped to fit closely the established management structure of the corporation concerned. The intention is – at least in theory – for historical inertias to be questioned; for people to come together to work across departmental boundaries on selected major issues; and often also to involve representatives of other significant interest groups, such as employees, residents or public service clients.

However, the basic management structures of most corporate organisations can still be seen as designed primarily as a means of responding efficiently to certain recurrent *categories* of decision problems, for which clear policy guidelines and rules of delegated responsibility can be defined. Where problems are of a more fluid, indistinct shape, experience shows that formal planning arrangements which reflect the established corporate structure can quickly break down. It is then that more informal, adaptive approaches take over – with the impetus usually coming from those points in the management system where the pressures for decision are most intense. It is in the face of repeated pressures of this kind that organisational arrangements for planning based on the hierarchical control structure begin to lose credibility, because their contribution to the making of key management decisions becomes increasingly hard to demonstrate.

So, to express the decision-centred philosophy of the strategic choice approach, an alternative guideline to the design of organisational arrangements is required. As an operational guideline, intended to reflect the orientation towards interactive participation as against individual working, the idea of a focus on **lateral connections** will now be introduced. The significance of this term in relation to a decision perspective is made more clear in Figure 31, which is an extension of the view of three contrasting responses to uncertainty in decision-making as first presented in Chapter 1 (Figure 3).

Figure 31 starts from the situation of an individual or working group currently concerned with some particular decision or planning problem – whether it be complex or more limited in scope – and experiencing some degree of *difficulty* in deciding what should be done. Different aspects of this current difficulty can be analysed in relation to the three basic categories of uncertainty – UE, UV and UR – and each of these types of uncertainty can be seen as having organisational implications of a somewhat different kind. In each direction, too, there may be various levels of investment to consider, reaching out increasingly far beyond the particular organisational setting in which the problem is currently being addressed. The possibilities may range from the level of quick and informal contacts with people who are relatively close in organisational terms, to the level of more deliberate, and possibly formal, approaches to others who are organisationally more remote.

When working outwards in the *UE direction*, the concern is essentially to acquire additional *information* relevant to the decision-makers' working environment. Some kinds of information can be acquired easily enough by means of informal enquiries from close colleagues; others may involve somewhat more formal approaches across departmental or corporate boundaries, while others again may mean initiating substantial survey, assessment or forecasting exercises, perhaps involving formal contractual arrangements with specialist consultants.

Turning next to the *UR direction*, there may again be several possible levels of investment in outward linkage to consider. However, the people approached now appear not merely in the role of knowledge providers, but also in the role of decision-makers in related fields. So any communication across boundaries will tend to take on a rather different flavour, involving more explicit elements of negotiation in so far as each party may be in a position to help the

FIGURE

31

Organisational Choice: Levels of Response to Uncertainty

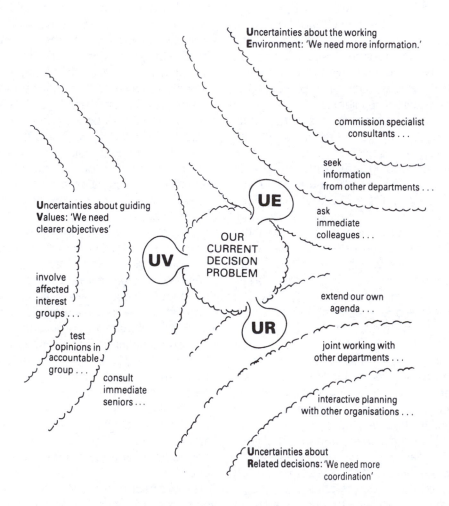

Uncertainties about the working
Environment: 'We need more information.'

commission specialist
consultants . . .

seek
information
from other departments . . .

UE

ask
immediate
colleagues . . .

Uncertainties about guiding
Values: 'We need
clearer objectives'

UV

OUR
CURRENT
DECISION
PROBLEM

involve
affected
interest
groups . . .

extend our own
agenda . . .

UR

test
opinions in
accountable
group . . .

joint working with
other departments . . .

consult
immediate
seniors . . .

interactive planning
with other organisations . . .

Uncertainties about
Related decisions: 'We need more
coordination'

other in reducing some of the uncertainties that they face. The organisational options to be considered in the UR direction can range from occasional bilateral exchanges – whether by telephone or other means – to more interactive working arrangements calling for substantial time commitments by the parties concerned.

Turning finally to the *UV direction*, the most familiar and straightforward means of seeking to reduce uncertainty about guiding values involves referring upwards within a hierarchy to a superordinate point of authority. Beyond this, there may be a possibility of referring for guidance to a meeting of some collective body – a Board, Council or Committee – in which formal authority resides; accepting that at this level there may be many competitive pressures on its agenda and only limited discussion time available. Beyond this again, there may be opportunities to launch special consultative exercises to probe the value positions of interest groups which have a major stake in the present decision problem, whether by use of existing representative channels, by convening open meetings, or by some combination of the two.

The successive levels of response shown in Figure 31 are intended to give no more than a broad indication of the opportunities for working across organisational boundaries that might emerge at any moment in a planning process. Some more specific examples were presented in Chapter 3 (Figures 24 and 26), and further illustrations will appear in Chapter 8. Sometimes it will be appropriate to refer upwards or downwards within a hierarchy, especially as a means of addressing significant areas of uncertainty of the UV type. However, the main orientation in strategic choice is essentially towards building connections in a *lateral* way, working outwards from a specific problem focus rather than downwards from a point of central authority.

Often, there will be choices to be faced as to whether particular connections should be activated through formal or informal channels. In particular, there is always the possibility that

conscious investment in building close working relationships with particular individuals will provide a foundation for quick and informal consultation later, when particular issues or circumstances arise. In managing a process of strategic choice, it is generally the choices about lateral working in the UR direction that pose the most subtle challenges; for, as was earlier indicated (Figure 5), it is in this direction that the boundaries of the decision problem itself become enlarged. So, the question now emerges as to how far the range of people involved in interactive working can be extended without the momentum of progress being lost.

Taking these considerations together, the significant areas of management choice in organisational terms can be seen as extending beyond the formal *structuring* of arrangements for internal co-ordination, as the hierarchical command perspective of planning organisation might suggest. For important choices must also be made about arrangements for bilateral *linking* and multi-lateral *grouping*, in response to particular problems as they arise. The choices about linking relate to the informal cultivation and activation of networks of interpersonal working relationships by specific participants in the process. On the other hand, the choices about grouping relate to judgements as to when and how to initiate interactive group working with others, or to enlarge the boundaries of an existing interactive process. It should not be forgotten too that choices may arise as to when and how to disband a group which has outlived its usefulness, or otherwise to modify the lattice of arrangements through which a process of interactive working is pursued.

In confronting such choices, it has to be recognised that invitations to participate in interactive group processes will not always be welcomed without reservation. Resistances may be encountered because of fears about loss of autonomy, or straightforward time pressures, or conflicts of interests, or various other factors of a broadly political kind. Factors such as these can contribute to making the emphasis on interactive participation more

FIGURE
32

Process Choice: Opportunities for Movement Between Modes

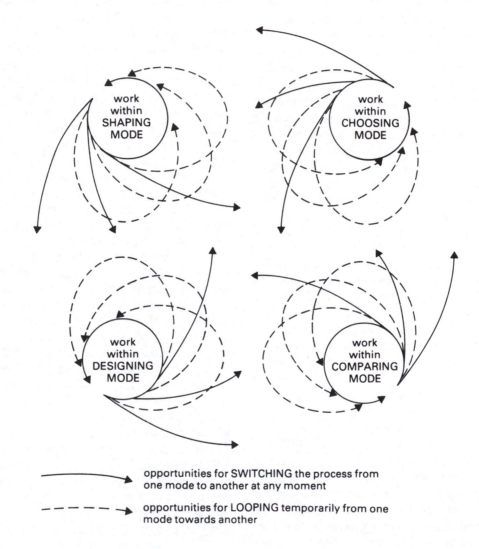

work within **SHAPING MODE**

work within **CHOOSING MODE**

work within **DESIGNING MODE**

work within **COMPARING MODE**

opportunities for SWITCHING the process from one mode to another at any moment

opportunities for LOOPING temporarily from one mode towards another

PROCESS

A-TOPP

ORIENTATIONS

difficult to interpret in practice than it might appear. The point to be underlined is again that there are always choices of *balance* to be considered. Not least, there is always a balance to be struck between the extremes of reactive and interactive working (Figure 2). This is a balance which must be expected to change through time in an adaptive, evolutionary way – and which can only realistically be judged by those directly involved in the process.

GUIDANCE IN PROCESS CHOICE

To talk of a process of strategic choice as being essentially a learning process may seem to be no more than to repeat a statement which, applied to planning, has now become so widely accepted as to have become little more than a cliché. But this orientation, like the corresponding orientations towards open technology and interactive participation, has proved to be very difficult to put into practice in a satisfactory way. This is because the question of what it is most important to learn in relation to complex problems can be by no means easy to answer with any confidence in advance. Often, it is only after interactive work has begun on such a problem that the participants can begin to form any kind of informed, coherent view as to what the most serious obstacles to progress are, and therefore what course their learning process should take.

Most of the more conventional approaches to planning and complex decision-making have advocated a process based on clearly specified sequences of steps or stages, following the norm of linearity which is widely accepted in the design of procedures for dealing with more recurrent, clearly structured decision problems. Following this principle, specific timetables are laid down for consecutive stages of the planning process, covering such activities as survey, formulation of objectives, design of alternatives, evaluation and plan preparation. In those situations where the aim is to add a more purposive direction-seeking emphasis to an existing system of corporate management and control, such steps are then fitted into a periodic – often annual – planning cycle. Arrangements of this kind have the virtue of apparent predictability; this can be important in organisational settings where substantial human, financial or other resources are being committed to the planning task, creating a demand that their use be subject to due procedures of accountability. However, the risk is that the requirement to adhere to a pre-ordained sequence of activities will constrain people to concentrate their effort on learning the wrong things at the wrong times, so far as the more important pressures for decision are concerned. Instances frequently arise, both in business and in public planning, where lengthy and expensive exercises in survey, forecasting or evaluation are carried out to a pre-arranged timetable, yet turn out to yield results of little relevance to the more crucial problems of the day.

So, in describing the process emphasis of the strategic choice approach, the general orientation towards a learning process will be interpreted more specifically in terms of an operational guideline of *cyclic continuity*. In this, the conventional representation of a process in terms of a linear sequence of stages is replaced by a more flexible set of possibilities for movement between one mode of decision-making and another. It may be useful for some purposes to follow an agreed sequence of progression to ensure that all modes are considered in a methodical way; but to maintain the emphasis on a learning process in a complex and evolving problem situation, decision-makers must be prepared to adopt a much more flexible approach.

Often the shape of a problem is only dimly perceived, and there are many partially formed viewpoints to be exchanged. Then the participants have to be ready at any time to move backwards to modes in which substantial work has already been done, so as to challenge and modify past assumptions. Equally, they must be ready to skip forward to modes where it might seem premature to work in any depth, according to a more conventional sequential view. Indeed, the very concept of a decision area implies a readiness to look ahead to what is to be decided at various points in the future, effectively skipping forward from the shaping to the choosing mode.

In Figure 32, the guideline of cyclic continuity is expressed more specifically in terms of the types of *process management choice* which it implies. Starting from the view of a process of strategic choice as involving a continuing interplay among four basic modes of activity, there are two types of choice that can be made in considering how to direct the learning process. First, there are choices about when and how to *switch* out of the primary mode of the moment and into any of the others, for a spell of deliberate working within that other mode. Then there are those more frequent, often informal, choices that people make about when and how to *loop* briefly outwards from the primary mode of the moment in the direction of another mode, to deal with some limited source of difficulty, before returning to pick up again the momentum of work already established in the primary mode.

Much of the advice to be offered in the next four chapters relate to forms of switching and looping judgement that people can consider when working in each of the four modes. Therefore, each of the next four chapters will end with a diagram which elaborates the relevant 'corner' of Figure 32 by summarising the types of switching and looping judgements that can be made when working in that particular mode.

The broader significance of the guideline of cyclic continuity is that, when people are consciously following the strategic choice approach, the conventional linear process of agenda control, as regulated through an appointed chairperson, no longer need apply. Instead, it becomes replaced by a more subtle, adaptive process of route finding with many possible paths among which to choose. In this process, both switching and looping judgements have to be made continually. Brief loops out of the primary mode of the moment towards another mode are often made subconsciously; however, in group working it

can be a significant contribution to the learning process if they can be more consciously recognised and discussed. Switching judgements, on the other hand, have a wider significance in the management of the process as a whole. So it is all the more important that they should be openly debated within a group, if a conscious emphasis on an interactive learning process is to be maintained. More specific advice on how to manage such switches of mode in the course of interactive group working will be given in Chapter 9, reflecting accumulated practical experience as to how best to sustain the emphasis on relevant learning at all times.

The significance given to switching and looping judgements here does not mean that more conventional *scheduling* decisions can be ignored in the management of a process of strategic choice. Each participant in the process has inevitably to make at least some advance arrangements to organise his or her working life, in which there will usually be other relatively fixed commitments to fulfil. So periods of interactive working will often have to be scheduled in advance, even if the organisation of work within such a period is kept as flexible as possible by following the precept of adaptive route-finding in place of that of linear agenda control.

In practice, problems can arise in reconciling the demands of cyclic continuity with expectations of linear procedure, not only in the advance scheduling of work but also in accounting to other people retrospectively for the way in which any conclusions or recommendations have been reached. To argue that a particular set of proposals has been arrived at as a result of a cyclic, adaptive, learning process may be to do no more than describe the realities that underlie any process of working at complex problems. But it is only natural that those not directly involved should wish to see some kind of rational argument by which the conclusions offered can be justified, without becoming drawn into the full subtleties of the learning process. The requirement for some degree of 'post-rationalisation' can be a vital one in some circumstances, and it will be the subject of further discussion in Chapter 9.

GUIDANCE IN PRODUCT CHOICE

The shift in orientation of the strategic choice approach in relation to the products of the process is expressed (Figure 29) in terms of a shift away from an emphasis on definitive resolution of problems at specified end points of the process, and towards a more subtle emphasis on making **incremental progress** through time. Where problems can be treated as simple and discrete, it may make sense to deal with them in accordance with some linear schedule or agenda, with the aim of settling each item of business in full before moving on to the next. When people encounter issues which are more interrelated and complex, the tendency is often to translate this desire for complete solutions into a concern with the production of *substantive plans* at as comprehensive a level as possible. The conventional wisdom is that such plans should *be implemented* in an equally complete manner through more specific operational decisions, budgets and programmes, after they have been steered through the required procedures of authorisation within the organisation.

However, it is a common experience for people to encounter very considerable difficulties in attempting to conform to such principles in practice. Indeed, the more comprehensively they may seek to view the scope of a strategy or plan in terms of the range of substantive issues it should cover, the more these difficulties tend to proliferate. It is in such circumstances that the alternative orientation towards incremental progress comes into its own.

Within the strategic choice approach, the operational guideline which is offered as a more specific interpretation of this idea is that of generating a balance between different kinds of **strategic products** through time. The spirit of this idea is captured in the concept of the commitment package, as introduced towards the end of Chapter 3 (Figure 26).

The structure of the commitment package is designed to help people in thinking and talking about what level of *balance* between commitment and flexibility is appropriate at any moment of a continuous process. This entails their weighing up the various urgencies and uncertainties impinging on the choices with which they are currently concerned, and also considering how foundations for the making of future decisions can be built. Such considerations are of only marginal value in a conventional problem-solving approach, but are of profound importance in a process of strategic choice where the need for continuity is explicitly recognised.

The concept of the commitment package provides a particularly clear expression of the principle of treating *commitment as a variable* rather than as something to be conceived in all-or-nothing terms. Yet a commitment package is essentially a product of the work of the choosing mode; and it is important to recognise that there are also products of work in the various other modes of strategic choice which can make a direct contribution to progress in a broader sense. A wider view of the various types of strategic product which can contribute to the momentum of progress in strategic choice is offered in Figure 33.

Figure 33 presents a two-dimensional framework for identifying different types of strategic product, first in terms of a distinction between products of substance and those relating to the process; and, secondly, in terms of a distinction between visible products and those of a more invisible or intangible form. The essence of the distinction between substance and process can be illustrated by referring again to the commitment package framework (Figure 26), the aim of which is, essentially, to present the products of work in the choosing mode in a clearly visible form.

Within a commitment package, the products which relate most directly to the *substance* of the decision problem are those appearing in the first column, concerned with immediate actions. It has to be recognised that

FIGURE
33

Product Choice: A Classification of Strategic Products

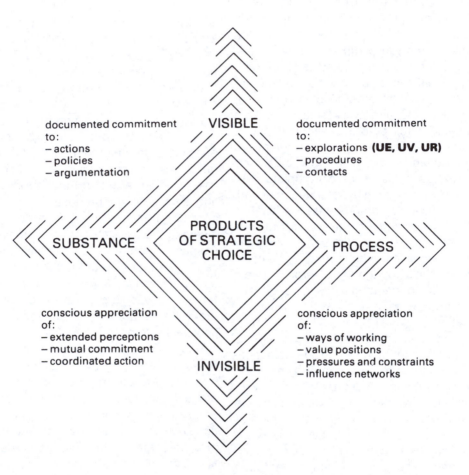

VISIBLE

documented commitment to:
– actions
– policies
– argumentation

documented commitment to:
– explorations **(UE, UV, UR)**
– procedures
– contacts

SUBSTANCE

PRODUCTS
OF STRATEGIC
CHOICE

PROCESS

conscious appreciation of:
– extended perceptions
– mutual commitment
– coordinated action

conscious appreciation of:
– ways of working
– value positions
– pressures and constraints
– influence networks

INVISIBLE

PRODUCT

A–TOP**P**

ORIENTATIONS

these actions may take various forms, including statements of policy and agreement on responsibilities, budgets and deadlines, as well as the commitment to here-and-now actions under the direct control of those involved in the process. There is also a substantive content within the right-hand half of the commitment package framework – that relating to the future decision space. For this includes information about decisions which have been deferred or are seen as contingent on future events.

The existence of *process* elements within a commitment package is implicit in its very nature as an incremental step in a continuing process. Those parts of a commitment package which are most directly process related include the arrangements for managing uncertainty, along with any proposed arrangements for scheduling; for future decision-making procedures; and for linking with other people with a part to play in the wider process.

There are also other kinds of visible products which are not directly represented in the commitment package framework. These include any documented evidence of progress made through work done in the shaping, designing and comparing modes. Work done in these modes can lead to clearer expressions of the participants' shared views about:

- the nature of the decision problems they face;
- the range of options or schemes available;
- the consequences of different alternatives;
- the uncertainties that make it difficult to express preferences between them.

It is common in planning for such kinds of information to be assembled as part of a reasoned *justification* of recommended courses of action. There are various conventional forms – written, diagrammatic, numerical – in which such information about problems, opportunities, criteria, constraints and sources of uncertainty can be assembled and documented whenever important moments of formal commitment to policies and actions arise. But the various concepts and conventions illustrated in Chapters 2 and 3 are specifically intended to help people build up a visible record of progress in all modes in a more continuous way. This is of particular importance when work is proceeding interactively in groups. There is still a task of *interpreting* visible products expressed in such ways into forms which are intelligible to those not directly involved; but there are practical ways of addressing this task, and these will be discussed further in Chapter 9.

Important as these various visible products may be, it is vital also to recognise that any process of strategic choice generates *invisible products* which can have a profound influence in the longer term. First, in terms of the *substance* of problems, people can expect to extend their perceptions in ways that cannot be fully reflected in any documented evidence of progress that is produced. Such extended perceptions may embrace all aspects of substantive progress already discussed at the more visible level, including problems, opportunities, effects and uncertainties. Such personal shifts in perception will generally be in the direction of increased sharing of views among those involved in interactive working; or increasing *intersubjectivity*, to use a term which others have found useful in relation to group processes (Eden, Jones, Sims and Smithin, 1981). Moves in this direction can be of considerable significance beyond the boundaries of the group involved in the interactive working process; for they can affect the ways in which individuals seek to influence the views and behaviours of colleagues, superiors and associates within their wider working environment.

Also, more realistic perceptions of the external political realities surrounding a problem can be an important invisible product of a process of strategic choice. However, such a product must be seen as relevant as much to future process as to the substance of particular problems; so this leads naturally into the discussion of the final quadrant of the product classification of Figure 33.

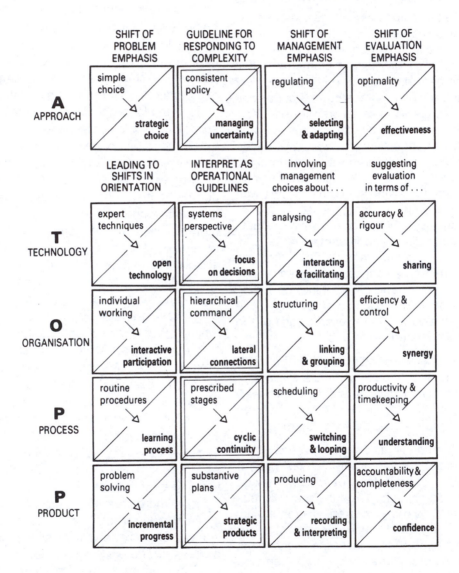

FIGURE
34

Technology, Organisation, Process and Product: An Interim Review

	SHIFT OF PROBLEM EMPHASIS	GUIDELINE FOR RESPONDING TO COMPLEXITY	SHIFT OF MANAGEMENT EMPHASIS	SHIFT OF EVALUATION EMPHASIS
A APPROACH	simple choice → strategic choice	consistent policy → managing uncertainty	regulating → selecting & adapting	optimality → effectiveness
	LEADING TO SHIFTS IN ORIENTATION	INTERPRET AS OPERATIONAL GUIDELINES	involving management choices about . . .	suggesting evaluation in terms of . . .
T TECHNOLOGY	expert techniques → open technology	systems perspective → focus on decisions	analysing → interacting & facilitating	accuracy & rigour → sharing
O ORGANISATION	individual working → interactive participation	hierarchical command → lateral connections	structuring → linking & grouping	efficiency & control → synergy
P PROCESS	routine procedures → learning process	prescribed stages → cyclic continuity	scheduling → switching & looping	productivity & timekeeping → understanding
P PRODUCT	problem solving → incremental progress	substantive plans → strategic products	producing → recording & interpreting	accountability & completeness → confidence

ORIENTATIONS

Among the important invisible products which relate more to process than to substance is fuller understanding of:

- other people's values;
- their ways of working;
- the pressures and constraints acting on them.

In most cases, this is backed up by extensions to the communications networks of individuals involved in the interactive working.

In interactive working, it is important to consider how far the full range of visible and invisible products can be expressed in more accessible forms, so that they can be better understood at a collective level. This raises important management choices in the areas of *recording* and *interpretation*. Recording is simply a question of keeping track of progress, as it is made. Various methods for recording progress on the substance of problems – and the more visible aspects of progress on the process side – have already been illustrated through the telling of the South Side story in Chapters 2 and 3; but recording of invisible progress in terms of process is often less straightforward. However, conscious efforts to document shifts in understanding of others, and in communication networks, can be important if these aspects of progress are not to become lost.

It is important to recognise that any conscious documentation of progress requires a process of *interpretation* as well as recording. This must involve the translation of jargon used in group working – whether verbal or graphical – if progress is to be reviewed in terms accessible to others rather than in terms which are intelligible merely to those directly involved. This is important enough in the documentation of visible products, but is even more essential in attempting to document progress at the more invisible level. It is especially important, from a longer-term perspective, that people should be helped to recognise invisible products through explicit review of the directions in which progress is – or is not – being made. Some practical advice on these aspects of the management of strategic products will be presented in Chapter 9.

ORIENTATIONS OF STRATEGIC CHOICE: A GENERAL REVIEW

The various points made under the four headings of Technology, Organisation, Process and Product are summarised in Figure 34. This is intended to form a point of reference in following the more concrete guidance to be offered in the next five chapters. The first two columns do little more than present in a more compact form the contrasts in orientation which were highlighted earlier (Figure 29), where the structure of a tetrahedron was introduced to convey the essential unity of the A-TOPP framework.

So, in general terms, the strategic choice approach is interpreted in terms of shifts of emphasis from conventional ideas about technology, organisation, process and product towards the four preferred *orientations* of open technology, interactive participation, learning process and incremental progress. These comparatively general, exhortative statements are then translated in the second column of Figure 34 into the four *operational guidelines* of focus on decisions, lateral connections, cyclic continuity and strategic products. All these can be seen as linked to the more general guideline of the conscious *management of uncertainty*, which distinguishes the strategic choice approach as a practical means of responding to complex problems. Each of these four guidelines can be contrasted with more conventional guidelines for responding to complexity which, in practice, are often disappointing in their effects. These more conventional guidelines – systems perspective, hierarchical command, prescribed stages and substantive plans have all been used as points of reference in discussing the strategic choice alternatives in the four preceding sections. So these too are brought within the comparative framework in the second column of Figure 34, linked to a more general guideline of consistent policy at the level of overall approach.

The third column of Figure 34 extends this framework to indicate the main areas of management choice which it is important to bear in mind when attempting to follow the recommended operational guidelines in practice. Again, these areas of management choice have already been introduced in the preceding sections of this chapter; but it will be helpful to gather them together here.

- In terms of *technology*, it is important to keep in view choices about ways of **interacting and facilitating** as well as about methods of analysis as such.
- In *organisational* terms, the important choices concern ways of **linking and grouping** across sectional or organisational boundaries, as well as about the design of more formal co-ordinating structures.
- In *process* terms, there are choices of **switching and looping** to be considered while working interactively, as well as the more familiar choices about scheduling of meetings and deadlines.
- In terms of *products*, there are choices to be made about ways of **recording and interpreting** progress, as well as the more familiar choices about production of formal reports which emphasise substantive actions and policies.

All these aspects of management choice can be seen as describing different facets of a more general task of managing the strategic choice approach. This means maintaining a spirit of *selectivity and adaptiveness* in planning and decision-making, as contrasted with a more familiar emphasis on the regulation of more simple decision-making tasks. Yet another level of contrast is added by the fourth and final column of Figure 34, which introduces a set of contrasting emphases in terms of the continuous *monitoring* of the quality of a process of strategic choice. In brief, the message is that judgements about the use of limited resources have to be approached not just in terms of some clearly defined criterion of optimality but more in terms of a broader concept of **effectiveness**. In the successive rows of the framework, this concept is seen as embracing such concepts as *sharing, synergy,*

understanding and *confidence*, in addition to more conventional indicators of success.

These evaluative issues will be discussed more fully in Chapter 9. They remain relevant whether the concern is to make quick prospective judgements about what to do next in the course of an interactive process, or to review progress in a more reflective vein. The important point is that it is not necessary to discard completely such traditional concerns as accuracy and rigour in technology; efficiency and control in organisation; productivity and timekeeping in process; or accountability and completeness in product. It is merely that other crucial considerations have to be explicitly considered as well. Indeed, this point applies to all the contrasts offered in Figure 34; to advocate a shift in emphasis from the top left section of each square towards the bottom right is not to be taken as implying that these more conventional emphases do not have their place. It has to be recognised that all organisations require a base of stability and predictability on which their more adaptive activities can be built; and the concern here is that this should be effectively complemented rather than undermined.

The concern with identifying areas of choice and evaluation which emerges in the third and fourth columns of Figure 34 may suggest that some of the core strategic choice concepts such as those of the decision area and the comparison area could be applied in structuring the management of the process of strategic choice itself. There is no reason in principle why this should not be possible. However, any explicit use of strategic choice methods for this purpose must not distract the participants from the real problems of substance that they face. So it is suggested that Figure 34 be treated as background rather than foreground in reading the chapters that follow. Working on the well-established principle that there is nothing so practical as a good theory, this framework can be referred to as and when required, as a broad philosophical context within which all the practical guidance offered in the next five chapters should make sense.

5 Skills in shaping

INTRODUCTION

This chapter offers some practical guidance on approaches to the shaping of complex decision problems. It does so by building on the basic concepts of the shaping mode which were presented in the first half of Chapter 2 – the concepts of the decision area, the decision link, the decision graph and the problem focus. Each of these ideas is quite simple in its essence. Within the overall technology of strategic choice, they together provide a foundation for the more technical activities of generating options and exploring their mutual compatibility which distinguish the work of the designing mode.

The importance of work in the shaping mode arises from all the difficult and subtle judgements that can be involved in expressing practical problems in terms of decision areas and linkages between them, and then in agreeing a problem focus on which to work within the resulting decision graph. This can be an especially challenging task in situations where the nature and scope of the choices to be made are far from clear cut and where there are many participants in the process, each with a different understanding of what is at stake. Experience has repeatedly shown that it can be worthwhile spending a substantial amount of group time working to achieve more satisfactory formulations of a decision graph. This may mean changing the 'map' of decision areas and their connecting links several times, as the level of shared understanding grows. Indeed, such a process of recycling is of value not only when a group of people is still in the early stages of working together. It can also be well worthwhile for the group to return and carry

out further work in the shaping mode after they have consciously moved ahead and invested effort in the work of the designing, comparing and choosing modes. This point is inherent in the guideline of cyclic continuity in the process, which was emphasised in Chapter 4 and gave rise to the various switching and looping opportunities indicated in Figure 30. Taking a longer-time perspective, the idea of the commitment package demonstrates how incremental progress towards commitment will usually mean deferring choice within some of the decision areas within a decision graph. Any such deferments will, in turn, create opportunities for the reshaping of decision areas and their relationships at future points in time – when other quite new areas of choice may possibly have come to the fore through the unfolding of external events.

In Chapter 2, it was suggested that the choice of problem focus within a wider decision graph marked an important point of transition between the work of the shaping and the designing modes. There are, however, many different considerations which can be taken into account in this process of 'cutting a problem down to size'. Some of these considerations – urgency, degree of importance, level of interconnectedness, degree of influence on the part of a particular set of decision-makers – may be much more important in some decision contexts than in others. Indeed, their importance can vary with the passage of time, even within the same decision context. So the whole process of problem-shaping can be seen as one in which a continuing tension must be expected between the desire to expand the boundaries of a problem to encompass all conceivable elements of

FIGURE
35

SOUTH SIDE
EXAMPLE

Building up a Tentative List of Decision Areas

DECISION AREA	LABEL
road line across South Side?	ROAD LINE?
shopping centre location?	SHOP LOC'N?
use of central site?	CENT'L SITE?
use of gasworks site?	GAS SITE?
closure of Main Street?	MAIN ST?
timing of construction of new road?	ROADTIM?
policy on rehousing?	REHOUS?
traffic management in South Side?	TRAF MGT?
West Street improvement?	WEST ST?
closure of Griffin Road school?	GRIFF SCHL?
investment in life of district?	DIST LIFE?
re-routeing of local bus services?	BUS ROUTES?
cutbacks in municipal spending?	CUTBACKS?
extent of further housing clearance?	HOUSCLEAR?
policy on housing repair?	HOUSRPR?
policy on contracting out design work?	DESIGN WK?
procedure for property acquisition?	PROPACQ?

initial quick
listing by
group working
collectively

further
additions
suggested
after
individual
reflection

SHAPING

SKILLS

The building up of an unstructured list of decision areas such as this can be a useful step when a group
is just starting work. The list can be extended, altered or restructured as understanding grows, with
some entries transferred to lists of comparison areas or uncertainty areas. Individuals can be invited to
list their own suggestions either at the start or later in the process.

choice, and the desire to keep its dimensions more manageable so as to secure a sense of progress towards action.

APPROACHES TO BUILDING UP A SET OF RELEVANT DECISION AREAS

Given some agreement to carry out work in a difficult but as yet unstructured problem field, the task of beginning to build up a set of decision areas to represent the choices within that field is one that can be organised either at an individual or a group level. It is broadly akin to the process of 'agenda building' which is, literally, no more than the construction of a list of things to be done, or matters to be addressed. However, in strategic choice, the task is not simply to arrange these things to be done into some appropriate order so that they can be tackled sequentially. This is because some of them at least are likely to be interrelated, in a way which implies that they should perhaps be grouped or clustered so that they can be examined together.

Wherever an individual or group is working to a reasonably well-defined remit, as in the problem of looking into the implications of the proposed new road through South Side, then it may not be too difficult to decide where the process of building up a list of decision areas should begin. For example, among the seven decision areas listed in Figure 10, it might be that the first four at least would suggest themselves fairly readily to anyone familiar with the local planning context. Yet in other circumstances, where the remit may be broader or looser, and the elements of choice less clear or less urgent, difficulties are to be expected in agreeing the way in which even the most basic elements of choice should be expressed.

Such difficulties may, of course, arise even where an individual is working alone; but where people are working as a group they can be expected to surface rapidly in the form of debates and disagreements between one person and another. Usually, the different members of the group will bring different kinds of perception to bear, rooted in different kinds of experience, different bases of professional or technical knowledge and different responsibilities to people outside the group, apart from any deeper differences in ways of construing the world around them. Such differences can be valuable in so far as they can help the group develop a more rounded appreciation of the choices which they face.

In South Side, for example, it might be expected that any engineers in the group might see the relevant choices in terms of road alignments, construction techniques and other technical matters to do with elevations, access roads, surface drainage arrangements or bids for resources on capital programmes. Urban planners might see them in terms of opportunities to specify intended uses or other controls relating to particular areas of land; economists might see them in terms of investment levels, amortisation of fixed assets, balance between private and public expenditures, and incomes. Then again lawyers, administrators, project co-ordinators, politicians and any other participants in the process might all have their subtly different perspectives on the range and content of the choices to be considered.

In a group setting, one good way to start the process of building up a set of decision areas is simply to begin with a large sheet of blank paper on the wall, on which an initial list of issues or matters of concern is recorded by one participant in such a way as to be clearly visible to all the others. Figure 35 gives an example of the kind of tentative list that might be built up by the South Side Working Party at the outset of its work, before any kind of sorting or grouping of decision areas has been attempted. What matters at this stage is primarily to encourage the involvement of as many participants as possible in the listing of an initial set of elements, however imperfect it may seem. The spirit called for is one of organised brainstorming, in which ideas put forward by one participant can trigger off new directions of thought by others.

An alternative way of starting is to ask each participant to spend a few minutes writing

FIGURE
36

SOUTH SIDE
EXAMPLE

Sorting Decision Areas by Categories and Levels

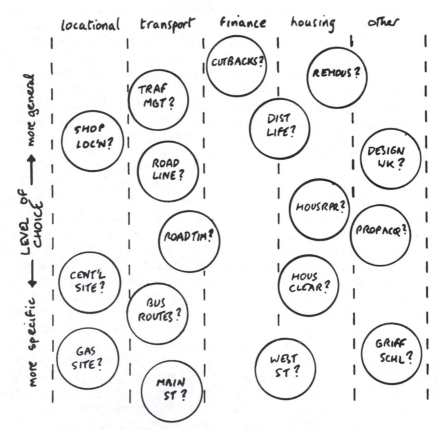

CATEGORY OF CHOICE

locational   transport   finance   housing   other

LEVEL OF CHOICE
more general ↑
more specific ↓

SHOP LOC'N?
TRAF MGT?
CUTBACKS?
REHOUS?
DIST LIFE?
DESIGN WK?
ROAD LINE?
HOUSRPR?
PROPACQ?
ROADTIM?
CENT'L SITE?
BUS ROUTES?
HOUS CLEAR?
GRIFF SCHL?
GAS SITE?
WEST ST?
MAIN ST?

SHAPING

SKILLS

It can be useful to rearrange decision areas by fields or levels — or both — whenever an unstructured list seems to be becoming too long or unwieldy. This can help in redefining or clustering similar decision areas; in considering the possibility of an multi-level problem structure; and in choosing a problem focus where there are many decision areas.

down a list of a few decision areas he or she believes to be important, before the interactive group process begins – or at least before it has built up a momentum of its own. If each individual uses a separate sheet of paper or card to record each suggested decision area – and if these sheets are not too large then the results can be shared by spreading all the sheets prepared by the participants out on a table top or, perhaps, merely on a patch of clear floor space in the centre of the room. Wall space can, of course, be used for displaying these sheets of paper, provided there is a simple, non-permanent means of sticking paper to the wall.

This kind of approach can be helpful in generating an initial sense of involvement by all participants in a group. Of course, it is also likely to lead to a degree of redundancy in the information generated, because some of the more obvious decision areas are likely to be thought of independently by different people. But this kind of redundancy may be no bad thing at an early stage in a group process, both because any area of choice which is identified by many people can be given more weight on that account, and because the elements of a problem may be perceived in subtly different ways by different participants. Such differences can then provide a focus for constructive debate when it comes to the point of formulating decision areas in more precise terms.

In this kind of activity, it is only to be expected that doubts will arise as to whether some suggested elements of a problem should be considered as decision areas at all. Some areas of choice may seem to lie largely outside the direct sphere of influence of the participants, in which case they might perhaps seem better expressed as uncertainty areas. Other 'decision areas' offered may seem more in the nature of statements or choices to do with generalised aims, criteria or desiderata, in which case there would be a possibility of reserving them to be introduced later as comparison areas. As will be seen later, comparison areas and uncertainty areas can always be transferred to separate sheets of paper on the wall, for further consideration when the process moves into other modes. However, there is no reason why they should not be included in a single unstructured list of problem elements in the first instance, with a view to further rearrangement when the group decides to move ahead.

SORTING DECISION AREAS BY CATEGORIES AND LEVELS

Where the problem to be tackled has no clear boundaries, and especially where many participants are involved, it is not uncommon for the process of generating decision areas to develop a momentum of its own. Each new addition to the list can then prompt further suggestions; so that the process begins to appear a never-ending one. But once the list of decision areas reaches around 15 or 20 – as in the example of Figure 35 – then questions will begin to arise as to whether it is useful to continue any further in this way. Participants may then well begin to ask whether, before thinking of any further additions, those decision areas already on the list should not be sorted or rearranged in some way, to identify possible overlaps and gaps in the problem formulation as it has shaped up so far.

One obvious way in which to begin to restructure a list of decision areas is to introduce some framework of *categories* of choice which are felt appropriate to the present decision setting. In a setting such as that of the South Side Working Party, for example, it might be felt that the decision areas in the list could be rearranged into broad fields of choice to do with transport, with land use, with finance and, perhaps, with other familiar functional areas such as housing, education, legal or personnel matters. In an industrial management context, the key functional areas might well be different, with categories such as production, marketing, purchasing, maintenance and product development forming the most natural frame of reference for the participants.

The differentiation of *levels* of choice offers another obvious means of sorting decision areas, especially where either the nature of the remit or the diversity of the participants leads to the generation of a list of decision areas some of which are expressed in more generalised terms than others. For example, in the list in Figure 35, the decision area about 'cutbacks in municipal spending' could be seen as impinging not just on South Side but on the population of the municipality as a whole; while that on investment in the continued life of the South Side district could be seen as clearly broader than that to do with the comparatively local West Street improvement issue.

Figure 36 illustrates one approach to the sorting of decision areas both according to category and to level of generality at the same time. Each decision area is here positioned, vertically, in relation to a spectrum ranging from the most specific operational choice to the most generalised choice of policy orientation. It is also located, horizontally, according to some set of functional categories which, for this purpose, need not be very precisely defined. These two dimensions can be marked out either on a large sheet of paper on a wall, or on a sufficiently large area of floor or table space, depending on the preferences of the group and the facilities of the room in which they are working. The use of floor or table space, with decision areas represented by movable cards, sheets of paper or discs, has the advantage that their positions can be shifted around easily, until the participants agree that the resulting layout represents a good enough 'map' as a basis for further shaping work. Of course, the same flexibility can be achieved on a wall, provided the technical problems of adhesion and easy repositioning can be dealt with – for example, by use of semiadhesive 'Post-It' type notes.

The main purpose of this sorting and positioning procedure is to build a broad picture of the overall balance of the set of decision areas so far generated; a picture within which it is possible to search for both overlaps and gaps. There may, for example, be very good reasons why, in Figure 36, there should be several comparatively specific transport decision areas, whereas the only financial decision areas seem to appear at the more generalised level: but at least it becomes possible to debate whether there are overlaps that should be eliminated or important gaps to be filled. Overlaps are, of course, especially likely to arise where some or all of the decision areas have been generated by individuals independently, rather than as part of a group process. Often, overlaps will point towards opportunities for more careful reformulation of decision areas, using the kind of guidelines to be discussed in the next section.

Where decision areas seem to be poorly balanced between levels, a useful way of proceeding is to review whether any of the comparatively specific decision areas can be thought of in terms of choices of *means* towards more general *ends*, or whether some of the more general ones can be thought of in terms of choice of *ends*, suggesting more specific choices of *means*. For example, the general CUTBACKS? decision area might, on reflection, suggest more specific choices to do with the relative severity with which any particular departmental budget or capital programme was to be cut back in a coming annual review cycle; while the specific issue of closure of the Griffin Road School might, on reflection, suggest broader areas of decision to do with educational reorganisation policy in a wider area.

This kind of ends/means investigation is likely, in practice, to cut across whatever divisions were agreed as a basis for organising decision areas into functional categories. For instance, choices about the closure of the Griffin Road School might be seen as leading towards broader policy choices beyond the field of education – especially if possible noneducational uses were being kept in view for the buildings or site, with implications for other policies and budgets.

Experience tends to indicate that categories are often simplest to distinguish in the middle range of the general type/specificity spectrum, while tending to converge both at the broad policy level, and in some cases at the level of specific local impact. So the vertical divisions in

Figure 36 can be thought of as rather like lines of longitude on a globe, which gradually converge as they are extended upwards or downwards towards the polar regions where they meet.

As in the construction of an initial tentative list, one outcome of this process of sorting by levels and categories may be a growing recognition that some decision areas may be better expressed either as comparison areas or as uncertainty areas, so may be best set aside for later consideration in this light. Also, as in the preliminary listing process, it is important not to spend too long in re-sorting decision areas according to categories and levels; this is because of the connections across levels and categories which are of more fundamental importance to the work of the shaping mode.

REFORMULATING DECISION AREAS

For a group to establish momentum, it is good practice to formulate decision areas loosely and informally in the first instance, without worrying about the finer points of how they should be worded or the specific nature of the choices which may be available within each. However, this can mean bypassing issues of definition which can be of much importance in practical terms; and it can be well worthwhile returning to consider such issues more carefully once the participants in the process feel satisfied that they have built up a good enough set of decision areas to form the basis of an initial decision graph. This kind of pause for reformulation of individual decision areas will be particularly important where there appear to be overlaps between somewhat similar decision areas; overlaps which could be overcome by more careful formulation of what is meant, so that the decision areas can either be merged or else more clearly distinguished from each other.

There are two kinds of difficulty which often arise in the initial listing of decision areas, especially among people who have not previously been accustomed to thinking explicitly in decision area terms. One is that decision areas are confused with options within decision areas: for instance, the decision area described as 'West Street Improvement' could be read as the specific proposal to improve rather than the area of choice as to whether to improve or not. It is this kind of scope for misunderstanding that makes it useful to maintain the discipline of writing a question mark at the end of both the shorter description and the shorter label of every decision area.

The other source of confusion encountered in practice is a tendency to express decision areas in terms of choice of preferred *state*, rather than choice of preferred *action*. For instance, depending on the powers at the disposal of the decision-makers, it may be one thing to consider whether the vacant central site in South Side should be in residential or industrial use at some future time; yet quite a different thing to consider which zoning should be indicated on a local plan to be prepared and published as a guide to future development decisions. So 'choice of zoning' may be a more realistic phrasing than 'choice of use', when considered in relation to the levels of influence which the public decision-makers in South Side can actually bring to bear. The choice of action within their control may relate, strictly speaking, to the action of setting down a policy statement in print, accompanied by the action of shading a map in one tone rather than another; this act may have some influence over the way the land is used, but perhaps by no means the only influence once market pressures and other policy influences come to bear.

In some contexts, refinements in the expression of a decision area may not matter very much: but in others they may be crucial. In essence, the attempt to express decision areas in more careful and realistic terms involves looping outwards from the shaping mode towards the designing mode. It means thinking about options within decision areas, in order to arrive at a clearer view of the nature of the decision areas themselves. Figure 37

95

FIGURE

37

SOUTH SIDE
EXAMPLE

Refining the Expression of Decision Areas

BRIEF INITIAL FORMULATION (as in figure 35)	MORE CAREFUL FORMULATION
ROAD LINE? road line across South Side?	which route to reserve on the South Side local plan map for the proposed new arterial road?
SHOP LOC'N? shopping centre location?	which site to designate in the South Side local plan as the location for a more concentrated local shopping centre?
CENT'L SITE? use of central site?	what type of land use to specify in the South Side local plan for the central area of cleared housing land?
DIST LIFE? investment in life of district?	what public statement to issue about level of intended investment in the continued life of South Side as a residential district?
WEST ST? West street improvement?	whether or not to propose to the Housing Committee that the West Street area be added to the priority list for improvement area status?

It is worth giving some thought to the more careful formulation of particular decision areas if they appear to overlap with other decision areas, or if they appear at any time to be emerging as part of a problem focus for the design and comparison of alternatives. The operational meaning of decision areas can become especially crucial when it comes to the design of possible commitment packages.

illustrates this point by offering some more careful formulations for five of the seventeen decision areas for South Side which were tentatively listed in Figure 35. These same five decision areas will also be found in the set of seven decision areas that were first presented to illustrate the general concept of a decision area (Figure 10). For that purpose, they were defined with more care than in the tentative listing of Figure 35, but with less precision than in Figure 37. This illustrates the general point that there is often considerable scope for debate and judgement in the way any particular decision area is expressed.

The closer formulation of decision areas can be seen not just as a means of reaching a clearer understanding of problems, but as a check against wishful thinking – in particular, against the illusion that the participants are in a position to choose between end states, in situations where in reality they may have only limited opportunities for intervention or influence in relation to the decisions of others. So this kind of probing can lead to subtle distinctions between decision areas in terms of decision-making agencies and roles. In a situation such as that of South Side, for instance, there could be an important distinction between professional officers, who are expected to offer recommendations on particular matters, and a politically accountable council or committee, which has the power and the responsibility to accept, modify or reject these recommendations as a basis for executive action. Such distinctions can become crucial when turning to the work of the choosing mode, and when considering the design of commitment packages in particular. This means that any attempt to formulate decision areas more clearly in action terms can be seen as a form of looping outwards in the direction of the choosing mode.

Of course, too much reflection on such subtleties may inhibit progress in the construction of a decision graph. So again it is important to avoid becoming too deeply immersed in this kind of activity. However, in moving ahead it is important to record any progress which is made in the more exact formulation of decision

areas – as in the example of Figure 37 – so that it is available for reference if and when required.

INTRODUCING LINKS BETWEEN DECISION AREAS

As was emphasised in Chapter 2, the drawing of a decision link between any pair of decision areas represents no more than a working assumption that it could make a difference if the choices available within those two decision areas were to be considered together rather than independently.

As in the generating of the decision areas themselves, it is useful to treat the introduction of decision links and the resulting build-up of a decision graph as a creative group process, in which one person begins by suggesting one or two obvious linkages, stimulating other participants to join in and suggest others. Where the number of decision areas is large, it can be advisable to defer this process until they have been arranged in terms of categories and levels, as in the example of Figure 36. However, it is more usual in practice to start from a set of decision areas which has not been arranged in this way, but can be extended and rearranged freely as the group interaction gathers momentum. Whichever approach is used, it is important to follow a selective approach to the introduction of decision links, omitting any which seem less significant than others. This is because a decision graph can become hard to understand if it shows virtually every decision area as joined up to every other. Indeed, as soon as the pattern becomes as complex as this, it can quickly lose any value it might have had as a guide to the understanding of problem structure within the group.

Once the decision graph begins to take shape, a useful way to proceed is to look at each decision area in turn and ask which of the other decision areas – if any – are likely to affect it to a significant degree. It is only to be expected that doubts will arise from time to time over whether the connection between one decision area and another is clear enough or important enough to be shown as a link on

FIGURE
38

SOUTH SIDE
EXAMPLE

Building up a Picture of Decision Links

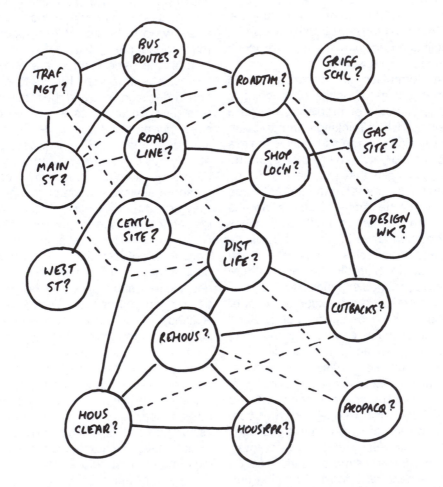

SHAPING

SKILLS

It is important to begin introducing links between decision areas at a comparatively early stage of work in the shaping mode, recognizing that many of the decision links will be only tentative at this stage. The pattern of decision links can if preferred be generated by using non-graphical methods, and the example from practice presented in Figure 45 gives an example of an alternative matrix format.

a decision graph; and it is only to be expected that participants will disagree with each other over judgements of this kind. Where this happens, progress can be sustained by adding a broken line to the graph, to indicate an uncertain or debatable decision link, as shown in the example of Figure 38. Sometimes, indeed, it may be worth expressing more than one level of doubt about the status of decision links, for instance by distinguishing between broken lines and more tentative dotted lines which identify links of even more dubious status.

As more and more links are added to a decision graph, it usually becomes apparent that it would be helpful to redraw it with some of the decision areas moved across to different positions, so as to avoid or reduce the confusion caused by criss-crossing lines and thus to bring out the underlying structure of relationships more clearly.

If the aim were merely to represent the inherent structure of relationships within the graph – its topological structure to use mathematical language – there would be no need to spend time altering the positions of decision areas to avoid inelegant features of graphic design. However, because the purpose of the decision graph is primarily to facilitate communication within a group, the attempt to 'clean up' its representation can be well worthwhile in practice. A confused and untidy picture with many bent or intersecting lines can obscure aspects of problem structure which, with a little rearrangement, could be brought out much more clearly; and this in turn can help members of a group to identify possible clusters of decision areas which they might wish to explore more closely within an agreed problem focus. So it is worth at this point introducing some simple guidelines for rearrangement and clustering of decision areas within a decision graph.

REARRANGING A DECISION GRAPH

There are various working rules, some of them simple and obvious enough, which can be used as an aid to the reshaping of a complex decision graph. First, it is usually not hard to pick out any decision areas which have no more than one decision link connecting them to the rest of the graph, as in the case of WEST ST? in Figure 38. Sometimes, indeed, there may be one or two completely isolated decision areas which were originally seen as important when drawing up a preliminary list, but then turned out to have no links to other decision areas at all. There may also be 'chains' of decision areas – such as that connecting GRIFF SCH? and GAS SITE? to SHOP LOC'N? in Figure 38 – which have only limited connections with the rest of the problem structure. So a useful preliminary step in the restructuring of a graph is to identify such comparatively isolated parts and set them aside, as a step towards exploring more carefully the configuration of the decision areas that remain. Typically, there will be several 'triads' of three fully interlinked decision areas in a decision graph of any size. In Figure 38, for example, there are seven such triads, if only solid links are counted, and several more if broken links are counted as well. It will be less common to find totally connected clusters of four or more decision areas. However, in Figure 38 it is possible, with perseverance, to pick out three such clusters by eye, if broken as well as solid lines are counted. All three, it may be noted, incorporate the same ROAD LINE? decision area, which emphasises its importance to the overall problem structure.

Figure 39 presents the result of one attempt to redraw the graph so as to bring out some of these structural features more clearly. Through the use of visual judgement and graphical dexterity alone, some of the decision areas have been shifted in position, mainly to reduce the number of criss-crossing lines, while preventing the more isolated decision areas from cluttering up the middle of the picture. Also, to identify closely linked clusters more clearly, boundary lines have been drawn around two clusters of four decision areas and one of five. Not all of these clusters include totally interconnected sets of decision areas, and there is no need to be rigid in this respect. What the

FIGURE

39

SOUTH SIDE
EXAMPLE

Rearranging a Decision Graph

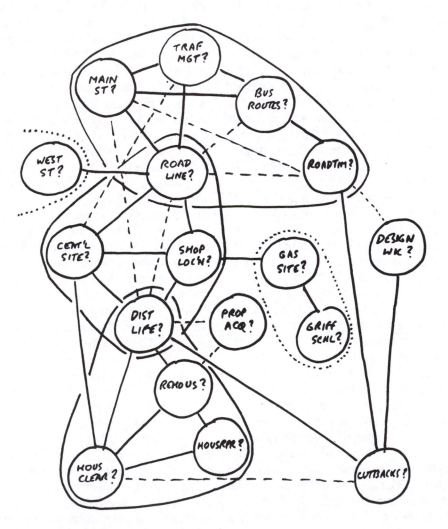

SHAPING

SKILLS

Where the structure of a decision graph is difficult to make out visually because there are too many decision links connecting decision area which are far apart on the graph, it can be important to give time to the repositioning of at least some decision areas to bring out the underlying structure more clearly. It is useful to start by identifying more isolated decision areas and closely connected clusters.

clustering in Figure 39 does reveal is that there are three closely connected clusters which in this case connect up in a chain: an observation which offers an important aid in comprehending the overall structure of this particular graph.

It is not easy, nor perhaps too helpful, to try to codify more precisely the kind of rules to be used in this kind of structuring process. This is because any attempt to codify creates a need to agree more precisely what status a broken link should be given as compared with a solid link, and this may be to place too much meaning on what is intended as no more than a loose and informal convention for making assumptions about relatedness between decision areas. Yet it is always possible to develop and apply more precise codes of rules for the limited range of situations where this could be a worthwhile aid to the work of the shaping mode. For instance, decision links can always be formulated as yes/no or zero/one entries in a two-way table or matrix of mutual relationships between pairs of decision areas: and question marks or other symbols can then be introduced to represent doubtful links if desired. Then that matrix can be rearranged according to some set of logical rules which, in turn, may indicate how the decision graph could, with advantage, be redrawn.

Resort to such methods is most likely to be worthwhile in circumstances where a graph is so complex that visual inspection offers few clues to its underlying structure, so that any attempt to disentangle it without resort to a computer is likely to involve judgements of an arbitrary and therefore misleading kind. In practice, experienced users of strategic choice methods usually stop well short of this level of elaboration in the size of a graph – not least because input of structural information to a computer can mean slowing down the pace of interactive working within a group.

HIGHLIGHTING MORE SIGNIFICANT DECISION AREAS

A decision graph may have to be rearranged more than once to bring out its structure as clearly as possible, and to draw attention to closely linked clusters without other decision areas getting in the way. However, this kind of structural information on its own cannot be expected to bring out all those characteristics of a problem situation which might be significant in choosing a more restricted problem focus or foci within which to switch to the work of the designing mode. In particular, the participants will often be aware that some decision areas are more important to them than others, in the sense that they represent choices where there is more at stake. Also, there may be some decision areas which may carry particular urgency even if they are not so significant in themselves – and it could be unwise to exclude these from any more restricted problem focus which the participants might choose.

It is always possible, however, to add information on importance, urgency or other considerations to a decision graph, by the simple device of introducing further symbols to highlight those decision areas which are believed to call for particular attention on any such grounds. Figure 40 illustrates how this can be done by simply adding to the graph various kinds of symbol to distinguish decision areas which the participants see as significant to them on different grounds. Here circles are marked in one way to indicate particular urgency of decision, and in another way to indicate particular importance in terms of their consequences. An asterisk is used to indicate decision areas within which there are thought to be comparatively clear alternatives, because these offer a prospect of straightforward progress when turning attention to the work of the designing mode. A different convention again is used in Figure 40 to highlight those individual decision areas which have a particularly high level of connectedness to other decision areas. The symbols chosen in this illustration are of a kind to allow them to be used in conjunction with each other, if necessary. So, for example, the CUTBACKS? decision area is identified as both urgent and important in its consequences; the ROAD LINE? decision area is identified as

FIGURE
40

SOUTH SIDE
EXAMPLE

Highlighting More Significant Decision Areas

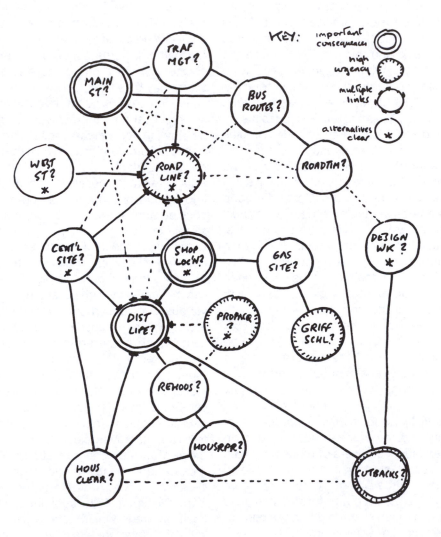

Where there are several possible problem foci within which work in other modes might be carried out, it becomes useful to use colour or other coding to highlight key decision areas on grounds of urgency, importance of consequences and any other such characteristics additional to those which are to be found in the structure of the decision graph itself.

both urgent and highly connected; the DIST LIFE? decision area, meanwhile, is identified as important in its consequences and also highly connected, if not thought to be so urgent at this stage.

The identification of highly connected or 'nodal' decision areas is of course one aspect of this process that can be carried out by working from the structural information contained in the decision graph itself. In the graph of Figure 40, it is not too hard to pick out ROAD LINE? and DIST LIFE? as the two most interconnected decision areas, as each has eight links to others, if the more doubtful links are included.

However, judgements about urgency and level of importance have to be made on the basis of information which comes not from the graph itself but from people's perceptions of the particular pressures and responsibilities that they face. It is, therefore, only to be expected that there will be differences of opinion as to relative urgency and importance where the participants are working as a group. There is no reason why different codings should not be used to pick out importance to different sets of interests; and when working with coloured wedge-tip pens, contrasting colours can always be used to build a richer picture than can be presented in a black and white diagram, such as that of Figure 40. For instance, one colour could be used to pick out decision areas of particular importance to local people in South Side, and another to pick out those of broader importance to the municipality as a whole, as a means of ensuring that neither perspective is lost sight of when it comes to choice of an agreed problem focus.

It is very much in the spirit of the strategic choice approach that differences of perspective should be debated openly within the group, while in the process of adding information on urgency and impact to the decision graph. In the course of such a discussion, specific arguments may emerge as to why one participant sees a decision area as urgent which another sees as not so urgent; or again, in the case of another decision area, it could emerge that one

participant has foreseen that the choice could have serious importance for some sector of the community with which other participants were not so closely concerned. So the highlighting of more critical decision areas on the grounds either of urgency or importance can bring valuable benefits in terms of increased mutual understanding – involving as it does elements of anticipation of timing and evaluative considerations that the participants may wish to explore in more depth when it comes to future work in other modes.

SUPERIMPOSING ORGANISATIONAL RESPONSIBILITIES ON A DECISION GRAPH

A further type of consideration, which can be used to differentiate between decision areas within a decision graph, relates to the degree of *influence* or control which the participants expect to be able to exercise. In South Side, for instance, the members of the working party might see themselves as collectively having a direct influence on the decision as to where the shopping centre for South Side should be located and, possibly, also on the choice of designated use for the central site. However, they might recognise that their influence was more limited when it came to recommendations on the line of the road; and their influence might be even more marginal in relation to the high-level corporate budgeting decisions which are implied by the CUTBACKS? decision area. Therefore, they might wish to discuss whether CUTBACKS? would be better reformulated as an uncertainty area instead of a decision area at this stage.

One means of reflecting judgements about relative influence or control is simply to designate another symbol with which to distinguish individual decision areas on a decision graph, along the lines of those used to indicate urgency and importance in Figure 40. This approach is indeed often used in practical applications of the strategic choice approach. However, in many situations it is useful to

FIGURE
41

SOUTH SIDE
EXAMPLE

Superimposing Organisational Boundaries on a Decision Graph

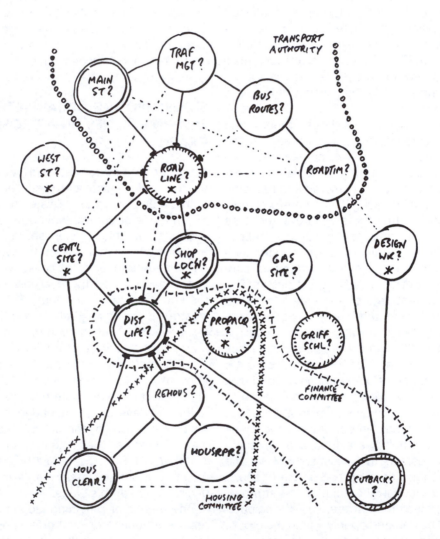

SHAPING

SKILLS

It is often important in practice to distinguish between different areas of organisational or departmental responsibility in the manner indicated above, using different coloured boundaries where possible. This can help in considering who should participate in the work of other modes, and in what ways linkages to the work of other parties might be maintained.

go further than this by distinguishing several different zones of organisational responsibility and influence, and to do this by superimposing a new set of boundary lines on the decision graph as a whole.

For example, Figure 41 once more takes the overall decision graph arrived at for the South Side problem and superimposes three new sets of boundaries, to do with transport decisions; housing decisions; and financial decisions – each of these relating to a zone of organisational responsibility which is recognised in this particular decision setting. Such organisational boundaries will sometimes overlap; and both the patterns of overlap and the patterns of decision links across the boundaries can then reveal much about the issues of inter-departmental or perhaps inter-corporate co-ordination that would arise if any particular set of decision areas were chosen as a prospective problem focus.

The kind of information used to develop the graph in this way will often be similar to that used to sort a preliminary list of decision areas into functional categories, as illustrated in Figure 36. So the results of any earlier work in sorting decision areas by categories can be drawn on in the process of superimposing a map of organisational responsibilities onto a decision graph. However, it is important to stress that the decision graph is intended primarily as a picture of problem structure rather than organisational responsibilities. Its value in organisational terms is that it can be expected to highlight issues of co-ordination which could have remained hidden, had the process of problem formulation been carried through in a more traditional way.

Of course, there is a danger that the introduction onto the same decision graph of information about organisational boundaries, on top of all the other information it contains, will present the participants with too rich and complex a picture for them to comprehend in its entirety. This is why Figure 41 – while highlighting particular decision areas as in Figure 40 – omits the cluster boundaries which appeared earlier in Figure 39. However, when a decision

graph is being built up on a large sheet of paper on a wall, the risk of confusion can again be much reduced through the use of contrasting colours to distinguish different sets of boundaries. For colour distinctions have a much clearer impact than distinctions among lines containing various patterns of dots, dashes and crosses, as used in Figure 41. Furthermore, they take less time to draw, which can be a significant factor where there is a momentum of group interaction to be sustained.

CONSIDERATIONS IN CHOICE OF A PROBLEM FOCUS

The work done in adding all this further information to a decision graph can offer a basis either for further rearrangement and reformulation or – once the participants are satisfied that they have a good enough representation of the problems before them – for moving on to look more closely at choices within selected parts of the graph. It is only if the graph as a whole contains no more than four or, at most, five decision areas that a group – or for that matter an individual – is likely to find it useful to move into the work of the designing mode without limiting the problem focus in some way. To attempt to explore combinations of options within a set of more than five decision areas is to risk moving into a depth of analysis which can be very time-consuming and, as experience shows, only rarely productive in terms of the progress to which it leads.

Indeed, it is advisable to err on the side of too narrow a problem focus in the early stages of analytical work, by choosing a set of no more than three linked decision areas – perhaps two, or even only one. Alternatives can then be carefully developed and compared within that focus before attempting to broaden the problem focus out again, possibly by introducing only one additional decision area at a time.

In the original example used to illustrate the concept of problem focus – Figure 13 of Chapter 2 – the choice of focus was a simple one. For there were only seven decision areas

FIGURE

42

SOUTH SIDE
EXAMPLE

Selecting Multiple Problem Foci

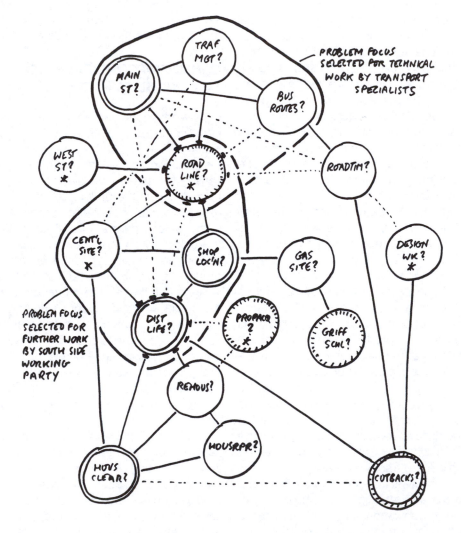

PROBLEM FOCUS
SELECTED FOR TECHNICAL
WORK BY TRANSPORT
SPECIALISTS

PROBLEM FOCUS
SELECTED FOR
FURTHER WORK
BY SOUTH SIDE
WORKING
PARTY

SHAPING

SKILLS

It becomes useful to distinguish more than one problem focus within a decision graph in any situation where it is possible to identify areas for more specialised analysis; where it is desired to define tasks for sub-groups of a large working group; or where there is a concern to schedule a succession of linked analytical task over a period of time.

in all, and three of those clearly occupied comparatively outlying positions. But, when a set of participants is presented with a more complex picture, such as that of Figure 41, where should the process of choosing one or more foci for more intensive analysis begin? This judgement must inevitably depend on the context, as it is only the participants themselves who are in a position to judge what weight to give to decision areas they have marked as urgent compared to those they have marked as important or easier to influence; and it is only they who will be able to appraise the advantages to be obtained through working at clusters of issues which cut across departmental or corporate boundaries. Furthermore, it is only they who can weigh these advantages against any possible political difficulties they foresee, drawing on their own knowledge of the history of working relationships – good, bad or indifferent – between the individuals, professions or organisational units concerned.

In some situations, there is a case for adopting not just one problem focus but two or more, on which different groups of people can work simultaneously. This possibility is illustrated in Figure 42. Here it is supposed that it has been agreed in South Side to adopt two overlapping problem foci as a basis for deeper investigation. One of these contains four of the five linked decisions within the transport sphere of responsibility, so is likely to raise comparatively few organisational difficulties. Within this particular problem focus it is quite possible that the work of the designing mode can be treated as a purely technical exercise, though the work of comparing and choosing may still involve challenges of a wider political nature.

The second problem focus – which the reader may recognise as corresponding exactly to the set of four decision areas selected as the original problem focus in Chapter 2 – overlaps with the first focus in that it contains the ROAD LINE? decision area. It includes one urgent decision area and two of high importance, along with one other decision area which is connected to all these three. Three of the four decision areas are marked as containing

reasonably clear alternatives; but the fourth, DIST LIFE?, is a broader policy-level decision area which presents more difficulties in this respect. This problem focus, in contrast to the other, does not lie entirely within a well-defined field of organisational responsibility; so it might well be agreed that the South Side Working Party, or some sub-group of those concerned, would afford the most appropriate setting for the next stages of the work.

It will be noticed in Figure 42 that some urgent and important decision areas are still omitted from either focus. So questions will, of course, arise as to what should be done about them – especially the more urgent ones. It may be agreed that some urgent decision areas such as PROPACQ? can best be explored further on their own at this stage, in effect forming a 'focus of one' in terms of the problem focus concept. And it may be that other decision areas such as HOUS CLEAR? and CUTBACKS? raise issues which can hardly be tackled without taking various wider organisational relationships into account. So it might be agreed that any deeper consideration of these issues should be set aside by the members of the South Side Working Party at this stage, accepting that they might wish to return to them in later work.

SUMMARY: PROCESS JUDGEMENTS IN THE SHAPING MODE

There is not much which is inherently difficult in the concepts of the decision area and the decision link, which have remained as the basic building blocks of the approach to shaping of problems throughout this chapter. Where the challenge lies is in applying these simple concepts to the representation of complex problems, in such a way as to capture as much as possible of the understanding of these problems which is to be found among the participants; to bring out differences of view wherever these are significant; and to help them find ways of moving forward towards an agreed collective view.

FIGURE

43

Process Choices when Working in the Shaping Mode

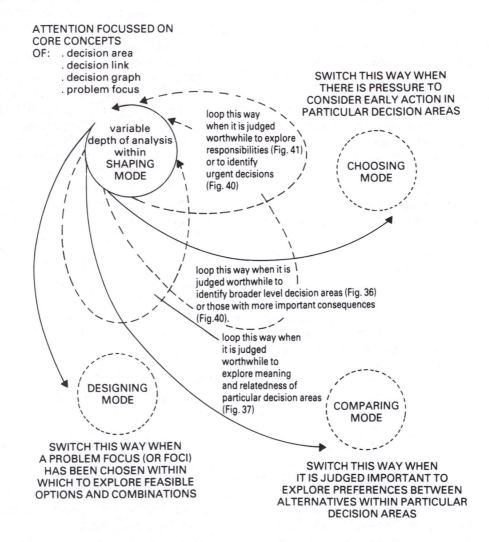

ATTENTION FOCUSSED ON
CORE CONCEPTS
OF: . decision area
       . decision link
       . decision graph
       . problem focus

variable
depth of analysis
within
SHAPING
MODE

loop this way
when it is judged
worthwhile to explore
responsibilities (Fig. 41)
or to identify
urgent decisions
(Fig. 40)

SWITCH THIS WAY WHEN
THERE IS PRESSURE TO
CONSIDER EARLY ACTION IN
PARTICULAR DECISION AREAS

CHOOSING
MODE

loop this way when it is
judged worthwhile to
identify broader level decision areas (Fig. 36)
or those with more important consequences
(Fig.40).

loop this way when
it is judged
worthwhile to
explore meaning
and relatedness of
particular decision areas
(Fig. 37)

DESIGNING
MODE

COMPARING
MODE

SWITCH THIS WAY WHEN
A PROBLEM FOCUS (OR FOCI)
HAS BEEN CHOSEN WITHIN
WHICH TO EXPLORE FEASIBLE
OPTIONS AND COMBINATIONS

SWITCH THIS WAY WHEN
IT IS JUDGED IMPORTANT TO
EXPLORE PREFERENCES BETWEEN
ALTERNATIVES WITHIN PARTICULAR
DECISION AREAS

SHAPING

SUMMARY

Because the concepts and tools used when working in this mode are simple in themselves, it is possible to take on board more complexity in the dimensions of the decision problems being looked at than would be the case with more sophisticated methods. So it can be quite realistic in practice to build up a decision graph containing 20 or even more decision areas, within which more limited foci for further analysis can be picked out, using some combination of the methods illustrated in this chapter. This is not, however, to say that it will invariably be useful to build up a graph of that size or complexity. If it is readily agreed that a problem can be represented in terms of only four or five important areas of choice – or indeed only one or two – there is no point in striving to make its representation more complex.

When working in the shaping mode, one of the few opportunities there is for moving to greater elaboration in analytical methods lies in the use of matrix conventions for representing the structure of a decision graph. Such methods were briefly touched on earlier in the discussion of ways of rearranging a complex decision graph and identifying clusters of closely linked decision areas. This kind of approach can normally be useful in a situation where a decision graph contains such a complex pattern of links that it is unclear from visual inspection alone how it could be rearranged to bring out its inherent structure more clearly; and where there are, therefore, dangers that human bias will play a significant part in its interpretation. Figure 91 in Chapter 10 illustrates the format in which a decision graph is displayed when using the STRAD 2 software, and the accompanying text discusses briefly some of the ways in which the software can help in redrawing the graph and in suggesting possible problem foci. The value of the software is that it can enable changes to be made more freely than when working on flip charts. However, the role of the computer is only to make recommendations on possible foci; the final judgement must remain one for the people concerned.

Here, as in other aspects of the strategic choice technology, the essential point is that depth of analysis can be treated as a variable to be controlled. Yet, experience shows that the creativity of the process of shaping problems is best sustained by keeping the level and methods of analysis as simple as possible, especially when working in groups. This is because it keeps the process open and transparent, and provides flexibility for changes in formulation as the work proceeds. For instance, it may be only after a comparatively complex graph has been gradually built up on the wall, by collective effort, that there is a shared basis for discussing what new decision areas might be added, and whether existing ones should be merged or expressed in different ways. The obvious next step will then be to start again on a clean sheet of paper, keeping the earlier version as a secondary record of the process rather than throwing it away. It is quite common for a group to go through many different formulations of a decision graph, before they can agree it offers a good enough basis for moving ahead. But such recycling of effort will only be creative if there is a shared sense that those involved are continually making progress in terms of mutual understanding of the underlying problem structure.

Figure 43 summarises the main points of this chapter, with reference to the concepts of switching and looping as explained in Chapter 4 (Figure 32). The types of judgements to be made within the shaping mode include not only choices of appropriate depth of analysis when working within that mode, but choices of when and how to move on into any of the other modes. Where some sub-set of linked decision areas has emerged as a useful problem focus, then the obvious next step is to move into the designing mode and, whether through AIDA or other methods, to search for feasible combinations of options among the decision areas concerned. But it is always possible that attention will be quickly drawn to just one crucial decision area, where the options are already clear cut; in that case, it may be possible to move directly to an examination of the consequences of those options within the comparing mode. Then, if there is little doubt which option is to be preferred, it may be possible to move almost straight away into the choosing mode, where a commitment to act on that particular option can be made. This describes the kind of fast route through a decision process which is often followed by an individual working on hunch or experience; but it is less characteristic of groups formed to work on difficult decision problems, the consequences of which for other interests may be profound.

If two or more different problem foci have been identified within a large decision graph, then the process can, of course, be carried forward by agreeing to move from the shaping mode into more than one of these other modes, more or less simultaneously – perhaps by sub-dividing the working group for this purpose, provided that the case for some continuing linkage between their activities is kept in view. Apart from indicating the various possibilities for switching out of the shaping mode, Figure 43 also shows three shorter loops which represent brief excursions in the direction of the other three modes, while continuing to work primarily within the shaping mode. For instance, any attempt to formulate decision areas more precisely, in terms of the kinds of alternative actions likely to be available, involves a loop in the direction of identifying options – and therefore towards the task of the designing mode. Any attempt to balance a set of decision areas according to some framework of categories or levels, as in Figure 36, means looping in the direction of the comparing mode, because the broader levels of choice offer a potential evaluative framework. The highlighting of especially important decision areas within a decision graph can also be seen as a form of looping

in the direction of the comparing mode. Meanwhile, the highlighting of more urgent decision areas on the decision graph tends to involve looping out towards the choosing mode; so does the superimposing of different organisational domains where responsibilities for action lie. This brief review of relationships with other modes only serves to emphasise the underlying unity of the process of strategic choice. It is important to stress the value of making these choices of movement between modes in a flexible, evolutionary way, rather than feeling constrained to conform to any more rigid and prescriptive sequence of operations. Some practical guidelines to help in managing this wider adaptive process will be offered in Chapter 9.

ILLUSTRATIONS FROM PRACTICE

On the three double pages that follow, the reader will find a set of three contrasting illustrations from practice which have been chosen to supplement the points about skills in shaping which have already been made in this chapter with reference to the South Side problem.

The illustrations are taken from applications in very different contexts – in Brazil, in the Netherlands and in Russia. The first includes photographs of people in action, to give some impression of the way in which decision graphs can be built up and reshaped through interactive group working. The second demonstrates how simple forms of ends-means mapping can be used to generate decision areas and to explore relationships between levels of decision. The third illustration describes how a focus was selected in a strategy workshop addressing issues of metropolitan food distribution and retailing, making use of both Post-It stickers and computer methods in priority-setting.

FIGURE

44

Illustrations from Practice – Shaping 1

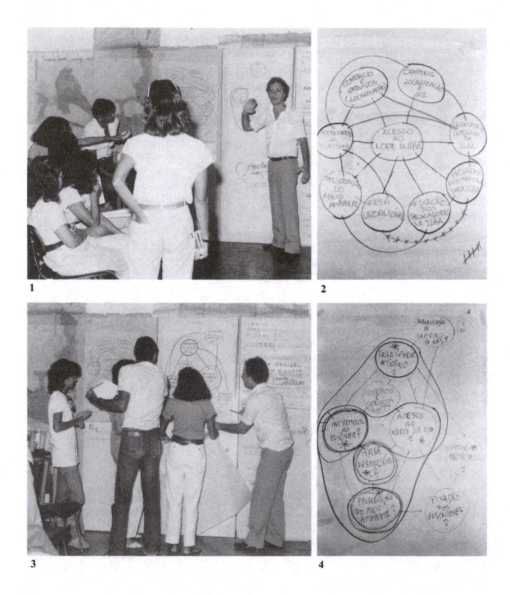

1

2

3

4

Theme: Group Interaction in Problem Structuring using Decision Graphs to find a Working Focus.
Problem: Policy Formulation in a Comprehensive Development Plan for an Offshore Island.
Context: Five-Day Workshop with a Local Inter-Disciplinary Planning Team, Recife, Brazil, 1984.

COMMENTARY ON FIGURE 44

These photographs were taken during the second day of a five-day workshop held in November 1984 in Recife, in the tropical northeast of Brazil. The task was to apply strategic choice methods to the exploration of alternative land use, economic, social and infrastructure policies for the offshore island of Itamaracá in the Recife Metropolitan Planning Region. This island, with an area of about 60 square kilometres and a permanent population of around 8000, was connected to the mainland by a road bridge and had become subject to intense pressures for development, which had to be reconciled with concerns about the conservation of the natural environment and of the islanders' traditional way of life.

The group which participated in the workshop included members of an interdisciplinary planning team from FIDEM, the metropolitan planning agency, two of whom were attached to the island's local municipal council. The process was facilitated by two Brazilians who were already familiar with the strategic choice approach, with John Friend as visiting consultant. The workshop was jointly sponsored by FIDEM, the Federal University of Pernambuco, the State Transportation Department and the British Council. The two decision graphs on the wall in the top left photograph are shown in detail to the right. The first was developed by focusing on a single important decision area selected from an initial set of about 60; this concerned the choice of road access to the undeveloped north of the island. The group then identified eight other decision areas which were directly linked to this, and some cross-links were inserted (2). On the second decision graph (4), this set of nine decision areas was rearranged to bring out clusters more clearly, and different colour codings and symbols were used to highlight decision areas of special significance on grounds of urgency and importance (the codings being listed on the wall on a sheet below the graph itself). Of particular interest in this case was the use of different colours to pick out not only decision areas of metropolitan importance, but also those of particular local importance to the islanders themselves. This distinction was made in response to a concern among some members of the group that the analysis might ignore issues about which the residents themselves were concerned. There was a great deal of lively discussion over the choice of a problem focus for further analysis, as shown in the second group photograph (3) where the second decision graph has just been replaced by a redrawn version showing the pattern of links rather more clearly.

It was later agreed to explore and compare alternatives within a focus of three decision areas chosen with both metropolitan importance and importance to the islanders in view. A later stage in the comparison of alternatives within this focus is illustrated in Figure 69 of Chapter 7.

FIGURE
45

Illustrations from Practice – Shaping 2

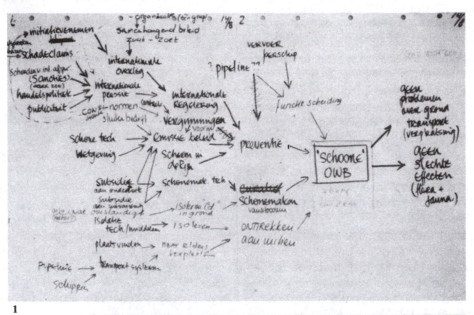

1

2

3

SHAPING

PRACTICE

Theme: Use of Ends-Means Mapping to identify Decision Areas which are then analyzed to find a Problem Focus.

Problem: Disposal of Accumulated Polluted Silts dredged from the Rhine Delta.

Context: Inter-Ministerial Government Working Group, Den Haag, The Neterlands, 1985.

COMMENTARY ON FIGURE 45

These charts were made during one of the middle sessions in a series of exploratory workshops held in Den Haag, The Netherlands, in the period May–August, 1988. The project was set up to explore the extent of the problem, and the feasibility of inter-ministerial working in this case. It also formed part of an action-research project aimed at developing ways of managing uncertainty in environmental decision-making. The problem centred on recent findings about heavy metals in the sediments lying under Holland's extensive water surfaces. Particular urgency created a focus on the Rhine estuary. Here a deep passage has to be kept clear to the harbour of Rotterdam. Unfortunately the sludge is replaced by the river currents almost as fast as it is removed. Thus to stop dredging is no solution – and there is an immediate need for a decision as to where to place the removed sludge. Sources of the pollution are known to extend far up the Rhine and its tributaries so there are international aspects to be taken into account also.

The working group was formed from various directorates of the Rijkswaterstaat (traffic, waterways and water supply) and the Ministry of VROM (housing, physical planning and environment), with Allen Hickling as Process Consultant.

The ends/means mapping (1) provided a way of helping the group to focus at several levels on what could be done to manage the situation. Thus, starting with 'clean underwater soils' (in the rectangle), the first means to be identified included prevention, cleaning and isolation of the toxic sludge. Ends (to the right in the diagram) were very broad, including the elimination of bad effects on flora and fauna. The next level down (to the left in the diagram) brings out possibilities with respect to the technology for cleaning, policy over emissions, approvals – and, of course, the international dimension. These lead to more specific issues of law-making, subsidies, publicity, transportation and so on.

The list of decision areas (2) was one of those developed out of the ends-means activity. The two first words of each line demonstrate the discipline of using 'choice of' ('Keuze van' in Dutch) as the opening phrase of all descriptions of decision areas. In this case they are mostly associated with publicity, claims for damages, various initiatives, and (at the bottom) one which is crossed out because it was thought to be too all-embracing and in need of working out more detail.

This was done in the decision graph (3) next to the list of decision areas. The messiness of the chart is typical of work done when the learning process is going quickly. The analysis to find a working focus was by use of the basic decision-making criteria of urgency, impact, controllability and connectedness. Two candidates for such a focus have been identified – a cluster of three decision areas at the top of the chart, and a set of two at the bottom. In fact the upper one was chosen, together with the very important central decision area concerning different ways of integrating the organisations involved.

FIGURE
46

Illustrations from Practice – Shaping 3

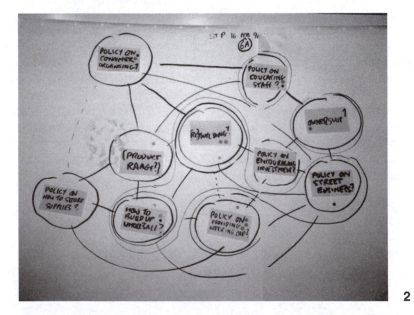

1

2

SHAPING

PRACTICE

Theme: Listing of Issues, drawing of a decision graph and choice of a problem focus.

Problem: Development of food distribution and retailing systems for a major metropolitan area.

Context: A project in St Petersburg, Russia, conducted by Danish consultants for a European Commission technical assistance programme.

COMMENTARY ON FIGURE 46

These photographs come from a two-day workshop in which John Friend was invited to act as facilitator to five members of a project team from the Danish Technological Institute shortly before the final reporting stage of a twelve-month contract for the European Commission TACIS programme (Technical Assistance to the Commonwealth of Independent States) to help in developing food distribution and retailing policies for the metropolitan area of St Petersburg in Russia.

After an initial listing of 27 issues covering three flipcharts – only one of which is shown here (1) – ten of these issues were classified as decision areas, and brief descriptions of these were transcribed to adhesive 'Post-It' notes. These were transferred to another flipchart and rearranged to bring out their interrelationships, using connecting lines to represent decision links and outer rings to represent importance and urgency (2). One of the team members had received some introductory training in the use of the STRAD software. She was therefore able to enter the resulting decision graph into the computer so as to generate a recommendation for a reduced set of decision areas which might form the core of a proposed problem focus. This recommendation was then debated critically before a problem focus of four decision areas was selected.

6 Skills in designing

INTRODUCTION

In Chapter 2, the set of concepts for shaping complex problems led into the introduction of a further set of concepts for designing feasible courses of action within any selected problem focus. These further concepts together provided a set of foundations for a design method – Analysis of Interconnected Decision Areas, or AIDA – which could be applied quite generally to any problem that could be expressed in terms of multiple areas of choice, however diverse these might be.

This chapter will build on those foundations by discussing the challenges which can arise in applying the conventions of AIDA to untidy decision problems, and the types of judgement which are called for in meeting these challenges in practice. The chapter will draw on working experience in applying strategic choice methods to problems of many different kinds. Although a number of elaborations of the basic concepts and techniques will be introduced, it is not intended to suggest that these forms of elaboration are always either necessary or desirable: it is simply that they are available to the skilled user of the strategic choice approach, wherever they can be of help in overcoming practical difficulties as they arise.

The principal advantage of the AIDA method of problem formulation is that it can allow many different kinds and levels of choice to be expressed in the same general language. So it offers a means of opening up the process of problem structuring to participants who may see the elements of a decision situation from quite different professional or representative perspectives. Its strength is that it has no inherent bias towards any particular frame of reference, whether financial, locational, engineering, marketing, administrative, political – or, indeed, anything else.

This high level of generality is, however only achieved at a cost. For it may be necessary to accept quite drastic simplifications when striving to represent complex design choices in terms of once-and-for-all decision areas, with a finite range of discrete options within each. There are, of course, other design methods which offer the possibility of overcoming these constraints – but usually these mean moving to a more specialised frame of reference, so as to view the problem primarily – for example – as one of engineering design; or of land-use planning; or of financial budgeting; or of scheduling a set of interconnected activities through time.

More specialised approaches to problem structuring can, of course, have an important place in practice, especially within management contexts where similar kinds of choice tend to arise recurrently over time. Choices can then often be expressed in terms of repeated adjustments to continuous control variables, rather than choices between discrete options within more transient decision areas. The AIDA approach to problem structuring was not developed with these comparatively well-structured management situations in view. Nevertheless, situations sometimes arise when it can be used to complement, rather than replace, more refined methods of problem structuring within particular specialist frameworks. Indeed, an initial quick analysis of options and relationships within the simplified conventions of AIDA can often form a useful prelude to deeper analysis by other methods. Its particular value can lie in opening up the debate about problem structure to

FIGURE
47

SOUTH SIDE
EXAMPLE

Testing the Range of Options within a Decision Area

DECISION AREA	OPTIONS	FURTHER OPTIONS?	COMMENT
ROAD LINE?	- NORTH - SOUTH	- MIDDLE ROUTE?	not feasible without massive demolition, so EXCLUDE
		- NO NEW ROAD AT ALL?	possibility not at present being considered, so EXCLUDE (re-introduce later?)
SHOP LOC'N?	- MAIN - KING - GAS	- FOOTBALL GROUND SITE?	only possible if club decides to move. Looks unlikely, so EXCLUDE for now
CENT'L SITE?	- IND - HOUS - OPEN	- MIXED USE OPTIONS?	some possibility that housing in west of site could be combined with either open space or (light) industry in East. Possibly INCLUDE composite options in later design work
DIST LIFE?	- 10 YRS - 20 YRS - 40 YRS	- LONGER SPAN? (eg 60 YRS)	similar to 40 YR option in consequences & option bars, so EXCLUDE
		- SHORTER SPAN? (eg 5 YRS)	politically inconceivable because of promises to residents, so EXCLUDE

DESIGNING

SUMMARY

Both when first identifying options within decision areas, and at intervals thereafter, it is useful to question briefly whether any additional options should be included to make the set of options more representative of the full range of choice available. This is often done verbally and informally, but a record of arguments for exclusion or inclusion can provide a useful point of reference for later.

a wider set of participants, and affording a clearer perspective of how far more specialist examination of particular parts of the problem may, or may not, be justified when set against the pressures for decision which the participants currently face.

IDENTIFYING SETS OF OPTIONS WITHIN DECISION AREAS

In generating a set of options within a decision area, the most important consideration is that they should be mutually exclusive; that the choice of any one option should foreclose the choice of any of the others. In an idealised, analytical world, such a set of options should, where possible, also be exhaustive: in other words, it should be a complete list of all the possible courses of action available. But in practice, this may be quite an unrealistic condition to impose, and it is usually necessary to settle for a set of options which is agreed to be *representative* of the full range of choice available, rather than one which covers every conceivable possibility.

For instance, in South Side, it might be possible to think of other lines for the new road apart from the northern and southern routes which were identified earlier (Figure 14). It could equally be possible to conceive further locations for the proposed shopping centre, or other quite different uses for the central site. Turning towards the broader policy decision on level of public investment in South Side, this was expressed in terms of choice of time horizon; and the choice of time horizon is one which could, of course, be regarded as a continuous variable, to be extended more or less indefinitely into the future. So the question arises here of whether the particular horizons of 10, 20 and 40 years are to be considered sufficiently representative of the full range of alternatives available in practice. It may be that this is readily agreed to be so – perhaps because, in the municipality responsible for South Side, these represent familiar periods of amortisation for different kinds of capital assets. Yet any such assumption can always

be challenged, debated and then modified if the participants agree.

Figure 47 illustrates the process of questioning which is involved in reviewing whether or not additional options should be included in a process which can be conducted either purely within an individual's head, or through interactive debate within a group. Whatever the method of search may be, it can be useful in practice to keep a record of possible options which have been considered but excluded, with reasons for the exclusion noted as in Figure 47. These options can always be reintroduced at a later stage if a case for doing so can be made.

The examples of possible additional options which appear in Figure 47 – relating to each of the four decision areas which were chosen as an initial problem focus (Figure 13) – illustrate various types of consideration which can arise in judging whether a proposed set of options is both representative and mutually exclusive. In the case of ROAD LINE?, for instance, the question arises of whether what is sometimes called a *null option* should be included, to reflect the possibility of building no new road at all. In this case, the null option is supposed to be excluded because of the particular brief given to the South Side Working Party: but of course this brief could, at any stage, be changed and the list of options modified accordingly. As will be seen later, the possibility of null options can arise again, more directly, when working in the choosing mode, when possibilities for deferring choice into the future begin to come to the fore.

Another question that can sometimes arise in practice is whether or not an option should be included when it is *uncertain* whether or not the conditions will occur which would make it possible. In Figure 47, this question arises in the case of the football ground as a possible location for the new shopping centre; and the assumption is recorded that this option should be excluded for now, possibly to be reintroduced at a later stage. Turning to the review of the DIST LIFE? decision area in Figure 47, it will be noticed that the 40-year option has been

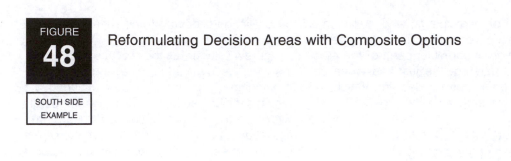

FIGURE
48

SOUTH SIDE
EXAMPLE

Reformulating Decision Areas with Composite Options

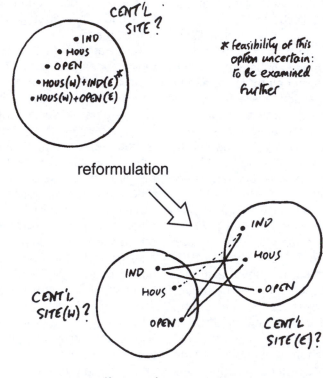

reformulation

··· indicates uncertain option bar

DESIGNING

SKILLS

Occasionally, it is helpful to examine the possibility of breaking a decision area down into two or more separate but connected decision areas, especially if the number of possible options is large and some of them appear to be composite in form. Such a reformulation can help in examining whether the set of alternatives indicated is fully representative, and in exploring structural assumptions.

taken to represent the 60-year horizon, on the grounds that this possible additional option is believed to be broadly similar to the 40-year option in its consequences, and also in its pattern of option bars. Indeed, this latter test casts doubt on whether it is even necessary to distinguish between the 20- and 40-year options; for a glance back to Figure 16 will show that these two options are identical in their patterns of option bars within the chosen problem focus.

REFORMULATING DECISION AREAS CONTAINING COMPOSITE OPTIONS

Another situation often encountered in practice is that in which doubts arise as to whether the initial list of options can realistically be considered as *mutually exclusive* – or whether, perhaps, some mixture of one option and another might be possible. For instance, in the case of the CENT'L SITE? decision area in South Side, the question could arise – as is suggested in Figure 47 – of whether it is possible to combine different uses on the same site and, if so, which particular combinations of use might be possible.

If the possibility of such 'composite' options arises, then it can be important to explore more carefully what the full range of possibilities might be. For instance, if it were possible to mix housing and industrial uses on the central site, could this imply an integrated design in which housing and light industry might be closely woven together throughout the site? Or would physical or other considerations suggest that housing should be sited towards one end and industry towards the other? Would different proportional mixes be possible, and how far could these different possibilities be reflected in the reformulation of options within the decision area?

The answers to such questions might sometimes depend on technicalities such as soil and drainage conditions, or on structural factors such as existing land uses on other adjacent sites. Figure 48 illustrates one simple way of dealing with this kind of complexity, which involves simply dividing up the original decision area into two more specific decision areas. In this example, the composite options within the CENT'L SITE? decision area in South Side have been dealt with by defining two simpler decision areas covering the western and eastern parts of the site respectively.

Whether this is a realistic and a useful way of reformulating the choices available will often depend on an understanding of local realities. In this case, it is assumed that the site is such that a division into two parts along some east/west boundary line makes sense. The new formulation embodies an assumption – which can always be challenged and reviewed at any time – that industrial use in the west is incompatible with housing in the east. Whether the opposite combination is possible is supposed, in this case, to be more doubtful; and this is indicated by a broken line connecting the option of housing in the west to the option of industry in the east. So this example introduces a new convention, a tentative or *uncertain option bar*, represented by a broken line connecting the options in question. So, a broken line is used to express a feeling of uncertainty over the existence of an option bar – just as it was used to express uncertainty over existence of a decision link when working in the shaping mode.

The expansion of a decision area into two or more linked decision areas, in order to arrive at a clearer formulation of composite options, means re-examining any option bars which might have linked the original decision area to others in the wider problem focus. For example, it could be that those bars in Figure 16 which originally excluded the combination of industrial use on the central site with the option of the southern road line, and also with the option of the King Street shopping location, apply to industrial uses at one end of the central site but not necessarily at the other.

FIGURE

49

SOUTH SIDE
EXAMPLE

Recording Assumptions Underlying Option Bars

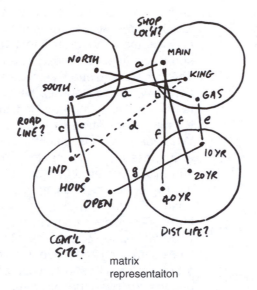

SHOP
LOC'N?

NORTH
SOUTH
MAIN
KING
GAS

ROAD
LINE?

a   b

c   c   d   f   e

f

IND
HOUS
OPEN

10 YR
20 YR
40 YR

CENT'L
SITE?

DIST LIFE?

matrix
representaiton

**EXPLANATIONS
FOR OPTION BARS:**

a   shops would be
    cut off from homes

b   uneconomic
    combination

c   site too near road
    to be developed

d   industry on central
    site might make
    King Square
    shopping uneconomic

e   shops on gas site
    not a short term
    option

f   main street shopping
    not a long term
    option

g. open space use not
    possible in short term

ROAD LINE?

		-NORTH	-SOUTH		SHOP LOC'N?					
SHOP LOC'N?	-MAIN	•	a		-MAIN	-KING	-GAS			
	-KING	•	a							
	-GAS	b	•							
CENT'L SITE?	-IND	•	c		•	d?	•		CENT'L SITE?	
	-HOUS	•	c		•	•	•		-IND	-HOUS	-OPEN
	-OPEN				•	•	•			
DIST LIFE?	-10YR	•	•		•	•	e		•	•	g
	-20 YR	•	•		f	•	•		•	•	•
	-40YR	•	•		f	•	•		•	•	•

The recording of assumptions behind the inclusion of particular option bars can be useful both as a record and as a means of challenging or justifying their validity in the course of interactive working. Cross-references to such assumptions can be included either on an option graph or a compatibility matrix. If some assumptions are deemed weaker than others, these can be removed on a trial basis.

RECORDING ASSUMPTIONS BEHIND THE INCLUSION OF OPTION BARS

There are many possible grounds for making a judgement that some pair of options from linked decision areas should be viewed as incompatible. Sometimes, the incompatibility will arise from the inherent logic of the situation. For instance, one option within the decision area about the use of the gasworks site (Figure 10) might relate to its development as the location of the new district shopping centre. This option would then be logically incompatible with any option in the SHOP LOCN? decision area which involved locating the new centre in Main Street, at King Square or on any other conceivable site apart from the gasworks site itself.

Often, however, option bars are used to rule out combinations which are not so much incompatible in strict logical terms, but agreed to be undesirable on other grounds; perhaps, because they may violate some agreed policy, or because they are thought likely to incur consequences which are agreed to be unacceptable. For example, there might be some design configurations for South Side which would present such severe engineering difficulties that they could only be overcome at unthinkable expense – for example, by the construction of a tunnel or deep cutting for the proposed new arterial highway.

The assumptions behind the inclusion of different option bars may be many and varied, and it is important to keep track of these assumptions so that they can be re-examined at any time. Figure 49 illustrates one simple way in which this kind of documentation of assumptions can be handled. This involves attaching a symbol to each option bar, whether as an addition to the information on the option graph itself or as a substitute for the simple cross used earlier (Figure 15) to register an incompatibility in the option compatibility table.

The symbols used in this example are simply letters of the alphabet, with an accompanying key to indicate the nature of the judgement involved in each case. Thus the two option bars marked 'a' are included because these combinations would both involve the unthinkable combination of locating a shopping centre where it would be cut off by an arterial road from its local residential catchment area. The combination marked 'b' is ruled out because it is judged not to be viable in economic terms; and the two combinations marked 'c' are excluded because they would mean permitting housing or industrial development on a restricted site unacceptably close to a busy main road. The more doubtful option bar marked 'd' reflects a more debatable assumption; the assumption that industrial use of the central site might erode the attractiveness of shops at King Square to local shoppers, who might then be able to take their custom to alternative shopping centres further afield.

While assumption 'd' has been picked out as more debatable than the rest, it may also be possible to distinguish in other ways between the levels of conviction with which option bars are to be regarded as imposing unacceptable constraints. This can be important if there are so many option bars as to seriously constrain the range of possible schemes that can be taken forward for comparison, in which case there will be an incentive to relax some of the less stringent of the option bars.

As a guide to this procedure, it is sometimes found useful to adopt a rough-and-ready judgemental scale to differentiate between option bars according to the relative ease or difficulty of breaking the constraints they imply. On a three-point scale, for example, the highest grading – perhaps indicated by three crosses – might indicate very strong grounds for an incompatibility judgement; the second grading, with two crosses, could indicate an incompatibility which might be broken if there were strong enough grounds for doing so; while the single cross grading could mark a weaker or more doubtful incompatibility. Such symbols for grading the strength of incompatibility could be used instead of more specific reference letters either in a compatibility matrix or an option graph. The procedure for developing a set of

FIGURE
50

SOUTH SIDE
EXAMPLE

Introducing Multiple Option Bars

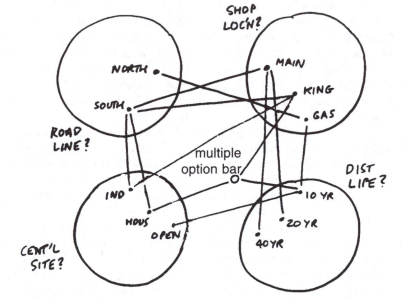

It is only occasionally in practice that it is worth trying to identify multiple option bars, to rule out particular combinations of options from three or more different decision areas. In practice, they can often be avoided by reformulation of the decision areas. The device of expressing a multiple option bar as a dummy decision area is useful mainly when generating schemes by computer.

feasible schemes can then be repeated, either with or without the 'weaker' option bars, to test what effect different assumptions would have on the range of choice available. It should be emphasised, however, that the grading of option bars offers no more than a crude filtering device which can occasionally be helpful when working in the designing mode. It always carries the risk of suppressing deeper evaluative issues, of a kind which can be subjected to more explicit scrutiny when working in the comparing mode.

INTRODUCING MULTIPLE OPTION BARS

One of the basic simplifying assumptions of the AIDA design method is the assumption that the majority of important design constraints can be represented as simple option bars: as relationships of incompatibility between pairs of options drawn from pairs of interconnected decision areas. Indeed, it is this kind of simplification which makes AIDA such a versatile and transparent means of exploring complex problems. In most problem situations encountered in practice, design constraints can indeed be represented in this way, at least for working purposes. Occasionally, however, important design constraints arise which can only realistically be represented in terms of a more complex form of incompatibility, involving some combination of options from not just two decision areas but three or more considered together.

Where some combination of three or more options from different decision areas is incompatible, this can be formulated through an extension to AIDA conventions known as a *multiple option bar*. For example, in South Side there could be subtle economic arguments why it should be considered impractical to consider a district life as short as 10 years if the particular combination of housing development on the Central Site and a King Square shopping location were chosen — even though a 10-year life might be quite conceivable in combination with either of these options taken on

its own. So, a triple option bar could be formulated to connect the particular triad of options combining KING in SHOP LOC'N?, HOUS in CENT'L SITE? and 10YR in DIST LIFE?. One quite simple means of representing such a triple option bar on the option graph is illustrated in Figure 50. Here, an unlabelled node on the graph is shown linked to each of the three options in different decision areas which are to be excluded in that particular combination.

It is usually not too difficult to add a limited number of triple or even four-fold option bars to a decision graph in the manner shown in Figure 50. But, in general, the introduction of multiple option bars tends to make the structure of a problem more difficult to comprehend, and is to be avoided unless it is clearly of pivotal importance to the present problem focus. It is, therefore, comparatively rare — though by no means unknown — for multiple option bars to be introduced during periods of interactive working, when the main concern is to develop a picture of problem structure which can contribute to mutual understanding within the group.

However, circumstances do arise in practice when it is important to explore what effects the introduction of multiple option bars might have on the range of decision schemes available. If the range of choice has already been displayed in the form of a tree, it is not too difficult to filter out those branches in which multiple option bars appear: for instance, it is not hard to see that there is only one of the nine decision schemes for South Side presented in Figure 17 – Scheme C – which would be eliminated if the KING-HOUS-10YR multiple option bar were introduced.

Multiple option bars can also be introduced into computer programs for developing the range of feasible decision schemes available within any specified formulation of a problem. Even if the program is designed to deal with incompatibilities between pairs of options alone, the higher-order option bars can be handled through the device of the *dummy*

FIGURE

51

SOUTH SIDE
EXAMPLE

Coalescing Closely Linked Decision Areas

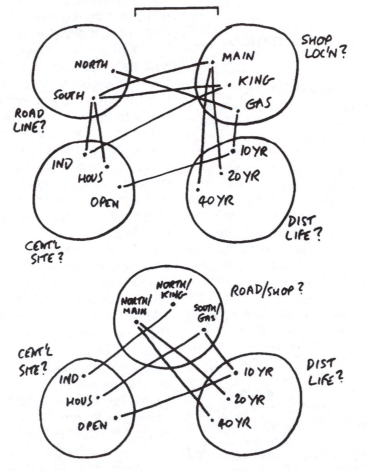

coalesce to form one decision area

It is usually only worth coalescing two or more decision areas into a single decision area in situations where the number of options and option bars can be significantly reduced by this step, and where the resulting set of composite options can be readily visualised and compared. In many cases, it will be possible to reformulate these composite options at a broader level of generality for subsequent reference.

decision area.[1] The dummy decision area is defined to include as many options as the number of decision areas which are linked through the multiple option bar – three in the case of the multiple option bar introduced in Figure 50. Each of the options affected in these other decision areas is then excluded by an option bar linked to a different one of the options in the dummy decision area, as shown by the set of three additional compatibility matrices in Figure 50. The dummy decision area has the effect of excluding this particular combination of three options, but no other combinations of two among the three. The three simple option bars can then be used as computer input in place of the triple option bar, and the search for feasible routes through the tree can proceed in the normal way. The dummy decision area can also, if desired, be shown directly on the option graph; in the example of Figure 50, this would involve replacing the unlabelled node by a full-sized circle to represent a decision area labelled DUMMY?, including options labelled 1, 2 and 3, each with its appropriate connections to an option within one of the other decision areas. However, this kind of representation has little value in practice, as – unless the dummy decision area can be so labelled to draw out some deeper significance to the substantive decision problem – it is likely to serve more as a distraction than as a source of illumination to the participants.

COALESCING DECISION AREAS

Wherever there is a high density of option bars connecting the various options within any pair or cluster of decision areas, the number of feasible combinations which remain available within that part of the problem focus is likely to be quite small. There may then be a case for coalescing two or more of the decision areas concerned into a single decision area containing a smaller set of composite options. This is, in effect, the converse of the device illustrated

earlier (Figure 48), where a single decision area containing composite options was split up into two separate decision areas with option bars connecting particular options within them. An example of the device of coalescing decision areas appears in Figure 51 which is again based on the three closely linked decision areas for South Side considered in Figure 50. Here, there is a high density of option bars between the ROAD LINE? and SHOP LOC'N? decision areas, which has the effect of excluding three of the six possible combinations. Therefore, these two decision areas can be coalesced into one, here labelled ROAD/SHOP?. This decision area includes the three composite options of NORTH/MAIN, NORTH/KING and SOUTH/GAS, each with its corresponding pattern of option bars linking it to options in the remaining CENT'L SITE? decision area.

In general, it is not likely to be worth coalescing decision areas where the result would be to create a decision area containing more than three or, at most, four composite options; as would be the case, for example, if the ROAD/SHOP? decision area in Figure 51 were to be further coalesced with either the CENT'L SITE? or the DIST LIFE? decision area, creating a set of seven composite options in the first case, or six in the second. Nor are composite options of much value once they cease to be readily intelligible in design terms. In Figure 51, for example, it is not too hard to look at each of the three options within the ROAD/SHOP? decision area as a coherent physical option for the broad-scale design of a future South Side neighbourhood. However, the ability of participants in the decision process to conceive alternatives in this way could easily be lost if any additional dimensions of choice were to be introduced as well.

As soon as a first attempt has been made to identify options and option bars within a selected problem focus, various opportunities may be identified both for expanding some decision areas and for coalescing others. Changes in either direction will depend on the judgement of participants as to which aspects of their

---

1 Introduced by Hunter in his early work on the development of an AIDA computer program.

FIGURE
52

SOUTH SIDE
EXAMPLE

Estimating the Number of Feasible Decision Schemes

method of
estimation
(cumulative)

ROAD LINE?

- NORTH -SOUTH

		-NORTH	-SOUTH
SHOP LOC'N?	-MAIN	·	×
	-KING	·	×
	-GAS	×	·

number of feasible combinations
of options in first pair of
decision areas [= 3]

↓

SHOP LOC'N?
-MAIN -KING -GAS

× number of options in   × 3
next decision area

CENT'L SITE?	-IND	· ×	· × ·
	-HOUS	· ×	· · ·
	-OPEN	· ·	· · ·

× proportions of feasible
combinations in new   × 6/6 × 5/9
compatibility tables

↓

CENT'L SITE?
-IND -HOOS -OPEN   [= 5·3]

↓

× 3

DIST LIFE?	-10YR	· ·	· · ×	· · ×
	-20YR	· ·	× · ·	· · ·
	-40YR	· ·	× · ·	· · ·

$\left[× \frac{6}{6}\right] × \frac{6}{7} × \frac{8}{9}$

[= 9·5]

comparison of estimates with actual numbers of feasible
combinations [as shown in figure 17]

	ESTIMATE	ACTUAL
FIRST 3 DECISION AREAS [ROAD LINE? SHOP LOC'N? CENT'L SITE?]	5.3	6
FIRST 4 DECISION AREAS [DIST LIFE? added]	9.5	9

DESIGNING

SKILLS

This kind of procedure for obtaining a rough estimate of the range of feasible schemes is rarely used explicitly in interactive working. It can however provide a useful quick aid to judgement when deciding whether or not to extend an option tree by adding further branches — especially when a tree has grown to a point where it is beginning to become difficult to comprehend the overall range of choice it contains.

problems are of greater or of lesser importance, as well as on more analytical considerations to do with the number of options within a decision area and the densities of option bars which connect particular pairs. In general, the aim will usually be to arrive at a design formulation which the participants feel to be well balanced in relation to their current perceptions of the choices before them. In this respect, they are likely to find that their work within the designing mode yields changes in their perceptions of the decision areas and their links, and so contributes to a sense of progress in the work of the shaping mode.

Once a problem has been expressed in terms of a pattern of options and option bars connecting some set of decision areas, it becomes possible to work out the number of feasible decision schemes by arranging the decision areas in some chosen sequence and then working systematically through the branches of the resulting tree of possibilities, in the manner illustrated in Figure 17. However, it is sometimes useful to make a rough estimate of the number of schemes before embarking on this systematic process; and there is a rule of thumb which is sometimes useful in this respect.[2]

The basis of the rule is simply to work out a series of fractions, one for each pair of decision areas, representing the proportion of option combinations which remain feasible after any option bars are taken into account. Then the total number of combinations which would be available in the option graph, if there were no option bars, is multiplied by each of these fractions in turn. The outcome is an estimate – usually quite a close one – of the number of schemes that could be available if all the combinations were to be worked through in full.

Figure 52 illustrates how this process works for the four decision areas in the original

South Side option graph of Figure 16. The process of estimation is built up in a stepwise fashion, starting with only two decision areas and adding one more at each stage. At the first stage, the number '3' simply reflects the information that only three of the six combinations in the first small table are still available once the three option bars are taken into account. When the third decision area is added, the number of combinations available in the first two decision areas – three in all – is first multiplied by the number of options in this new decision area, which is also three; the result is then multiplied by the two fractions 4/6 and 8/9 representing the proportions of feasible combinations in the two additional option compatibility tables. This gives an estimate for the number of schemes now available for the three decision areas taken together.

The process of estimation indicates that approximately 5.3 out of the conceivable 18 combinations so far are likely to be feasible; this compares with the exact number of six as revealed by the tree of Figure 17. Figure 52 then takes the estimation procedure a step further, showing that the estimate remains quite close – 9.5 compared to 9 – when the fourth decision area is added. It is, of course, quite possible to work directly from the option graph when building up the estimates, if the information is not already set out in the form of compatibility tables. Wherever there are no option bars between a pair of decision areas, the appropriate 'multiplier' fraction is 1; a point which can greatly simplify the computations involved.

This kind of estimating procedure can be carried out by hand, as in Figure 52, or it can be built into an interactive computer program; it can be especially useful as an aid to deciding whether or not to add an additional decision area to an option tree in which the range of feasible decision schemes so far has already been estimated or enumerated. The estimation process can also help in making quick assessments of the consequences of adding or removing option bars; if an estimate shows that a problem is so constrained as to be likely

2   This was first suggested by John Luckman and consequently became known as 'Luckman's Lemma'; a lemma in mathematics meaning no more than an unproven rule.

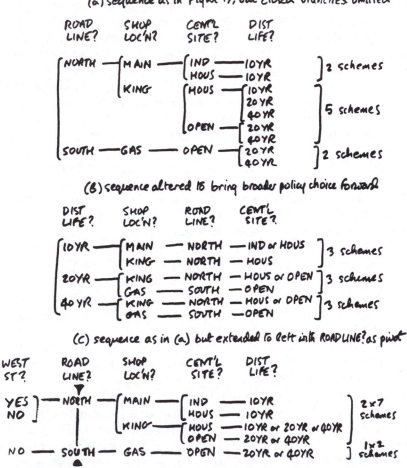

FIGURE

53

SOUTH SIDE
EXAMPLE

Altering the Sequence of Decision Areas in a Tree

DESIGNING

SKILLS

At any moment when the range of possible decision schemes is set out in the form of a tree, it can be helpful to try changing the sequence of decision areas to explore different structural features. In particular, this makes it possible to focus on more urgent, important or controllable decision areas by bringing them further forward, or to develop combinations on either side of a pivotal decision area.

to leave open a very small number of feasible schemes, then this may suggest that certain of the more doubtful option bars should be removed in order to open up a wider range of choice. Where there is a large number of decision areas within a problem focus, the procedure can be used to estimate the likely number of schemes to be found either in the formulation as a whole or in particular branches of the tree. In other words, it is a flexible tool which is by no means essential to the strategic choice 'toolbox' – but which can sometimes save time, and alter the course which further analysis may take.

ALTERING THE SEQUENCE OF DECISION AREAS IN A TREE

Figure 17 illustrated one kind of standard format in which it is possible to display the set of decision schemes that is feasible under any chosen set of assumptions about options and option bars. This format indicates those points where option bars have been encountered, by means of the device of displaying 'dead' branches wherever they arise in the development of the option tree. However, various alternative forms of presentation are possible, including a format which simply suppresses information on dead branches, to make the resulting picture more compact (this simplified form was adopted in Figure 22). Another possibility is simply to list the set of feasible schemes in straight tabular form, or to list them using repeat signs wherever the same option in a decision area recurs on successive lines. This gives a presentation which is logically similar to that of the tree, but avoids any use of graphics; so it offers a useful alternative format in the production of formal documents.

A more fundamental choice that arises in developing a set of feasible decision schemes concerns the choice of sequence in which the decision areas should be considered. By bringing different decision areas to the fore, different structural features can be displayed. This point is illustrated in Figure 53, which

begins by comparing just two of the twenty-four possible sequences available for arranging the four decision areas in the South Side problem focus. The first sequence is that originally used in Figure 17, with the information about dead branches omitted. It draws attention to the information that the majority of feasible schemes involve choice of the northern road line and that, of these, five out of seven involve choice of King Square as location for the shopping centre.

The second sequence illustrated in Figure 53 brings the DIST LIFE? choice to the fore – a rearrangement which might be decided upon in the light of the broad policy significance of this particular choice. To save space, options in the final decision area are this time listed horizontally rather than vertically. This alternative sequence demonstrates that the three branches relating to the 10-, 20- and 40-year horizons, all allow equal numbers of possibilities in the remaining decision areas. Furthermore, the combinations available under the 20- and 40-year life policies are otherwise identical – a point which might indeed have been spotted from the structure of the option graph, but is demonstrated more clearly in the structure of the option tree.

The third example in Figure 53 illustrates another kind of format, in which an option tree is developed in two directions, both to the left and the right of a selected 'pivotal' decision area. This can be particularly useful in circumstances where a decision graph can be partitioned into two parts which are only connected through a single decision area or decision link. In this example, just one decision area is introduced to the left of the pivotal ROAD LINE? decision area – the WEST ST? decision area, which was linked in the decision graph of Figure 12 to the ROAD LINE? decision area alone and, for that reason, was omitted from the original problem focus (Figure 13). It is supposed here that there is just one option bar which involves the WEST ST? decision area – an option bar which rules out the YES option in combination with the southern road line. This piece of information can be introduced quite

FIGURE 54

SOUTH SIDE EXAMPLE

Exploring Consistency Between Levels of Choice

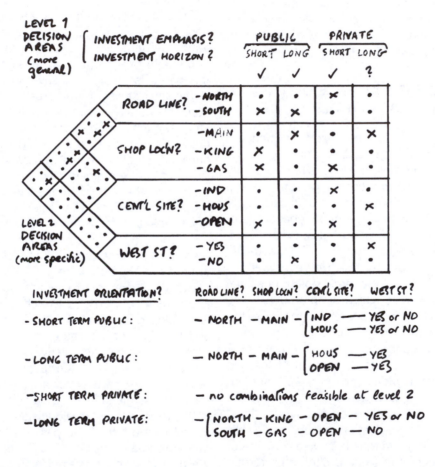

LEVEL 1 DECISION AREAS (more general)

INVESTMENT EMPHASIS? INVESTMENT HORIZON?	PUBLIC		PRIVATE	
	SHORT	LONG	SHORT	LONG
	✓	✓	✓	?

			PUBLIC SHORT	PUBLIC LONG	PRIVATE SHORT	PRIVATE LONG
ROAD LINE?	– NORTH		•	•	✗	•
	– SOUTH		✗	✗	•	•
SHOP LOC'N?	– MAIN		•	✗	•	✗
	– KING		✗	•	•	•
	– GAS		✗	•	✗	•
CENT'L SITE?	– IND		•	•	✗	•
	– HOUS		•	•	•	✗
	– OPEN		✗	•	✗	•
WEST ST?	– YES		•	•	•	✗
	– NO		•	✗	•	•

LEVEL 2 DECISION AREAS (more specific)

INVESTMENT ORIENTATION?	ROAD LINE?	SHOP LOC'N?	CENT'L SITE?	WEST ST?
– SHORT TERM PUBLIC:	– NORTH	– MAIN	IND — YES or NO / HOUS — YES or NO	
– LONG TERM PUBLIC:	– NORTH	– MAIN	HOUS — YES / OPEN — YES	
– SHORT TERM PRIVATE:	– no combinations feasible at level 2			
– LONG TERM PRIVATE:	NORTH – KING – OPEN – YES or NO / SOUTH – GAS – OPEN – NO			

DESIGNING SKILLS

Distinctions between broader and more specific levels of choice offer a valuable means of dealing with complexity where the number of decision areas is large. When exploring choices over many interrelated fields of policy, it can occasionally be helpful to introduce a hierarchy of three or even more levels of generality, using feasible combinations at the broader levels as a framework for evaluation at other levels.

simply when the new decision area is added to the left of the tree, adjacent to the only other decision area to which it is directly related.

The wider potential that may sometimes exist for developing a tree separately on either side of a pivotal decision area can be appreciated by glancing back at the larger decision graph of Figure 42, where the ROAD LINE? decision area forms the sole point of overlap between two potential problem foci. If the pattern of option bars in the transport cluster of decision areas was an intricate one, then the range of possible decision schemes within the transport focus could be explored by developing another option tree branching out to the left of the pivotal ROAD LINE? decision area.

Mention has already been made of the potential of computer methods in developing sets of feasible decision schemes. Computer methods can of course make short work of the multiple basic 'logic-crunching' operations that are involved, as will be discussed further in Chapter 10. When there are only three or four decision areas in focus, it is not too arduous to go through the procedure without computer support. However, experience has shown that it is easy for humans to make errors in this process, so a computer can always provide a useful check. It is of course technically feasible for the computer to handle quite large numbers of interconnected decision areas, but it is another matter to present the results in a form that can be readily absorbed by the participants. Where the power of the computer can be especially useful is in the realm of sensitivity analysis, for it can quickly be tested whether different assumptions about the inclusion of any doubtful options or option bars have any significant impact on the range of decision schemes available.

EXPLORING CONSISTENCY BETWEEN LEVELS OF CHOICE

There is another variation on the procedure for developing feasible combinations of options from several decision areas, which has been found particularly useful wherever there are some decision areas expressed at a higher level of generality than others. This is sometimes the case where a set of people are reviewing choices of broad policy orientation at the same time as more operational choices which might be consistent with some policy positions but not with others. In such circumstances, the options or combinations at the more operational level can be evaluated not merely according to their anticipated consequences in certain agreed comparison areas, but also according to their consistency with different policy orientations which could be adopted at a broader level. An example will help to illustrate how this analysis of consistency between two levels of decision can work in practice. Figure 54 shows an example of a consistency matrix (or table) relating to South Side, in which four of the seven decision areas from the original problem formulation – including the WEST ST? but excluding the DIST LIFE? decision area – have been regarded as forming together the more operational level of choice.

For purposes of exploring relationships between levels the DIST LIFE? decision area has been reformulated here as a broader policy-level choice of investment horizon with only two options – short and long. To this choice is added another choice at the broader policy level concerned with emphasis on public versus private investment – reflecting perhaps a well-recognised ideological difference on the municipal council. There are then four combinations of emphasis at the policy level, which have been expressed as four columns in the matrix of Figure 54. In this case, it is judged that there is an element of doubt over whether a private investment emphasis can be considered compatible with a longer-term investment horizon in view of prevailing economic circumstances. So there is one possible option bar within the broader level of choice, which may possibly eliminate one of the four columns in its entirety.

The main cells of the matrix are then completed by entering a cross wherever an option within a decision area at the more operational level is judged inconsistent with a policy orient-ation represented by a combination of options at the broader level. As always, there can be scope for argument as to whether or not partic-ular entries in the table should be included, and any such argument can yield useful products in terms of learning and mutual adjustment among the participants. Any incompatibilities between options among decision areas at the more operational level can also be displayed within this kind of format; and the triangular grid that appears to the left of the main mat-rix of Figure 54 offers one compact means of adding information of this kind.

The consequences of any set of assump-tions about incompatibilities can then be worked out and displayed in terms of a series of separate option trees covering the more operational decision areas, one correspond-ing to each broader choice of orientation. So it is possible to explore what range of choice is available for any one of the broader policy orientations, and to present the res-ults in the normal branching form. It is often found that a particular choice of orientation will pre-determine the choice of option in some decision areas, while leaving open a range of alternatives in others. In Figure 54, for example, a choice of a shorter-term public investment emphasis restricts choice of ROAD LINE? to the northern option, and choice of shopping location to Main Street, while leaving the WEST ST? choice completely open.

Where there are many decision areas it can be useful to draw out such structural features by varying the sequence of decision areas between one branch and the next, to bring any 'no choice' decision areas to the front and to set back any 'free choice' decision areas to the end of the sequence; this will sometimes leave a 'conditional choice' zone in between, the structure of which can be examined more closely. This kind of representation is some-times referred to as a decision stream; it can be especially useful in displaying structural char-acteristics of problems which include a large number of decision areas, and then seeking reactions from policy-makers before going on

to search for compromise schemes which may sometimes be consistent with more than one policy orientation.

This kind of analysis of consistency between levels of choice, in effect takes the process of strategic choice in the direction of the comparing mode. For it introduces a form of evaluation which stresses the assessment of alternatives not so much directly in terms of their consequences, as in terms of their per-ceived consistency with different political ori-entations or aims. In effect, the comparison areas described in Chapter 3 are replaced by the broader-level decision areas – illustrating how one kind of strategic choice concept can be replaced by another in a flexible, adaptive way. This therefore provides a fitting point at which to conclude this chapter and to review the various points made about skills of working within the designing mode.

SUMMARY: PROCESS JUDGEMENTS IN THE DESIGNING MODE

The various points made in this chapter have taken the process of strategic choice into a somewhat more technical domain than those made in Chapter 5 – reflecting a general shift of emphasis in moving from work in the shap-ing mode to work in the designing mode. It is worth first re-emphasising the general point that work in the designing mode may some-times be very important, but at other times much less significant. In the extreme case, there will be little designing work to be done at moments where the problem focus has been restricted to a single decision area, and the options within that decision area are not too hard to identify. However, even in these circumstances, it may be difficult to choose between these options because of uncertain-ties of type UR relating to possible future decisions in related fields; so sooner or later other decision areas may be brought back within the problem focus, and the range of pos-sible combinations may begin to broaden out again.

When working in the designing mode, as in each of the other modes, the choice of appropriate level of analysis is always a matter of judgement. In general, there is a case for inclining towards simplification in the first instance, and only then moving in the direction of further elaboration if or when there seems justification for doing so. In the work of the designing mode, simplicity generally means working within a limited focus of no more than three, four or five decision areas, usually with between two and four options in each. At this level, the number of option bars will usually be manageable and the process of developing a set of feasible decision schemes will not be too complex.

The simpler the structure, the more practicable it will be to develop the set of schemes in a way which keeps all the participants involved. But when participants are working in the designing mode, as opposed to the shaping mode, there is more likely to be a case for handling at least some of the complexity in other ways. In particular, a computer can be used in checking combinations in terms of feasibility; in rapidly changing the sequence of a tree to display different structural information; and in testing the consequences of removing or adding option bars, or options, in terms of the overall range of choice available. But the computer can become a distraction in an interactive group situation; and its benefits in terms of speed and flexibility may be of little value if the momentum of group working is thereby disrupted.

Figure 55 shows the various directions of movement out of the designing mode towards other modes. One frequent direction of movement will be towards the comparing mode, to develop a basis of comparison among the various decision schemes that are available. But, as was explained in Chapter 3, there are different levels of comparison from which to choose. If there are only two or three schemes available in all, then it becomes possible to compare them all in considerable depth, taking uncertainty explicitly into account; but if there are many schemes, it may be more practicable

to compare them first at a much broader level, to form a more limited working shortlist as illustrated in Figure 22.

Alternative directions of exit from the designing mode take the process into the choosing and the shaping modes respectively. Exit directly into the choosing mode will be possible where the participants agree that one course of action in a particular decision area is clearly superior to the others. For example, the participants in the South Side exercise might be so convinced by the advantages of the northern road line, after realising that it presents a far wider choice in other decision areas than the southern alternative, that they agree to make a recommendation for the northern line straight away, without conducting any further analysis. And there are also many circumstances in which an exit from the designing to the shaping mode will make sense. In particular, a very restricted range of alternatives within a problem focus may suggest that this focus might easily be extended, whereas a very wide range may suggest it should be narrowed down.

Also, as indicated in Figure 55, there are various ways in which the guidance offered in this chapter can involve more modest process 'loops' in the direction of the other modes. A loop towards the shaping mode is implied both in the coalescence of decision areas and in the breaking down of decision areas with composite options into two or more linked decision areas. A loop towards the comparing mode is implied in the step of separating out different levels of choice for the development of consistency matrices. It is also implied in the device of annotating option bars to indicate different kinds of arguments for introducing assumptions of incompatibility between options; arguments which in many cases will be grounded in value judgements of a debatable kind. Finally, the resequencing of a set of decision areas to bring more urgent decision areas to the fore implies a form of looping towards the choosing mode, where the pressures for action begin to dictate the direction in which the process moves.

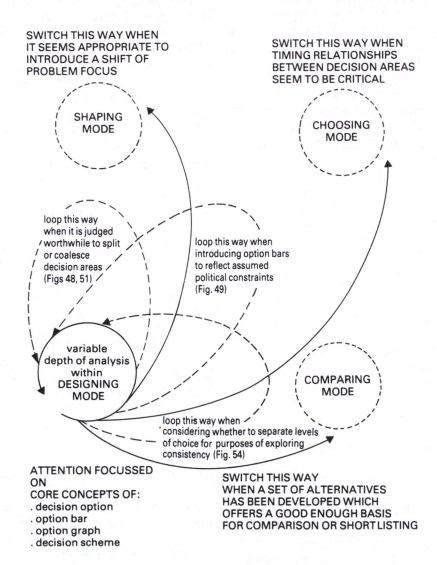

FIGURE 55 — Process Choices when Working in the Designing Mode

SWITCH THIS WAY WHEN
IT SEEMS APPROPRIATE TO
INTRODUCE A SHIFT OF
PROBLEM FOCUS

SWITCH THIS WAY WHEN
TIMING RELATIONSHIPS
BETWEEN DECISION AREAS
SEEM TO BE CRITICAL

SHAPING
MODE

CHOOSING
MODE

loop this way
when it is judged
worthwhile to split
or coalesce
decision areas
(Figs 48, 51)

loop this way when
introducing option bars
to reflect assumed
political constraints
(Fig. 49)

variable
depth of analysis
within
DESIGNING
MODE

COMPARING
MODE

loop this way when
considering whether to separate levels
of choice for purposes of exploring
consistency (Fig. 54)

ATTENTION FOCUSSED
ON
CORE CONCEPTS OF:
. decision option
. option bar
. option graph
. decision scheme

SWITCH THIS WAY
WHEN A SET OF ALTERNATIVES
HAS BEEN DEVELOPED WHICH
OFFERS A GOOD ENOUGH BASIS
FOR COMPARISON OR SHORT LISTING

DESIGNING

SUMMARY

ILLUSTRATIONS FROM PRACTICE

Following the precedent set in Chapter 5, a set of three diverse illustrations from practice is presented on the pages that follow. They have been selected to illustrate some of the more important practical points that arise in relation to the work of the designing mode,

The first illustration, based on extracts from documents published in connection with a land-use policy plan for an English rural area, demonstrates one way in which information about options and their mutual consistency can be presented clearly for public discussion. The second illustration, from an application in the Netherlands, shows how members of a group can work together in developing a set of feasible schemes from the information contained in an option graph. The third illustration is taken from a group exercise in organisational choice, and anticipates some of the points to be made in Chapter 9 about systematic documentation of the progress made through interactive working on flip charts around the walls of a room.

FIGURE
56

Illustrations from Practice – Shaping 1

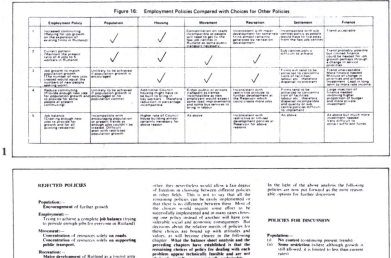

1

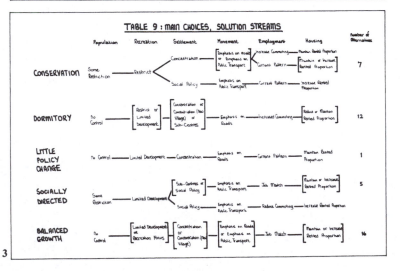

3

Theme: Presentation for Public Discussion of Policy Options, Incompatibilities and Choices within Orientations.

Problem: Preparation of a Structure Plan as a Policy Framework for a Rural Area.

Context: Planning Team for Rutland with Various Community Groups, County of Leicestershire, England, 1975–76.

COMMENTARY ON FIGURE 56

These three extracts are taken from documents published by the County Council of Leicestershire in central England as part of the process of preparing a first official Structure Plan for Rutland. Rutland is a predominantly rural district of some 30 000 inhabitants which at that time (1975/76) had recently lost its independent County status (since recovered).

The table at the top is one of a series of six similar tables presented for public discussion in November 1975, as part of a consultation document entitled 'Let's talk about Rutland'. This particular table focuses on employment policy for Rutland, and lists in the first column a set of five possible options for employment, treated as a single decision area. Each row of the table contains notes on the incompatibility of that particular employment option with specific options in other decision areas concerned respectively with population change, housing, movement, recreation, settlement pattern and finance. For presentation purposes, the individual options in these other decision areas were not shown in separate sub-divisions of the columns as in the standard format of option compatibility tables. This kind of simplification is most desirable in published documents. It will be noticed that the table does however briefly indicate the arguments on which particular option bars are based, so that the underlying assumptions can be challenged by readers.

Below the table appears an excerpt from a subsequent page of the same document (2), arguing for the exclusion of certain options on the strength of the foregoing analysis – among them the fifth of the employment policy options, excluded on the grounds of its excessive financial implications. After a description of the challenge of policy design and evaluation that remains (paragraphs 9.11 and 9.12), the report then goes on to list out the main options that remain in the various decision areas (only those for the first two decision areas, concerned with population and employment, being included in this extract).

The final illustration opposite is taken from a technical document written to present the analysis on which the submitted Structure Plan was based. The five 'solution streams' had been developed to indicate the range of choice available in the six main decision areas (excluding the financial decision area) for each of five broad policy 'orientations' or emphases which could be clearly envisaged by the County and District Councillors. It was indicated by the planners that the set of policies finally selected might be based on a compromise between orientations rather than the selection of any one orientation in its pure form. The final decision was to go for a set of policies based on a position part way between the conservation and the socially directed orientations.

FIGURE
57

Illustrations from Practice – Shaping 2

1

2   3

Theme: Deriving Alternative Schemes from an Option Graph and forming an Option Tree.
Problem: Implementation Policy for the Law against Nuisances, in an Environmental Policy Plan for a Municipality.
Context: Action-Research with the Project Group, Municipality of Emmen, The Netherlands, 1982.

COMMENTARY ON FIGURE 57

These photographs were taken at a working session of the project group during the second month of a 1-year project to produce a Municipal Environmental Policy Plan. This work was undertaken by the Municipality of Emmen in the Province of Drenthe in the north of the Netherlands as part of an action research project sponsored by the Central Government.

The project group was drawn from various parts of the organisation and contained a mixture of administrators, planners, engineers and other professionals. The alderman responsible for the plan was often present for parts of such sessions. Allen Hickling and Arnold de Jong, who were conducting the research, acted as process consultants.

A high level of unemployment in this part of Holland, and around Emmen in particular, had led to the environment receiving very low priority in the recent past. This had been especially the case with respect to industry and commerce. Thus the need for an Environmental Policy Plan was a matter of debate. Environmentalists argued it to be essential if not too late, while others considered it not only unnecessary, but even harmful.

The focus of the work in this sequence of photographs is the implementation of controls of various kinds – legal, planning and so on (1). It represents a good example of how different levels of choice can be combined in an option graph – although this may be only of value early in a project. Here there are decisions about whether to produce detailed local plans for the industrial areas; whether to be involved in zoning and the setting of norms; and the thoroughness of the implementation plan to be made for the law about nuisances. At the same time there were more general considerations about the attitude to management of controls and the relaxation of by-laws.

The process of deriving the decision schemes on the wall is important (2). In this instance there were three members of the group directly involved, and this helped to keep track of the logic. The option tree itself (3) is typical in that an unexpected number of schemes had to be accommodated, leading to a very asymmetrical layout. This does no harm to the learning process and was corrected in the official loose-leaf record of the meeting. Here also the reasoning and assumptions underlying the option bars were recorded. In this case recycling occurred soon after, and the whole problem was broken out into its constituent levels for further analysis.

FIGURE
58

Illustrations from Practice – Shaping 3

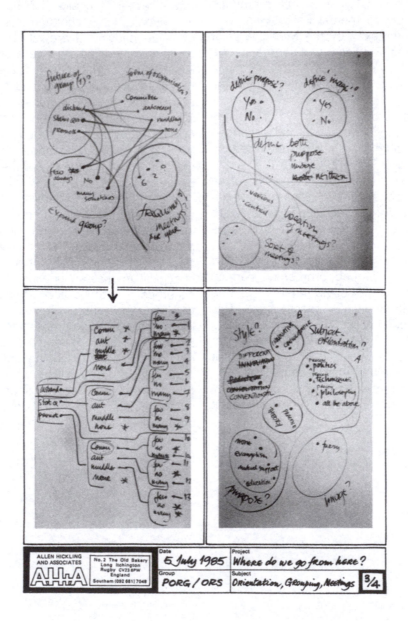

DESIGNING

PRACTICE

Theme: Documentation using a Photo-Record of Progress in Designing Alternative Decision Schemes.
Problem: Organisational Choice in Developing a Programme of a Study Group of a National Society.
Context: Process of O.R. Study Group, Operational Research Society, Birmingham, England, 1985.

COMMENTARY ON FIGURE 58

The four illustrations opposite show how even relatively quickly drawn, exploratory flip charts produced in the course of a working session can be incorporated in a documentary record to help the participants recall afterwards something of the spirit of the process in which they were involved. The flip charts are part of a set of 17 generated during a one-day workshop held at the University of Aston in Birmingham by a study group of the Operational Research Society of Great Britain. This study group, called the Process of OR Study Group (PORSG), had been formed several years earlier by a set of members of the Society with an interest not just in the analytical techniques of operational research but in the wider process of carrying out operational research projects in organisations.

Nine members of the study group took part in the workshop, the task of which was to consider possible directions for the future of the group after a period in which its momentum seemed to have been slipping. Allen Hickling had agreed to act as facilitator to the workshop, of which John Friend was also a member. Because only a few hours were available, and because not all those present were familiar with the strategic choice approach, Allen Hickling did not involve the group as a whole in building up the record of progress on the wall; instead he combined the facilitator and recorder roles, attempting to capture the contributions of others on flip charts in a rapid, free-flowing way.

Quite early in the workshop, the initial concerns expressed by participants were structured loosely in the form of an ends/means diagram rather similar to that shown in Figure 45; from this, an initial set of 17 decision areas was generated. The two wall charts on the right hand side reflect attempts to examine some of the broader decision areas more closely. It will be noticed that some questions arose in discussion about whether the labels of particular options should be changed, and whether or not options could be treated as mutually exclusive.

The more 'finished' option graph in the top left corner includes a set of three key decision areas concerned with the future of the group; the form of organisation, and the question of expansion of its membership – a further decision area on frequency of meetings having been first included but then set aside. The analysis of this option graph indicated a choice of 14 decision schemes. A debate on preferences was centred on four comparison areas, some of which were treated as constraints; these were concerned with commitment, relevance to others, availability of enough willing people and effect on OR education.

The upshot of the meeting – corresponding broadly to scheme 10a in the tree – was the formation of a committee to work on a promotional strategy with a six-month deadline in view. The committee then went on to devise a programme of joint meetings with regional groups of the Society, thus opening up the debate about the practical process of conducting operational research projects to the wider membership of the Society.

7 Skills in comparing

INTRODUCTION

In this chapter the aim will be to explore, more fully than was possible in Chapter 3, the subtle judgements that arise when working in the comparing mode. The relevant core concepts were introduced in Figures 19–22; they are those of the *comparison area*, the *relative assessment*, the *advantage comparison* and the *working shortlist*. These concepts are all very general ones, which can be adapted to guide the work of the comparing mode at a variety of levels, ranging from the most rough and ready appraisal of 'pros' and 'cons' of some proposed action, to the most elaborate exercises in quantification and predictive modelling.

However, experience so far in applying strategic choice methods to practical decision problems supports the view that it is only very rarely that the more elaborate forms of comparison exercise can be justified. In the first place, it will usually take an exceptionally weighty decision to justify the time and resources called for in collating and analysing large amounts of data: more fundamentally, however, the strategic choice philosophy draws attention to the question of whether extensive investment in analysis will produce a good enough return in terms of the level of confidence with which decisions can be taken, once the full range of uncertainties bearing on that decision has been considered.

So experience indicates that it usually pays to concentrate on quite simple, crude approaches to the comparison of alternatives. Yet it is important to stress that there is always scope for *choice* in the ways alternatives are to be compared. There are choices to be made in the formulation of comparison areas; choices in methods of relative assessment; choices in ways of presenting broader advantage comparisons; and choices in the extent to which simplified numerical or other indices are introduced to narrow down the full range of alternatives to a more limited working shortlist. The guidance offered in this chapter is intended to help users in addressing these choices of evaluative method and style in a more conscious and effective way.

It is important to recognise that the work of comparing alternatives can become very difficult in practice, however simple or elaborate the chosen methods of evaluation may be. The difficulties encountered can be political as much as technical, especially where there are many different constituencies of interest which might be affected – some perhaps directly represented in the decision process and others not. Furthermore, the procedural setting itself may be far from simple, and may change as the problem focus shifts. For these reasons, the guidance in this chapter will be shaped according to the principle of dynamic comparison, which has already been touched upon in the concluding section of Chapter 3. This principle captures the evaluative implications of the wider view of planning as a process of choosing strategically through time: a process in which there may be a succession of 'evaluative moments' as the focus of comparison changes or as new information comes to light, whether through unforeseen circumstances or through explorations deliberately set in train.

FIGURE
59

SOUTH SIDE
EXAMPLE

Developing a Set of Relevant Comparison Areas

DECISION AREA [-options]	RELEVANT COMPARISON AREAS	check relevance to other decision areas within present problem focus:			
		ROAD LINE?	SHOP LOC'N?	CENT'L SITE?	DIST LIFE?
ROAD LINE? [-NORTH -SOUTH]	• CAPITAL OUTLAY • IMPACT ON RESIDENTS • FLEXIBILITY of future development opportunities	• • •	✓ ? ✓	✓ ✓ ✓	? ✓
SHOP LOC'N? [-MAIN -KING -GAS]	• INCOME from rents • CONVENIENCE TO SHOPPERS • CONTINUITY FOR TRADERS • ROAD SAFETY		• • • •	✓ ✓	
CENT'L SITE? [-IND -HOUS -OPEN]	• LOCAL JOBS created • contribution to HOUSING POLICY • VISUAL IMPACT on local environment			• • •	✓
DIST LIFE? [-10 YR -20 YR -40 YR]	• CONFIDENCE of South Side residents				•

COMPARING

SKILLS

In building up a set of comparison areas which are relevant to a specific problem focus, it can be useful to start by examining each of the decision areas in turn, identifying the more important areas of difference between options as indicated here. When working interactively, this kind of activity is usually carried out verbally, and can be combined with the use of various brainstorming methods.

IDENTIFYING APPROPRIATE COMPARISON AREAS

In general, a set of comparison areas should be chosen to be as relevant as possible to the scope of the decision problem currently in view, and also to the political domain within which decisions are to be made. With problems of any complexity, there is always a danger that these considerations taken together will draw the participants in the direction of quite an elaborate evaluation frame, with a longer list of comparison areas than can be conveniently managed when working under practical pressures. So, as with the definition of decision areas, it can be worth devoting some time and effort to the formulation of an appropriate yet manageable set of comparison areas. Yet again, as with decision areas, people's views on comparison areas may change as a group process builds up momentum and the level of shared understanding grows; so the formulation of comparison areas is better viewed as a continuing matter of concern than as something which should take up a great deal of time in the early stages of an interactive process. Where a current problem focus is expressed in terms of a set of linked decision areas and a choice of options within each, one practical way in which to begin generating comparison areas is to take each decision area in turn – perhaps starting with those which are believed to be most important – and then to consider what kinds of consequences or effects are thought to be most relevant to the comparison of options within each. One way of organising such a process is illustrated in Figure 59.

In this example, the first question concerns the consequences of choosing between the northern and the southern road line through South Side. It might be immediately apparent that these options are likely to differ in terms of capital outlay and also in terms of impact on local residents. Further discussion might then suggest that there is another important consequence to be considered, relating to the flexibility to pursue further local development

options in the future. So the consideration of this one decision area has indicated a set of three different comparison areas straight away. These are listed in Figure 59 using brief and tentative definitions. Such definitions can always be extended later, in the manner illustrated earlier in Figure 19, and can be modified, if need be, as the work proceeds. Some of these comparison areas may, of course, also be relevant to other decision areas as well; this is indicated in Figure 59 by checking off subsequent columns in the table where this is thought to be the case, or where there is some doubt over this point.

Turning to the second decision area – that on location of the shopping centre – an additional set of comparison areas may emerge as important. These again are listed in a tentative way, using the options within the decision area as one source of guidance in reviewing what kinds of comparison areas are likely to be significant. As further decision areas are added, the list is extended further – though it becomes more and more likely that some at least of the relevant comparison areas will have already been generated at an earlier stage. In the example of Figure 59, it will be seen that a set of 11 tentative comparison areas has been generated once the four decision areas within the chosen problem focus have been considered in turn.

But a list of comparison areas generated in this way is unlikely to provide a well-balanced base for comparing alternatives, until some further work has been done on the structure of the list. For a start, the list may well be too long for working purposes; furthermore, it may contain a certain amount of repetition or overlap, raising doubts about the level of generality or specificity with which comparison areas should be expressed. For example, in considering the ROAD LINE? decision area, it was at first considered good enough to talk simply of 'impact on residents' without distinguishing one group of residents from another. Further down the list, in comparing options for DIST LIFE?, it was however felt to be appropriate to formulate a rather more specific comparison

FIGURE

60

SOUTH SIDE
EXAMPLE

Building a Balanced Evaluation Framework

(1) FRAMEWORK OF POLICY CONCERNS (purposive approach)

ECONOMIC
- restrict municipal expenditure commitments
- increase local wealth / tax base
- create new local employment

SOCIAL
- avoid disrupting established communities
- reduce inequalities in access to welfare facilities

ENVIRONMENTAL
- segregate vehicles and pedestrians
- enhance quality of urban landscape
- reduce level of air pollution around steelworks

(2) FRAMEWORK OF INTERESTS TO BE CONSIDERED (responsive approach)

RESIDENTS
- Dockport urban area as a whole
- South Side district
- local neighourhoods affected by particular proposals

UNEMPLOYED
- adults
- school leavers

LOCAL TAXPAYERS
- households
- businesses

EXTERNAL INTERESTS
- national taxpayers
- users of inter-city highways

COMPARING

SKILLS

Even where a set of comparison areas has been generated initially with reference to a particular problem focus, it can be useful to check the list for balance and coverage by cross-reference to broader evaluation frameworks. Different perspectives can emerge by referring to frameworks expressed in terms of organisational purposes and of political interests, so use of both types of framework can be worthwhile.

area concerned with the level of confidence of South Side residents in the future of the area. If the West Street decision area were to be added to the list, then a further question could arise of whether impacts on this more compact group of residents should be considered separately from those on the larger South Side community.

In many practical problem situations, questions will arise about discrimination between different affected groups, between different kinds of impact on the same group and, possibly, between different time horizons of impact as well. In the South Side situation, it might indeed be very important that the working party should debate what different categories of impact on residents there might be: whether, for instance, it could be important to distinguish the severe and immediate consequences for those few residents facing the possibility of physical demolition of their homes from the less severe but continuing nuisance to others from high levels of traffic vibration and noise.

DEVELOPING A BALANCED EVALUATION FRAME

Participants in a decision process do not normally work entirely from scratch when building up a list of comparison areas relevant to each new decision problem that comes up. Usually, each member of a group begins with some preconceptions about a relevant frame of evaluation; a frame which may either have evolved as a purely intuitive response to felt political pressures, or may have been articulated more systematically as an expression of formal organisational policies or aims.

One of the more explicit forms that a frame of evaluation can take is a written statement of guiding objectives of the type often developed by those responsible for the management and control of large corporate organisations. Such a statement may sometimes be structured in a hierarchical form, with expressions of broad aspirations at one level and expressions of more specific policy intentions at another. In

other situations the elements in the framework may be expressed in less aspirational and more pragmatic terms; perhaps in terms of broad problem areas to be addressed, such as poverty or unemployment, rather than in terms of idealistic aims to be achieved. Usually, however, a statement expressed in terms of amelioration of problems can be rewritten in terms of achievement of goals, or vice versa; the underlying sense of purpose may be quite similar in either case.

Underlying such statements of purpose, however, may be more subtle political pressures, relating to the structure of accountability within which the participants are operating. Sometimes, this sense of accountability will differ significantly from one participant to another: one member of the South Side Working Party, for example, might feel a special responsibility for the interests of South Side residents, and another for the interests of unemployed school leavers throughout the wider municipality. Such variations are likely to be influenced by some mix of personal commitments, representational roles and the principles of accountability on which the membership of the working group has been selected.

Figure 60 illustrates how it is possible to use more than one type of evaluation frame as a point of reference in the search to develop a more structured set of comparison areas for a process of strategic choice. In the first list, based on a more purposive approach, a set of broad headings and more specific sub-headings is used to develop a framework of policy appropriate to the South Side problem; in the second list, a different sets of headings and sub-headings is used to identify relevant interests or 'stakeholder' groups, reflecting a concern to be responsive to varied political pressures.

Either list would probably have to be extended quite considerably before it could be considered to be at all complete in its own terms. Nevertheless, these two examples of evaluation frames are both reasonably typical of their kind. The first is typical of the kind of hierarchically ordered statement of objectives which is sometimes formally adopted as a set of central guidelines for the work of a corporate organisation; while the second is typical of the range of interests to which a set of publicly accountable decision-makers might see themselves as having to respond. If the setting were one of a commercial rather than a political organisation, the headings might, of course, be different – for example, the interests to be considered might include shareholders, employees, customers, suppliers – but the organising principles would be much the same.

Either type of list could, of course, be used directly as a set of comparison areas within which to evaluate alternative courses of action. However, in addressing any specific decision problem it will often be more helpful to generate comparison areas directly in the first instance, as illustrated in Figure 59. Then the tentative comparison areas generated in this way can be matched against whatever more structured lists of policy concerns and interests may be available, to help generate insights into ways in which the set of comparison areas to be used might be reformulated in a more logical and consistent way.

Although the two types of framework illustrated in Figure 60 are organised on different principles, there will often be more similarities between them than might at first appear. For example, a concern with employment appears in both lists, expressed in different ways, as does a concern with municipal expenditure levels. The value of this kind of cross-reference between contrasting frames of reference is that it illuminates the scope for *choices* in the way comparison areas are expressed. Among them are choices between different levels of specificity or generality, and between levels of aggregation or disaggregation which might be considered appropriate to a particular decision process and a particular 'evaluative moment' within that process.

One particular opportunity for evaluative choice concerns the possibility of reformulating some comparison areas as decision

areas, relating to choices of policy orientation at a quite general level. This opens up the opportunity for an alternative approach to evaluation which was introduced in Chapter 6 (Figure 54), based on the exploration of *consistency* between different levels of choice. This can be particularly helpful where there is uncertainty or disagreement about choices of appropriate policy stance; for example, lack of agreement on whether corporate expenditure commitments should be held to their present level, allowed to increase to some degree, or perhaps deliberately reduced. Such matters can often be the subject of long-standing political controversy, which cannot always be addressed too explicitly in a process of strategic choice – but which even so can be accommodated in the analytical work.

APPROACHES TO THE COMPARISON OF ALTERNATIVES IN TERMS OF FLEXIBILITY

Whatever the range of policy concerns or interests that may be relevant to a decision problem, there is one particular aspect of comparison that is of fundamental importance to the process of choosing strategically through time. This is the comparison of alternative courses of short-term action in terms of the *flexibility* of future choice which they allow. One approach to this aspect of comparison was illustrated in Figure 25, where five possible action schemes for South Side were compared in terms of the range of longer-term decision schemes left open by each. This range was first presented in terms of a straight count of schemes; but then a robustness index was used to indicate how many schemes in each case met a specified threshold of acceptability, reflecting the concerns of one of the more important of the various interest groups affected in this case.

In general, flexibility of future choice tends to be valued positively by decision-makers. This is because the more courses of action are left open for the future, the greater in general will be the prospects of successful adaptation to whatever changes in circumstances the future may bring.[1] However, it may not always be realistic to treat flexibility of future choice as one simple comparison area, because the value of such flexibility may differ between one area of future choice and another, and also between one set of interests and another. Indeed, flexibility to one party may sometimes mean restrictions of opportunities to others. In South Side, for example, the opportunities for residents to improve their homes, or to exercise other kinds of choices in their own domestic lives, might become more restricted if certain options for development on nearby sites were not foreclosed.

Where many alternatives are being compared in broad terms, it may be adequate to treat flexibility or some such term as a single broadly defined comparison area, as in the list of Figure 59. At other times, however, it may be important to relate this aspect of comparison more carefully to some evaluation framework which identifies a range of affected interests or policy concerns, as in the two examples in Figure 60. This finer level of flexibility analysis becomes practicable in any situation where opportunities for future choice have been structured in terms of decision areas and options, so that flexibility in some decision areas can be given greater weight than flexibility in others. For example, in the situation of Figure 25, the first of the five short-term action schemes could be regarded with particular favour as it is the only one to leave open the opportunity of developing the central site for industry – an aspect of flexibility which could be viewed as of particular importance to the local unemployed.

Another possibility – which will be discussed more fully in Chapter 8 – is that the preservation of options in some decision areas might be

seen as of particular significance as a means of responding to certain specified contingencies that might arise in future. For example, the opportunity to zone the central site in South Side for industry might be seen as of particular significance if the contingency of closure of the local steelworks were to occur.

Circumstances sometimes arise in practice where another related aspect of flexibility has to be considered; the flexibility not just to choose between alternative courses of action in future but to alter courses of current action at some point in time after an initial commitment has been made. Where decision areas and options have been rigorously defined in terms of immediate action commitments of an irrevocable nature, this possibility should, strictly speaking, not arise. However, when people are working on problems under pressure, this kind of rigour is not always appropriate. This is a point that is of particular significance in relation to choices of broad policy orientation, which may be publicly adopted at one moment but can be modified or reversed later, should circumstances change.

One means of approaching this question of flexibility to modify a policy position at some future time is illustrated in Figure 61. This example builds on the comparison of South Side policy orientations presented earlier (Figure 54). Figure 61 starts by presenting the courses of possible action at an operational level which are left open by each of the three possible policy orientations – omitting the short-term private orientation because no schemes at all at the operational level were found to be consistent with it.

Also, it was indicated in Figure 54 that a long-term private investment orientation was believed to be of doubtful feasibility. In such circumstances, one working assumption might be that such an orientation could not be adopted in the short term, yet that the choice of a short-term public investment orientation now could leave open the possibility of a later switch to a long-term private orientation, should a sufficiently interested and influential private investor appear. The full logic of this

---

1 This can be seen a essentially an expression of the cybernetic law of requisite variety, first enunciated by Ross Ashby in his 'Introduction to Cybernetics' (Ashby, 1956). At its simplest, the law states that 'it takes variety to control variety'.

FIGURE

61

SOUTH SIDE
EXAMPLE

Expressing Interchangeability in Policy Choice

LEVEL 1 (POLICY) CHOICE   LEVEL 2 CHOICES

INVESTMENT ORIENTATION?   ROAD   SHOP   CENT'L   WEST
                      LINE?   LOC'N?   SITE?   ST.?

POLICY   POLICY
NOW?   LATER?

— LONG TERM ———[no change] ├— NORTH — MAIN —[HOUS - YES
   PUBLIC   [possible] │   [OPEN - YES

— SHORT TERM —— CONTINUE ├— NORTH — MAIN —[IND —[YES
   PUBLIC   [NO
                                          HOUS —[YES
                                             [NO

 *   CHANGE TO ——[NORTH — KING — OPEN —[YES
            LONG TERM   NO
            PRIVATE   [SOUTH — GAS — OPEN — NO

* opportunity to change
  to this policy orientation
  may arise later IF
  a major private developer
  should express interest

[note that choices in some of
these level 2 decision areas
may become foreclosed if they
are subject to pressures for
decision before opportunities
for policy change arise]

Where decision areas relate to choices of policy stance or other positions which allow future modification, it can sometimes be useful to compare short-term alternatives in terms of the possibility of changing to other positions at some future time. Such comparisons are usually made informally and interactively, but this example of a more formal comparison illustrates the general principles involved.

situation is represented in Figure 61, where POLICY NOW? and POLICY LATER? are formulated as separate areas of choice, in place of the composite decision area which was originally labelled INVESTMENT ORIENTATION?. The choice now of an orientation towards short-term public investment can then be compared to the choice now of a long-term public investment orientation – or, indeed, any other alternative – in terms of the additional flexibility it offers in terms of its changeability to a different policy position in future. However, it should be noted that, in this example, the flexibility available in the 'Level 2' decision areas may be limited if some of them are of high urgency, calling for commitment at or before the time the initial policy is agreed. This kind of difficulty will be considered further in Chapter 8.

CHOICE OF METHOD OF ASSESSMENT WITHIN A COMPARISON AREA

Just as there are different ways in which alternative courses of action can be compared in terms of their relative flexibility, so more generally there are different ways in which alternatives can be compared within any other kind of comparison area. This means that there are always judgements to be made as to how any kind of comparative information should be presented to help people make comparisons between specific alternatives – not least where information from varied sources has to be compressed into a compact and intelligible form. Among the practical choices to be faced are choices relating to the use of different forms of language for communication such as words, figures and graphs, as well as choices about the ways in which feelings of uncertainty should be expressed. Some of the differences of approach that can be considered in both these directions were considered in Chapter 3 (Figures 20 and 21).

Underlying such choices of presentation, however, may be deeper choices about the actual techniques or procedures to be used in making assessments of alternatives, and the sources of information or judgement on which those procedures should draw. Such choices of assessment procedure can sometimes have an important bearing on the levels of effort and time to be devoted to different comparison areas, and also on the levels of confidence with which assessments can be expressed.

Some procedures of assessment are highly intuitive, while others involve precisely defined sequences of calculation. For example, to form an assessment of the relative capital outlays involved in different development options for the central site in South Side, there could be a choice of either asking a single financial or engineering expert for a quick 'off the cuff' guess, based on accumulated personal experience; or calling for a more painstaking calculation taking several weeks, in which several different experts might be asked to play some part. However simplified or elaborate the procedure may be, it is important to remember that the range of underlying sources of uncertainty will be the same – the choice being one as to whether or not effort should be invested in exploring them in a conscious way.

Whenever a particular procedure of assessment is thought to be critical to the decisions currently in view, there is always the opportunity to pause and explore its structure in more depth, in a search for a fuller understanding of the pattern of elements and operations on which it is built. One systematic means of conducting this kind of exploration is illustrated in Figure 62. For illustrative purposes, this example is restricted to one comparatively tangible aspect of the assessment procedures in South Side – that of the relative assessment of capital outlays for two of the development options for the central site.

The breakdown of elements and operations in Figure 62 begins by taking two of the apparently straightforward numerical assessments of capital cost which were first presented in Chapter 3 (Figure 22): the estimates of 450 k and 200 k entered against the industrial and housing options for use of the central site.

The baseline for each of the assessments in Figure 62 is assumed to be the 'null option'

FIGURE
62

SOUTH SIDE
EXAMPLE

Uncovering the Elements in an Assessment Procedure

ELEMENTS IN ESTIMATION OF
CAPITAL COSTS OF SERVICING
CENTRAL SITE FOR
ALTERNATIVE USES:

CENT'L   SITE?

-ind   -hous

	CENT'L SITE? -ind	-hous
estimated cost of servicing this site	450k	200k
estimated usable site area	30 ha	25 ha
full area of site	40 ha	40 ha
⊖ estimated extent of buffer zone	-10 ha	-15 ha
⊗ estimated site servicing cost/ha	×15k/ha	×8k/ha
knowledge of unit servicing costs on other comparable recent sites	11-14 k/ha	6-7 k/ha
predicted rate of cost inflation for site servicing contracts	5% per year	5% per year
extent of any engineering difficulties expected on this site	not exceptional	not exceptional
policy on range of site infrastructure services to be provided by municipality	comprehensive for industrial sites	minimal for housing sites

[simple arithmetical operations]
marked ◯

COMPARING

SKILLS

This kind of systematic exploration of the elements contributing to an assessment procedure is not usually worth carrying out unless and until the focus for comparison has been narrowed down to a few alternatives which differ critically in terms of assessments in particular comparison areas, making it important to explore key sources of uncertainty and alternative ways in which they might be managed.

of leaving the site in its present derelict state – an option which may be purely hypothetical in so far as it is not considered a realistic alternative within the present South Side problem formulation but, nevertheless, might offer a well-defined starting point for the application of standard cost assessment techniques.

In Figure 62, the assessments of capital outlay for the industrial and housing options are both shown broken down in a stepwise way into various contributory elements of assessment. Some of these take the form of other more basic estimates of a quantitative kind – for instance, estimates of the usable site area and the unit cost of site servicing per hectare – while others take the form of non-numerical statements of assumptions which are still worth recording explicitly, especially where they remain open to challenge. For example, one engineer might assume that engineering difficulties on the central site were 'not exceptional'; yet another might cast doubt on this assumption in the light of a somewhat different appraisal of drainage problems or geological conditions. Again, some participants might wish to challenge an underlying policy assumption that industrial sites should be provided with a comprehensive range of infrastructure services before being advertised for rental or sale, whereas only minimal infrastructure should be provided if housing development were being considered.

The breakdown of assessments into contributory operations and elements is a procedure that could, in theory, be pursued almost indefinitely, exposing more and more hidden assumptions all the time. However, this depth of investigation will not normally be justified unless it is suspected that it will expose new areas of uncertainty which might have a critical effect on work within the choosing mode. Under practical time and resource pressures, it is more usual to trust the judgement of the experts; however, the opportunity is always there to ask probing questions about the assumptions underlying any expert assessments, and Figure 62 illustrates one general procedure that can be used to probe systematically the range of assumptions on which particular assessments rest.[2]

Of course, the nature of the assumptions and the underlying procedure of assessment may be quite different in different types of comparison area. For instance, any assessments of annual incomes for the two alternatives in Figure 62 could depend on judgements about the year-by-year build up of incomes over some fixed period of future years, with mounting levels of uncertainty as the time horizon extends. And, wherever there is no obvious numerical unit of assessment on which to rely – as in the assessment of the impact any course of action might have on existing residents of South Side – then the breakdown of contributory assumptions is likely to be a less straightforward matter. But the same principles apply; and the method of stepwise investigation of assumptions illustrated in Figure 62 remains valid even when most or all of the contributory assumptions have to be explored by interrogating an expert whose assessments are based purely on personal experience and informed judgement.

EXPRESSING FEELINGS OF UNCERTAINTY WHEN ASSESSING ALTERNATIVES

Because any assessment of the effects of pursuing a course of action involves at least some elements of conjecture, anybody who is asked to contribute towards the process of assessment must expect to encounter feelings of *uncertainty* – whether these feelings are addressed consciously or at a more unconscious level. Referring again to the example of an assessment procedure considered in Figure 62, it might be possible for a local planner to feel very confident about quoting a figure of 4 ha for the full area of the central site,

2 Other examples relating to actual planning studies carried out by Coventry City Council were presented in Local Government and Strategic Choice (Friend and Jessop, 1969/77, pp. 69–95).

FIGURE

63

SOUTH SIDE
EXAMPLE

Eliciting Limits of Surprise

would it surprise you if it were suggested that the CAPITAL COST
PER HECTARE to service industrial development on this site could be:

below 5 k/ha? (YES!)   above 30k/ha? (YES!)

below 10k/ha? (YES)   above 20k/ha? (YES)

below 12k/ha? (NO)   above 18k/ha (NO)

So take range of assessments as [12k/ha to 18k/ha]
point assessment (best guess) as 15k/ha

would it surprise you if it were suggested that the BALANCE OF
ADVANTAGE between schemes A and B in terms of the CAPITAL:
comparison area could be:

extreme in favour of A? (YES!)   extreme in favour of B? (YES)

considerable in favour of A? (YES!)   considerable in favour of B? (NO)

significant in favour of A? (YES)

marginal in favour of A? (YES)

negligible either way? (YES)

marginal in favour of B? (YES)

significant in favour of B? (NO)

So take balance of advantage in terms of CAPITAL:
to be [significant to considerable] in favour of B

COMPARING

SKILLS

This kind of stepwise questioning process is usually carried out verbally, and can be introduced briefly
and informally at any stage of interactive working where it is proving difficult to arrive at an assessment
either on a numerical or a more judgemental scale. It can be used either to overcome unwillingness to
offer any assessment at all, or to probe the level of uncertainty surrounding a point assessment.

accepting that details of boundary demarcation could make a marginal difference. Yet the extent of the proposed buffer zone – assumed to be wider in the case of the housing than the industrial option, so as to provide a higher level of insulation from traffic noise – might be seen as a rather more debatable matter. And the assessment of site servicing costs per hectare might be expected to involve higher levels of uncertainty again – as was indeed suggested in Figure 62 by the fuller breakdown of this element into four different contributory elements, not all of them of a readily quantifiable form.

People who are asked to make assessments under uncertainty – even if they be professional experts in their field – do not always behave in a similar or consistent way. One expert, for instance, might prefer to quote a single estimate of 15 k per hectare for industrial servicing costs, as if it were quite incontrovertible, treating any feelings of uncertainty as a purely personal concern. However, another expert might profess such a high state of uncertainty as to be reluctant to offer any figure at all – perhaps for fear of being called to account, should any estimate offered later be falsified by events. To overcome such feelings of reluctance in quoting figures – or conversely, to get a sense of the level of uncertainty which surrounds a single apparently confident estimate – it is often worth adopting a simple questioning procedure which has become known as the *surprise limit method*. This method is illustrated with reference to South Side in Figure 63.

The surprise limit method can be applied to any element within an assessment procedure which calls for judgements along some numerical or equivalent scale. It involves asking a series of questions of a person who holds information in that field – the *knowledge source*, in expert systems language – as to what levels on that scale would cause them surprise, starting with extreme levels at either end and gradually working inwards until a range of 'non-surprising' possibilities remains.

Figure 63 demonstrates two different levels at which this approach can be applied to the comparison of capital outlays for Schemes A and B in the South Side problem situation. In the first set of questions, it is supposed that an expert – in this case perhaps a civil engineer – starts from a position of reluctance to give any estimate of the capital cost per hectare of servicing the central site for industrial development. So the interrogator begins by taking what is likely to be an unrealistically low level – in this case 5 k per hectare – and asking whether it would cause the expert any surprise if the servicing cost per hectare were as low as this. If the expert says 'yes' then the question is repeated with successively higher levels until a level which no longer causes surprise is reached. The same kind of question can also be asked, starting from what is initially judged to be an unrealistically high level and working downwards.

Usually, the questioner works from the two ends more or less alternately, accepting that there will be a tendency to 'overshoot' the limits of surprise from time to time. The process is, therefore, one of gradual narrowing down from both ends until a view is arrived at, with the *range* of tenable assumptions in between. Such a procedure, of working by successive approximation towards a feasible range, can usually persuade even the most reluctant expert to give some expression to his or her limits of surprise, even when starting from a position of refusal to make any estimate at all. In the opposite situation, where an expert refuses to deviate from a single point on the scale, it becomes possible to test the limits of surprise by working outwards from that point rather than inwards from the extremes. In practice, the procedure is usually conducted purely through verbal questions and answers; it is mainly for illustrative purposes that Figure 63 sets out the successive steps in written form.

The second illustration in Figure 63 shows how the surprise limit method can be applied even when the scale is a non-numerical one. The scale here is the generalised one of degree of *comparative advantage* which was first illustrated in Chapter 3 (Figure 21). The process of asking surprise limit questions in relation to this non-numerical scale is essentially the same as

FIGURE
64

SOUTH SIDE
EXAMPLE

Combining Advantage Judgements Across Comparison Areas

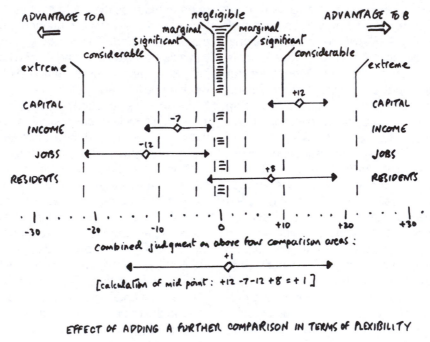

It is occasionally worth calibrating an advantage comparison scale numerically as in this illustration, either to provide a firmer basis for arriving at judgements of advantage across different comparison areas for a particularly important pair of alternatives, or to carry out periodic checks for the types of bias that can arise in combining judgements of ranges in a more informal and judgemental way.

before; this example demonstrates how relative assessments can be arrived at even within comparison areas where there is no basis for comparing alternatives other than in terms of some intuitive sense of level of advantage – marginal, significant or whatever – within the specific setting in which decisions are to be made.

There is, of course, no reason why surprise limit questions should not be addressed to more than one expert. Indeed, the possibility that there may be several different knowledge sources opens the way to the use of systematic approaches such as the Delphi method (Dalkey, 1969) for pooling the judgements of several individuals with differing kinds or levels of expertise to contribute. Such experiments, if used as a background for discussion rather than a substitute for it, can expose all kinds of hidden differences in the assumptions of different individuals. One exercise in which a surprise limit approach was used to explore differences in perception between colleagues in the same team – an administrator, a planner and an engineer – has been fully reported elsewhere (Friend, Power and Yewlett, 1974, pp. 140–158).

COMBINING ADVANTAGE JUDGEMENTS ACROSS DIFFERENT COMPARISON AREAS

It can be difficult enough at times to arrive at judgements of the balance of advantage between alternatives within any single comparison area: it can be even more difficult to judge the overall balance of advantage across a set of dissimilar comparison areas. This was illustrated by the comparison in Chapter 3 (Figure 21) of two alternative schemes for South Side across the four comparison areas of CAPITAL:, INCOME:, JOBS: and RESIDENTS:, each represented by a range of points on a common advantage comparison scale. It is at such moments of evaluation across comparison areas that major feelings of uncertainty about value considerations tend to come most directly to the fore, and have to be taken into

account, alongside whatever other feelings of uncertainty may have been encountered in making assessments within the separate comparison areas taken one at a time.

It is never an easy matter to bring diverse sources of uncertainty within a common analytical framework. But it is necessary to do so if it is intended to compare alternative approaches to the management of uncertainty within the choosing mode; and it was as a step in this direction that a broad-based method of advantage comparison under uncertainty was introduced in Chapter 3. The judgement was presented (Figure 21) that Scheme B had the advantage over Scheme A in terms of capital outlay and probably also in terms of impact on residents; but that Scheme A had the advantage in terms of income and jobs. But the levels of advantage were subject to much uncertainty – uncertainty deriving in part from the process of assessment within each comparison area and, in part, from the value judgements involved in conversion to the common advantage comparison scale. These uncertainties made it all the more difficult in that example (Figure 21) to judge where the overall balance of advantage lay when all four comparison areas were taken into account.

This kind of balancing process is one which people continually have to undertake in practice, if only in an intuitive way. However, once a comparative advantage scale has been used to record an explicit picture of judgements and assumptions, it becomes possible to supplement that intuition – and to carry out checks on its reliability – by resort to rather more systematic methods. One way of doing this is illustrated in Figure 64. In Figure 64, a numerical scale of advantage assessment has been introduced as a means of *calibrating* the distinctions between bands on the original non-numerical scale, and thus as a basis for combining judgements across the different comparison areas. The calibration of the scale is a matter of convenience: the particular numerical scale used in Figure 64 treats the point of no advantage either way as zero, and takes the boundary between the 'significant' and 'considerable' bands as 10 points in either direction – one direction being treated as negative and the other positive so as to keep the arithmetic straight.

Such a scale allows the mid-point of the range for each comparison area to be expressed as either a negative or a positive number. These numbers can then be added together to arrive at a rough estimate of the mid-point of the range of belief about overall comparative advantage, for any set of comparison areas taken in combination. In the illustration of Figure 64, there is a total of 20 'advantage points' in favour of B to be counted by adding the mid-points of the CAPITAL: and RESIDENTS: ranges, against 19 points in favour of A obtained by adding the mid-points of the INCOME: and JOBS: assessments. The net effect is a marginal single point of net advantage in favour of B when all four comparisons are combined.

But then there is the influence of uncertainty to be considered, which is considerable in this case. A rough rule of thumb, which is good enough for most practical purposes, is that the range of belief for a combined advantage comparison will be a little wider than the range of belief for the most uncertain of the separate advantage comparisons within the individual comparison areas; if there are two comparison areas with an equally wide span of uncertainty, then a span about half as wide again as either of them can be assumed. In the illustration of Figure 64, it will be noticed that the range for both RESIDENTS: and JOBS: extends about 10 points on either side of the mid-point, whereas the range for both CAPITAL: and INCOME: assessments is significantly less. So the rule of thumb suggests that a range of about 15 points on either side of the mid-point will be roughly right as an expression of the total range of uncertainty when all comparison areas are combined. As shown in Figure 64, this means there could be a significant or even considerable advantage to either alternative when all sources of uncertainty are taken into account; so there is a case for some serious thought about how the overall range of uncertainty

could be managed, before a preference in the direction of either alternative is expressed.

This kind of procedure for combining advantage comparisons can also be carried out in a step-by-step way, introducing one new comparison area at a time. This possibility is illustrated in Figure 64 by the introduction of FLEXIBILITY: as an additional comparison area; the range of positions on the scale being based, in this case, purely on a quick intuitive judgement about the relative flexibility of A and B. In the event, Figure 64 shows that this addition makes only a marginal difference to the mid-point and range arrived at for the other four comparison areas combined. With practice, it becomes possible to use a non-numerical advantage comparison scale in a quick and informal way, either as a group activity or by asking people to work individually on pre-prepared sheets, then comparing and collating the individual judgements which they make. It usually takes a little experience to arrive at consistent interpretations of the different levels of significance within a particular working situation; for people have to learn to use the successive bands of a comparative advantage scale in a broadly similar way.

For example, in a particular context, it might seem to make sense to rate one alternative as having a 'considerable' advantage over another in each of two comparison areas, but little sense to regard their combined advantage as 'extreme'. In that case, it might be decided to extend the width of the 'considerable' band on the scale until such inconsistencies tended to disappear. Also, methods based on statistical theory can provide a check on any more intuitive rules of thumb by which ranges of uncertainty are combined.[3] However, in interactive

---

3 If a set of variables are independent and can be assumed to follow the normal (Gaussian) probability distribution, then the standard deviation of their sum can be taken as the square root of the sum of the squares of the separate standard deviations. So if the ranges shown in Figure 64 are assumed to represent two standard deviations on either side of the mean, the corresponding distance for the first four comparison areas combined would be the square root of $(4^2 + 5^2 + 10^2 + 10^2)$, which is about equal to 16.

group working, such checks are mainly of use on an occasional basis, as a means of building confidence that intuition is not generating results which are at too much variance with logic.

APPLYING CONSTRAINTS IN THE CHOICE OF A WORKING SHORTLIST

Where there is a large number of decision schemes to be compared, it will usually be quite unrealistic to subject more than a few of them to the kind of carefully structured pair comparison process under uncertainty which has just been discussed; so the need to choose a more restricted working shortlist becomes acute. One approach to the choice of such a working shortlist was illustrated in Chapter 3 (Figure 22), where all schemes which were estimated to come above a specified threshold of capital cost were set aside, as were all those which did not meet a specified minimum level on the non-numerical residents' confidence index.

The application of such minimum or maximum constraints on selected indices of assessment is a useful, if obvious, means of arriving at a working shortlist where there is a very large number of possible decision schemes to be considered. This is especially so where the options within the individual decision areas can be assessed separately on numerical or equivalent scales, and assessments for at least some of the combinations of options can be made simply by adding the option assessments together. In practice a monetary index is often used as a constraint, because there are many situations in which it is politically appropriate to apply some upper limit to the overall cost of a decision scheme. However, in other situations a constraint might be placed on the minimum number of jobs created, or the maximum number of residents to be displaced, or the minimum ratio of annual return to investment. In general, it will, of course, only be worth introducing a constraint on any scale if it corresponds to a con-

cern which is important in the particular context in which the participants are working.

When applying a constraint to a large and complex set of decision schemes, it is not always necessary to work through all possible schemes in full. One means of simplifying the procedure is illustrated in Figure 65. Here, assessments of capital cost are indicated for the set of possible decision schemes for South Side, these being presented in the form of a tree as in Chapter 3 (Figure 22) – but with some adjustments introduced to illustrate particular points. First, the WEST ST? decision area has been added, which increases the total range of schemes. Secondly, the options within the SHOP LOC'N? and DIST LIFE? decision areas are assessed jointly rather than separately – because it is supposed now that there are certain costs associated with choosing options in particular combinations in these two decision areas – and the sequence of decision areas has been modified so as to bring these two decision areas together. Thirdly, the capital cost assessments in each column have been recalibrated so that the alternative with the lowest capital cost is taken as zero and the expected capital cost of every other alternative is assessed as a positive figure relative to this minimum amount. Such recalibration can be useful where it is desired to apply a constraint of expected relative cost – but of course in many situations cost limits may be conceived in more absolute terms.

Because only positive cost figures can now appear, it is possible to set a constraint on the maximum cumulative figure which is acceptable at any branching point in the tree. In Figure 65, a capital cost limit of 500 k monetary units has been introduced. This has the effect of terminating the branches emanating from choice of the southern road line quite early on, and also closing some of the other branches before the full set of feasible schemes has been developed. In this example, only four feasible schemes remain which do not violate either the option bars or the cumulative capital cost constraint of 500 k. These four schemes have been given the labels P, Q, R and S for

FIGURE
65

SOUTH SIDE
EXAMPLE

Applying Constraints in Generating Decision Schemes

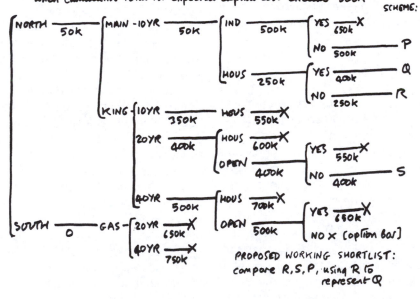

expected capital costs in k [recalibrated
with least cost alternative in each column = 0]

joint assessment

ROAD LINE?		SHOP LOC'N?	DIST LIFE?		CEN'TL SITE?		WEST ST?	
-NORTH	50k	-MAIN	-10YR	0	-IND	450k	-YES	150k
-SOUTH	0	-KING	-10YR	300k	-HOUS	200k	-NO	0
			-20YR	400k	-OPEN	0		
			-40YR	450k				
		-GAS	-20YR	650k				
			-40YR	750k				

PROPOSED RULE FOR ELIMINATING HIGH-COST SCHEMES: close any branch
when cumulative total for expected capital cost exceeds 500k

SCHEME:

PROPOSED WORKING SHORTLIST:
compare R,S,P, using R to
represent Q

Wherever options or combinations can be assessed in terms of a simplified scale, it becomes possible to cut down the range of schemes for closer comparison by introducing, on a trial basis, some constraint on the maximum or minimum acceptable level. It can save time and effort to close off entire branches at an early stage, and recalibration to make all relative assessments positive can facilitate this.

working purposes, and together they offer one basis for a manageable working shortlist. If desired, the working shortlist can be further reduced by grouping together schemes which are rather similar in terms of their options, then using one of them to represent the other members of that group at this stage in the comparison process. In the example of Figure 65, the judgement has been made that Scheme R can represent Scheme Q within a more restricted shortlist of only three schemes, because the two schemes differ only in terms of the West Street option and R is the less costly of the two.

Often, it can be difficult to judge, in practice, at what level a constraint should be set, if the purpose is to develop a working shortlist which is neither too large nor too limited to serve as a base for more careful comparison of alternatives. The level of the constraint can, of course, always be raised or lowered in retrospect, if the level first chosen does not have the desired effect. Where computer support is available, then such adjustments can be carried out quickly; indeed, if desired, the level of constraint can be varied automatically in accordance with specified rules. One possibility is to specify in advance the number of schemes required in the working shortlist, leaving the computer to adjust the level of the constraint accordingly. Another possibility is to specify the maximum level of difference to be considered between the least-cost scheme and any other scheme to be included in the list recognising that, as in the example of Figure 65, the level of cost for the least-cost scheme cannot be known at the outset if there is a possibility that the combination of all the zero-cost options will be excluded by option bars.

SHORTLISTING ACROSS MULTIPLE COMPARISON AREAS

The application of constraints in relation to numerical or similar indices can provide an effective way of reducing the range of schemes where this is very large. But this reduction can carry a cost, because it can mean ignoring for the time being any other comparison areas which cannot be treated in this way; and also because potentially vital information about uncertainty has to be temporarily set aside. So, it is often wise to view the use of constraints as only a crude filtering phase in the formation of a shortlist, leading to an intermediate list of schemes to which other methods of shortlisting can subsequently be applied.

As was also illustrated earlier (in Figure 22) the ranking of alternatives according to order of preference in different comparison areas offers another useful reference point in selecting promising alternatives for closer examination. Simple rankings can be deduced quickly wherever decision schemes can be compared in terms of numerical or equivalent indices, with tied rankings wherever the indices for two or more alternatives are the same; and it is not difficult to scan two or more comparison areas simultaneously, once the information has been reduced to this form. But a set of alternatives can always be arranged in a tentative rank order in other comparison areas, where assessments cannot be quantified – so long as there is some basis for judgement which allows one scheme to be rated, however hesitantly, as more desirable than, less desirable than, or roughly similar to any other.

Figure 66 develops this point by comparing the nine schemes, A–I of Figure 22, in terms of their rankings on all four of the comparison areas which were originally introduced. The CAPITAL: and RESIDENTS: rankings are as earlier indicated in Figure 22; but the INCOME: and JOBS: rankings have been added on the basis of quick intuitive judgements about orders of preference within each of these two additional comparison areas.

On the basis of a set of rankings such as that in Figure 66, it may be possible to pick out one or more schemes which are dominated by particular others, in the sense that any dominated scheme is inferior to, or at least no better than, the other in each of the rankings in the different comparison areas. So, in South Side, there are four schemes – C, F, H and I – each of

FIGURE

66

SOUTH SIDE
EXAMPLE

Shortlisting Across Multiple Comparison Areas

RANKING OF 9 SCHEMES BY EACH OF 4 COMPARISON AREAS:

SCHEME	CAPITAL:	RESIDENTS:	INCOME:	JOBS:	dominated by:
A	2nd=	4th=	(1st)	(1st)	–
B	(1st)	2nd=	7th	8th	–
C	4th=	4th=	6th	6th	A
D	7th=	2nd=	4th	5th	–
E	9th	(1st)	2nd	4th	–
F	2nd=	7th	9th	9th	A, B
G	4th=	4th=	8th	7th	–
H	6th	8th=	5th	3rd	A
I	7th=	8th=	3rd	2nd	A

RANK ORDERINGS OF 9 SCHEMES BY DIFFERENT COMPARISON AREAS:

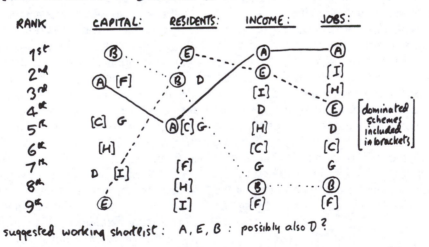

suggested working shortlist: A, E, B : possibly also D?

The ranking of alternatives taking several comparison areas separately offers a simple but useful aid to comparison where the set is neither too large to be readily handled in this way — in which case constraints can be introduced — nor so small as to make this step unnecessary. The setting aside of dominated schemes and the picking out of those ranking highly on several comparison areas can then aid the shortlisting process.

which is dominated by Scheme A in terms of this set of four comparison areas; and among them, Scheme F is dominated by Scheme B as well. So it could be judged appropriate to exclude these four schemes from any short-list selected as a basis for closer evaluation, accepting the risk that the excluded schemes might score quite highly in other comparison areas not considered at this stage, and also the risk that the rankings might change if major areas of uncertainty were to be investigated and new information uncovered.

As an alternative means of displaying the same information, it can often be useful to rearrange a set of rankings by reference to the principle of rank ordering, as shown in the second listing of Figure 66. Here the set of alternatives is arranged in four different orders of preference, each based on their rank order in one of the four comparison areas; so schemes which rate highly in terms of two or more comparison areas will tend to rise towards the top in the corresponding columns. It can be seen in this instance that Scheme A – which comes top in two of the columns – rates quite well also in the other two columns, while Scheme E – the most attractive from the residents' viewpoint – scores well enough in terms of income and jobs but is the least favourable in terms of capital cost. So, the comparison of A with E could be a promising one to explore more closely from the point of view of exposing underlying value issues; thus these two alternatives might well be taken forward to a committee of elected representatives for debate, perhaps after further assessment of their relative consequences has been carried out.

Further inspection of Figure 66 might suggest also that Scheme B be carried forward for closer comparison with A and E, in view of its high ranking in terms of both the residents and capital assessments – despite its low ranking in each of the other two comparison areas. Conceivably, too, Scheme D could be carried forward as a possible compromise alternative, making a quite manageable working shortlist of four schemes in all – A, E, B and D – to be used as a basis for closer pair comparisons taking uncertainty more explicitly into account. And this in turn could provide a basis from which to switch into the work of the choosing mode.

FURTHER EXTENSIONS IN COMPARING METHODS

In Chapter 10 there will be found a brief discussion of the use of computer software to support the work of the comparing mode, and examples of three of the main window layouts used to support this mode in STRAD 2 for Windows will be presented in Figure 92. In the design of this software, the opportunity has been taken to make significant extensions in the methods of comparison presented in this chapter, although these remain based on the four basic concepts of the comparison area, the relative assessment, the advantage comparison and the working shortlist. These extensions are possible because, provided assessments of option differences have been entered for all combinations of decision areas and comparison areas where these differences are judged to be significant, the computer can aggregate this information rapidly. The user can then introduce any adjustments which may be judged necessary to take account of expected effects of combining options from linked decision areas in particular ways.

The computer can carry out this process of aggregating differences not only across decision areas but also across comparison areas, provided some assumptions have been entered about their relative weightings or trade-off rates. A particular feature of the STRAD software is the way it enables intuitive assumptions of these weighting factors to be entered at an early stage of the comparing work, and subsequently adjusted as and when required.

SUMMARY: PROCESS JUDGEMENTS IN THE COMPARING MODE

This chapter has discussed various choices of method and emphasis that are continually

FIGURE
67

Process Choices when Working in the Comparing Mode

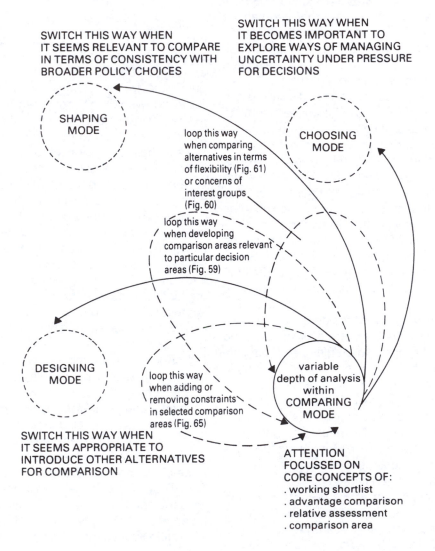

SWITCH THIS WAY WHEN
IT SEEMS RELEVANT TO COMPARE
IN TERMS OF CONSISTENCY WITH
BROADER POLICY CHOICES

SWITCH THIS WAY WHEN
IT BECOMES IMPORTANT TO
EXPLORE WAYS OF MANAGING
UNCERTAINTY UNDER PRESSURE
FOR DECISIONS

SHAPING
MODE

CHOOSING
MODE

loop this way
when comparing
alternatives in terms
of flexibility (Fig. 61)
or concerns of
interest groups
(Fig. 60)

loop this way
when developing
comparison areas relevant
to particular decision
areas (Fig. 59)

DESIGNING
MODE

loop this way
when adding or
removing constraints
in selected comparison
areas (Fig. 65)

variable
depth of analysis
within
COMPARING
MODE

SWITCH THIS WAY WHEN
IT SEEMS APPROPRIATE TO
INTRODUCE OTHER ALTERNATIVES
FOR COMPARISON

ATTENTION
FOCUSSED ON
CORE CONCEPTS OF:
. working shortlist
. advantage comparison
. relative assessment
. comparison area

COMPARING

SUMMARY

encountered in practice when working in the comparing mode. They are choices which involve repeated judgements about the balance between simplification and elaboration in evaluation method; a balance which, as argued at the beginning of the chapter, is more usefully conceived in dynamic than in static terms. To maintain an appropriate balance through time can involve alternating between rough and ready comparisons among many alternatives, and closer comparisons of a selected few; however, this balance is one that has to be judged not only in the light of the application of broad guidelines such as those offered in this chapter, but also in the light of political and administrative considerations which can vary from context to context. These will include the perceived importance of different decisions; the range of interests affected; and the nature of their representation, direct or indirect, in the processes by which comparisons and choices are to be made.

Underlying many of the evaluative choices to be made are questions of response to uncertainty – feelings of uncertainty being, in practice, inseparable from the necessary processes of conjecture about what the consequences of alternative courses of action might be. The concepts of relative assessment and of advantage comparison developed in this chapter have provided a way of coming to grips with these feelings of uncertainty, at least so far as their influence on comparative judgements is concerned. But the closer analysis of perceived areas of uncertainty, and the consideration of what might be done about them, is a matter that will be deferred for discussion in Chapter 8, as it is more germane to the work of the choosing than the comparing mode.

Figure 67 summarises the points made in this chapter, in terms of the various types of looping and switching judgements which centre on the comparing mode. Within the comparing mode itself, the idea of dynamic comparison, involving alternation between crude sifting of many alternatives and closer evaluations of a selected few, offers a key to the process judgements that have to be made. Considering first the brief loops that can be made out of the comparing mode towards other modes, Figure 67 indicates a loop in the direction of the *choosing mode* in situations where some rough and ready assessment of flexibility of future choice seems important; a loop in the direction of the *shaping mode* when developing a set of comparison areas relevant to a particular problem focus; and a loop in the direction of the *designing mode* whenever, for current working purposes, it is felt useful to reduce the range of alternatives by imposing additional constraints – or, for that matter, to extend the range by removing constraints previously assumed.

Turning to the question of less transitory switching into other modes, the normal progression in a conventional sequential process of decision-making would be from the comparing into the choosing mode – not necessarily to make a definitive choice among the alternatives that have been compared, but at least in order to make incremental progress in that direction. However, where a process is guided by the strategic choice philosophy, other directions of progress are possible. A move into the shaping mode will often be appropriate where the balance of advantage between alternatives across different comparison areas seems so problematic that choices of policy orientation should be brought more explicitly into the problem focus itself. At a more technical level, a switch back into the designing mode makes sense whenever it seems that a reformulation of options and option bars could lead to a clearer expression of the set of alternatives to be compared.

ILLUSTRATIONS FROM PRACTICE

There now follows a set of three illustrations from practice illustrating some further practical points about the work of the comparing mode.

The first of these, from a planning exercise for North Holland, illustrates the merging of contributions from different members of a group in the building up of an initial set of comparison areas, and the collation of opinions about their relative importance. The second illustration, from northeast Brazil, shows a variant of the advantage comparison method in which a list of uncertainty areas is built up as difficulties are encountered in arriving at group judgements. The third illustration presents an example of the successful use of advantage comparison methods with the management committee of a housing co-operative in a disadvantaged former mining community in South Yorkshire, England, leading to a broader appreciation of the positions of some significant external stakeholders.

FIGURE
68

Illustrations from Practice – Comparing 1

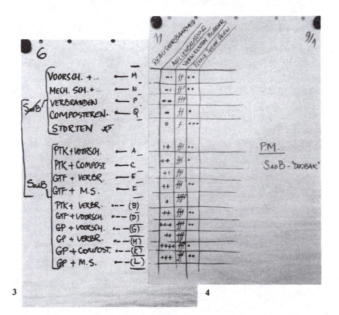

Theme: Developing Key Comparison Areas for Exploring the Differences between Decision Schemes.
Problem: A Provincial Development Plan for the Disposal of Household Waste.
Context: Inter-organisational Planning Team, Province of Noord Holland, The Netherlands, 1986.

COMMENTARY ON FIGURE 68

These flip charts were drawn up during the final day of the first of a series of four workshops, held to bring together the thinking of planners from the province of Noord Holland, the Central Government and the Municipality of Amsterdam on the problem of disposal of solid waste. The workshops were held in Heemstede, the Netherlands during January and February 1986, with Allen Hickling acting as process consultant to a team of two facilitators from the Directorate General for the Environment.

A number of alternative decision schemes had already been formulated, and these were set out in a list. A set of comparison areas ('criteria') was then composed in order to differentiate among these. The first step in this procedure involved the use of cards on which participants were encouraged to write their suggestions. All these were stuck up on the wall and then sorted according to three categories: physical ('fysiek'); social ('soc. maatsch.'); and economic ('fin. econ.') (1). Some cards naturally fell between categories, and were therefore positioned so as to overlap sector boundaries; others were found to be duplicates ('dubbelle').

From this, a straightforward list was drawn up, in no particular order, defining each criterion more clearly. Stickers were issued to the participants, who were asked to place them next to the comparison areas which they

thought most significant in relation to the range of alternatives under consideration. The area of greatest concern emerged as practical feasibility ('realiseerbaarheid'), followed by environmental damage ('milieubelasting'), cost of disposal to local citizens ('verwijderingskosten', 'burger') and flexibility of waste disposal method ('flexibiliteit techn. verwerking') (2).

Assessments were then made by consensus in the group using very simple scales. A scale of + and − signs was used for the environment; the more plus signs the better. The Dutch symbol for Guilders (f) was used for cost; the more symbols, the higher the cost. Spots were used for flexibility; the more spots, the more flexible. The note by the side headed 'PM' is merely an elaborated definition, describing the system of separating the waste at source.

This work in the comparing mode was not taken further on that day, because it was felt to be more important to explore further the uncertainties and assumptions which had been thrown up; these were listed elsewhere on the wall. As is quite usual with work carried out in the early stages of a strategic choice workshop, this particular part of the analysis was not resumed later. By the time the group was ready to move back to work in the comparing mode, the formulation of the alternatives and comparison areas had changed again, reflecting the further understanding of the problem that had been gained in the meantime.

FIGURE
69

Illustrations from Practice – Comparing 2

Theme: Generating a List of Uncertainty Areas during an Advantage Comparison of Shortlisted Decision Schemes.

Problem: Policy Formulation in a Comprehensive Development Plan for an Offshore Island.

Context: Five-Day Workshop with a Local Inter-Disciplinary Planning Team, Recife, Brazil, 1984.

COMMENTARY ON FIGURE 69

These two photographs were taken in Recife, Brazil, during the course of the workshop already described in Figure 44, concerned with policies for the offshore island of Itamaracá.

At the moment when the first photograph was taken, attention had become focused on a comparison between two sharply contrasted decision schemes, numbered 2 and 5, which had been picked out of a set of six feasible combinations of options from three linked decision areas. These covered respectively the choice of economic base for the island; the area chosen for urbanisation; and the access route to the undeveloped north. Scheme 2 involved retention of a traditional economic base, centred on farming and sea fishing, with a brake on any urban development beyond existing commitments; Scheme 5 involved an emphasis on tourist development with additional allocation of land.

Initially, five comparison areas were chosen, concerned with fulfilment of metropolitan aims; with levels of income for the islanders ('renda'); with preservation of their way of life ('vida'); with conservation of the natural environment ('ambiente'); and with demands on a limited water supply ('agua'). A sixth comparison area was added later, concerned with internal transport for the islanders; it is interesting (Figure 44) that some of these comparison areas had earlier been viewed as decision areas.

In the top photograph, a member of the group has just filled in the top row of an advantage comparison chart, using a nine-point scale labelled (e c s m n m s c e). This is essentially similar to that introduced in Figure 21 – the words extreme, considerable, significant, marginal and negligible all having close equivalents in Portuguese. On the first row in the photograph, excluded parts of the scale have been blocked out. So there was thought to be no possibility that the balance of advantage on the metropolitan benefit comparison area could be in favour of Scheme 2 to any degree, or as much as considerable or extreme in favour of Scheme 5. For the group to arrive at this judgement, they had to confront many areas of uncertainty; and a tentative list of uncertainty areas is being started up on another chart underneath. The three uncertainty areas encountered in debating metropolitan benefit are to do with which groups might benefit; with the actions of another agency; and with assessing how far investors would be attracted.

The second photograph shows the same two wall charts at a later moment when all rows of the advantage comparison table had been completed and the list of uncertainty areas extended accordingly. The various uncertainty areas have now been classified (the Portuguese equivalents of UE, UV and UR being IA, IV and IR, respectively). Also appearing in the second photograph is a second advantage comparison chart, in which Schemes 2 and 3 are compared. In this case, the process was carried out initially by each individual completing a smaller version of the chart. One member then collated the results and presented them to the group in the form of the mode and range of the frequency distribution for each row, as shown here.

FIGURE
70

Illustrations from Practice – Comparing 3

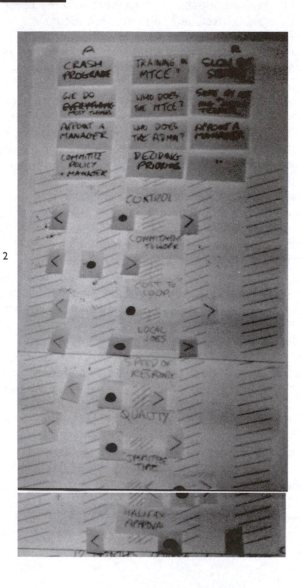

2

1

3

<table>
<tr><td>COMPARING</td><td></td></tr>
</table>

COMPARING

PRACTICE

Theme: Comparing the advantages of a 'crash programme' versus a slow but steady approach to takeover of housing maintenance.

Problem: Strategy for Tenants' Co-operative in taking over responsibility for maintenance of houses on their estate having recently become owners.

Context: Support from the Community Operational Research Unit to the Thurnscoe Tenants Housing Co-operative in South Yorkshire.

COMMENTARY ON FIGURE 70

This illustration from practice comes from the first in a series of workshops carried out in 1988 with the management committee of the Thurnscoe Tenants Housing Co-operative, serving a former mining community in South Yorkshire, England. The members of this group had just taken over the ownership of their estate of about 300 houses from British Coal, previously the National Coal Board. Having fought a successful campaign to become owners of the estate – with loan finance from a large mortgage company and professional support from a regional housing association – the tenants (1) were now faced with taking over the very different responsibilities of estate managers, involving decisions on matters such as rent levels, maintenance and sales that directly impinged on their relationships with their neighbours and friends.

This first one-day workshop was facilitated by John Friend, acting as a consultant to the Community Operational Research Unit that had recently been established at Northern College near Barnsley, working with Peter Long of the Operational Research department of Sheffield City Polytechnic – now Sheffield Hallam University. The focus of the workshop was on the choice of arrangements for housing maintenance. It quickly emerged that one of the most critical early choices was whether the co-operative should plan for a gradual transition to setting up its own organisation for medium-scale maintenance work over a 3-year period, as had been originally envisaged, or whether it should commit itself to a faster 'crash' programme leading to a takeover of this work within about 12 months – as most members of the committee preferred.

The main picture (2) shows an advantage comparison that was made between the scheme for a crash programme and a more 'slow but steady' alternative – defined in terms of options for doing the work, for administration and for priority setting. Quick assessments were first made in terms of the six criteria of control; commitment to the work; cost to the co-operative; local job creation; speed of response; and quality. Stickers were used to indicate the participants' view on the likely balance of advantage (spots) and the range of uncertainty (arrows) on each row. There were agreed to be significant sources of uncertainty on several criteria, and these were added to an accompanying list of uncertainty areas (3) on another flip chart. Overall, however, the advantage on each of the six criteria was judged to lie with the crash programme.

This prompted the facilitator to ask why, if all the advantages seemed likely to lie on one side of the balance sheet, a decision should not be made straight away. Might there be any obstacles to making it happen? Might there not be other interests that had not yet been thought of that would suggest other advantages to the slow, but steady, alternative? Prompted by these questions, two additional comparison areas were added, where the balance of advantage was thought likely to lie in the opposite direction: these were concerned with the load on committee time and the attitude of the loan provider. The participants then went on to review the actions that they might take to deal with those uncertainties that appeared to be most critical, and to develop an action plan to address these – leading to a decision point on whether to appoint a maintenance manager in a few months' time.

This episode demonstrates that a facilitator may sometimes find it necessary to play a 'devil's advocate' role in questioning whether there are any biases among workshop participants in the range of comparison areas that they initially select as significant, especially when all the advantages seem to lie to one alternative.

8 Skills in choosing

INTRODUCTION

The work of the choosing mode calls for quite different kinds of judgements to the work of the comparing mode. In essence, they are judgements to do with the management of uncertainty and the development of commitment through time; for this is the mode in which the time dimension comes to the fore, and the pressures for urgent action have to be balanced against any concerns that the decisions faced may be too difficult to address before further explorations have been carried out.

The pressure for a switch towards the choosing mode can frequently be observed in the course of a conventional committee decision process. Typically, some participants start to become impatient, look at their watches and say 'isn't it time we reached a decision and moved on to the next business?', or 'isn't it time we brought the meeting to an end?'. In practice, however, the issues involved in making progress through time become most complex and challenging where the problem under consideration is itself complex in structure, embracing many interrelated elements to which different urgencies and uncertainties apply.

Even though the challenges of making progress through time are readily recognisable from personal experience, they have received much less attention in the literature of planning and management methods than the more technical challenges of evaluation. This may be because judgements to do with choosing through time are much less easy to separate from the particular organisational or political

context in which they arise than are judgements to do with comparison of specific alternatives, which scholars have generally been able to treat in a more detached, analytical way.

So in practice, the shift from the comparing to the choosing mode means a shift from the technical domain towards the political arena. But one political arena can differ sharply from another, in terms of the configurations of conflict, competition, consensus and coalition which influence the ways in which decisions are made; and such differences can reflect not only variations in the ways in which the participants themselves have shaped their own internal working relationships through time, but also deeper, underlying differences in their accountability to others with a stake in the decisions to be made. Even where progress is being sought towards action commitments by a set of participants who come together repeatedly in the same group setting – as has been supposed to be the case with the South Side Working Party – the members may differ from each other in terms of their external accountability. Indeed, in practice, the wish to include representation of all the most relevant departments, agencies or interest groups is often one of the explicit principles on which involvement in a decision process is designed.

So, in addressing complex issues, the working group in which all members share exactly the same accountability tends to be more the exception than the rule. Not only problems but also personal responsibilities may be perceived differently by different members of a group; and this in turn means that any guidance on the work of the choosing mode cannot always be addressed to all members of a working group as if they formed a single coherent team. There

FIGURE
71

SOUTH SIDE
EXAMPLE

Building up a Working List of Uncertainty Areas

UNCERTAINTY AREA (tentative description)	TYPE	note on how/why this uncertainty first encountered
? RATE OF EXPECTED REDUCTION OF LOCAL AIR POLLUTION	UE (UR?)	preliminary discussion of problem
? TIMING OF CONSTRUCTION OF NEW ROAD	UR	early work on shaping of decision graph and selection of problem focus
? CUTBACKS IN MUNICIPAL EXPENDITURE	UR	
? POLICY VALUE OF JOB CREATION	UV (UR?)	
? FEASIBILITY OF OTHER ROAD LINE OPTIONS	UE	work in the designing mode
? AVAILABILITY OF FOOTBALL GROUND SITE	UE	
? FEASIBILITY OF COMBINING HOUSING ON CENTRAL SITE WITH SHOPS AT KING SQUARE	UE	
? SERVICING COST PER HA. ON CENTRAL SITE	UE	assessment of alternatives within particular comparison areas
? ATTRACTIVENESS OF CENTRAL SITE TO EMPLOYMENT - INTENSIVE INDUSTRIES	UE	
? STEEL CORPORATION DECISION ON FUTURE OF STEELWORKS SITE	UR	advantage comparison schemes A vs B
? POLICY VALUE OF RESPONSIVENESS TO RESIDENTS' CONCERNS	UV	
? EASTWELL DISTRICT SHOPPING COMPLEX – SCALE AND TIMING	UR	advantage comparison schemes B vs E
? POLICY VALUE OF MEETING TRADERS' DEMANDS	UV	

CHOOSING

SKILLS

It is useful to build up a rough-and-ready listing of uncertainty areas progressively in interactive working, as new areas of uncertainty can surface when working in any mode. The use of the UE/UV/UR typology helps in drawing attention to any under-represented types as well as borderline cases. Notes on origination are here included for illustrative purposes and would be omitted in practice.

is no shortage of useful advice that can be offered in this chapter, at a generalised level, building on the four core concepts of the *uncertainty area*, the *exploratory option*, the *action scheme* and the *commitment package*.[1] But readers should not be surprised when questions of whose uncertainty, whose exploration, whose action and whose commitment keep breaking through. Yet even in contexts where it is unrealistic to expect that views about these matters will be freely shared, there remains the possibility that individuals will be able to make good use of the concepts and methods offered here as a guide to their own personal contributions to a decision process.

BUILDING A WORKING LIST OF UNCERTAINTY AREAS

The concept of the uncertainty area can be used to represent any area where alternative assumptions can be made about matters which are of some importance to decision-making. Such assumptions may relate to various aspects of the *working environment* within which people are trying to make decisions; they may relate to aspects of the *policy values* to which they are expected to pay heed; or they may relate to other *related decisions* where commitments have not, as yet, been made. The labels UE, UV and UR, which were introduced in Chapter 1 to differentiate these three types of uncertainty, serve not only as a means of classifying particular uncertainty areas as they are identified, but also as a useful reminder of the broad scope of the uncertainty area concept. Such a reminder can be especially appropriate to participants of an analytical bent, who are often pre-disposed to view the management of uncertainty primarily in terms of prediction or survey exercises using established statistical techniques.

In Chapter 3, the concept of the uncertainty area was first illustrated at a point in the South Side story where the focus of comparison had been narrowed down to a particular pair of alternative schemes, A and B, for which the overall balance of advantage across comparison areas was far from clear cut. However, it is only to be expected that people will experience personal feelings of uncertainty at many moments in a decision-making process, and that these feelings will change continually as they are exposed to what other participants have to say. People may feel uncertain as to where the boundaries of their problem should be drawn; they may feel uncertain as to whether or not particular decision areas should be seen as interconnected; they may feel uncertain as to whether particular options or combinations of options should be considered feasible; and they may feel uncertain as to the terms in which particular comparison areas should be formulated. Then, when it comes to comparing specific alternatives, they are bound to experience feelings of uncertainty both in attempting to assess their consequences within particular comparison areas and in judging where the overall balance of advantage lies; and it is at such moments that it becomes most important to find ways of viewing all areas of uncertainty together as sources of difficulty in choosing – some of which may be more significant than others – using the methods which will be discussed in this chapter.

Because feelings of uncertainty may surface at virtually any moment in a process of strategic choice, it is often useful in group work to set aside a sheet of paper on the wall where a cumulative list of uncertainty areas can be developed, recognising that such a list can always be restructured, and the items within it reformulated, at some later time. An example of a relatively unstructured list built up gradually in this way is presented in Figure 71. This illustration follows broadly the development of the South Side story, as recounted in earlier chapters, so the listing of uncertainty areas follows the broad sequence of shaping, designing and comparing in a more or less linear way – after starting by registering one uncertainty

---

1 As will be explained later, this is now often referred to by the alternative phrase *progress package*.

area, to do with air pollution, that is in this case supposed to have been so clearly recognised among the participants that it could be placed on record even before the group activity of shaping problems began. In practice, however, the more work is carried out within a group, the more the group is likely to switch freely between one mode and another; so the longer a list of uncertainty areas becomes, the more mixed it will tend to become in the modes of activity from which successive uncertainty areas are drawn.

In a group process, the recording of each uncertainty area on the list implies a working assumption that the feeling of uncertainty it contains is shared among different members of the group. Sometimes, of course, one member may express a feeling of uncertainty which is promptly dissolved because of some piece of information which another member of the group can supply, from a position of greater knowledge or authority in some particular field. Sometimes, too, there may be areas of uncertainty which remain largely *latent* until exposed within the group. For example, one member of the South Side Working Party may feel quite confident in assuming that the football ground will be available for redevelopment, only to discover in discussion that another participant is equally confident that it will not; and they may then discover that neither is in a position to refute the other's assumption on the grounds of superior knowledge. Whereas neither participant had feelings of uncertainty on this point before the group interaction started, both share a feeling of uncertainty after some communication has taken place; so a new uncertainty area is recorded, and the decision process has become the more realistic as a result.

Because a working list of uncertainty areas may be subject to considerable restructuring before it is put to operational use, it is usually not worth while assigning brief labels to the uncertainty areas at the time they are first recorded, in the manner that was illustrated in Figure 23. It can, however, be helpful to register from the outset whether each new

uncertainty area seems to be of type UE, UV or UR, even if there remains some doubt over which classification is most appropriate. For the attempt to classify uncertainty areas in this way can provide a valuable check against any tendency to bias towards or against any one of the three basic types – a bias towards concern with uncertainties of type UE being a common experience among participants of a more analytical, apolitical cast of mind. Often there is a tendency in an initial list to include comparatively few uncertainty areas of type UR – most of them referring to decisions over which the participants feel they have relatively little control. This is natural enough at a stage of the process before a clear problem focus has emerged, because the tendency will have been to include most of the significant areas of choice within the decision graph itself. However, as soon as particular decision areas begin to be excluded from the problem focus, they become potential candidates for the list of uncertainty areas of type UR.

Finally, it is often helpful, as in Figure 71, to include brief notes against all the various uncertainty areas on the list, referring to the mode or moment in the process where each of them first surfaced. The value of this can be appreciated by noticing that some of the marginal notes recorded against particular uncertainty areas on Figure 71 – though not all of them – can help in making reference back to earlier chapters which covered other stages in the development of the South Side story.

PUTTING UNCERTAINTY AREAS INTO A CLEARER DECISION PERSPECTIVE

Each uncertainty area on a working list, such as that of Figure 71, will have been recorded because at some moment in the process it appeared to have at least some relevance to the decision problems being addressed. However, the longer a list grows, the more it will usually become apparent that some of the uncertainty areas are more relevant than others – and that some of the less prominent ones might perhaps be set aside, or amalgamated with others to which they may seem closely related. So there will always be opportunities for the use of judgement and creativity in reformulating particular uncertainty areas, and in restructuring the overall list: opportunities of a similar kind to those already addressed in Chapter 5 in relation to the reformulation of decision areas.

Although a long and unstructured list of uncertainty areas can be tidied up at any time, where obvious opportunities for so doing can be seen, it is in practice usually worth saving any serious efforts towards restructuring until a moment arrives when there are pressures to explore preferences within a quite restricted working shortlist – perhaps a set of three or four promising schemes or, in many cases, only two promising alternatives – within which it is difficult to see where the overall balance of advantage ties.

The argument for leaving more detailed formulation and investigation of uncertainty areas until such a moment stems from the observation that in practice the relative prominence of different uncertainty areas can change quite dramatically as the decision perspective shifts. For example, some of the uncertainty areas listed in Chapter 3 (Figure 23) as relevant to the choice between Schemes A and B could well be overshadowed by others if some third scheme – such as Scheme E – were brought into the comparison as well. One way of picking out those uncertainty areas which are most relevant to a particular decision perspective is simply to use asterisks or some other symbol to pick out those in a longer list which are agreed to be the most important in that particular light. However, Figure 72 illustrates one alternative form of presentation, which is sometimes found useful because it reflects the emphasis on creative use of graphics in communications, which is characteristic of the strategic choice approach.

Figure 72 is an example of an *uncertainty graph*, in which the more relevant uncertainty areas are represented by labelled circles, using rather similar conventions to those of the decision graph. But there is an important difference, in that the positioning of uncertainty areas on the uncertainty graph is judged in relation to a particular decision perspective that has been selected in advance. In the centre of the graph is indicated the current focus of comparison, in this case the set of three schemes, A, B and E, which was selected in Figure 22. Different directions of movement outwards from this central focus then correspond to the three basic categories of uncertainty, UE, UV and UR, occupying broadly the same sectors of the graph as in the general introductory diagram of Figure 3. However, the graph leaves the boundaries between the three sectors undefined, so that any borderline cases can be plotted in intermediate positions. In addition, the more *relevant* uncertainty areas are positioned closest to the centre of the graph; these being the ones which are judged to bear most closely on the difficulty experienced in making choices among the particular alternatives currently in view. As an aid to this aspect of positioning, two or three concentric rings can be drawn around the centre of the graph. When working with wall charts and coloured pens, these rings are best drawn in an unobtrusive colour, such as yellow, so that they do not get in the way of the other, more specific, information which the graph is intended to convey.

Working from an unstructured list such as that of Figure 71, it is usually best to begin by scanning it to pick out the most relevant uncertainty areas first. These can then be positioned within the innermost ring, working methodically outwards to add others of lesser relevance. Another approach is to begin by placing on the graph those uncertainty areas that are best understood and use these as points of reference in positioning others. It is not usually necessary to overload an uncertainty graph by attempting to locate within it all uncertainty areas, however insignificant relative to others; and it is rarely in practice worth going beyond a set of eight or nine uncertainty areas

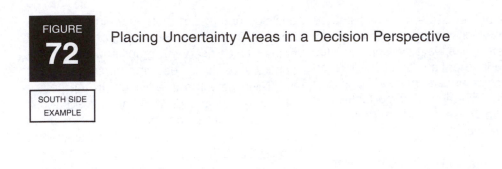

FIGURE
72

SOUTH SIDE
EXAMPLE

Placing Uncertainty Areas in a Decision Perspective

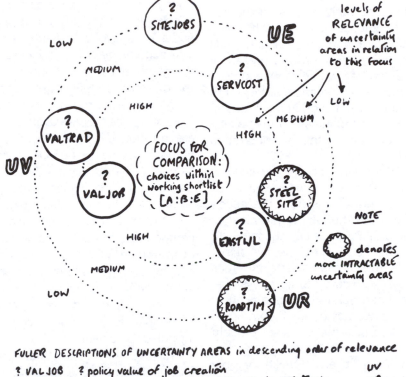

FULLER DESCRIPTIONS OF UNCERTAINTY AREAS in descending order of relevance

? VALJOB	? policy value of job creation	UV
? EASTWL	? Eastwell District shopping complex: scale and timing	UR
? SERVCOST	? servicing cost per ha. for development on central site	UE
? STEELSITE	? steel corporation decision on future use of steelworks site	UR (UE?)
? VALTRAD	? policy value of meeting traders' demands	UV
? SITEJOBS	? attractiveness of central site to employment-intensive firms	UE
? ROADTIM	? timing of construction of new road	UR

CHOOSING

SKILLS

This kind of radial uncertainty graph offers a useful way of putting the more important uncertainty areas into a decision perspective, and bringing together judgements about type, relevance and tractability. It is usual to start by plotting the more clearly understood uncertainty areas, and position others with reference to these, reassessing the first few when this process is complete.

which are judged to be of particular relevance in relation to the current focus of comparison. Although the classification of uncertainty areas as UE, UV or UR may have been noted on the original working list, the act of plotting them on the uncertainty graph can provide a useful opportunity for second thoughts and for further debate on any doubtful cases. Usually, at least some of the more relevant uncertainty areas will have come to the fore in the comparing of particular schemes, for example, the three uncertainty areas ?VALJOB, ?SITEJOBS and ?STEELSITE all emerged from the original comparison of Schemes A and B in Chapter 3 (Figure 23). However, other uncertainty areas may have surfaced while comparing other pairs of alternatives, or even in the work of the shaping and designing modes – for instance one or two of them might reflect doubts as to whether particular options should be considered feasible or whether particular options bars should be assumed.

Various additional kinds of information can be added to the basic information conveyed by an uncertainty graph about the type and relevance of different uncertainty areas. But too much elaboration can confuse rather than inform; so the only additional information introduced in Figure 72 is the use of a serrated ring to pick out particular uncertainty areas which are judged to be more *intractable* than others. The message is that there is thought to be very little that could be done to reduce the current state of doubt in each such uncertainty area, whereas in the case of other uncertainty areas it is possible to conceive of at least some form of exploratory action whereby current feelings of uncertainty might be reduced. In the case of these more tractable uncertainty areas, any decision to carry out this exploratory action will then have the intended effect of pushing that uncertainty area some distance further outwards from the centre of the graph; however, in the case of a more intractable uncertainty area, this possibility either does not exist, or is assumed to be realisable only at an unacceptable cost.

RESTRUCTURING COMPOSITE UNCERTAINTY AREAS

Once attention has been focused on a few of the most relevant uncertainty areas – whether through use of an uncertainty graph or simply through picking out the most important uncertainty areas on a list – it is only to be expected that doubts will begin to arise as to whether they have been formulated clearly enough. In some cases, closer investigation will suggest that a particular uncertainty area is composite in form, and could with advantage be broken down into two or more separate elements for which different kinds of exploratory action would be appropriate. Some of these elements might then be found to be more relevant than others to the present focus of comparison; furthermore, the elements might occupy quite different parts of the uncertainty graph in terms of the UE/UV/UR classification. Therefore, the reformulation of composite uncertainty areas in terms of their more significant elements can sometimes lead to quite a radical restructuring of the content of the uncertainty graph, and a reappraisal of the picture of opportunities for managing uncertainty which it conveys.

It is possible to explore such possibilities for restructuring uncertainty areas by working directly from the uncertainty graph. But the graph itself can become overloaded and confused if too much information of this kind is added. Figure 73 illustrates a way in which the elements of composite uncertainty areas can be explored on a separate sheet, with a view to possibly modifying the graph at a later stage. The first example of a composite uncertainty area relates to the policy value of job creation; this is an uncertainty area occupying quite a central position on the graph of Figure 72, which was classified as of type UV. In Figure 73, this value uncertainty is broken down into two different value elements, one of them relating to the general priority given by the municipal council to job creation as against other policy aims; and the other relating to the more specific question of whether there is

FIGURE
73

SOUTH SIDE
EXAMPLE

Reformulating Composite Uncertainty Areas

UNCERTAINTY AREA - elements	TYPE	RELEVANCE to [A:B:E] focus	PROPOSED RESPONSE - exploratory options
? VALJOB ? policy value of job creation	UV	<u>HIGH</u>	<u>EXAMINE ELEMENTS</u>
? value of job creation v. other policy aims [as stated; higher; lower]	UV	LOW/MID	• examine no further
? whether to discriminate in favour of low income areas in creating jobs [yes; no]	UV	<u>MID/HIGH</u>	• label as ?JOBDISC - refer to policy committee - consult leaders
?EASTWL ? Eastwell shopping complex scale/timing	UR	<u>MID/HIGH</u>	<u>EXAMINE ELEMENTS</u>
? scale of Eastwell shopping [as in plan; larger; smaller]	UR	<u>MID/HIGH</u>	• label as ?EASTWLSC - full analysis - brief liaison
? timing of Eastwell shopping development [sooner; later]	UR/UE	LOW	• examine no further
?SERVCOST ? cost of servicing central site	UE	<u>MID/HIGH</u>	<u>EXAMINE ELEMENTS</u>
? additional buffer zone in ha. if HOUS [3;5;7] *	UE	VERY LOW	• examine no further
? unit servicing cost in k/ha if IND [12;15;18] *	UE/UV	<u>MID</u>	EXAMINE ELEMENTS FURTHER
? geological /soil factors	UE	LOW/MID	• examine no further
? policy on range of services	UV	MID	• intractable: no action

* SENSITIVITY ANALYSIS : refer to Figure 62 for basic calculations

- additional buffer zone in ha [3;5;7] → | cost of site servicing | → [266;250;234] ±6%
- unit servicing cost in k/ha [12;15;18] → | difference IND + HOU | → [160;250;340] ±36%

CHOOSING

SKILLS

This splitting down of composite uncertainty areas into more specific elements is often carried out directly on the uncertainty graph, reassessing type and relevance in the process. Judgements about the relevance of different elements can be seen as a type of informal sensitivity analysis, and the more explicit form of sensitivity analysis illustrated here is used comparatively rarely.

to be discrimination in favour of economically deprived neighbourhoods, such as South Side, in the attraction of new jobs to different parts of the municipal area. The meaning of each element is made more explicit in Figure 73 by spelling out, in parenthesis, a set of two or more alternative assumptions which can be regarded as representative of the current range of doubt. Such a set of alternative assumptions is exactly analogous to the set of options used to represent the range of choice within a decision area; indeed, within an uncertainty area, similar problems of how best to represent a complex or open-ended range of possibilities may sometimes have to be faced.

In this instance, it is possible that the participants will be experiencing doubts over whether the general priority attached by members of the municipal council to job creation has shifted upwards or downwards since its last written policy statement on this issue was agreed. But it may be judged that this element of uncertainty is not so important as the element of uncertainty relating to positive discrimination is in favour of particular localities, about which there might recently have been much political controversy. Therefore, Figure 73 shows the latter element rated as of medium-to-high relevance and so worth subjecting to further scrutiny straight away; while the former – rated as of only low-to-medium relevance – can perhaps be set aside for the time being. The latter element is assigned a brief label – ?JOBDISC – with a view to this replacing the composite uncertainty area ?VALJOB on the uncertainty graph. As a further step in analysing this more carefully defined uncertainty area, a note is made of the kinds of exploratory option which could be considered to reduce its relevance further. In this example, it is indicated that two alternative levels of policy soundings might be considered as possible exploratory options – the first of them more formal and the second comparatively quick and informal.

Turning to the second of the uncertainty areas in Figure 73 – labelled ?EASTWL – its original description in terms of 'scale and timing'

of the proposed Eastwell shopping complex indicates that it also is composite in form. It is supposed here that further discussion of its content leads to the judgement that it is uncertainty over scale which is much the more prominent element. In the case of ?SERVCOST, it is supposed in Figure 73 that the analysis of elements can be taken further with the help of some more explicit sensitivity analysis, of a kind that only becomes possible in circumstances where assessments can be made on the basis of well-defined sequences of calculations or logical steps.

The particular procedure of sensitivity analysis used in Figure 73 can be appreciated more fully by referring back to Figure 62. This indicated a sequence of operations involved in estimating the costs of providing site services for either industrial or housing development. Some of these steps involved calculations of a straightforward arithmetical kind, but others depended on expert judgements – and the logical structure of these will often be much less transparent.

In the particular example of sensitivity analysis included in Figure 73, it has been supposed that it is the cost of servicing the site for industrial use rather than housing use which is the source of most of the uncertainty; and the relative contributions to this uncertainty of two contributory elements are explored. The difference in usable site area for the two alternative uses was estimated as 0.5 ha (Figure 62) – the difference between 2.5 ha for housing and 3.0 ha for industry. In Figure 73 it is supposed that the range of uncertainty over this estimate has been assessed, through a process of surprise limit analysis, as extending from a minimum of 0.3 ha to a maximum of 0.7 ha. In the same way, a range from 10 to 20 k/ha has been assessed for the cost per hectare of servicing the site for industry (see Figure 63); the equivalent cost of servicing for housing being taken as a more predictable 8 k/ha.

Repeating the sequence of calculations in Figure 62 with the minimum and maximum figures substituted for the original estimates, first

FIGURE
74

SOUTH SIDE
EXAMPLE

Comparing Alternative Responses to Uncertainty

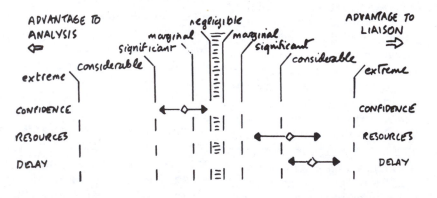

UNCERTAINTY AREA	EXPLORATORY OPTION	COMPARISON AREA	RELATIVE ASSESSMENT
?EASTWLSC (Scale of Easterly shopping complex) — as in plan — larger — smaller	—ANALYSIS (systematic analysis of alternative shopping configurations for Eastern sector of municipal area)	CONFIDENCE : RESOURCES : DELAY :	more confidence in judging balance of advantage E:B / extensive survey & analysis work (c. 100 planner days) / 4 months
	—LIAISON (brief exploratory discussions with leading staff of shops planning team)	CONFIDENCE : RESOURCES : DELAY :	somewhat more confidence in judging advantage E:B / a few hours discussion / 1-2 weeks to arrange meeting

ADVANTAGE COMPARISON [LIAISON vs ANALYSIS]

ADVANTAGE TO ANALYSIS ⇐   negligible   ADVANTAGE TO LIAISON ⇒

marginal / significant / considerable / extreme   marginal / significant / considerable / extreme

CONFIDENCE
RESOURCES
DELAY

It is only in the case of highly relevant and relatively intractable uncertainty areas that it is likely to be worth comparing different exploratory options in as much depth as illustrated here. Nevertheless, the general principles apply to any judgement about alternative responses to uncertainty, including judgements about whether to take no current action but prepare contingency plans.

for the loss of site area and then for the servicing cost per hectare, Figure 73 shows that the former element causes very little variation in the estimated servicing cost for the site, while the latter element contributes considerably more.[2]

In pursuing this example further, it will be noted (from Figure 62) that this estimated site servicing cost per hectare can itself be broken down into four more specific elements of assumption – some expressed in numerical form and others not. So the process of breaking down elements of uncertainty can, in this case, be extended further. In Figure 73 this point is illustrated by indicating the two more important sub-elements of the uncertainty over industrial site servicing cost – the more significant of them in this case being of an intractable policy nature. This illustrates the general point that analysis of elements within an uncertainty area can lead to a revision of views about its classification within the UE/UV/UR framework.

ASSESSING EXPLORATORY OPTIONS WITHIN CRITICAL UNCERTAINTY AREAS

Once attention has been focused on a few crucial uncertainty areas, attention can be turned to the question of what might be done about them. This involves examining more closely any exploratory options that are seen as realistic – whether they have already been identified or whether they only come to mind at this stage – and weighing up what the consequences of following these exploratory options might be.

In Chapter 3, one approach was illustrated (Figure 24) by which the implications of following any particular exploratory option could be

compared with the consequences of not pursuing it. In this, the three comparison areas of *confidence*, *resources* and *decision delay* were used to represent the three most important dimensions of evaluation that normally arise when making judgements about how uncertainty should be managed. In practice, it is only rarely that it is worth while evaluating exploratory options in this explicit way. But the principles involved are crucial to the management of uncertainty in strategic choice; so Figure 74 illustrates how the comparison of exploratory options can be taken a step further in relation to any especially critical uncertainty areas where this deeper level of analysis may be justified.

Because the proposed scale of the Eastwell district shopping complex has emerged as an especially relevant uncertainty area (Figure 74), the implications of taking different exploratory actions in response are reviewed in Figure 74. The first exploratory option to be considered is that of undertaking a full and systematic analysis of alternative combinations of district and more local shopping centres in the broader eastern sector of the municipality that includes both Eastwell and South Side. But, in addition, a more modest exploratory option is also considered, which might go at least some way towards reducing the level of doubt within this same uncertainty area; this is the option of engaging in some informal liaison with leading members of a specialist team of planners which the municipality has set up to look at shopping provision within its overall administrative area. This second option may mean relying on the specialist team's own expert judgement of the consequences of adopting different shopping patterns, rather than on any more rigorous methods of survey and analysis. Nevertheless, it could be well worth considering as a more modest – but possibly more effective – way of reducing the level of doubt in this same uncertainty area.

Figure 74 records the judgement that the first exploratory option – labelled ANALYSIS – is expected to lead to more confidence in judging the overall balance of advantage

---

2 This is a contrast which can be quantified if statistical methods are used to calculate – on conventional assumptions of independence and normal distributional form – that the latter element explains some 97% of the combined variance.

between Schemes E and B – this pair comparison being a more appropriate one to consider than A:B within the working shortlist (A:B:E) because A and B do not differ in terms of options within the SHOP LOC'N? decision area. But the more modest LIAISON option is also judged likely to lead to 'somewhat' more confidence in relation to the same pair comparison – and to do so at considerably less cost in terms of both demands on resources and decision delay. The call on resources for the ANALYSIS option is here assessed in terms of a rough estimate of the number of planner days required – although of course it could have other dimensions such as the use of computer time and the cost of origination of data, possibly involving the recruitment of interviewers through agency or other channels.

To weigh up whether it is likely to be worth pursuing the full ANALYSIS option as against the more modest LIAISON option, it becomes essential to take the urgencies and resource pressures of the current decision situation into account. In practice, this will usually be done intuitively. But intuitive appreciations of urgency may differ from one participant to another; so it can sometimes be a useful aid to communication, in the case of especially critical uncertainty areas, to introduce an advantage comparison framework as an aid to this kind of judgement. This possibility is demonstrated in the lower part of Figure 74.

In this case, the advantage comparison indicates a view that the additional gain in confidence from adopting the ANALYSIS rather than the simpler LIAISON response to the uncertainty about the scale of the Eastwell shopping centre should be placed in the marginal-to-significant range. Yet Figure 74 shows that this benefit is likely to be outweighed by the considerable additional investment of resources required, along with the even more serious implications – in this particular decision situation – of a four-month delay before the decision in question can be made. This example merely makes explicit the kind of judgements that are being made all the time in an intuitive way, when people have to decide

how far to invest in any kind of exploratory action to improve the confidence with which important choices can be made.

This particular example concerns an uncertainty area of type UR; but the judgement of whether or not to invest in exploratory action can be expressed in a similar way whether an uncertainty area of type UE, UV or UR is involved – as was indeed demonstrated earlier in Chapter 3 (Figure 24). Quick and informed judgements of this kind can be debated with reference to the comparative information about the relevance of different uncertainty areas which is contained in an uncertainty graph such as that of Figure 72. As a general rule, it is rarely worth making major investments in exploratory action directed towards uncertainty areas of lower relevance, so long as uncertainty areas of higher relevance remain.

RELATING EXPLORATORY ACTIONS TO THE TIMING OF DECISIONS

As was discussed in Chapter 3, the consideration of what to do about particular uncertainty areas can bring concerns about the *timing* of choices in different decision areas directly to the fore. For any exploratory action invariably takes some time to carry through – whether this be measured in minutes, hours, days, weeks, months or even years – arid can thus imply delays of a more or less serious extent in the taking of those decisions they are designed to inform.

The opportunities for taking immediate actions in some decision areas while deferring choice in others were approached in Chapter 3 through the core concept of the *action scheme*, chosen to cover some but not necessarily all of the decision areas within a problem focus. An example was then presented (Figure 25) of how action schemes could be compared in terms of the relative *flexibility* of choice left open, and various possible approaches to the comparison of flexibility were discussed in Chapter 7.

There are, therefore, two types of timing judgement which have to be considered in practice. On the one hand there is the judgement of how far to invest in pursuing exploratory actions which imply delays in at least some decision areas; on the other hand there is the judgement of how far to make commitments to action in some decision areas in advance of others. This means that any consideration of the time dimension can make the structure of interconnected choices for participants more subtle and complex; indeed, this is a reality that has to be faced whether or not the concepts of strategic choice are being applied in an explicit way.

In dealing with these choices, a useful guideline is to focus first on any decision areas where considerations of both urgency and uncertainty arise. This is illustrated in Figure 75, which takes as its point of departure the set of nine possible decision schemes first developed in Chapter 2 (Figure 17) for the four decision areas in the original South Side problem focus. In Figure 75, these schemes are arranged (as in Figure 25) with the two more urgent decision areas – ROAD LINE? And DIST LIFE? – brought to the fore; then, focusing more closely on the comparison of schemes within the more limited working shortlist of A, B and E, Figure 75 identifies the points of greatest difficulty in the decision process, by means of question marks positioned at the relevant branching points of the tree.

It can now be seen that the DIST LIFE? decision area is the more urgent of the two decision areas in which there are differences between the shortlisted schemes A, B and E; and it has already been discovered (Figure 74) that the ?EASTWLSC uncertainty area has an important bearing on the choice of routes at this branch point of the tree. So it could be especially important to explore how to deal with this particular uncertainty area if the urgencies of the problem situation are to be addressed. So, in the second picture of Figure 75, the first part of the option tree is shown expanded to introduce, as additional branching points, a choice of two exploratory options

within the ?EASTWLSC uncertainty area. The first is the 'null option' of taking no exploratory action at all, and the second is the quick option of a brief liaison exercise with the shops planning team – it being here supposed that the more costly and time-consuming option of fuller analysis has been ruled out after the kind of advantage comparison exercise illustrated earlier (Figure 74).

In Figure 75, the assumption is made that the DIST LIFE? decision should definitely be *deferred* if the LIAISON exploratory option is to be followed through. It is also supposed there may possibly be an argument for deferring choice of DIST LIFE?, as an alternative to early commitment to any specific option, if it is decided to take the 'no explorations' route. For such a deferement could make sense if there were any likelihood that some event might occur which could clarify the choice within DIST LIFE? without any explicit exploratory action being taken. For example, it might be known that there was a meeting of a South Side community forum scheduled in a week's time to debate this very issue.

The introduction of an option to defer choice within the DIST LIFE? decision area has the effect of subtly altering the meaning of that decision area; for it now represents a choice as to what should be done *now* about the life of the district, rather than what should be done in any more timeless sense. However, the main point about the expanded option tree in Figure 75 is that it displays five possible combinations of current choices and exploratory options that can be compared with each other as a basis for incremental progress; and these five paths can quickly be compared in terms of how many of the nine decision schemes remain available in each case. In Figure 75, the schemes remaining open are listed for each path, drawing attention in particular to the availability of the three shortlisted Schemes A, B and E.

In general, this analysis indicates that those courses of action involving immediate commitment in the DIST LIFE? decision area carry a

FIGURE

75

SOUTH SIDE
EXAMPLE

Weighing Uncertainty against Urgency in Decision-Making

CHOOSING

SKILLS

In considering how far to defer decisions in strategic choice, it is useful to focus on any decision areas which may be urgent yet subject to major uncertainties which could be reduced through exploratory action. The judgement of whether to decide now or defer while explorations are carried through is usually made informally in constructing a commitment package, but the principle is as illustrated here.

risk of subsequent *regret*, through the fore-closing of particular decision schemes which might have been found to be advantageous had the explorations been followed through. For example, commitment now to a 40-year life for South Side might lead to regret if the work of planning team of the specialist shops were to result in a proposal for a particular sector-wide shopping pattern which made it uneconomic to develop a new South Side local shopping centre on the King Square site; while commitment now to a 10-year life might lead to regret if geological difficulties on the central site were later found to be so severe that no uses other than open space could realistically be considered there.

In general, the choice of whether to opt for commitment or deferment in an urgent decision area involves some process, however intuitive, of weighing the risks of early commitment against the negative consequences of delay – including any political or professional penalties that might be incurred. In the particular circumstances of Figure 75, the deferment being considered is only a couple of weeks, so might well be considered worth while; unless, perhaps, there were an imminent meeting of the municipal council, or a closely fought local election, to introduce an added note of urgency over the commitment to district life, even within this otherwise insignificant time scale.

ACCOMMODATING UNCERTAINTY BY PREPARING FOR ALTERNATIVE CONTINGENCIES

Various approaches have now been discussed to the comparison of alternative courses of immediate action, in terms of the flexibility of future choice which they allow. At the simplest level, an intuitive judgement can be made that one alternative is likely to leave open more opportunities for future choice than another, without any analysis of what these opportunities are.[3] At another level, the patterns of future

choice left open can be analysed and presented for visual comparison, or the comparison can be simplified by introducing some form of robustness index (Figure 25).

However, it is possible to go further in circumstances where there has been some analysis of the relative importance of different uncertainty areas, and where some attempt has been made to represent the more important of these in terms of the range of alternative assumptions that could be held. Where this is so, then it is possible to bring those alternative assumptions more directly into the comparison of current actions, and to explore how far some such actions could have advantages over others in their capacity to respond to particular eventualities that could arise. One way of taking the analysis in this direction is illustrated in Figure 76. In Figure 76, two alternative action schemes for South Side are compared, each of which involves commitment to the northern road line and also to a particular option in the DIST LIFE? decision area. Referring to Figure 75, each such course implies that no exploratory action is being taken in relation to the important ?EASTWLSC uncertainty area. So the feelings of uncertainty over the scale of the proposed Eastwell shopping complex remains unchanged; and this uncertainty area has already been represented in terms of a choice of three possible assumptions labelled AS IN PLAN, LARGER and SMALLER (Figure 76).

According to which of these assumptions is held, either the feasibility or the relative attractiveness of different courses of future action may be affected. In Figure 76, the judgement is made that the uncertainty about the scale for the Eastwell shopping complex is of such direct relevance to the choice of shopping location for South Side, that the King Square development must be ruled out on grounds of economic viability if the Eastwell complex is to be significantly larger than proposed in the current plan. Turning to the second of the action schemes in Figure 76 – Action Scheme III – this appears to allow no alternative to the King Square site; but it does afford protection

---

3 This was the kind of approach adopted when 'flexibility' was introduced as an additional comparison area in Figure 64.

FIGURE
76

SOUTH SIDE
EXAMPLE

Accommodating Uncertainty in the Future Decision Space

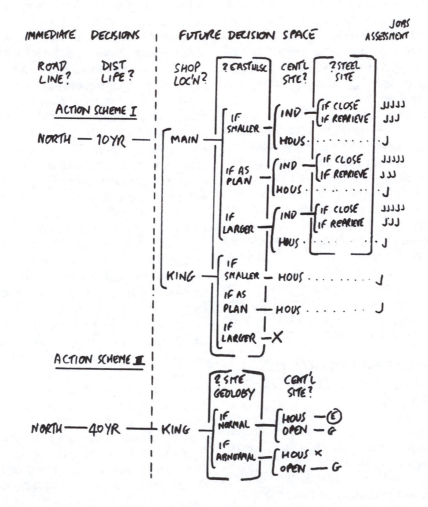

Uncertainty areas in which the choice of assumptions can have a critical effect on the choice of path through a tree may become an important focus for contingency planning. This consideration is usually introduced only when attention is turned to the design of a commitment package, but the extension of the tree to show contingencies as extra branching points can be a useful aid to communication.

against another contingency – the perhaps remote contingency of abnormal geological conditions being discovered on the central site, precluding the possibility of any use except that of open space.

However, another point in favour of Action Scheme I is that it leaves open the option of industrial use on the central site; provided geological conditions make this option feasible, Figure 76 shows that its attractiveness as a means of creating alternative local jobs could be enhanced, should the contingency of early closure of the steelworks arise. So, the consideration of flexibility to accommodate different kinds of uncertainty can become more complex, the more contingencies are explored. Sometimes this kind of analysis can lead towards a searching re-examination of earlier assumptions. For example, the assumption that there is no possibility of using the central site for open space if a 10-year district life were chosen might now seem a rather unnecessary constraint. Referring back to the structure of the problem as reflected in the option graph (Figure 16), the reasoning behind this particular option bar could well now be challenged. The result could be an agreement that the option bar was no longer necessary, so removing an apparent advantage towards Action Scheme III on grounds of capacity to accommodate geological uncertainty.

Once the possibility is considered of introducing some of the more crucial uncertainty areas into the structure of possible paths through the problem situation, as illustrated in Figure 76, then it becomes possible to move in a number of different directions of further analysis, depending on whether these crucial uncertainty areas are of type UE, UV or UR. In the case of a UE-type uncertainty area – such as that over geological conditions in South Side – it may be important to ask whether the contingencies reflected in the alternative assumptions are of high or low probability: and questions then arise of how far it is worth safeguarding or insuring against specific risks. If these questions are of sufficient importance, then the analysis can be taken in the direction of the classical form of *decision analysis* in which numerical probabilities are assigned to different contingencies treated as alternate branching points in a decision tree.[4]

Any important uncertainty areas of type UV can, if desired, be absorbed into the analysis of decision areas expressed at a broader policy level – and such a step will open up the possibility of introducing the methods already illustrated for analysing relationships between *levels* of choice (Figure 54). Again, any crucial uncertainty areas of type UR can be absorbed into the problem structure as additional decision areas, thus in effect extending the problem focus. However, where these new decision areas relate to choices which are entirely or partially under the control of other parties – and, where there are elements of conflict or competition in relationships with those other parties – then the decision situation may have to be considered as more like one of a *game* in which moves, counter-moves and points of potential stability might have to be explored: 'If they did this, we could retaliate by doing that'. This points to another direction of analysis, based on the ideas about the management of conflict and collaboration discussed by authors such as Howard (1989) and Bennett, Cropper and Huxham (1989).

MOVING TOWARDS THE DESIGN OF POSSIBLE COMMITMENT PACKAGES

This chapter has, so far, covered various kinds of judgement which are relevant to the design of a commitment package, conceived as a proposed incremental step towards commitment through time. The four basic sections of a commitment package were first illustrated in Figure 26: a set of immediate decisions covering both *actions* and *explorations* to reduce

---

4 See, for example, Raiffa, 1968.

FIGURE

77

SOUTH SIDE
EXAMPLE

Building an Appropriate Commitment Package

COMMITMENT PACKAGE IA
- based on <u>SHORT-TERM PUBLIC</u> investment policy

	IMMEDIATE DECISIONS		FUTURE DECISION SPACE	
	ACTIONS	EXPLORATIONS	DEFERRED CHOICES	CONTINGENCY PLANNING
SOUTH SIDE local planning	DISTRICT LIFE ✱ - commitment now to 10 YEAR LIFE			IF a major developer can be attracted THEN consider extended life 1
	SHOP LOCATION ✱ - no action	- leaders to arrange discussions with local traders	IN 6 MONTHS - decide Main St. OR King Square	IF scale of Eastwell complex, increased, THEN reject King Sq. 2
	CENTRAL SITE ✱ - no action	- commission quick geological survey	IN 6 MONTHS - decide industry OR housing IF Main Street shops stay (C2)	3
	WEST STREET - no action	- initiate design and costing studies	IN 12 MONTHS - decide whether to improve West St.	4
TRANSPORT	ROAD LINE ✱ - recommend NORTH route through South Side			IF north route rejected, THEN appeal 5
	MAIN STREET - no action		WHEN road is in firm programme, THEN consider closing street	IF new road not to be built in next 5 years, THEN extend parking 6
ECONOMIC DEVELOPMENT		ask M.E.O. to approach steel corporation to discuss joint jobs initiative		7

A   B   C   D

✱ identifies main set of interconnected decisions

SUMMARY OF COMPARISON with alternative package IIIA (LONG-TERM PUBLIC INVESTMENT)

CAPITAL: IA to cost 100k-300k LESS than IIIA
INCOME: IA likely to generate marginally LESS income
RESIDENTS: IA offers BETTER outlook
JOBS: LITTLE DIFFERENCE if B7 successful
FLEXIBILITY: IA preserves options in shop location

CHOOSING

SKILLS

The basic framework of a commitment package offers a framework for discussion in considering how to act which can be extended in a number of different ways, according to context. When working with large sheets of paper it is useful to add marginal notes against immediate decisions specifying agreed organisational responsibilities, resource commitments and deadlines.

uncertainty; then a set of proposed arrangements for *deferred choices* and *contingency planning* within a future decision space. In any setting where decisions call for formal commitment of organisational resources, there will be moments when it is important to give careful attention to the design of *alternative* commitment packages. Yet it is important to emphasise that at other times, when there is a desire to move ahead informally, or to respond to particular urgencies of the moment, a commitment package may be much more skeletal in its content, and will not necessarily be recorded in written form.

In practice, important points of judgement can arise not only in developing the content of a commitment package, but also in judging the *format* in which it should be presented. This applies in particular to the rows as opposed to the columns of the framework. In the simple example presented in Chapter 3 (Figure 26), the problem structure was brought out by designating a separate row for each decision area. This presented no difficulty in that particular case, because each of the exploratory actions proposed to address uncertainty could be directly linked to a particular area of deferred choice. In practice, however, the number of decision areas to be brought together within the compass of a commitment package can sometimes be larger, and the relationships between explorations and deferred choices less straightforward. In these circumstances, it can be more practicable to group two or more decision areas together in the same row, perhaps relating to some designated sphere of responsibility. This way of presenting a commitment package is illustrated in Figure 77.

This example of a commitment package presents one coherent set of proposals which is, in effect, an expanded version of the first of the two alternative action schemes compared in Figure 76. The rows of the framework are organised into three broad spheres of responsibility, concerned respectively with local South Side matters, with transport issues and with economic development in the

municipality as a whole. Only the first of these is within the direct sphere of responsibility of the South Side Working Party; and even then there may be procedures of formal authorisation or endorsement of proposals to be followed, requiring some consideration of contingency planning if any recommendations should be rejected or opposed. In the transport and economic development spheres, all the working party may be able to do is to make representations to other parties, and to use whatever influence or leverage they can exert to follow those representations through – perhaps again with some thought to possible contingency actions, should the proposed representations or negotiations fail.

In Figure 77, asterisks are used to indicate the principal set of interconnected decision areas around which the commitment package has been built, as a reminder that it may be difficult to consider changing course in any one of these, without considering what implications there might be for the others. However, there may be more scope for considering variations in other elements of the package; and the number of elements shown in this particular illustration, though quite large, is only a limited selection from those that could have been included if all the decision areas and uncertainty areas discussed in the course of the last few chapters were to be included. For example, extra spheres of housing or financial responsibility could have been included to reflect these other organisational interests in the South Side problem (Figure 41). Various other decision areas from this wider decision graph might then have been considered, in the shaping of either proposed actions or deferred choices. Further kinds of technical exploration could also have been suggested. For example, explorations could have been proposed into the feasibility of doubtful options, such as the possibility (examined in Figure 48) of combining some industrial with some housing development of the central site. Further explorations into policy values might also perhaps have been recommended: for example,

FIGURE
78

SOUTH SIDE
EXAMPLE

Helping Decision-Takers to Make Progress

Meeting of Policy Committee, 10 June 1986

DOCUMENT 7 : Interim Report of South Side Working Party

ALTERNATIVES

The two most urgent decisions in South Side concern the alignment of the new arterial ROAD through the area and its continued LIFE as a residential neighbourhood. It is now clear that the balance of advantage lies with the northern road line; but the commitment to continued life of the district could range from the 10 years already pledged to a significantly longer horizon of around 40 years.   The following alternatives have been examined in depth:

–a SHORTER TERM INVESTMENT HORIZON (committed life 10 years) would allow options of either consolidating the local shopping centre on Main Street or moving it to King Square. In either case the now vacant central site could be developed for housing – but industrial development would be an alternative were the shops to remain on Main Street;

–a LONGER TERM INVESTMENT HORIZON (committed life 40 years) would mean relocating the local shops in King Square, with the central site used for either housing or open space.

THE SHORTER TERM HORIZON offers advantages in terms of flexibility and response to the concerns expressed by residents, as well as in terms of nett expenditure by this authority. The following RECOMMENDATIONS are therefore put forward at this stage:

RECOMMENDED IMMEDIATE ACTIONS

(1) A case be formally submitted to the Transport Authority for adoption of the NORTHERN ROAD LINE (see accompanying map);

(2) A renewal of the pledge to residents of a 10–YEAR period before further housing demolition, with public investment in environmental improvements geared accordingly.

LATER DECISIONS

(3) A decision on the location of the LOCAL SHOPPING CENTRE be taken in 6 MONTHS, after consultation with local traders and consideration of the impending proposals of the shops planning team on the scale of the new Eastwell shopping complex;

(4) The use of the now vacant CENTRAL SITE also to be decided in six months, in conjunction with (3) above.

CONTINGENCY PLANNING

It is just possible that the recommendation of the northern road line will be rejected by the Transport Authority; in which case a formal APPEAL is recommended, backed by evidence from the working party's analysis to date.

It is also possible that a major private developer may be attracted to South Side at some time; in which case, an EXTENSION to the life of the district can be considered.

FURTHER EXPLORATIONS

Because there still remain some important areas of uncertainty affecting future decisions in South Side, the working party proposes to continue carrying through a programme of explorations and consultations with other bodies. Priorities for further work will be outlined verbally at the meeting.

CHOOSING

SKILLS

With ingenuity, it is often possible to present action proposals to decision-takers in forms which do not appear to deviate significantly from familiar forms of report, yet which reflect the underlying structure of a strategic choice analysis, as in this illustration. Use of diagrams should be viewed with caution and contingency plans may not be indicated explicitly where sensitive negotiations may arise.

into the issue of discrimination in job creation in favour of low-income neighbourhoods.

So, however broad in scope it might appear, any commitment package is designed to be *selective* rather than comprehensive in its content, reflecting the various resource constraints, urgencies and priorities of the specific decision setting within which it is shaped. For it is intended as an incremental step in a continuing process of commitment, rather than as a conclusive response to the full range of problems that has been identified. Even so, there are many additional subtleties that can be introduced informally into a decision process while a commitment package is being designed, extending its scope beyond that of the analysis as so far pursued. For example, Figure 77 introduces for the first time the possibility that the uncertainty about the steelworks closure might not be so immune to municipal influence as earlier assumed, once the idea of a joint initiative to attract small business enterprises to the site has been conceived.

So, within the commitment package framework, a considerable amount of richness and complexity can be encompassed, even where a conscious effort is made to present its content in a form which is intelligible to people who may not have been involved in the analytical work which has gone into its presentation. Cross-referencing between elements in the package itself can be indicated by discreet annotations; in Figure 77, for example, row and column codes are used – sparingly – for cross-reference both within the commitment package and also in the brief statement of comparative information which appears below. The intention is that the format selected for the commitment package should offer a basis for structured debate about choices and assumptions; for closer comparison of alternatives, either within particular elements or on a broader scale; for modification to reflect new insights or representations; and – when the moment is ripe – for progress through commitment to decisive actions.

HELPING DECISION-TAKERS TO CHOOSE

Even a carefully organised and selective commitment package such as that of Figure 77 can present an overload of information for those decision-takers who may be called upon to authorise decisive actions. This problem of potential overload is of course not specific to the strategic choice approach; it applies equally to any form of decision technology, wherever actions have to be endorsed by busy people with multiple roles and responsibilities, who may not have the time to keep themselves closely acquainted with the progress of any analytical work.

However, if decision-takers are to exercise their right to choose *responsibly* in other than a token and ritualistic way, it can sometimes be important that they be presented with more than one commitment package from which to choose. Judgements must then be made about how many alternative packages should be presented, how much back-up information should be offered in support; and what the balance should be between different forms of communication – text, graphics, numerical tabulations, verbal presentation – as opposed to documents circulated in advance. These are judgements which will depend on the particular decision context, and the way in which its opportunities and constraints are understood by those who carry the responsibility of presenting proposals to decision-takers.

Figure 78 gives one example of the way in which the members of the South Side Working Party might decide to present their initial recommendations to the policy committee to which they report. It is here assumed that the latter group, with many pressures on its agenda, is accustomed to acting mainly on the basis of written documentation of a condensed summary form – backed up, if need be, by fuller information introduced in the course of discussion.

Figure 78 therefore takes the form of a one-page summary report, presented in fairly conventional written form, offering guidelines which can be followed, questioned or challenged at the discretion of the decision-takers – in this case, the members of the municipal policy committee, meeting as a group with the authority to commit resources to whatever course of action they may agree. To keep the report brief and readable, it is restricted in its focus to two main alternatives expressed in terms of contrasting policy orientations – one of these being a condensed version of the commitment package of Figure 77, and the other a contrasting package based on a 40-year horizon for the life of South Side as a residential area. In the interests of brevity, all but the most crucial characteristics of the two packages are omitted from the report; for the main aim of the summary is to indicate what are the main differences in structure between the two.

It is likely that the main structural assumptions behind the alternative proposals will have been put to quite stringent testing well before this reporting stage; but it is important that they should be checked again carefully before the report is finally submitted. For example, if there were any serious residual doubts as to whether the 40-year life might, after all, allow the Main Street shopping centre to be retained, or as to whether industry on the central site might, in some circumstances, be compatible with the King Square shopping location, then the whole structure and emphasis of the report could be subject to challenge. The proposals might then either have to be redesigned in their entirety – or at least revised to allow this element of uncertainty to be acknowledged and an appropriate response prepared.

In any case, it will be only prudent that the working party members should prepare themselves carefully for the sorts of debate that could conceivably develop at the meeting, on the basis of their prior knowledge of the responsibilities of committee members, their interests, their power relationships and the idiosyncrasies or prejudices of particular members. As a first step, they could be well advised to prepare more detailed descriptions of each of the alternative commitment packages – perhaps using wall charts or other visual aids to present a broad picture of actions, explorations and future choices of the kind illustrated in Figure 77. They might also agree to come to the meeting armed with this kind of picture not only for the two contrasting packages highlighted in the report, but also for a 'compromise' 20-year package, to demonstrate how marginal the differences were between this and the 40-year alternative. Indeed, they might agree that it was a good move to prepare a further commitment package based on the southern road line, to indicate how limited a future it offers to South Side and what a strong case the Council has in recommending the northern alternative to the transportation authority.

Knowing the political inclinations of the committee members – which might cover quite a broad spectrum – the working party members might also feel it was important to prepare carefully the case for an emphasis on public rather than private development, in terms of the constraints presented by the local situation in South Side. They might, however, anticipate that the first contingency planning element of the package in Figure 77 offers a possible basis for helping the committee to converge on an agreed compromise view. They might also anticipate some surprise from committee members that this package is thought to offer local residents better short-term economic prospects than one based on a longer-term investment horizon. The explanation could be that a longer-term commitment to the future of South Side was expected to lead to rising house prices followed by gradual disintegration of the existing deep-rooted community structure; so they might have to be prepared for some challenging debate in the committee about the subtle issues of policy values this could raise.

The example of a commitment package given in Figure 77 is of a form which assumes that the decision-takers to whom it is addressed have significant influence not only in the sphere of responsibility of the Working Party itself, but also in their relationships with others. But this may not always be the

case; and a decision situation involving negotiation between two or more autonomous or
semi-autonomous parties may call for a different approach – especially if the parties are
potentially in conflict, in which case it might not
be thought tactically wise that all elements of
the commitment package should be declared.
For example, if the working party did not feel
that the Council was in a position powerful
enough to ensure that its recommendation
of the northern road line would be accepted by
the transportation authority, then it might have
to rethink the whole commitment package in
terms of a more subtle negotiating stance.
To take another example, it might be thought
more tactful – and more likely to yield results –
if the idea of a joint small business initiative on
the steelworks site were seeded informally in
the mind of the Municipal Enterprise Officer,
rather than suddenly presented to him or her in
a background document during a formal committee meeting. So, the overt content of written proposals and background documents can
be as much a matter of choice as any other
aspect of the decision-making process.

To round off this particular episode in the
South Side story, it will be supposed that
some particular commitment package is accepted by the committee as a basis for action –
whether this be Package IA, as presented in
Figure 77; or some variant of it which has
attracted support in the course of discussions;
or possibly some quite different package, perhaps embodying a higher level of commitment;
or perhaps a lower level. For it is the committee
that has the final responsibility and authority to
decide.

Whatever the outcome of the meeting, the
use of strategic choice concepts and methods
does not mean that the problems of the South
Side community are now 'solved' in any final or
comprehensive way, any more than it is ever
realistic to expect in a case as complex as this.
But progress has been made; and it is progress
both in the direction of action and of learning.
For both the decision-takers and their advisers
should have gained valuable insights into not
only the problem but also the process; insights

which will help to lay foundations for more confident decisions when further chapters come
to be written in the continuing South Side
story.

In Chapter 10, an illustration will be presented of the way in which the format of the
commitment package has been adapted in
the design of computer software to support
the strategic choice approach. While the basic
grid format of Figures 26 and 77 is closely followed in the design of the software, the phrase
progress package is adopted in this context as
a generic description as opposed to the phrase
commitment package.

The aim of this is to encourage users to
develop alternative packages, which can be
stored in different data files, before proceeding
to the further step of adopting a preferred progress package as an agreed basis for action.
The STRAD software offers options of adopting any progress package either as a basis for
commitment, in a situation where those generating the package have sufficient authority
to do so, or as a basis for recommendation to
others, or as a strategic option to be compared
with other strategic options by those who carry
the primary responsibility to decide.

PROCESS JUDGEMENTS IN THE CHOOSING MODE

Of course, not every moment of commitment
in a continuous planning process need be
approached as formally or with as much preparation as this last episode in the South Side
story might suggest. Sometimes, a commitment package might contain no more than
a single action commitment on some aspect
of the problem under consideration; and this
action may fall within the personal sphere of
responsibility of a single decision-maker. Perhaps this action may be accompanied by a
decision to embark on some form of exploratory action to provide a clearer basis for other
choices that have been deferred. Perhaps too –
though not of necessity – that small step in

FIGURE
79

Process Choices when Working in the Choosing Mode

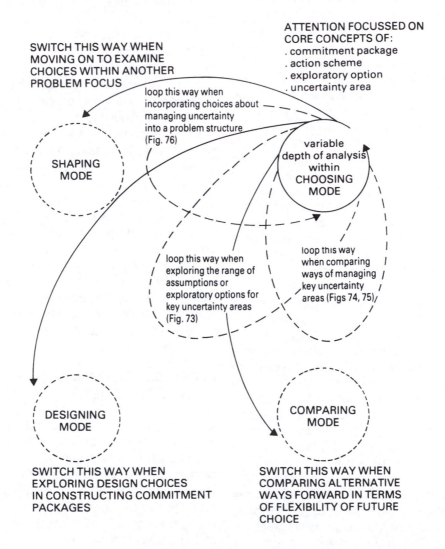

ATTENTION FOCUSSED ON
CORE CONCEPTS OF:
. commitment package
. action scheme
. exploratory option
. uncertainty area

SWITCH THIS WAY WHEN
MOVING ON TO EXAMINE
CHOICES WITHIN ANOTHER
PROBLEM FOCUS

loop this way when
incorporating choices about
managing uncertainty
into a problem structure
(Fig. 76)

SHAPING
MODE

variable
depth of analysis
within
CHOOSING
MODE

loop this way when
exploring the range of
assumptions or
exploratory options for
key uncertainty areas
(Fig. 73)

loop this way
when comparing
ways of managing
key uncertainty
areas (Figs 74, 75)

DESIGNING
MODE

COMPARING
MODE

SWITCH THIS WAY WHEN
EXPLORING DESIGN CHOICES
IN CONSTRUCTING COMMITMENT
PACKAGES

SWITCH THIS WAY WHEN
COMPARING ALTERNATIVE
WAYS FORWARD IN TERMS
OF FLEXIBILITY OF FUTURE
CHOICE

CHOOSING

SUMMARY

the process will include some agreed arrangements for the making of those other choices at a later time.

But the latest episode of the South Side story does illustrate some of the subtle considerations of dialogue between advisers and decision-takers that can arise whenever a more formal moment of commitment arrives. And the story has at least touched on some of the complexities that can arise where there is more than one authoritative decision-taking body, and where different parties may be continually pulling in conflicting directions. In these circumstances, progress may well depend on quite complex negotiations across organisational boundaries – raising issues which will be discussed further in the next two chapters.

This chapter has shown how the work of the choosing mode can draw on prior work in any or all of the other modes – shaping, designing and comparing – sometimes in a very subtle way. Also, as summarised in Figure 79, the work of the choosing mode itself presents many opportunities either for looping briefly in the direction of these other modes, or for switching more deliberately to work for some time in a different mode, if it is judged that the moment for making commitments has not yet arrived. In particular, once a commitment package is adopted as a basis for immediate decision, there will remain the deferred choices to be dealt with at some later time. When this time arrives, all the various opportunities for shaping, designing, comparing and choosing will arise once again – perhaps in different forms, influenced by events and reappraisals over the intervening period. For the process of strategic choice is above all a continuing one which cannot be isolated from the processes of change within the wider environment in which it is set. The content of Figure 79 will not be discussed in detail, as was the content of the equivalent figures at the end of the last three chapters. Rather, it is left as an exercise for the reader to reflect on the various switching and looping opportunities which it indicates. Indeed, the reader is encouraged to reflect on these not only in relation to the development of the South Side story in earlier actions, but also in relation to personal experience in choosing strategically in his or her own working life.

ILLUSTRATIONS FROM PRACTICE

This chapter again concludes with a set of three illustrations from practice selected to illustrate further points about the work of the choosing mode.

The first illustration shows how uncertainty areas can be mapped and sorted quickly and informally in a group setting. The second illustration shows the use of a commitment package framework in presenting the proposals from a national policy development project, showing the wide range of actions and explorations involved in putting them into effect. The third illustration shows how uncertainty areas were explored and a first trial commitment package was developed on flip charts in a workshop in Venezuela to explore options for response to a major flood disaster.

FIGURE
80

Illustrations from Practice – Choosing 1

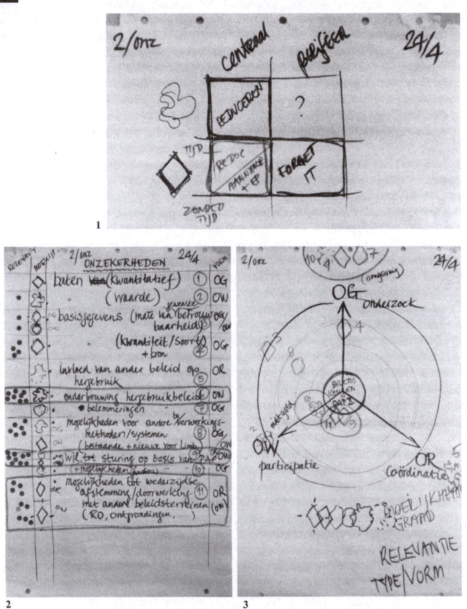

CHOOSING

PRACTICE

Theme: Putting Uncertainty Areas into Perspective through the Use of an Uncertainty Graph.
Project: Development of an Integrated Policy Framework for the Management of Solid Waste.
Context: Workshops with an Inter-Organisational Project Team, Province of Limburg, The Netherlands, 1986.

COMMENTARY ON FIGURE 80

These charts record work done by a project group at the end of the first day of a series of three two-day workshops, designed to get a more substantial planning project under way. The group consisted mainly of Provincial Government employees, and was charged with preparing a policy plan to integrate the management of different kinds of solid waste.

In the first instance, uncertainty areas were listed as they occurred to members of the group, drawing on their everyday experience and on understanding gained through earlier analysis (2). They ranged from the quite specific (quantity, type and source of solid waste) to the relatively general (basis for recycling policy). When this process slowed, the analysis proper was started, although the list was left open for additions if there were any.

Firstly, each uncertainty area was classified according to type, as can be seen down the right-hand side of the list ('OG' = UE in Dutch, 'OW' = UV, 'OR' = UR). As usually happens, a number of the uncertainty areas were seen as falling between categories and so given dual classifications.

The second stage of the analysis then identified views about the difficulty or otherwise of reducing uncertainty in the various areas. A pictorial distinction between 'diamonds' (hard to reduce) and 'jellies' (easy to reduce) was adopted as a starting point. As might be expected, this quickly developed into a more subtle range which is shown just below the uncertainty graph (3).

The third stage of the analysis involved assessment of relevance to the plan. For this, use was made of stickers. Each member of the group was given four stickers and asked to place them next to the four uncertainty areas which they considered most relevant to the policy plan. The results appear down the left-hand side of the list. The three boxed uncertainty areas emerged as more relevant than the others. They included the uncertainty over support for a policy of recycling; over level of commitment to making the plan work; and over possibilities for combining with other fields of policy.

All this information was then transferred to the uncertainty graph (3), which has as its centre the focus: 'Beleidskeuzen in PAP II' (policy choices in the second Provincial Waste Management Plan). This was further analysed in line with principles outlined by means of a simplified 2×2 taxonomy (1). As a result the decision was taken to reduce uncertainty area number 6 about the level of support for a policy of recycling. However, because the project was still at an early stage, it was possible to give some more thought to ways of tackling the other central uncertainties which seemed more difficult to reduce. Had the process been nearer the end, they would probably have been tackled by making assumptions, perhaps backed up by some contingency planning.

FIGURE
81

Illustrations from Practice – Choosing 3

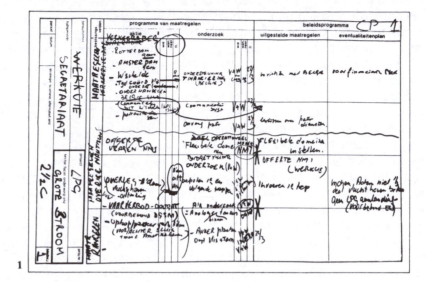

1

An excerpt of the commitment package for Dutch national LPG policy (1984)

Action set

Actions:
- traffic regulation: increase regulatory measures for LPG ships on the main national waterways;
- LPG inland tankships: adapt design and construction in order to effectively prohibit large LPG outflows;
- LPG railcars: large contingents should always be shipped in block trains; in case (for smaller contingents) of shunting some extra measures are specified;
- LPG road tankers: extra design adaptations are introduced to further decrease probabilities of LPG outflows;
- Stationary installations: specifications for zoning around such installations are given;
- Road transport routes: will basically be limited to the Dutch dangerous goods network. New stationary installations will be located in places compatible to this network.

Explorations:
- research into the safe domains around seaships will be done;
- the collision safety of seagoing tankers carrying pressurised LPG will be analysed;
- the possibilities of repressing fire around LPG inland tankers will be analysed;
- the further analysis with respect to effective and economic means of prohibiting Bleve's on LPG road tankers will be conducted.

Policy set

Delayed actions:
The result of the above mentioned analysis will be implemented in the relevant policy decisions and it will be introduced in national regulation and in international regulatory bodies.

Contingency plans:
- in case an LPG-terminal in Amsterdam is conceived then a refuge location for LPG tankers will be constructed;
- in case international regulatory bodies do not accommodate the proposed measures then the general character of such measures must be guaranteed along other lines;
- in case the analysis with respect to prohibiting Bleve in road tankers does not give satisfactory results then other means will be used to create an acceptable situation;
- in case measures with respect to LPG filling stations prove to be intractable due to local situations, then a decision will be made regarding other necessary measures or removal of the filling station.

2

CHOOSING

PRACTICE

Theme: Finalisation of a Policy Statement using a Commitment Package Framework.
Project: National Policy on the Handling and Distribution of Liquid Petroleum Gas (LPG).
Context: A Multi-Disciplinary Inter-Ministry Working Party, Den Haag, The Netherlands, 1983–84.

COMMENTRY ON FIGURE 81

This illustration is taken from a published case study (van de Graaf, 1985; see also Hickling, 2001) of the application of strategic choice methods to the development of a new national policy in the Netherlands for the landing, transportation, storage and distribution of Liquid Petroleum Gas (LPG). The author of the published paper was a civil servant in the Dutch Ministry of Economic Affairs who played a leading role in the project alongside representatives of other Ministries, with Allen Hickling and Arnold de Jong in the role of process consultants.

The situation was one in which the basic assumptions of the previously adopted policy had become eroded, because it had not proved possible to concentrate the landing of this economically attractive but hazardous hydrocarbon – of international importance as a fuel and feedstock – at a single installation at the mouth of the Rhine, with distribution by pipeline. For 2 years, the search for an alternative policy had exercised the attention of civil servants from the Ministry of Economic Affairs, the Ministry of Transport and the two Directorates of the Environment Ministry concerned with land-use planning and environmental protection. Progress had been blocked by the well-known tendency to defend departmental positions. The explicit use of a more interactive approach based on strategic choice methods allowed rapid progress to be made towards an agreed set of policies. However, the participants found it useful to switch back from time to time to a more adversarial mode of working, so as to appreciate more clearly the policy and other constraints they would have to contend with outside the context of the working group.

The working document reproduced here (1) was one of several in a set which were needed to cover all aspects of the problem. The printed framework adopted here is one that can be used large (A1 size) on the wall or small (A4 size) in a loose-leaf file. Notice the explicit accommodation of responsibility ('wie' – who), deadlines ('wanneer' – when) and budgets ('fl.' – guilders (money)). The decision-taker is listed on the left ('secretariaat'), as is the orientation ('grote stroom'). Otherwise it is a standard commitment package framework.

The condensed extract from the final recommendations (2) is presented using the four headings of the commitment package framework – as was the actual set of proposals. These were formally adopted in February 1985 by the second chamber of the Dutch national parliament. It will be noticed that the explorations are primarily of a technical and economic nature, reflecting concern with uncertainty areas of the UE type. However, the significance of uncertainty areas of type UR is clearly indicated in some of the proposals listed under the contingency plan heading – the other decision-makers identified ranging from international regulatory bodies to local agencies concerned with the siting and safety of filling stations. Uncertainties of type UV in the form of the conflicts between economy, safety and other criteria were accommodated in the design of the inter-ministry working process.

FIGURE
82

Illustrations from Practice – Choosing 2

1

2

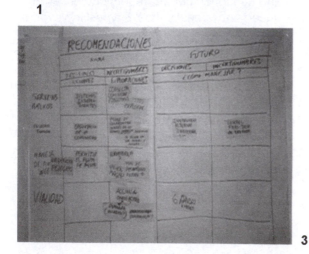

3

CHOOSING

PRACTICE

Theme: Developing proposed actions in response to key uncertainty areas, so as to build an initial progress package.

Project: Post-disaster reconstruction in the Province of Vargas, Venezuela.

Context: Second session of inter-agency workshop convened by Ministry of Planning and Development, Caracas, Venezuela, March 2000.

COMMENTARY ON FIGURE 82

These three photographs illustrate the process adopted to make rapid progress towards a first trial progress package during the second day of a workshop convened in March 2000 by the Vice Minister of Planning and Development in the Venezuelan government. The purpose of the workshop was to explore options for responding to the challenges of reconstruction within the coastal State of Vargas, and in the adjoining States that together comprise the metropolitan region of Caracas, in the wake of the disastrous mudslides that had inundated the coastal communities of Vargas in December the previous year.

Representatives of several government departments, emergency services, technical support agencies and planning consultancies involved in the reconstruction programme were invited, at short notice, to participate in two exploratory workshop sessions to be held on consecutive afternoons.

During the first session, some twenty decision areas were generated in the full group and prioritised, by the use of stickers, for deeper investigation. There appeared to be few direct links between the most critical decision areas, which varied from the relatively technical – to do with the design of early warning systems for floods – to wider questions of the future economic role of the region. There was energetic debate over the issue of how far ecological as well as engineering considerations should influence the design of works to protect for the upper river valleys.

Five decision areas were carried forward to the second session, when five sub-groups were formed and invited to explore one decision area each in more depth. Each sub-group was asked to concentrate on a pair of realistic yet contrasting options and to draw up a pair comparison of these on a flip chart, taking all relevant comparison areas into account. They were asked to indicate ranges of uncertainty for their assessments on each comparison area, and to arrive at a group judgement on whether or not their overall preference between the alternatives was clear (1). They were then asked to indicate the main sources of uncertainty on another chart, showing any exploratory actions they would recommend to deal with these, before presenting the results of their work to the full group (2).

While they were presenting these conclusions, the main proposals were being logged using 'Post-It' slips on a pair of flipcharts formatted in the form of a progress package – or commitment package – grid. At this stage of the workshop, it was not surprising that there were fewer entries in the first column, concerned with recommendations for decisions now, than in the second column, concerned with explorations to inform future decisions. It was stressed by the facilitators that most entries in a package generated by such a workshop would be expected to take the form of recommendations to the responsible decision-taking authorities rather than firm commitments, as most of the participants in the workshop had been specialised advisers rather than managers with authority to commit their agencies.

The workshop was facilitated by a team in which John Friend, as visiting consultant, was accompanied by Ana Maria Benaiges as recorder and occasional co-facilitator, using the STRAD software as a recording device. Others in the facilitation team were José Madrid, Head of the Ministry's Strategic Analysis Unit, and John Foley of the Central University's Planning School. Issues of Spanish/English translation were handled by this team in a flexible and adaptive way, with little evident disruption in the momentum of progress. The following month, John Friend returned to Caracas with Jonathan Rosenhead, and two further workshop sessions were held with senior representatives of key executive agencies. This time, Elisenda Vila and a Cuban consultant acted as co-facilitators.

9 Practicalities

TAKING STOCK

The last four chapters have completed a second and fuller cycle around the four basic modes of planning seen as a process of strategic choice. In contrast to the briefer, introductory tour made in Chapters 2 and 3, the emphasis has been on appropriate ways of drawing on the core concepts and basic methods of the strategic choice approach, when adapting to different working situations. Although certain elaborations of these concepts and methods have been introduced, it is important to stress again that moves towards elaboration should not necessarily be seen as moves towards 'better' use of the strategic choice approach. Simplification is usually a virtue when working under pressure; and in striking a balance between simplification and elaboration the most useful working rule is to favour simplification except where there are convincing arguments to the contrary.

At various points in Chapters 5–8, consideration was given to some of the organisational aspects of the strategic choice approach; to the switching of the process between modes; and to the forms that the more visible products might take. Also, those aspects of technology concerned with effective interaction and facilitation in a group setting were considered more closely than in the earlier introductory tour of core concepts and methods. But the exposition of the last four chapters has still followed the structure of the four modes in a sequential way. It has to be recognised that, the more effective a working group becomes, the more the process will tend to move freely and adaptively between modes through a succession of rapid switching and looping judgements. So the offering of operational advice on the management of the strategic choice approach cannot be organised according to the structure of the four modes alone. There is another level of practical advice which relates generally to the management of the approach as a whole. It is this kind of advice with which the present chapter is concerned.

The starting point for the advice to be offered here will be the general picture of the orientations of strategic choice presented at the end of Chapter 4 (Figure 34). That diagram used the framework of technology, organisation, process and product to compare the strategic choice approach with more conventional approaches that could be regarded as quite appropriate in dealing with simpler problems. In successive columns, contrasts were drawn first at the level of general orientations, then at the level of operational guidelines, then at the levels of emphases in management choice and in evaluation. This chapter will interpret these last two aspects in still more concrete terms, reflecting the body of experience in the application of strategic choice ideas that have been built up through working with many different people on a wide range of practical problems over a considerable period of years. First, this body of practical experience will be briefly reviewed. Then, the main lessons to be drawn from it will be presented; first in terms of the emphases on selectivity and adaptiveness which distinguish the overall approach, and then in terms of the four headings of technology, organisation, process and product, considering each in turn.

THE BASE OF EXPERIENCE

The advice that will be offered in this chapter is rooted primarily in the experiences of the authors, working with many other people in many different project settings, and the picture that has gradually developed through this experience of what constitutes 'good practice' in working with the strategic choice approach. This view of the current state of the art is one which is unlikely to stand still in the years ahead, as further experience accumulates. For the range of applications to different fields of decision-making can be expected to extend and, with it, both the variety of people and organisations involved, and the range of further adaptations made.

However, our current view of good practice is one which already has quite a broad base in terms of the range of planners, managers, specialists and lay policy-makers who have become exposed to the approach and played some part in its development. The people with whom we ourselves have worked have come from several different countries and decision-making cultures; and the types of working relationship through which we have collaborated with them have also been diverse. So, it will be a useful prelude to the advice of this chapter to indicate briefly what the range of these working relationships has been and, broadly, what has been learned through each type of experience. For this purpose, three broad headings will suffice – sponsored experiments, training events and consultancy projects. Each type of experience has complemented and reinforced the others: but the order in which they will be introduced here corresponds broadly to the historical sequence in which they first emerged.

Much of the early development work on the strategic choice approach took place through the medium of sponsored experiments, in which an organisation interested in the possibility of promoting new methods of planning and decision-making has been prepared to invest in a programme of one or more experimental applications of the strategic choice approach to 'on line' problems within its general area of concern. Leading examples included the initial LOGIMP experiment of 1970; the structure plan project of the mid-seventies; the Netherlands project on environmental policy plans in the early eighties; and successive projects in the states of São Paulo and Pernambuco in Brazil. Each exercise was sponsored not so much to help with specific decision problems, as to test the relevance of the strategic choice approach to a wider class of problems; yet success in helping with specific cases was quite central to this testing process. In each of the first three projects mentioned, between two and six 'live' planning problems were pursued in parallel, with the authors and other colleagues or associates acting as advisers to the local teams responsible for producing recommendations on these selected problems. The different teams would all meet together from time to time, to exchange experiences, review difficulties and provide mutual support – with representatives of the central sponsoring body maintaining oversight of the programme as a whole.

The overall style of working in these sponsored experiments has been one of *action research*, designed through negotiation with the dual aims of discovery and practical service to users in view. In contrast to the more classical action research studies (Clark, 1976), there was the added dimension that the action research team was engaged in collaboration with people not just from a single organisational context, but from a set of two or more local 'host' organisations together with a central sponsoring body, each with its own expectations of what the collaboration should achieve.

Inevitably, each sponsored experiment has involved elements of *training* in the strategic choice approach – partly in the form of 'on the job' training for the members of the local teams, and partly in the form of introductory lectures on philosophy and method. In addition, however, from 1971 onwards, free-standing training events have been arranged under the auspices of a wide range of other organisations, in various parts of the world. The duration of such an event has generally been short – ranging from as little as half a day to two weeks at the most – because those participating have generally been not full time students but decision-makers and planners with many other pressures on their time. The design formula for all but the shortest half-day events – a two- or three-day duration being most typical – has been for lectures to be interspersed with work in small groups on a realistic problem exercise. The aim is to move progressively through the shaping, designing, comparing and choosing modes, as in this book, with as much attention as practicable within the time available to the various opportunities for recycling that can be explored as understanding grows and circumstances change. The experiences of both sponsored experiments and consultancy projects have provided a rich source of case material for use in these training events, allowing the various facets of planning under pressure to be realistically reproduced. At the same time, the wide variety of management contexts and positions represented by those participating in the various training events has considerably enriched the process of feedback from practice through which strategic choice ideas and methods have gradually evolved.

Involvement in direct *consultancy projects*, where the primary aim has been to help with a specific planning or decision problem rather than to explore the relevance of the approach to some *class* of problems, has achieved momentum as the experiential foundations of strategic choice have become more secure. In almost all cases where we or others associated with us have been involved as consultants, arrangements for direct collaboration with people from client organisations have been treated as an important part of the project design, and opportunities for interactive working have been stressed.

The scale of such projects has varied from substantial engagements with national governments on national policy issues, to briefer assignments for commercial, public and voluntary organisations. Sometimes, too, brief exercises in mutual consultancy have been designed within short-term training events. Typically, an hour or two has been allowed for participants to talk about instances of specific problems which are currently concerning them in their own management situations.

While the various training and consultancy experiences have provided opportunities to experiment with many different styles in managing the process of strategic choice, the advice that follows is based primarily on one 'prototypical' style that has proved successful in many different settings and has been widely used both in sponsored experiments and in consultancy projects. It is a style that reflects the basic orientations and operational guidelines of Chapter 4, in that it is built around a programme of interactive group sessions of limited duration in the kind of working environment illustrated in the upper picture of Figure 30.

Within the group, the methods of strategic choice are used as an 'open technology', starting from some initial state of knowledge or uncertainty about the problem among the participants, that will gradually be revealed. The agenda is treated as flexible within the time constraints of the working session or sequence of sessions that has been arranged. Little or no backroom preparation is expected for the first session – though priorities for backroom work can build up as a shared view of issues and uncertainties develops within the group. Typically, a working session will cover two or three hours either in a morning or an afternoon, with the same kinds of pressures on time as in the more traditional committee setting depicted in Figure 6 – but with the important exception that there is no expectation of working through a preconceived agenda from start to finish as the session proceeds.

SELECTIVITY AND ADAPTIVENESS: THE TOOLBOX ANALOGY

It is most important that the strategic choice approach is not seen as a mere technique.

The straightforward application of techniques, with some well-defined rules as to how and when they should be applied, has all the attraction of simplicity and is easily taught in a classroom setting. But such an approach has severe limitations, unless the problems being addressed are 'bent' to fit it – something which in practice happens rather more often than it should. The strategic choice approach has been developed in a way designed specifically to avoid this difficulty. This means that there is no one right way to use the approach. There can be no 'correct' sequence in which to do things, and no prescribed combinations to adopt – whether these be viewed in terms of technology, organisation, process or product. It is all a matter of judgement as to what is appropriate to the circumstances at that particular time. Every problem is different. Each must be tackled on its merits.

Use of the strategic choice approach has been likened to the use of a toolbox. The analogy is extremely apt so long as it is remembered that in strategic choice the tools are many and varied – including a wide range of concepts, modes, frameworks, techniques, activities and media.

Imagine taking a toolbox to mend a car engine. Having opened the bonnet and looked at the engine, it is likely that a start has to be made by undoing a nut. Reaching into the toolbox, one selects a spanner, takes it out and tries it on the nut. The first time, almost invariably, it does not fit. So one puts it back and tries another. It may be that the nut is still stubborn, in which case one dips down into the toolbox and chooses another spanner, using now the two in combination. It may be that this combination fails too. If so, they can be put back and another combination tried; or perhaps some penetrating oil is used in addition, thus using three items in combination; and so on, until it works.

As progress is made through the job in hand, different situations will emerge requiring different combinations of tools – and so on, until the job is finished. Also, the next time it is necessary to do the same job, it will probably be appropriate to use different tools, in different combinations and sequences. Imagine that the same car engine requires the same maintenance three months later. It may now be easier to shift that nut, which was once so difficult that several spanners had to be used to shift it; perhaps because it was greased before being tightened. This time, the tools needed may be different again. Perhaps a pair of pliers will be enough to get it undone – or it may be found to be only finger tight in any case. Meanwhile, however, other things might have changed; a bolt might have become rusted in, or broken off, or weakened in some way. So yet more different tools, sequences and combinations might have to be tried.

This analogy illustrates well the two key ideas which govern all the operational advice offered in the sections which follow. The first is the idea of *selectivity*. This follows inevitably from the wide variety of choice available in the use of the strategic choice approach. Indeed, it is clearly implied in the toolbox analogy; there are many tools which obviously cannot all be used on a specific task, even if they were all appropriate – which is most unlikely. Even more inconceivable is the idea that they could all be used at the same time. Thus it is necessary to be selective; to choose carefully what to do and what not to do – and how, with whom and when.

The second idea is that of *adaptiveness*. This follows from the feelings of uncertainty which are endemic to working with complex issues – uncertainty about what the problem is (and is not); what the alternative ways of dealing with it may be; how they rate one against the other and, indeed, what to do about it. The idea that one can always, unerringly, select a good way of working in such a context is plainly unrealistic. It may serve some purpose to try to predict the course that the analysis should take; but to believe that it will be sensible to maintain that course whatever happens in the process is similarly far-fetched. So, there can be only one way of working; and that, paradoxically, is to be ready to work in many ways – in fact, to work adaptively via the explicit acceptance of the learning process, part of which is learning how to conduct that process. One's capacity to think about what to do; what not to do; how, when and in which context, is bound to evolve as one's understanding develops. It is only sensible, as long as time allows, to give that evolutionary process full rein.

Therefore, every opportunity has to be taken to promote that evolution – to keep the learning process going in a smooth and adaptive way. Referring back to the description of the toolbox analogy, there was an important moment when the first spanner selected proved to be the wrong one. This was not bad or inefficient – it was a vital step in the learning process. Being mistaken in this way is important because so much is learnt from it. Thus the second spanner was more likely to be right because the choice of it was so much better informed than the first. This is a classic example of learning from one's mistakes – a phenomenon well known in all cultures of the world, old and new. It leads to the idea of *learning by doing*. The only way to make mistakes is by doing something – so it follows that the more one does, the more mistakes will be made, and the more one will learn.

But this does not mean that selectivity is unimportant. Selections have to be made all the time, in order to keep the process going, and there are times when making a mistake can be costly. So it means that care must be taken in that selection; yet that too much time must not be wasted on it. Going back to the toolbox analogy again, a lot of thought could be given to the choice of which tool to use at any time. It is easy to hesitate when there are so many alternatives – not only which size of spanner to use, but also which sort of spanner and, indeed, whether a spanner was an appropriate tool in the first place. The important thing is not to agonise too long over the choice of which to use; but to try one, drawing as much as possible on past experience, with an open mind and in a spirit of learning. As a rough and ready rule, it is worth bearing in mind that the time spent thinking about it should not exceed the time it would take just to try one out.

Naturally, experience is a vital help in selectivity. This in itself can lead to the idea of each user having his or her own individual *repertoire*. This is the sub-set of all the available tools which that person tends to use more freely and frequently than others – a form of behaviour which is systematically reinforced because it is the most frequently used tools that tend to stay at the top of the toolbox, thus being the first for consideration the next time. Tools from lower in the toolbox only get used when the earlier ones do not work so well, or when the specific task is very well defined. Different people's personal repertoires are likely to have a number of tools in common, and these may be expected to be those with the more general application; the equivalent of hammers, pliers and screwdrivers, though even these may be of various sizes and types. For users of strategic choice, among these common tools would probably be the basic concepts of AIDA; though even here such core concepts as the option bar and the decision scheme can be represented and used in different ways, as earlier chapters have shown.

So, even the experienced consultant or practitioner in strategic choice will have a personal repertoire, which will be similar but probably by no means identical as between individuals. There will be differences in their personal styles as well as in their work experiences in collaborative settings. The two authors, for example, recognise some clear personal differences in the emphases they give to particular concepts and methods in their respective repertoires.

Most people already have personal toolboxes of their own and, indeed, their own repertoires with which they are likely to feel quite comfortable. What is more, they are probably reluctant to abandon these just to take up what could seem to be a self-contained box of tools for strategic choice, such as that presented here. In most cases, this is not necessary. The strategic choice approach is intended to be open and flexible – and most of its tools can be used in combination with other ways of doing things. Indeed, mention has already been made of certain other tools of evaluation and design at particular points in the preceding chapters. Further discussion of these relationships will be found in Chapters 11 and 12.

CHOOSING TOOLS UNDER PRESSURE

The most distinctive and significant feature of the strategic choice approach is that it is has been developed directly out of practice, working with planners and decision-makers who are usually working under pressure. Consequently, it is under these conditions that strategic choice is most useful, and it is generally where deeper and more lengthy analysis is relevant that some of the other approaches come into their own.

In developing the strategic choice approach, it has been found helpful to distinguish between contrasting ways of handling work under pressure – especially pressure caused by the shortage of time. These are what is often called the *quick and dirty way*, and what may be called the *fast and effective way*. Taking up the toolbox analogy again, they can both be likened to types of screwdriver. The quick and dirty way can be likened to the 'Brummigem' screwdriver, whereas the fast and effective way can be likened to the 'Yankee' screwdriver. The 'Brummigem' (which is a corruption of the name Birmingham) is, in fact, a heavy hammer. Although designed for other tasks, such as banging in nails, it can be a very quick way of driving in screws. Of course, there tends to be a loss of effectiveness in the result, although the appearance may sometimes be satisfactory. The 'Yankee' (actually a trade mark) is a specially designed 'plunge' type screwdriver which, by means of a helical thread inside the handle, turns the screw automatically as the tool is pushed on. It is very fast and, indeed, can be very effective. But the trouble is that it is not suitable for all situations and, unlike the 'Brummigem', it cannot be easily used for anything else. Thus, it can be seen that there is no clear-cut recipe for the use in practice of the strategic choice approach. Selectivity and adaptiveness are both essential and, by definition, require that choices be made. And, as was implied in the toolbox analogy, these choices mean balancing ideas about effectiveness against ideas about the expenditure of effort, time and resources – whether the balance is struck in a conscious or sub-conscious way. Here it is worth mentioning the Sutton Principle, which many users of strategic choice have found helpful as a simple, light-hearted way of reminding themselves of the issues involved.

The Sutton Principle is named after Willie Sutton, who was an infamous American bank robber. One day, when he eventually became available for interview, Willie Sutton was asked why he robbed banks. To this he came back with the now immortal reply: 'Because that is where the money is!' His reasoning was very simple. Given a limited amount of time and effort (in Willie's case his own), these resources should be directed where the rewards are likely to be greatest.

Without examining Willie Sutton's logic too deeply, two important lessons can be drawn. The first is that if one cannot deal with everything adequately then, rather than deal with all things inadequately, it is better to deal adequately with some things only. The second is that, in choosing which things to do, the process should always be steered in the direction where it is believed the greatest progress can be made. So it is also with deciding how to select tools from a toolbox – always remembering that in the strategic choice approach the toolbox includes modes, concepts, frameworks, media of communication and ways of working, as well as analytical techniques. The costs are generally the demands which the use of each tool places on the available resources and, in the management of a process of strategic choice, the resources in question tend to take many forms. They include elapsed time; the skills and experience of relevant people; access to relevant information; and access to the capacity to process such information by electronic or other means. The effectiveness of alternative ways of proceeding has to be weighed against the demands they make on resources of all these kinds and, as such resources tend to be limited, they can become constraining, limiting the range of choice. Or sometimes, of course, they can be bought in from elsewhere. Money has not been mentioned yet as a resource because it is rare for the selection of a tool from the toolbox to carry a direct financial cost. Where such costs do arise is in trying to make up for shortfalls in resource supply. This means giving consideration to improvement, support or, in some cases, replacement of the resources already available, in such forms as:

- more and more effective people (e.g. training and consultants);
- more and more relevant information (e.g. surveys and research);
- better and/or faster technological support (e.g. computers and software).

However, this is always assuming that there is enough calendar-type time available – and this is often the most inflexible constraint of all.

The effectiveness side of the resource effectiveness balance is difficult to judge in advance because it is so intangible and uncertain. It is concerned essentially with the potential of the tool; in particular, the potential progress it might generate in terms of those broad and comparatively subtle dimensions of evaluation which were indicated in the final column of Figure 34. Progress in the directions of sharing, synergy, understanding and confidence can be difficult enough to assess in retrospect, let alone to judge with any clarity in advance.

So far, this chapter has discussed the practicalities of working with the strategic choice toolbox in rather general terms. The aim has been to explain more fully the broad management emphasis on selectivity and adaptiveness which appeared in the top row of

Figure 34, and also to develop further the idea of effectiveness as an evaluative principle. To move to a more concrete level in this discussion of the practicalities of strategic choice, it will be necessary now to consider the overall approach in terms of its four components: technology, organisation, process and products.

TECHNOLOGY: MANAGING THE OPEN TECHNOLOGY IN PRACTICE

In Chapter 4, it was argued that the technology of strategic choice was designed above all as an *open technology*; as a means of assisting and encouraging effective communication and interaction within a working group and not just as an aid to backroom analysis by experts. It is because of this emphasis on sharing between participants with diverse perspectives to contribute, that the technology of strategic choice can be considered an *appropriate* technology for group working on issues the very shape of which may be both complex and confused.

The emphasis on an open technology was interpreted in Chapter 4 into an operational guideline of a *focus on decisions*. This guideline finds more specific expression in the set of core concepts to do with decision areas, decision options, decision schemes and the various other linked concepts which were introduced in relation to the work of the comparing and the choosing modes. In addition, an impression was presented of the kind of interactive work setting in which the spirit of an open, decision-centred technology can be achieved in practice (Figure 30). It was argued that choices about the use of rooms, furniture and equipment were just as much a part of the management of the strategic choice technology as were matters to do with the application of specific concepts and techniques. So there are various practical matters to do with these *physical* aspects of technological choice to be discussed in this section; after which, some further points will be made about the kinds of social technology that can be helpful in stimulating productive forms of interaction within a working group.

Some of the advice to be offered on effective use of walls, paper and pens may seem quite trivial and mundane. However, long experience in using the strategic choice approach with groups does indicate that the quality of group communication and interaction can be quite severely impaired by failure to pay heed to such considerations, especially in the early stages of group working, when patterns for future interaction are being set. It is important, firstly, to choose a room which is not so small in relation to the number of participants that their freedom of movement is restricted, constraining them to sit in fixed positions in relation to each other, as they would in the familiar committee setting. For the same reason, it is important to avoid creating a situation in which a table becomes the centrepiece. Indeed, a first step in preparing a room is usually to push any tables to one side, where they can still be used as required, for documents, refreshments, materials or note-taking, but do not create barriers between the participants as they move around. It is a matter of comfort and convenience to provide enough chairs for participants to be able to sit down whenever they desire. However, they are likely to spend much of their time standing and moving around when the process of interactive working is in full swing; and at such times the focus of attention will normally be on the ever-changing pictures of decisions and their relationships which are building up around the walls.

Fixtures such as blackboards or whiteboards do not allow this to happen. This is simply because the information they contain has to be 'wiped' once they are full; this is not consistent with effective working in a cyclic process, which requires the ability, at any moment, to go back to a previous point and to pick up where one left off, Nor do 'flip chart' boards on easels by themselves serve the purpose, because of their limited surface area.

It is important in strategic choice to display as much of the work as possible at any one time, thus encouraging instantaneous, ad hoc looping to take place. Participants should be able to compare the focus of the moment with previous work, skipping backwards and forwards through the process as freely as possible.

So, *walls* are important; and the interactive process can be impeded quite seriously if people are working in a room where the wall space is broken up by too many windows, or projecting panels, paintings or shelves; where access to the available wall space is restricted by too much furniture; or where the walls are uneven or richly decorated in a style which is designed to impress. This means that conventional boardrooms or council chambers do not make an ideal environment for this kind of interactive working; for tensions can often arise with other people who wish to preserve such rooms as settings for more orthodox meetings. Such tensions can usually be avoided by choosing to work in a more sparsely furnished and plainly decorated space. To work effectively on walls, plentiful supplies of *paper* of generous dimension are required. Continuous rolls of paper have sometimes been used; but pads of flip chart sheets of international A1 size have been found to be more flexible when it comes to rearranging and consolidating information as the work proceeds.

The more the sheets of paper accumulate around the walls of the room, the more important the practicalities of *paper management* become. Sheets of paper can be affixed to the walls either by masking tape or by a reusable putty-like substance such as 'Blu-tack'; pins only provide an acceptable substitute where walls are covered with cork or some similar soft surface. Blu-tack has been found to provide high flexibility in removing and repositioning sheets of paper quickly and, if properly handled, leaves no permanent marks on most types of surface. It is generally quite sufficient to fix each sheet by the top two corners only, placing the Blu-tack a centimetre or two in from the corner; each new sheet should be positioned with its upper edge a little above head height, for purposes of writing and of visibility. As wall space at this level becomes more scarce, sheets recording past work can either be moved down to a lower level or overlaid by others. However, in doing so, it is important to avoid hanging paper on paper – for the additional weight is then likely to pull the original paper away from the wall, usually to the distraction of all concerned.

It is not always possible to keep the papers on the wall neatly arranged – evenly spaced and vertical. However, well-ordered walls can help a group overcome the strangeness of working in this way and give a sense of organised purpose. Architectural features, such as joints in walls, door frames and even wallpaper patterns can be used for guidance – not only with hanging the papers but also with setting up lines, grids and matrices on them. Paper over-printed with a feint grid is also helpful in this respect. Large sheets of paper with pre-drawn frameworks, such as:

- compatibility and consistency matrices;
- concentric circles for uncertainty graphs;
- advantage comparison charts;
- commitment package frameworks;

not only make the work look more organised, they also promote faster, more effective working. They can be copied quite easily by the same processes that architects and engineers use. In this way, one can have a large enough supply not to have to worry about running out.

The paper used need not be of high quality, so long as it is not too porous when put to the test of being written on with coloured marker pens. The pens themselves should be sufficient in number for participants not to have to compete with each other when they feel moved to add something to the 'maps' of problems that are building up around the walls; and they should be sufficiently varied in hue to allow colour differentiation to be used freely as an aid to communication.

Experience has shown that some brands of marker pens are much more reliable than others in terms of ink flow. Those using water-

based coloured ink have been found to provide the best service; and those with a wedge-shaped felt tip, 3–5 mm wide, allow a variety of line thicknesses, and clear visibility in most interactive environments. Many experiences in group working have been impoverished by reliance on pens which can only make thin, pale lines; which squeak in a jarring way; or which are prone to dry up at important moments. However, this is not to say that pale colours are never useful. In particular, a barely visible yellow makes a good colour with which to pre-enter frameworks for guidance in adding more substantive information; for example, it can be used to draw up the rows and columns of a grid or matrix, or the concentric rings of an uncertainty graph. In drawing up an option graph for a selected problem focus, one useful 'trick' is first to draw a faint yellow ring intersecting each of the decision areas, then to space out the options within each decision area at intervals around this ring.

There are also more general points of calligraphy and style which regular users of flip charts have tried to cultivate – points about holding the pen, about drawing freehand lines and circles, about positioning of information on a new sheet of paper in a way that anticipates the further information that is still to come. Practice and discussion can lead to gradual improvements in these directions; but it is important above all that concern with the quality of the graphics should not be so pervasive that participants who feel they have few graphic skills should feel inhibited from taking part.

It is not to be regarded as a sign of failure to make mistakes, or to revise earlier views; it is a vital part of the learning process. So it is important to make corrections quickly and move on, rather than go to pains to erase any signs that a change has been made. Trivial mistakes can be covered up by self-adhesive labels; but less trivial changes or corrections are better left as part of the record on the wall, in so far as they represent a significant step in the learning process which people may wish later to recall. A decision graph or similar picture which has become too untidy and confused can always be redrawn and the new version placed over or alongside the old, treating the original as a secondary record only. Every now and again, too, it may be sensible for the participants to pause and rearrange the total set of flip charts around the walls, perhaps grouping together those to which they expect to refer most frequently in the course of subsequent work.

Turning to what has been called the *social* technology of strategic choice, there are further management choices which arise when working with a group of participants in which there is little or no prior experience of this style of interactive work. It is appropriate for the person or persons acting in a facilitating role to take the lead in the use of pen and paper in the early stages, if only to demonstrate the general method of working and set a style for others to follow. Yet, in training courses which include small group exercises, it is usually found that most people start working on the walls spontaneously enough, provided they have had at least a brief demonstration of the art of paper management beforehand.

How quickly and energetically moves are made to open up the process of writing on the walls to wider participation is a matter which has to be judged according to the situation and the sense of how well a group momentum is developing without active steps to promote it. Sometimes it will be easy to encourage people to start using the walls, paper and pens in an interactive way; sometimes, they will be more inclined at first to sit and talk and leave any writing to the facilitator, unless they are explicitly offered a pen and encouraged to use it. In a brief exercise with inexperienced users with only an hour or two to run, it may be acceptable that the facilitator continues to play the main recording role, concentrating on capturing what other people have to say; but the longer the time available, the more feasible it becomes to build up pictures around the walls in which the draughtsmanship of many participants has been merged, so that the sense of common ownership can take on a visible reality of its own.

Mention has been made in earlier chapters of the advantages of punctuating interactive group sessions with brief opportunities for individuals to work on their own. It can help to ask participants to write down their own ideas about relevant decision areas, uncertainty areas or other elements in their own words, using cards or small sheets of paper. These individual contributions can then be compared and merged in such a way that each participant feels he or she has participated directly in building up the shared pictures that are taking shape around the walls. The use of floor or table space to sort and regroup the various individual contributions can itself help to build up a spirit of interactive working.[1]

There is a related technique, which can be especially helpful in bringing invisible products to a conscious level. It involves the use of small circular-coloured stickers (about 2 cm diameter), for the structuring of informal interactive evaluation. For example, if it is thought a good idea to review the growth of joint commitment in the grouping, each participant can be asked to place one sticker on a scale from very good to very bad which has been drawn on the paper. Small stickers can also be used for identifying the most important items in a list – such as comparison areas or uncertainty areas. The resulting pattern is then used as the basis of a creative discussion of the subject, often leading to consensus in the group.

It can pay to introduce brief opportunities for individual working from an early stage in a group process, with further such opportunities whenever the momentum of interaction

---

1 Working on paper on the wall is not exclusively a strategic choice style. There are others who adopt a similar style of working (Doyle and Straus, 1976); but very few have a structured approach to the use of the papers themselves. One such approach, which has much to offer, originated in Germany in the early seventies. It is called Metaplan, and is based on the use of shaped coloured cards (oval, circular, rectangular) on which the participants write, before pinning them onto special screens (Schnelle, 1973). There are some close parallels with the use of cards in strategic choice group processes, which started about the same time.

appears to be flagging or dominated by a sub-group. In order to be ready when such opportunities occur, it is recommended that a supply of cards and stickers be on hand at all times – in addition to the pens and the paper. It is always possible to improvise by cutting or tearing sheets of paper into smaller pieces and marking them with coloured blobs; but a supply of cards and stickers in several sizes, shapes and colours gives the process an air of professionalism which can be reassuring to some participants.

In Figure 83, all these practical points about the management of the technology of strategic choice are drawn together, in a form intended for quick reference, both when preparing for an interactive group session and while reviewing progress subsequently. The key distinctions made are between choice of the physical setting, which usually has to be negotiated in advance; the provision of adequate supplies both for interactive participation and individual working, not forgetting refreshments; and, finally, the requisite techniques and skills to allow these resources to be used to good effect once the group process is under way.

ORGANISATION: MANAGING INTERACTIVE PARTICIPATION IN PRACTICE

It is neither practicable nor useful to attempt to draw a firm line to define where the management of technology ends and the management of organisation begins. There are some further points to be made about ways of managing the dynamics of a working group, and about opportunities for forming sub-groups and subsequently bringing them together. These points will be touched on briefly here, leaving some deeper points about the understanding of group dynamics to be opened up in later chapters. However, it is most important to recognise that any working group has to be seen as embedded in a wider organisational environment in which many other people may have a part to play. So important practical questions have to be asked about what levels and

forms of participation and of interaction will be appropriate for other people beyond the confines of the present working group; and these questions too will be dealt with in this section.

It is quite easy to think of good reasons for involving many and various people interactively in the process of decision-making. But it is not so easy to make a case for the meetings that this entails. It is regularly argued that meetings are a waste of time; that there are too many of them; and that the decisions made as a result cannot be proven to be better. This is entirely justified and will continue to be so, as long as meetings are organised in the conventional manner. Therefore, in using the strategic choice approach, changes have to be made. Already, in the last section, ways in which the conduct of meetings can be changed have been dealt with at some length. In this section the concern shifts to questions about how the meetings should be set up, especially with reference to who should meet with whom.

The form of association will vary from person to person and from time to time. Of all the people who might be involved, only some may wish to be; others may be content to be consulted occasionally, in a reactive rather than an interactive way. It has to be remembered that interactive working, for all its advantages, is demanding in terms of time and energy; and people in practice must always find ways of distributing their personal resources of time and energy effectively, depending on the overall range of responsibilities they carry.

The general picture of three kinds of uncertainty was used in Chapter 4 (Figure 31) to indicate some of the main ways of initiating connections with other people, whenever it was found difficult to deal with a current decision problem in the present working context – whether it be that of individual work or an interactive working group. However, there are various types of relationships which can be distinguished, with different implications for the grouping and linking decisions that have to be made. They reflect different roles people can play in relation to an overall decision process, as contrasted to the roles they might play

FIGURE
83

Management Checklist: Technology

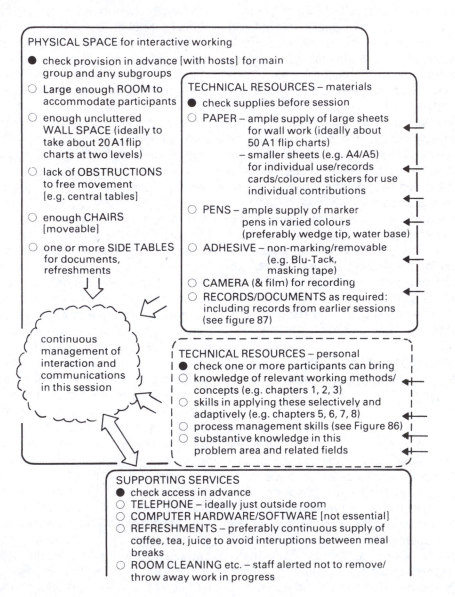

PHYSICAL SPACE for interactive working
- ● check provision in advance [with hosts] for main group and any subgroups
- ○ Large enough ROOM to accommodate participants
- ○ enough uncluttered WALL SPACE (ideally to take about 20 A1 flip charts at two levels)
- ○ lack of OBSTRUCTIONS to free movement [e.g. central tables]
- ○ enough CHAIRS [moveable]
- ○ one or more SIDE TABLES for documents, refreshments

continuous management of interaction and communications in this session

TECHNICAL RESOURCES – materials
- ● check supplies before session
- ○ PAPER – ample supply of large sheets for wall work (ideally about 50 A1 flip charts)
  – smaller sheets (e.g. A4/A5) for individual use/records cards/coloured stickers for use individual contributions
- ○ PENS – ample supply of marker pens in varied colours (preferably wedge tip, water base)
- ○ ADHESIVE – non-marking/removable (e.g. Blu-Tack, masking tape)
- ○ CAMERA (& film) for recording
- ○ RECORDS/DOCUMENTS as required: including records from earlier sessions (see figure 87)

TECHNICAL RESOURCES – personal
- ● check one or more participants can bring
- ○ knowledge of relevant working methods/concepts (e.g. chapters 1, 2, 3)
- ○ skills in applying these selectively and adaptively (e.g. chapters 5, 6, 7, 8)
- ○ process management skills (see Figure 86)
- ○ substantive knowledge in this problem area and related fields

SUPPORTING SERVICES
- ● check access in advance
- ○ TELEPHONE – ideally just outside room
- ○ COMPUTER HARDWARE/SOFTWARE [not essential]
- ○ REFRESHMENTS – preferably continuous supply of coffee, tea, juice to avoid interuptions between meal breaks
- ○ ROOM CLEANING etc. – staff alerted not to remove/throw away work in progress

in relation to the work of a particular group. It is helpful to think of people in seven proto-typical roles in relation to the decision-making process:

- those who are charged with *working* on the project in the sense of performing all the technical tasks involved in shaping, design-ing, comparing and choosing (as described in Chapters 5–8);
- those who undertake the continuous *pro-cess management* of the project, looking after the day-to-day co-ordination of all the various activities and groupings;
- those who are *accountable* for the decisions to be taken in a broadly political way;
- those who are directly *responsible* for guid-ing the conduct of the decision-making pro-cess, at a managerial or senior professional level;
- those to whom periodic *reference* should be made because they have roles in other fields of decision-making which are instrumental in this case;
- those who fill a *representative* role in relation to specific interests which may be affected by the decisions;
- those others who are *stakeholders* in the sense that they will be directly impacted by the decisions.

It is important to recognise that, in any given decision process, the exact way in which people in such roles should participate is a design question in its own right. This means that some of the roles – though not necessarily all of them – will be played by groups or semi-formal *groupings*. There will often be overlap-ping memberships and/or vacancies; and, in some cases, sub-divisions may be recognised. For example, it is common, in public agen-cies, to distinguish between internal and inter-agency reference groups.

Nevertheless, in discussing these roles and relationships, it is useful to take as a reference point the task of a particular *working group* – a group which, in the prototypical decision setting being considered in this chapter, may

be constituted as a more or less formal *pro-ject group* charged, like the South Side Work-ing Party, with working on an issue of some importance over a period of several months. However, most of the points to be made here are also relevant to briefer, more informal exer-cises. The typical relationships between these groupings, one to the other and all to the work-ing group, are illustrated in Figure 84. Broad distinctions are superimposed between those groupings which have a role to play in the technical domain and those with a role more in the political arena. In addition, a distinc-tion is drawn between groupings which are internal and those which are external to the main locus of responsibility for the decisions being addressed.

There are advantages to be gained by keep-ing the working group as compact as possible without losing the representation of important interests, especially with respect to the ease of calling the group together often at short notice. Therefore it has been found helpful to consider two sorts of participant:

- *Regular participant*: responsible for regular substantive input and team member func-tions;
- *Ad Hoc participant*: responsible for a spe-cific area of specialised substantive input and general team functions when present.

In the typical project situation, the role of maintaining continuity is usually handled by a small sub-set of all the people who form the main working group. The task of this process management grouping, or core group, is to pro-mote the effectiveness of the wider process in which members of all other groupings shown in Figure 84 may at different times be involved. It is a small group – generally two or three people – because it must have the capacity for extremely flexible behaviour, especially in its arrangements for meetings. It normally embraces the four specific intra-group roles:

- *Leader*: responsible for the substantive work, controlling the quality and quantity of the analysis and information input;

FIGURE
84

Organisational Responsibilities in Strategic Choice

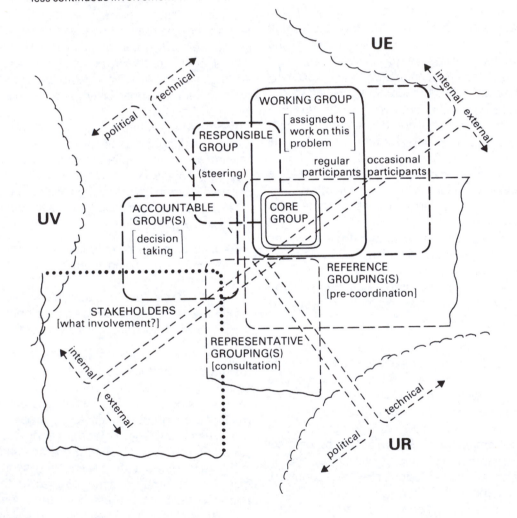

HEAVIER BOUNDARY LINES indicate
direct responsibilities in this field of decision
BROKEN BOUNDARY LINES indicate
less continuous involvement

UE

technical

political

internal

external

WORKING GROUP

[assigned to
work on this
problem]

RESPONSIBLE
GROUP

(steering)

regular
participants

occasional
participants

UV

ACCOUNTABLE
GROUP(S)

[decision
taking]

CORE
GROUP

REFERENCE
GROUPING(S)
[pre-coordination]

STAKEHOLDERS
[what involvement?]

REPRESENTATIVE
GROUPING(S)
[consultation]

internal

external

technical

political

UR

ORGANISATION

PRACTICALITIES

- *Co-ordinator*: responsible for process rather than substance, making sure that the right people are at the right place at the right time;
- *Facilitator*: responsible for internal group relations, guiding interactive sessions and helping with grouping and linking;
- *Recorder*: responsible for the visible results, co-ordinating the continuous output from the process and its distribution in appropriate forms.

Process management is sometimes seen as a function which can ultimately be handled by one person. When this occurs, that person is often described as the *project manager*. Unfortunately, neat as this arrangement may seem, all four roles are very difficult to play together. In particular the facilitator role sits uncomfortably with the other three. Also, it is often the case that the co-ordinator and facilitator have little direct knowledge of the specific problems being addressed. In such a case it is important to recognise the vital contribution which the leader can make. Thus, there are distinct advantages when such a project management function is given over to a small group. While any one person can take on any one role, there are a limited number of combinations of roles which any one person can play. These are the combinations of:

- leader and recorder (product manager);
- co-ordinator and recorder (secretariat);
- co-ordinator and facilitator (process manager).

Another issue which can arise in the choice of core group membership concerns the introduction of external consultants. While a capable process consultant should be able to take on any of these functions or roles, there are some to which they are better suited than others. For example, in many cases the facilitator role can be better performed by someone from outside the immediate organisational framework. Basically, there are two reasons, in addition to the extra manpower, why help of this sort can be useful. The first is that strategic choice skills may be lacking and need to be developed in the team; and the second, where several organisations are involved, is that an independent view may be required. In either case, it is important that the external consultant is given a *counterpart* from within the client group, to provide the detailed knowledge and experience of the problems, the people involved and the culture within which they work.

Next to be described will be the set of people who are formally accountable for the decisions with which the working group is primarily concerned. These can be thought of as the *decision-takers* in relation to a wider, more diffuse set of *decision-makers*, if the distinction is made between decision-making as a continuous process and decision-taking as something that happens at comparatively rare moments when formal authorisation of actions or policies is required. In the classical management hierarchy, decisions are taken at most levels throughout the process; but there is often a level of importance at which authorisation by some accountable group, such as a Board or Council, is required. In the public sector as opposed to commercial organisations, the stakeholders are usually more diffuse, so the principle of group accountability is rather more widespread. Sometimes, accountability is vested in joint organisations – joint committees or 'standing conferences'. In general, the more complex the problem, the more complex will be the politics of accountability; so a working group may have to relate to more than one accountable grouping in some cases.

There have been a few applications of the strategic choice approach where decision-takers in such accountable roles have become involved in interactive working with members of a working group.[2] This can bring powerful

---

2 Members of the accountable grouping tend to find such a role shift easiest through involvement in the responsible grouping, and there is extensive experience of this. However, there have been some examples of the direct involvement of local politicians in the working group. This occurred during preparation of the Structure Plan for the County of Hereford and Worcester in England, and also in the preparation of local environmental policy plans in the Netherlands.

benefits both in terms of the level of awareness with which formal decisions are taken and in terms of the direct input of political considerations into the work of the working group. However, it has to be recognised that senior decision-takers – whether appointed or elected – are often subject to multiple and severe pressures on their time. Their inputs can be particularly significant in the work of the shaping and choosing modes and, given limited opportunities to involve them in interactive working, it is important that their involvement should be focused in these areas.

Often, a link between a working group and a set of accountable decision-takers is made by means of a project *steering group*. Meeting more or less regularly, guidance is provided on the directions and priorities of the work, progress is reviewed and any difficulties discussed, especially so far as the handling of external relationships is concerned. In multi-accountable decision settings, such a responsible grouping will often have been deliberately designed to bring together representatives of different organisations or departments involved in sponsorship of the project work. The membership can be relatively small; leading members of the project group may be directly involved either as members or in a reporting capacity; and there should be opportunities between scheduled meetings to work through informal links with individual members.

So a great deal of informal *negotiation* about difficult or contentious matters can take place through the channels offered by the responsible grouping, both during and between meetings; and there will be opportunities here to use various aspects of the strategic choice approach. It is also through this set of relationships that members of the working group can retain the sanction of their departmental heads to continue acting on their behalf, and that changes in the membership of the working group can be discussed and approved. So the responsible grouping offers a channel through which the highly cyclic, adaptive work process of the working group can be adjusted to the more formally structured procedures and political realities of the wider organisational environment. It is, therefore, important to allow the time and resources for this element of the wider participative process to work in an effective way.

What is referred to in the prototypical working context as a *reference grouping* consists of delegates or representatives of all those other organisations whose co-operation will be important if proposals arising from the work of the project group are to be put into effect. Where the project group's task is to produce a relatively generalised 'plan' or set of policies, the application of which depends on actions of many other agencies, it is important that there should not only be co-ordination during some eventual 'implementation' stage; a realistic framework for *pre-coordination* is also recommended, by which these other organisations or departments can have the opportunity to participate at an appropriate level throughout.

Even in comparatively simple contexts of inter-agency or inter-departmental working, an element of pre-coordination can be important so that duplication, omission or contradiction in the provision of services can be anticipated and avoided. However, when working on broader problems of strategic choice, pre-coordination can involve more complex issues of adjustment of values and perceptions. In larger-scale exercises of policy planning it is sometimes appropriate to invite representatives of all related agencies to participate in occasional seminars. In these, some of the spirit of interactive working can be generated – even though, given time pressures, it might not be feasible to introduce the strategic choice methods in an explicit way.

There are two further types of grouping which it is important not to overlook; both fall into the external political arena. They are the *representative* grouping through which the political interests of specific sections of the population, such as car owners, conservationists or small businesses, are protected and promoted; and the wider *stakeholder* grouping of those others directly impacted by the decisions, such as residents, consumers, or employees. They involve those who are concerned directly from time to time through exercises in direct public or employee participation.

Conventional attempts at a more general sort of participation, involving 'the public at large', tend to end up being conducted with members of these groupings. Unfortunately, because such exercises are aimed at a broader audience, they most often take the form of seeking reactions to well-formulated proposals, which it is too late to influence in any fundamental way. A more sensitive appraisal of which people in which roles are being addressed – and are willing and able to contribute – is the key to selective design of participative frameworks in which a high level of creative feedback can be realised.

So the way in which all these types of relationships evolve through time forms part of the broad concern with *management of organisation* in a process of strategic choice. This applies not only in the prototypical project group situation that has been discussed here but also in other more modest working situations. Sometimes, in such cases, it can be more realistic to relate to those in other roles through more familiar patterns of bilateral contact and negotiation. So this is where patterns of linking through personal networks can play an important part in supplementing any grouping arrangements of a more formal kind. The extent to which strategic choice ideas can be used to guide such interactions will depend on the judgement of the user and the extent to which support has already been established.

The larger a working group, the more difficult it becomes to sustain a spirit of interactive participation through time. To make progress in such circumstances, it is useful at times to suggest that the group breaks into smaller sub-groups to pursue complementary aspects of the overall task. There are many possible grounds on which such

a sub-division of work can be made. Conventionally, work is sub-divided by disciplines, professions or organisational units; but, once some shaping of problems and their implications has been recorded on the walls of the room, other possibilities become available. The conceptual frameworks of strategic choice provide a rich source of logical ways for defining sub-groups. The four different modes of work taken individually, or in looped pairs, provide one useful division. And there are many other possibilities such as different problem foci, separate working shortlists, or commitment packages based on alternative orientations. Some such tasks for sub-groups may require considerable time, and so should be scheduled to be done in the periods between the main interactive sessions of the working group. However, there are many ways in which strategic choice structures can be used to identify briefer tasks for sub-groups within a working session. Examples of such tasks include designing options within decision areas separately; assessing alternatives by individual comparison areas; and exploring different areas of uncertainty. While such divisions of labour can be most helpful, it is important:

- to use the structure of the analysis as the basis of the division;
- to set, and keep to, a strict time limit;
- to allow plenty of time for the sharing of results afterwards;
- to use the structure of the analysis to integrate the various contributions.

Of course, in suggesting which people might be assigned to which sub-groups, the skilled facilitator should be able to take into account which participants work well – or not so well – with each other, and which individuals can be looked to in order to provide stimulus and leadership for the more reticent members of the group.

Then, if it is intended that there should be not just one working session but a series of sessions – whether concentrated within a few successive days or spread out over a longer

FIGURE
85

Management Checklist: Organisation

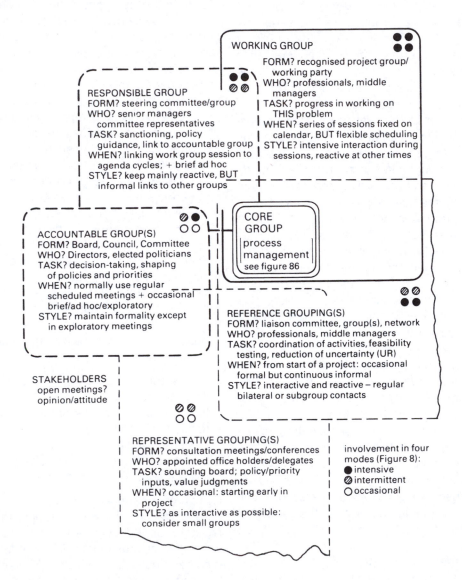

WORKING GROUP
FORM? recognised project group/
  working party
WHO? professionals, middle
  managers
TASK? progress in working on
  THIS problem
WHEN? series of sessions fixed on
  calendar, BUT flexible scheduling
STYLE? intensive interaction during
  sessions, reactive at other times

RESPONSIBLE GROUP
FORM? steering committee/group
WHO? senior managers
  committee representatives
TASK? sanctioning, policy
  guidance, link to accountable group
WHEN? linking work group session to
  agenda cycles; + brief ad hoc
STYLE? keep mainly reactive, BUT
  informal links to other groups

ACCOUNTABLE GROUP(S)
FORM? Board, Council, Committee
WHO? Directors, elected politicians
TASK? decision-taking, shaping
  of policies and priorities
WHEN? normally use regular
  scheduled meetings + occasional
  brief/ad hoc/exploratory
STYLE? maintain formality except
  in exploratory meetings

CORE
GROUP
process
management
see figure 86

REFERENCE GROUPING(S)
FORM? liaison committee, group(s), network
WHO? professionals, middle managers
TASK? coordination of activities, feasibility
  testing, reduction of uncertainty (UR)
WHEN? from start of a project: occasional
  formal but continuous informal
STYLE? interactive and reactive – regular
  bilateral or subgroup contacts

STAKEHOLDERS
open meetings?
opinion/attitude

REPRESENTATIVE GROUPING(S)
FORM? consultation meetings/conferences
WHO? appointed office holders/delegates
TASK? sounding board; policy/priority
  inputs, value judgments
WHEN? occasional: starting early in
  project
STYLE? as interactive as possible:
  consider small groups

involvement in four
modes (Figure 8):
● intensive
◙ intermittent
○ occasional

period – it is likely that the composition of the group will alter at least a little from session to session, whether by design or because of restricted availability on the part of some participants. Such changes can, of course, affect the momentum and patterns of interaction within the group. This means that there is a balance to be struck between a desire for continuity of membership, with the advantage that everyone is working from the same basis of shared group experience; and a desire to keep the membership open, so that new participants can join and others drop away.

This desire to keep the group boundaries permeable can be especially important where ideas about the shape of the problem are initially unclear. Where this is so, the focus of attention may shift in unexpected ways, suggesting that others should be involved who were not seen as relevant earlier on. But it is important to keep in mind the point that extending the boundaries of a working group is not the only way of extending the processes of communication and interaction: and this is where a whole range of possible ways of grouping and linking can be considered. For any complex problem which impinges on many different organisational interests, it is only to be expected that participation will also become a complex matter, with many people becoming associated with the process in one way or another.

Thus, the whole task of *managing the organisation* for strategic choice can be seen as a process of dynamic grouping and linking, in which there are many variables. It is not only a question of which people in which decision-making roles should be active, but of how frequently; in which combinations; and in what relationship they should be to each other, and the current decision situation. A summary of the considerations which arise in these areas of choice is put forward in Figure 85. This is intended as a guide for those faced with the task in practice – probably in the core group role. The key emphasis in evaluation of such organisational choices will be not so much on

efficiency and control, as in a classical hierarchical structure as on the creation of synergy which can be realised through the orientation towards interactive participation.

PROCESS: MANAGING THE LEARNING PROCESS IN PRACTICE

In the *process* aspect of the A-TOPP framework, the practical choices which people face are primarily to do with the effective use of time. Choices about the use of time have to be faced continuously during an interactive working session; and these have already been described at the end of Chapters 5, 6, 7 and 8, in terms of the various switching and looping judgements that have to be made in moving from one mode of work to another. This section will offer some further practical advice on how this switching and looping process can be managed within an interactive working session.

However, in a longer-term project, where there can be a commitment to a series of such working sessions over the project period, there are also important choices to be considered about the management of time in the intervals between one working session and another. During these periods, there will usually be backroom and investigative work to be done by at least some of the participants, individually or in sub-groups, and there will often also be various activities of a consultative or co-ordinative nature involving other people.

There are two interrelated tasks which are often overlooked, but which are of crucial significance – especially in situations where there are conflicting interests. These are the need for participants to:

- report progress made in the working group to their home organisation;
- and gather feedback as input to the group process in return.

If these activities are neglected, or given too little time, the result can be, at worst, that the work loses all credibility; or, at best, that there is a withdrawal of the backing that is necessary if the recommendations are going to be carried out.

Some of these tasks may have emerged directly from the activities of the working group, as ways of dealing with important areas of uncertainty; while some of them may have been explicitly recorded in the format of a commitment package. But of course, not everything that happens between sessions flows from the work done in this interactive setting. All participants will have competing claims on their time between sessions, some more than others. They may have to respond to unexpected events of quite separate origins: some of them may be involved in more than one interactive process or have pressing outside deadlines to meet. So there is a fine balance to be struck between adapting to these pressures and maintaining the momentum of progress in the agreed common task.

The core group task embraces all the mundane jobs associated with organising meetings: tasks which range from the time-consuming job of getting people together at the same time and in the same place, to the provision of appropriate spaces to work in and adequate sustenance for the participants. However, in addition, it involves proper preparation for and steering of the interactive working sessions themselves; and it can take continual effort to keep those not involved in these sessions in touch with what is going on.

One of the greatest cultural difficulties encountered when introducing the strategic choice approach to organisations is that most of these tasks are not conventionally considered to be 'real work'; or at most they are considered as simple administrative tasks which can be delegated to clerical staff to be dealt with in a routine way. Some aspects of the arrangement of meetings can, of course, be dealt with as a matter of routine; but experience has repeatedly shown that the time involved between meetings on the part of those who carry the main core group responsibilities should not be underestimated. Many negotiations about involvement in meetings

and related matters have to be handled informally on the basis of the rapport which is developing through interactive working; and a failure to allow time for this can soon begin to erode the quality of the process as a whole.

Even where there are several members of the working group who are committed to the project for much or all of their working time, some element of advance scheduling of meetings is essential. For example, the same day of the week can be scheduled for a number of weeks in advance, with the understanding that members of the working group will normally meet for two and a half to three hours in the morning and a similar period in the afternoon. Where possible, some flexibility should be built in by an understanding that, if necessary, the afternoon and/or evening before a session might also be used or perhaps the morning of the next day. In some cases it may be necessary to use two or more days together; while, in other cases, less time may be necessary, allowing sessions to be cancelled. At intervals, other types of meetings may be fitted into this kind of schedule. In particular, allowance can be made for meetings of the responsible grouping, which involves senior managers in a steering capacity, and of the reference grouping through which working liaison is maintained with other departments and agencies. This *flexible scheduling* approach means arranging in advance a series of meetings, in which there are some basic and fairly firm expectations about time commitment and participation in meetings, with the understanding that either may be extended or curtailed should circumstances require.

Between sessions, the core group should arrange to meet every few days, although such meetings need not be very lengthy. The periods immediately before group sessions, and also immediately after, are also important times to exchange notes on progress and ideas on how the dynamics of group interaction can be maintained in the current situation. Laying out the room, setting targets for the day, monitoring progress towards them, analysing the results and recording wall charts are among the vitally important activities which the core group must undertake during such sessions. Without them, progress and direction can quickly become lost. It is better than nothing to get together in the main working room a few minutes in advance of the others – but that is really not enough. On the other hand, it should not be necessary to organise such meetings formally – they should happen spontaneously – but it is important that they should not be so squeezed out by other pressures. It is also important that the core group meetings should not be seen as secretive. If other members of the working group happen to come into the room while the core group is discussing process management issues, it is important that they should not feel excluded from the discussions but should be explicitly brought in.

It is not recommended that a half-day working session be formally broken, for instance to go to another room for coffee or tea at some appointed time. For the loss of momentum can be serious and it is much preferable that coffee, tea or other light refreshments be available in the working room itself. Lunch breaks, on the other hand, are more essential; they can be important not only as respite for the participants and as consultation time for core group members, but also for other informal purposes. In particular, process consultants working for the first time on a problem, in an organisation of which they have little or no inside knowledge, will often find themselves being briefed during the lunch hour on aspects of the internal political background which are well enough known to most of the participants, yet cannot be openly discussed during the course of a working group session. Also, of course, social interactions in the evenings and weekends can play an important part in the cultural acclimatisation of all concerned, especially those who come from a distance to an unfamiliar organisational setting.

The facilitator role is of particular importance because it is concerned with the *group process*. The role is one with many parts and is sometimes handled flexibly between two or more people who are experienced in process management. This sort of *team facilitating* can be most effective, with the active facilitator role changing hands from time to time. It allows the benefits of active facilitating to be combined with simultaneous reflection on it, which improves the effectiveness of the review process. In many cases, it can enable process issues to be discussed openly between members of the group, with the input of two or more independent views of what is happening at any one time.

The facilitator has always to be ready to aid communication between the participants, especially where they may have difficulty in sharing their different perceptions, concepts, assumptions and priorities. The task is to prevent progress being blocked whenever possible, and to unblock it when it is. It means keeping all the participants feeling involved by creating opportunities for all to make their contributions effectively. It includes active guidance of the interactive work of the group and, in particular, guidance of the judgements associated with switching and looping between modes of work. In making switching and looping judgements, the main evaluative emphasis is on seeking always to move in directions where the growth of understanding is expected to be greatest in relation to the time and energies of the participants. It is not, of course, easy for anyone, however skilled, to make judgements in advance as to whether more will be learned by a shift of mode in one direction rather than another. These are, essentially, judgements about where the rate of potential learning is likely to be greatest; and here the idea of the *learning curve* is of value.

When starting work in any mode, there is usually an initial period of quick learning, the duration of which will depend on how much is already known – and shared among the participants – at that time. When little is known about a problem, it can be some time before the rate of learning – the learning curve – begins to level off. But where there is an established base of understanding, a tailing-off effect in learning is soon experienced, so more

FIGURE
86

Management Checklist: Process

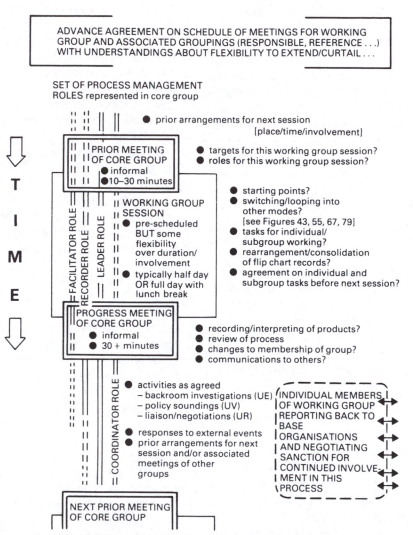

ADVANCE AGREEMENT ON SCHEDULE OF MEETINGS FOR WORKING
GROUP AND ASSOCIATED GROUPINGS (RESPONSIBLE, REFERENCE . . .)
WITH UNDERSTANDINGS ABOUT FLEXIBILITY TO EXTEND/CURTAIL . . .

SET OF PROCESS MANAGEMENT
ROLES represented in core group

T
I
M
E

● prior arrangements for next session
  [place/time/involvement]

PRIOR MEETING
OF CORE GROUP
● informal
● 10–30 minutes

● targets for this working group session?
● roles for this working group session?

FACILITATOR ROLE
RECORDER ROLE
LEADER ROLE

WORKING GROUP
SESSION
● pre-scheduled
  BUT some
  flexibility
  over duration/
  involvement
● typically half day
  OR full day with
  lunch break

● starting points?
● switching/looping into
  other modes?
  [see Figures 43, 55, 67, 79]
● tasks for individual/
  subgroup working?
● rearrangement/consolidation
  of flip chart records?
● agreement on individual and
  subgroup tasks before next session?

PROGRESS MEETING
OF CORE GROUP
● informal
● 30 + minutes

● recording/interpreting of products?
● review of process
● changes to membership of group?
● communications to others?

COORDINATOR ROLE

● activities as agreed
  – backroom investigations (UE)
  – policy soundings (UV)
  – liaison/negotiations (UR)
● responses to external events
● prior arrangements for next
  session and/or associated
  meetings of other
  groups

INDIVIDUAL MEMBERS
OF WORKING GROUP
REPORTING BACK TO
BASE
ORGANISATIONS
AND NEGOTIATING
SANCTION FOR
CONTINUED INVOLVE-
MENT IN THIS
PROCESS

NEXT PRIOR MEETING
OF CORE GROUP

NEXT MEETING OF WORKING GROUP (or RESPONSIBLE GROUP or . . .)

PROCESS

A-TOPP

PRACTICALITIES

rapid switching and looping are to be expected. A group which starts with little experience in strategic choice is likely to be dependent on a process manager or facilitator for judgements of this kind; but as a group becomes accustomed to this way of working, the breadth of participation in active process management can increase.

What is important is that people should be conscious of the mode in which they are currently working, and of the opportunities for switching and looping which exist at any particular moment. For this reason, it is a useful guideline that any group which includes members who have never worked with strategic choice before should have at least some experience of work in each mode during the course of the first working day. A flip chart showing the four modes (as in Figure 8) can be posted on the wall as a point of reference to which such people can refer; and occasional reference to the 'Sutton Principle' will help people to be conscious at any time of the opportunities to switch to the mode where they think the greatest rewards will be found.

But switching judgements can be difficult, especially if there is a sense of leaving work *unfinished* when moving into another mode. Part way through a lengthy analysis, the feeling often develops that there is little more to be learned by going on – so the learning curve is now becoming flatter – but nonetheless there is resistance to a switch because the analysis is incomplete. At this stage, a relaxed approach is recommended and the switch should be made. The analysis can always be completed later if, in coming back to it through the cyclic process, that seems a helpful thing to do.

A somewhat different form of this is experienced when people find themselves labouring to define some aspect of the problem, often in terms of a decision area, comparison area or uncertainty area the meaning of which is ambiguous, or the wording of which is difficult to agree. In such situations, the device of temporary labelling has been found very helpful in maintaining the pace of learning. The idea

is that a name is given to whatever is unfinished; it is put on one side; and then it can be picked up later if it is still relevant. This device has become known as the 'Rhubarb Principle,[3] and around it has developed the informal shorthand of putting unfinished work 'in the rhubarb sack'. In practice, the rhubarb sack is usually an open-ended list of unresolved items built up on a separate flip chart on the wall. This is then used during review, and as input to agenda building exercises for future sessions.

To summarise at this point, process management choices are vital to effective progress, though not often recognised adequately in conventional practice. It is important that they be made explicit wherever possible, and that adequate time be allowed for them. As an aid to this, a summary of relevant process issues is presented in Figure 86. Some of the most important aspects of process management to be considered are those associated with judgements about switching and looping within and between group sessions, combined with the passage of time. In evaluating the use of time through process choice, it is important to be guided by considerations of growth of understanding rather than just good time-keeping or productivity in terms of substantive plans; and these are judgements to which all members of a group can contribute, once they have become conscious of the considerations which arise.

PRODUCT: MANAGING INCREMENTAL PROGRESS IN PRACTICE

In a process of strategic choice, there are both invisible and visible products. Various forms can be identified (Figure 33), taking the substance–process dimension as well as

---

3 This name arose during early work on the formulation of policy choices for the Avon County Structure Plan, where the working group was struggling with the definition of a decision area about the quality of life. The impasse was resolved by one member suggesting that they label this decision 'rhubarb' for the time being and pressed on to something else.

the visible–invisible into account. The management emphasis is placed on the recording and interpreting of these products as well as the act of producing them (Figure 34).

In any interactive working session, visible products will be continuously building up on flip charts around the walls of the room – apart from any notes that may have been made by individuals. At the end of a session, the choice arises as to what should be done about these products. At one extreme, they can be thrown away, while at the other extreme, they can be left intact as a starting point for the next session, provided the space is not required for other purposes. But there is a range of other more practicable possibilities in between; and this is where the task of *recording* becomes important.

Flip charts can, of course, be saved at the end of a session; and where this is the intention it is useful that somebody charged with the recorder role should number them in the sequence they were first written on – and add a date – at the end of the session. But flip charts are bulky, and to save too many can be to create both a storage problem and potential information overload, with severe difficulties of access and retrieval.

One of the most useful and simplest means of recording is simply to *photograph* the set of flip charts around the walls of the room at the end of a session – and possibly also at critical moments during the course of a session, especially at any moment when the information on the wall is being reorganised, breaking up a pattern of relatedness between flip charts which has become familiar to the participants and which they might later wish to recall. Colour prints are recommended to capture the way in which coloured pens have been used; and use of a digital camera enables the results to be quickly displayed. It is important that the information in the *photo-record* be easily retrievable, and that closely related parts of the work are kept together. Mounting sets of three or four prints together on A4 sheets of paper has been found to serve such purposes well, especially if they are suitably

coded, dated, labelled and indexed (Figure 58). It is important that all members of a working group have access to copies of the photo-record. It is sometimes found useful to take some pictures of people working together as well – both as a reminder to the participants of the process, and as an indication to others of the general style of working within the group.

Another way of recording is to write up the key aspects of visible progress in the form of a *loose-leaf* record in a ring-back file, which can provide a more accessible set of reference points for the participants when they reconvene for another working session. This can of course be supplemented by photographs of the flip charts in groups on the wall – in which case, some or all of the charts themselves can be scrapped, or the reverse sides written on again where the paper is of sufficient quality.

Any act of recording – even one of mere photographic recording – involves some element of *interpretation* of information into another form – usually a more condensed form appropriate for later use. If the intended use is reference by the same working group at a later meeting, the extent of the interpretation may be quite small, because those concerned have become used to the language of strategic choice – the graphical conventions, the vocabulary, the abbreviated labels by which they have learned to communicate with each other. But it is important to remember that this sort of recording can easily become, in effect, another cycle in the process. In some cases this may not be too serious; in others it can be interpreted by other participants as an attempt by the recorder to manipulate the results. It is hardly necessary to point out that this could have very negative effects on the group process. Where there is a danger of this, and when there is enough time, it is better to make recording the explicit subject of another group session – perhaps using a photo-record as a starting point. Another way, if time is short, is to allow the recorder to go ahead, but also to allow a reasonable amount of time for questioning and clarification at the start of the next group session. This can be usefully combined with circulation of the record in a reactive style between sessions.

It is only to be expected that the members of a working group will develop their own form of *jargon* – graphical as well as verbal. This can be extremely useful insofar as it helps them talk about problems rapidly and effectively among themselves. But such jargon, of course, can be of little value in communicating with others and, indeed, it can have the effect of confusing more than it informs. In practice, there is always a temptation for members of a working group to try to communicate with others in such terms, presenting decision graphs or lists of alternatives described in terms of brief labels which have acquired significance to them through the process of interaction within the group. But such information cannot have the same significance to others not so intimately involved. There is a danger that findings and supporting information presented in terms of apparently esoteric jargon will annoy and alienate rather than bring any sense of involvement to those only intermittently involved – such as members of accountable, reference and representative groupings (Figure 84). So, in reporting progress to others, and in providing a basis for interactive discussions with those who are only occasionally involved, some more substantial form of interpretation into plain language is required.

A general impression of the progressive build-up of visible products is presented in Figure 87. This shows the development of a loose-leaf record drawn from the flip charts relevant to each mode and, from that, the further development of documents suitable for use outside the group. The process of production is one of *incremental documentation*. In practice, the loose-leaf record builds up and evolves gradually, providing at any one time a statement of the latest findings and possible recommendations coming out of the work. Whenever it is necessary to produce a formal statement or recommendation, it is then a matter of taking the relevant leaves

out of the loose-leaf system; assembling them in an appropriate order; and considering how to present the result. The remainder of the loose-leaf system provides the basis for any *reasoned justification* for the choice; a source of supplementary information; and a starting point for future cycles.

It is important in building up a loose-leaf record that it should reflect the products of work in all four process modes. It will, of course, be vital to record the content of a commitment package where the work of a session has culminated in a product of this form; but information on decision areas, decision graphs, problem foci, options, decision schemes, assessments, advantage comparisons, shortlists, uncertainty areas and exploratory options can be vital for future reference as well. On some major strategic choice projects, standard pre-printed forms have been used to record some of these kinds of information, so that it can be retained in as organised and immediately accessible a form as possible. What is most important is that the decision-takers should be in a position to question and challenge the presented argument; and that their advisers, when challenged, should be able to retrieve further information from the loose-leaf system wherein the fuller records of their work are stored. So the outer rings of Figure 87 are linked by loops which indicate a two-way flow of questions and responses. It is in this way that decision-takers, with many pressures on their time, can become interactively involved in the process – and can do so on their own terms, as it is they who set the questions on which the dialogue is based.

In taking a view of planning as a decision process in which uncertainties are managed continuously through time, it is vital to recognise the importance of process-related products. Nonetheless, it is the recommendations about the substantive problems which will be the focus of attention when the time comes for formal decision-taking. Even where they have been developed using a commitment package framework, these may differ little in visible form to recommendations made

FIGURE
87

Recording and Interpretation in Strategic Choice

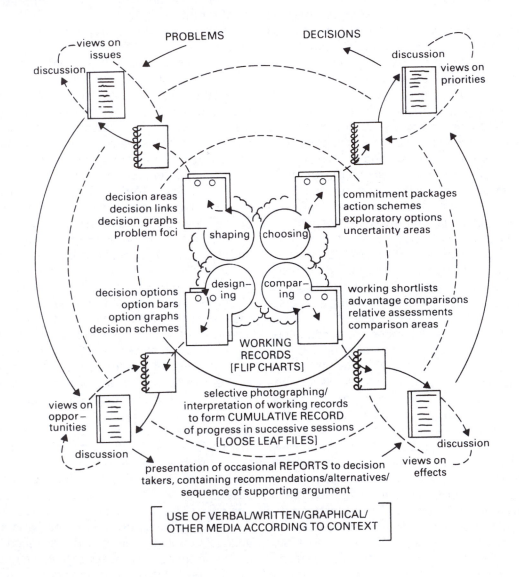

without the use of strategic choice methods.[4] But it has to be recognised that such recommendations may include many partial and interim actions, to complement those which are explicitly deferred or made contingent on future events. Although what decision-takers are being asked to sanction may be primarily the products of work in the choosing mode, the provision of some supporting information on the work of the other modes is essential if they are to feel that:

- the advice they are offered is soundly based;
- their advisers have explored the shape of the problem in a realistic way;
- they have looked at a wide enough range of alternatives;
- they have taken all the most significant consequences into account;
- they have attempted to deal with uncertainties in an adequate way.

To demonstrate these things can mean a degree of *post-rationalisation* of the highly complex and adaptive processes of switching, looping and recycling through which members of the working group in reality arrived at the findings they present; processes which could seem quite chaotic if any attempt were made to present them realistically in full.

As suggested in Figure 87, it is possible in strategic choice, as in other ways of working, for a reconstructed argument to follow a linear course from shaping, through designing and comparing, to choosing – though there is no reason why one or two feedback loops in the process should not be presented as well, if they are sufficiently critical in their implications. However, in strategic choice, such a linear

framework is not essential. Free of the constraint of a retrospective process-based logic, the reasoning can be based instead on the structure of the problem – with an increased emphasis on the prospective aspects of the continuous decision process.

Indeed, this kind of 'prospective process-based logic' is essential in strategic choice, where the decisions are structured over time. Future *procedures* form an important part of most commitment packages. Not only is there explicit provision for various forms of exploration to reduce uncertainty, but statements in the 'future decision space' are likely to be couched in terms of procedures to reach decisions, rather than definitive plans. Such recommendations are likely to be needed in order to:

- keep track of how proposed actions turn out, and review the need for adaptive planning;
- monitor the performance of assumptions so that critical misjudgements can be managed;
- provide for decision-making on a regular basis, as well as prepare for cases of emergency and/or unforeseen circumstances;
- allow for participation by individuals and relevant groupings with respect to expected and unexpected future decisions;
- maintain progress in implementation programmes related to time schedules and budgetary cycles.

In addition, documentation in relation to future processes is likely to include potential sources of information, as well as key individuals and organisations who are particularly relevant to the case in hand. However, it is often difficult to define procedures exactly – and especially uncertain is the behaviour of the individual people who will ultimately enable them to work. Therefore, it can be very helpful to have developed a high level of understanding among the participants during the decision-making process, so that there is a foundation of shared perception, mutual respect and trust which can be built on in the future. This entails not only knowledge of other ways of working, but also extended networks of communication within

---

4 This was particularly evident in the English Structure Plan project. However, sonic of the participating teams made use of structured frameworks of 'policy management information', to interpret commitment package concepts into forms of presentation which indicated how policies might be adapted through time. Assumptions were clearly stated, together with contingencies which would warrant change and constraints which would limit that change.

which these invisible products can be put to effective use.

Such products, which are continuously developing in a process of strategic choice, emerge from work in all modes and take shape in many ways. They take shape in the minds of individuals, as peoples' limited perceptions of problems, possibilities, implications and uncertainties gradually become replaced by richer perceptions through the sharing of views within an interactive group setting. Indeed, it can be said that invisible products build up in the 'hearts and souls' rather than just the minds of individuals, insofar as they come to share values as well as perceptions and to develop a sense of shared commitment to common directions of action or policy. These somewhat nebulous products can have an immediate value through the production of better integrated and more strongly supported decisions. But, in most cases, their full worth is experienced over time – paving the way for more effective working in the longer-term future. However, they are likely to escape unnoticed unless explicit efforts are made to help participants:

- first of all to become conscious of them;
- and then to find ways of harnessing them.

Invisible products can be brought to a conscious level most effectively as they happen; and the facilitator will be trying to do this. Unfortunately, this is no easy task; so it becomes important also to try to capture the invisible products retrospectively. Most commonly in a strategic choice exercise, this is done at the end of sessions, through allowing opportunities for reflection at that time. A quick recognition of the visible work done during the session is followed by evaluation not only in terms of progress on the wall, but also in terms of the growth – or lack of it – in understanding, consensus and commitment. People's ideas about matters of process as well as substance are likely to change; and these can also have profound implications for the quality of decision-making in the longer

term. So these also can be usefully included in any end-of-session sharing of views.

Taking a more extended view, it is worthwhile to suspend business for slightly longer after a series of working sessions, so that participants have an opportunity to consider the cumulative growth of invisible products increments of which may easily slip by without comment during more frequent evaluations. Longer, more formal surveys can be most effective at the end of a project.[5] Questionnaires can be focused on the potential of invisible products and ways in which participants intend to capitalise on them. Retrospective questions paired with prospective ones, addressing the same issue in different words, reveal changes in attitudes. These changes may have been perceived at an individual level but become much more powerful when they are seen as part of a group development. Naturally, as with any survey of this kind, feedback of the results to the respondents is essential.

But all of this emphasis on process-oriented products – visible and invisible – is to no avail if nothing happens as a result of the work. What is required also is a convergence of view towards a common understanding about what has to be done – or not done, as the case may be. For this sort of joint commitment, there must be a degree of sharing of perceptions about what the problems are; the solutions which are available; and their likely consequences. All of which can build up to a well co-ordinated set of feasible recommendations with the backing of all concerned – especially given a framework for structuring them over time.

Where a working group has an inter-departmental or inter-organisational membership, there is a need for a framework which

---

5 Evaluative questionnaires were used for this at the end of the LOGIMP experiment (Friend, Wedgwood, Oppenheim *et al.*, 1970) and, more recently, in a number of environmental policy projects in the Netherlands. On two occasions, follow-up studies have been carried out by means of interviews with participants three or more years after the event, and the findings presented in internal papers.

will enable the actions required of the various participants to be brought together. In the strategic choice approach, this can be achieved via a *mutual* commitment package. Each set of participants in a working group will have their own separate commitment packages, within their own spheres of responsibility which may be expressed in a variety of forms. Parts of each such commitment package can however be merged to form a composite statement of the way forward or mutual commitment package. But how much should be expressed in this form will be a matter for negotiation, as there may be various political sensitivities to keep in mind.

In such a multi-organisational group, the range of uncertainties encountered in agreeing how to move forward at any time may include areas of recognised conflict, which cannot be resolved at that point. But a decision process, structured within a commitment package framework, provides opportunities for the management of such conflicts. It allows decisions over which there is conflict to be deferred, whilst others over which there is agreement can be put into action. In many cases, when the time comes for the deferred decision to be taken, the conflict will have dissolved. Options can become infeasible over time, while new ones, over which there is more agreement, can emerge. In any case, even if the conflicts have not disappeared, at least those involved will by then have a better chance of understanding their consequences. Another source of conflict arises from uncertainty over events which may – or may not – occur. The commitment package includes space for contingency planning which can be used to handle this sort of uncertainty. Provision can be made to reduce the impact of adverse circumstances and thus remove the fear which is causing the conflict.

Of course, there may be times when it will be necessary to recognise deep-seated conflicts of interest, reflected in divergent pressures from different members of the group. Such conflicts are not often such as to block the opportunities for progress in a group using

strategic choice methods; but where this happens, resort may have to be made to other means of resolution, such as external arbitration or mediation. Sometimes, where there is not one accountable grouping but two or more, conflicting interests may have to be reconciled in an incremental way, through a process of gradual mutual adjustment over time.[6] Even here, the commitment package framework can still provide a dynamic structure to aid collaborative negotiation.

Figure 88 contains a summary of the range of products which might be considered – structured as in Figure 33, along the dimensions of substance/process and visible/invisible. Naturally, it is necessary to be selective in the choice of products as in the other aspects of strategic choice. The evaluative emphasis which is most appropriate to the consideration of products is an emphasis on confidence; the gradual accumulation of confidence among participants that they are moving towards decisions which are soundly based, at least so far as a realistic appraisal of uncertainties and time and resource pressures allow. This is the emphasis which was contrasted with the more conventional emphases on accountability and completeness of products (Figure 34), important as these more tangible considerations remain. And the evaluation of growth in confidence is a matter not just for the working group itself, but for all those other participants who may be involved in other process roles.

CONTINUITY AND THE INDIVIDUAL

In the prototypical working situation where substantial human and other resources are being committed to a major planning task, the rate of progress towards a more continuous way of working becomes an important test of the extent to which the philosophy of strategic choice is becoming diffused; especially so where there remains the expectation that

---

6 See, for instance, the case of Droitwich Town Development – Friend, Power and Yewlett (2001) or Batty (1977).

FIGURE
88

Management Checklist: Products

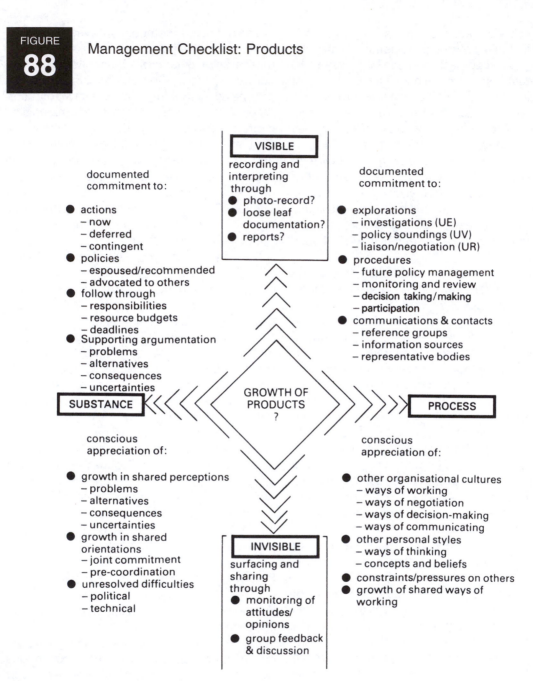

VISIBLE

recording and interpreting through
- photo-record?
- loose leaf documentation?
- reports?

documented commitment to:

- actions
  - now
  - deferred
  - contingent
- policies
  - espoused/recommended
  - advocated to others
- follow through
  - responsibilities
  - resource budgets
  - deadlines
- Supporting argumentation
  - problems
  - alternatives
  - consequences
  - uncertainties

documented commitment to:

- explorations
  - investigations (UE)
  - policy soundings (UV)
  - liaison/negotiation (UR)
- procedures
  - future policy management
  - monitoring and review
  - decision taking/making
  - participation
- communications & contacts
  - reference groups
  - information sources
  - representative bodies

SUBSTANCE ←← **GROWTH OF PRODUCTS ?** →→ **PROCESS**

conscious appreciation of:

- growth in shared perceptions
  - problems
  - alternatives
  - consequences
  - uncertainties
- growth in shared orientations
  - joint commitment
  - pre-coordination
- unresolved difficulties
  - political
  - technical

conscious appreciation of:

- other organisational cultures
  - ways of working
  - ways of negotiation
  - ways of decision-making
  - ways of communicating
- other personal styles
  - ways of thinking
  - concepts and beliefs
- constraints/pressures on others
- growth of shared ways of working

INVISIBLE

surfacing and sharing through
- monitoring of attitudes/opinions
- group feedback & discussion

PRODUCT

A-TOP**P**

PRACTICALITIES

the main substantive product will take the form of a fully integrated master plan, delivered by some appointed deadline. This shift in the direction of continuity has been called the 'continuisation' of a planning process (Hickling, 1982) and it becomes an important evaluative emphasis in process terms, to accompany the emphasis on growth of confidence in the more substantive products.

But the shift towards continuity has its limits, especially when combined with the emphasis on interactive working. People cannot work interactively all the time and, indeed, practical ways of managing the process and products are essentially to do with the management of those discontinuities that inevitably arise when people can only come together periodically and for limited lengths of time. Two expressions that are often heard from people involved in complex planning tasks are 'let's start from scratch' and 'at the end of the day'. In most real-life planning, there is no such thing as 'scratch' and people never do reach 'the end of the day' in that final sense. Yet successive working days will come to an end and new working days will begin – whether the new day is spent working on the same problem or on another. And these are the realities against which moves towards continuity of process and incremental products must be judged.

Inevitably, it is at the level of the individual that the experience of continuity finds its fullest expression. For individuals exist continuously, in states of consciousness punctuated by more or less regular periods of sleep. While conscious, they make choices of many kinds, some of them in a more or less programmed and automatic way. They make choices about eating, drinking, moving from place to place, about small-scale social interactions and economic transactions. Indeed, one of the first examples of a decision area quoted in Chapter 2 was of the choice facing an individual as to how to respond to an early morning alarm, as the first choice of all at the start of another decision-making day.

Some personal choices, of course, call for more deliberation – either through a process of *simple* choice (Figure 6), with work concentrated in the designing and comparing modes – or through a more subtle process of *strategic* choice such as that exercising the individual depicted earlier (in Figure 30) relaxing in an armchair and contemplating how some set of uncertainties should be managed – in which situation one possible response could be to rise out of the chair and to discuss it with someone else.

Choices for the individual arise over where to direct his or her attention at any moment; where to look; what to read; to whom to listen; and, indeed, how to use any of the various sensory mechanisms with which the body is equipped. These choices about *scanning* are continuously being made, more or less consciously, and are accompanied by choices in the realm of action, or *doing*, through the motor mechanisms of the body. So any complete model of individual decision-making must include some representation of these motor and sensory mechanisms which provide connections to the physical world outside.

Following this line of argument, any complete representation of a process of strategic choice should include scanning and doing modes in addition to the four already considered in depth in this book. A more complete six-mode representation appears in Figure 89. The two additional modes are shown as embedded in a *world of operations* in contrast to the *technical domain* of designing and comparing, and the *political arena* in which the shaping and choosing work are done. So what has been called the process of simple choice (Figure 6) in effect by-passes the political arena – unless and until difficulties are encountered which mean moving in the direction of increasing complexity and, therefore, increasing interactions with others whose values and perceptions may conflict.

Of course, organisations as well as individuals have their 'worlds of operations' which tend to provide the strongest strands of continuity and predictability in their work. Individuals who are employed by organisations will spend parts of their conscious lives making choices within

FIGURE
89

Strategic Choice as a Continuous Process

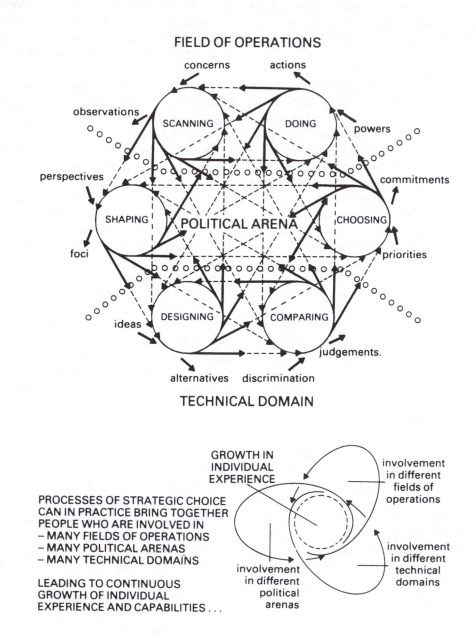

FIELD OF OPERATIONS

concerns   actions

observations

SCANNING   DOING

powers

perspectives

commitments

SHAPING   POLITICAL ARENA   CHOOSING

foci

priorities

DESIGNING   COMPARING

ideas

judgements.

alternatives   discrimination

TECHNICAL DOMAIN

GROWTH IN
INDIVIDUAL
EXPERIENCE

involvement
in different
fields of
operations

PROCESSES OF STRATEGIC CHOICE
CAN IN PRACTICE BRING TOGETHER
PEOPLE WHO ARE INVOLVED IN
– MANY FIELDS OF OPERATIONS
– MANY POLITICAL ARENAS
– MANY TECHNICAL DOMAINS

LEADING TO CONTINUOUS
GROWTH OF INDIVIDUAL
EXPERIENCE AND CAPABILITIES . . .

involvement
in different
political
arenas

involvement
in different
technical
domains

the framework of their employer's field of operations, and other parts of their lives making choices within more personal settings. Many of these choices will be simple, others more complex – possibly involving not just one technical domain or one political arena, but several, which may be interrelated in intricate ways. So the six-mode diagram of Figure 89 provides no more than a conceptual reference point in attempting to follow activities within a set of processes which may, in practice, have a very rich and complex texture – with threads of continuity provided by the scanning and doing activities of all the various individuals who may become involved.

The extended six-mode model of strategic choice will not be further developed here, but it can be used as a base from which to explore further what is involved in work in any of the four main process modes, with reference to the others. In particular, Hickling (1985) has developed a view of evaluation as a five-finger exercise, in which the comparing mode is treated as the palm of the hand, with the five 'fingers' of designing, shaping, scanning, doing and choosing being used in various sequences and combinations as the pianist consciously works to extend his or her skills.

KEEPING IT SIMPLE

The emphasis of this chapter has been on practical guidance in managing a process of choosing strategically through time. Attention has been given in turn to the four aspects of technology, organisation, process and product. These together comprise a coherent approach – or merely a 'way of working'

if these aspects are developed in an informal rather than a conscious way. In the use of the strategic choice approach, these four aspects have provided a structure for the design and management of comparatively large-scale exercises. In some cases, governmental bodies have committed substantial human and other resources over a period of months to work on important national, regional or local problems. It is in such settings that deliberate attention has been paid to the finer points of technological choice (Figure 83); to the relationships of different groupings (Figures 84 and 85); to the scheduling arrangements for meetings (Figure 86); and to the systematic documentation and interpretation of products (Figures 87 and 88).

Important as these practical points are, they cannot, of course, be taken into account so consciously in every application of the strategic choice approach. The most important guideline of all is to keep things simple wherever possible. Problems vary and pressures vary. If an opportunity suddenly emerges to draw on strategic choice ideas in the heat of working with a few other people on an urgent problem, the setting and materials may not be ideal; the working group may have to be treated as given and the time constraints may be severe. So the immediate products might have to be simple and direct. But a consciousness that there are management choices involved in each of the four aspects of technology, organisation, process and product can provide a valuable background to the snap judgements that have to be made, even in such informal working situations – and a framework for reflection once the moment of creativity has passed.

10 The electronic resource

WHAT ROLE FOR INFORMATION TECHNOLOGY IN STRATEGIC CHOICE?

Should electronic information and communication technologies have a central, and possibly an expanding, role to play in the future development of the strategic choice approach (SCA)? This has been a subject of sustained and vigorous debate since the early years of the design of the toolbox presented in earlier chapters. On the one hand, it is not hard to see that there are some aspects of the methods presented there that might be handled more quickly and painlessly by electronic means. On the other hand, some users have argued that there should be little or no place for electronic methods if the emphasis of the approach is to remain on interactive working among the *people* who are involved together in any decision process, drawing primarily on the knowledge and values that they carry with them rather than on shared sources of external data.

Yet the question of the role of electronics in strategic choice is one that has to be raised repeatedly, as circumstances change, for the pace of development in information and communication technologies continues to accelerate, and at the same time the breadth of access to these technologies continues to extend. Whereas the world of electronic communication might once have been seen as the province of the backroom expert, it has been since gradually extending its reach into the home, the schoolroom and the meeting places of local communities. Younger generations have begun to make casual and intuitive use of mobile communication devices which their elders have had to learn to use in a more conscious manner, if at all.

PROGRESS IN DESIGN OF SOFTWARE SUPPORT FOR THE STRATEGIC CHOICE APPROACH

Software to support some of the more technologically demanding methods within the strategic choice approach – specifically, the combinatorial aspects of the analysis of interconnected decision areas – has a history extending back as far as the early seventies, when a program to deal with the combinatorial aspects of AIDA was developed in FORTRAN by Hadley Hunter with other colleagues in the Institute for Operational Research.

Then it was at around the time when the first edition of this book was published in 1987, when microcomputers were beginning to become widely available at affordable prices, that pilot work began on the design of interactive software to support the wider process of working flexibly through the four modes of shaping, designing, comparing and choosing, helping decision-makers to move incrementally towards commitment over time.

Through a small family company formed by John Friend in the Sheffield Science Park,[1] work proceeded on the development and marketing of a prototype software package called STRAD – short for strategic adviser – designed to guide users interactively in drawing on the full range of tools as presented in earlier chapters. The design, writing and testing of the

---

1 See the *Planning Under Pressure* companion website or www.stradspan.com.

FIGURE 90

Design of the STRAD 2 software

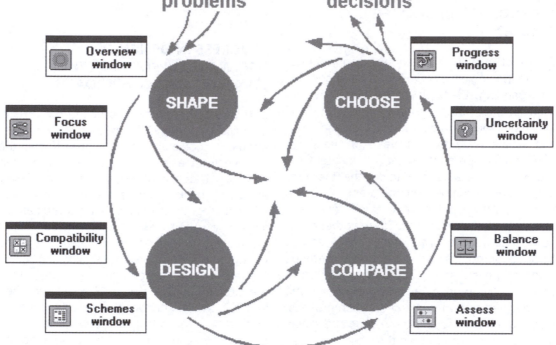

DESIGN PRINCIPLES:

STRAD 2 provides two *windows of access* to additional software resources for each of the four strategic choice modes. One window of each pair is primarily concerned with managing *inputs* to the work of the mode, while the other window is concerned with managing *outputs* from the work of the mode – see examples in Figures 91 and 92.

As a matter of principle, the management of the continuing decision process itself, including any switching or looping between modes, is treated as a matter for human judgement rather than machine.

program was carried out by John Friend's son Dave, who writes about some of his experiences in his contribution to Chapter 13.

The first commercial version of STRAD was published in 1991, designed for IBM-compatible microcomputers running under the MS-DOS operating system. Several potential users had previously advised that it would have been more appropriate for the development work on STRAD to be carried out in the alternative Apple Macintosh environment with its more user-friendly graphical interface. It was with reluctance that this suggestion was set aside; for it would have made it more difficult to test the resulting package with a wide range of potential users.

However, shortly after the launch of STRAD 1, Microsoft was to introduce the more flexible graphical user interface of MS Windows 3.1, with enhanced capabilities and a capacity to display more than one window on screen at a time. This made it possible for users to view simultaneously the progress they had made so far in the different modes of the strategic choice approach – thus simulating the way in which a workshop facilitator can switch attention flexibly from one flipchart to another, and from mode to mode, when working with the more familiar materials of paper and felt-tip pens. Initially, the storage limitations of early personal computers imposed severe limitations on this flexibility. However, it was not long before the development of more powerful microcomputers was to enable these constraints to be overcome.

STRAD 2 for Windows was first released in late 1994. Since then, it has been upgraded several times to enable it to operate with newer and more powerful versions of MS Windows. The scale of investment in marketing has remained modest, yet single user or network licences have since been purchased in over 30 countries, by users in a range of market sectors which gradually extended the previous range of application of the Strategic Choice Approach. Among the main types of user of the software have been managers in business and the public and voluntary sectors; planners, consultants and policy analysts involved in the management of both intra- and inter-organisational projects; and teachers, students and researchers in leading schools of management, planning and public policy.

WINDOWS OF ACCESS TO WORK IN THE FOUR MODES OF STRATEGIC CHOICE

In the early design work on the STRAD software, the first aim was to design a linked set of *program modules* corresponding as closely as possible to the four modes of strategic choice – shaping, designing, comparing and choosing. It was intended that these modules should replicate as closely as possible the graphical formats introduced in Chapters 2 and 3 of this book, and further elaborated in Chapters 5, 6, 7 and 8. From this point of departure, opportunities could then be explored to offer users access to additional procedures reflecting the analytical power of the computer wherever this might be helpful. For example, the computer might introduce new ways of supporting the choice of a focus within a complex decision graph; or the development of a set of feasible decision schemes where the range of choice is constrained by many option bars; or the comparison of alternative schemes taking multiple comparison areas and diverse sources of uncertainty into account.

In the design of STRAD 2, this logic was pursued further, through the design of eight *process windows*, two for each of the four modes, as shown in Figure 90. In general, the purpose of the first window relating to each mode is to help users in organizing *inputs* to the work of that mode, while the purpose of the second is to help in organizing *outputs*.

The principle behind this picture is that the process of sustaining flexible progress through the four modes of the approach, from shaping of problems to the achievement of incremental and continuing progress towards action commitments, should continue to be viewed as a *human process*, whether it entails people

FIGURE
91

Shaping and Designing with STRAD 2

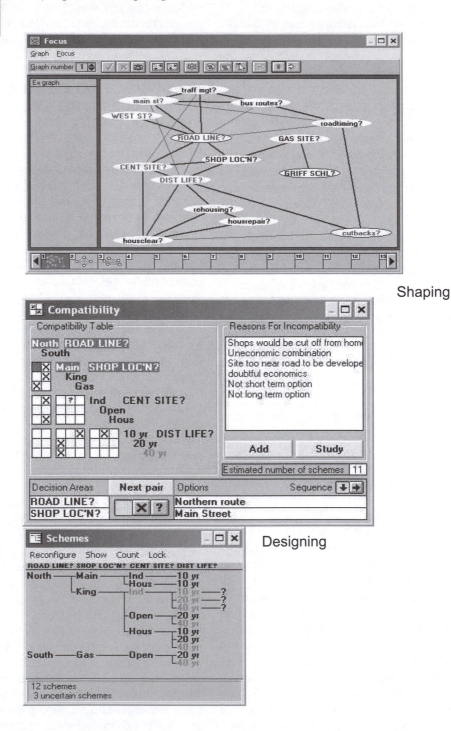

Shaping

Designing

working individually or collectively. What is represented by the eight associated process windows in Figure 90 is merely a set of windows offering *access* to certain supporting resources which the STRAD program can bring them in their endeavours.

The set of illustrations of screen formats that follows in Figures 91 and 92 illustrates how, in the design of STRAD 2, it has been possible to replicate several of the graphical formats used when working on flip charts, with adaptations to the alternative medium of the computer screen. Furthermore, they illustrate how, through these adaptations, the software can offer certain additional forms of support to users of a kind that is difficult to introduce when working on paper alone. The illustrations in these two Figures are all based on the South Side case that runs throughout this book, so as to facilitate comparisons with the freehand drawings that accompany earlier chapters.

EXTENDED TOOLS FOR SHAPING AND DESIGNING

Figure 91 brings together examples of three of the main types of window layout available in STRAD 2 to support the work of the shaping and designing modes.

The first stage in working on a problem is to set up a *project file* for the problem situation being examined, which can then be developed over the course of one or more working sessions, and stored at intervals under successive versions of the file name if desired. The function of the first window of the shaping module – the *Overview window*, not shown here – is to provide rapid access to current information on all decision areas, uncertainty areas and comparison areas at any stage of work.

The first picture of Figure 91 shows the format of the other main window of the shaping module, the *Focus window*, which is used in STRAD 2 to help the user in developing successive versions of the decision graph. The decision graph shown in this example contains the same decision areas and links as that presented in Figure 40 of Chapter 5. The focus

window enables various operations that correspond to those discussed in Chapters 2 and 5 to be followed through. Decision areas can be dragged to or from a list of those not currently included in the graph ('ex graph'), or they can be positioned and repositioned freely within the graph. Further dragging operations enable decision links to be inserted or removed. Colour distinctions are available to emphasise important or urgent decision areas; to distinguish uncertain from firm decision links; and to indicate differences in the 'ownership' of decision areas, much as when using flip charts in a workshop.

In addition, STRAD 2 offers a choice of aids to the development of a new problem focus that does not depend on visual judgement alone. A toolbar displays various buttons designed to help users in selecting a new focus – for example by highlighting a suggested 'triad' of three interlinked decision areas as a starting point, based on a user-adjustable points system which enables criteria such as importance, urgency and density of links to be taken into account. As a matter of principle, any such recommendations are always subject to the overriding judgment of the user. A strip at the foot of the window displays miniature pictures of all earlier stages in the development of a focus, enabling any of these earlier graphs to be called up again as a starting point for further work.

The second window of Figure 91 illustrates the layout of the *compatibility window*, which is used in STRAD 2 to organise inputs to the designing mode. A grid format similar to that of Figure 15 is used in preference to the option graph format of Figure 16, as this representation is simpler to work with in any situation where there are more than a few option bars. One of the option bars is here shown as uncertain (?) as in Figure 49.

Reasons for inserting option bars can be registered in a list that is available for future reference; and procedures are available to enable users to inspect, suspend or cancel any reason on the list, in order to expand the set of feasible schemes. Below this list, an estimate of

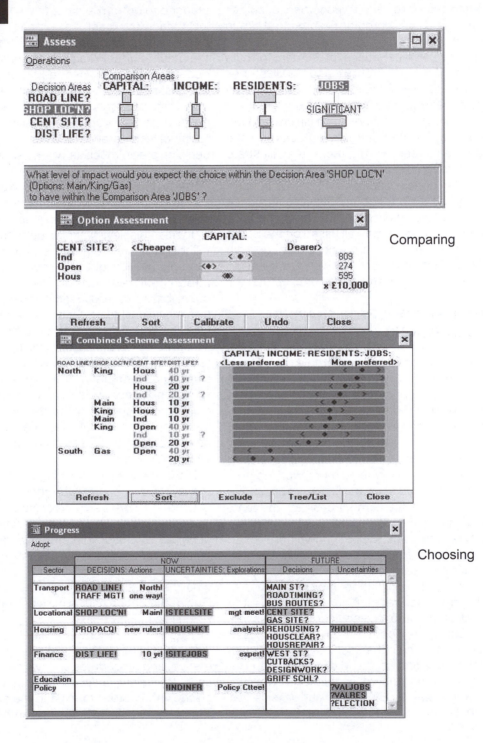

FIGURE 92 Comparing and Choosing with STRAD 2

the total number of feasible decision schemes is presented, using the formula explained on Figure 52.

The final window in Figure 91 presents an example of the *schemes window*, through which the set of decision schemes resulting from any specified pattern of option bars can be rapidly displayed – normally in the form of an option tree as in Figure 17, though an alternative list format is also available. In this window, there are procedures for altering the sequence of decision areas in the tree; for calling up a *count* of the appearances of each option; and for selecting and 'locking' a preferred option in the first one or more decision areas in the tree, working from the left. This is normally only done after some relative assessment of the schemes has been carried out, and a working shortlist has been developed through the assessment procedures now to be described; this gives effect to the principle of robustness discussed towards the end of Chapter 3.

EXTENDED TOOLS FOR COMPARING AND CHOOSING

In Figure 92, a set of four further illustrations of STRAD windows is presented, indicating some of the main procedures used to support the work of the comparing and choosing modes. To support the work of the comparing mode, STRAD introduces several features that go some way beyond the relatively crude methods advocated in Chapters 3 and 7. For the software makes it possible to carry out quickly various aggregating and sorting operations of a kind that it has been found scarcely practicable to introduce in a workshop setting if a climate of interactive working is to be sustained. The main *Assess window*, illustrated at the top of Figure 92, provides access to a set of secondary assessment windows, two examples of which appear below. This main window displays a grid of all decision areas currently in focus against all comparison areas that have been selected for current use. Within this grid, users can enter their first intuitive judgments about the relative levels of impact within

particular comparison areas of the choice open within each decision area, as a preliminary step before entering their assessments of differences between specific options. Having thus entered their initial judgments about the relative value weightings of comparison areas in an intuitive yet logically defensible way, they can then focus their attention on those cells of the grid in which they expect to find the most significant differences. They can modify these judgments later if they wish, by means of an optional display at the foot of the grid covering all decision areas combined.

Coloured rectangles indicate those cells where option differences have already been assessed; open ones indicate those in which this is not yet done. The width of any cell is initially set at zero, as in the case of the cell for ROAD LINE? with JOBS: in this example. However the cell width can be altered, by means of a dragging operation, to indicate anything between a marginal to an extreme impact, in answer to the question posed in the space below the grid.

A double click on any cell opens up a secondary *option assessment window* for that cell, as shown in Figure 92. Each option is initially represented by a marker in the centre of the range. These markers can be moved to new positions to represent the user's assessment of option differences. Each option also has a pair of symmetrically placed 'range markers', the distance between which can be increased to represent perceptions of uncertainty.

The scale used for assessment in any comparison area can be calibrated with reference to any specified numerical unit of measurement, wherever this can be defined. Yet STRAD does not require the user to make such a calibration in the case of less tangible comparison areas; for the software applies its own internal metric defined by the intuitive value judgments that have been entered in the main Assess window, and there are procedures for automatic adjustment whenever the limits of the working range of the window are exceeded.

The option assessments from all the filled cells of the assess window can then be automatically combined – across decision areas, across comparison areas or both. The combined scheme assessment window of Figure 92 shows the outcome of this process. It displays a set of multi-criteria assessments for all the feasible decision schemes displayed in the tree of Figure 91, after aggregating all the option assessments entered so far. The formula applies the weightings to the comparison areas as they were last adjusted in the main assess window, applying a standard sum of squares rule as a means of estimating the combined range for each scheme.

Any of these scheme assessments can be adjusted at this stage to reflect any further knowledge about the effects of combining options from different decision areas in particular ways; and STRAD can quickly sort the schemes to display them in descending order of preference. Schemes near the top of the sorted list can then be selected to form a working shortlist. Information on the schemes included in this shortlist will then be carried back to the schemes window, as a basis for the selection of robust actions in the more urgent decision areas.

The set of shortlisted schemes can also provide a starting point for closer comparisons of pairs of promising alternatives using the *balance window*. This window is similar in its layout to the type of advantage comparison chart shown in Figures 21 and 64, and is therefore not reproduced here. Also not shown in Figure 92 is the format of the uncertainty window, which is designed to help in the judgments about alternative ways of managing uncertainty, using the types of procedure illustrated in Figures 24, 71, 72 and 73.

Figure 92 concludes with an illustration of the layout of the *progress window* which is designed to bring together proposed outputs from the choosing module. This window displays the current state of progress towards decisions in the format of a commitment package grid, using a broadly similar format to those illustrated in Figures 26 and 77. In STRAD, the less definitive phrase *progress package* is adopted to describe the general format of the grid; then it is up to the user whether any such package is subsequently *adopted*, either as an explicit commitment, or as a recommendation to others; or as a strategic option to be saved and compared with any alternative strategic options which might have been designed. Clicking operations enable fuller details of any elements of a progress package to be entered, edited or inspected – including details of any proposals for implementation (who, when, how). There are print and export procedures that then enable the content of a progress package – or indeed of any other STRAD window display – to be printed out as hard copy that the user or users can take away as a record of what has been agreed at this stage in the process.

EXPERIENCES IN USING THE SOFTWARE

Since the first production version of the STRAD software was launched in 1991, and especially since this was followed by the first Windows-based version STRAD 2.1 in 1994, there has been enough feedback on its applications by users who have applied it in management, consulting, project co-ordination, teaching and research to provide us with several learning points to guide the further development of electronic support to users of the strategic choice approach.

It is also important to ask what implications this additional electronic 'compartment' in the strategic choice toolbox can be expected to have on the future development of the approach as a whole, and on the future range of its applications. For the provision of software for strategic choice, supported by tutorial and help files and a comprehensive user's manual, makes available an additional channel for disseminating understanding of the approach more widely on a broad international front.

Contacts have been maintained, through both personal and electronic channels, with many people in the developing network of users of the STRAD software. Also, opportunities have arisen in many countries to demonstrate the capabilities of the software to prospective users, ranging from policy-makers to local community development workers. It has been found that one of the most effective forms of demonstration is to begin from a live situation on the current development agenda of those present, then to start building up a project file based on a direct process of questioning by the facilitator/consultant. The result is a gradually developing picture of problem structure jointly constructed by the problem owner(s), the consultant and any others who may be present. One successful framework for generating such an informal computer-supported discussion is reported in the contribution by Rebecca Herron and Dennis Finlayson in Chapter 13.

SOFTWARE AS AN AID TO PROGRESS IN SMALL INFORMAL MEETINGS

One of the more surprising conclusions from the experience built up so far in the use of software as a problem-structuring aid is its potential in supporting the use of strategic choice methods by clusters of two or three people meeting casually and informally in their own working environment – so long as they have access to a desktop or laptop computer with a monitor large enough to enable all to follow progress. The contrast here is with the more spacious kind of workshop environment that becomes so important as a setting for the use of flip charts in wider groups. While the workshop process itself may be highly informal and adaptive, this is counterbalanced by the more formal preparation that may sometimes be necessary to reserve a suitable working space in advance; to requisition supplies of flip charts and pens; and to reserve dates in the diaries of those invited to participate.

There have now been several occasions when STRAD has been put to good effect in facilitating smaller, more *intimate* meetings of a few people grouped around a single workstation. All that is required is that at least one of those involved should be familiar enough

with the software; and should also have sufficient personal facilitation skill, to be able to drive the process forward. As in the case of a facilitated workshop, the art is in balancing the concern for steady progress against the concern to encourage each participant to contribute spontaneously as the picture of shared progress gradually builds for all to see.

At this scale of the small intimate group, the evidence is that it is quite feasible to sustain a creative synthesis between a process of spontaneous group interaction and a process of flexible interaction between human and machine. For this is a scale where people can switch their focus casually and repeatedly from the computer screen to the other participants grouped around it and back again. However the evidence is that this kind of informal switching can become more difficult as the size of the group increases; the content of the screen can of course be projected onto a wall, but there can then be a noticeable loss in terms of the interactive dynamics of the group.

One effect of the use of the computer is inevitably to make the developing picture of problem structure look more impersonal than if the picture had been built up freehand on a flip chart. Through the introduction of the computer, the shapes become more regular and the conventions more standardised. There is a risk that this may reduce the sense of ownership of the work; yet there can be compensating advantages in terms of focusing attention on matters of content rather than presentation.

Another consequence of the switch from flip charts to computer is that the record of past mistakes, and of the learning points to which they have given rise, may become less easy to retrieve. Yet there are facilities within the software to enable these learning points to be recorded, as systematically as the required pace of progress allows. This can be done by a combination of recording text notes on the key assumptions underlying any new information entered at each stage; and saving successive versions of the project file at intervals. In this way, a cumulative record of progress can be built up; and revisited later as an audit trail of the way in which steps towards important decisions were agreed.

COMPUTER-AIDED CONSULTING

The situation of a consultant using STRAD interactively with an individual client – or with a small informal client group – is in most respects little different from that of the small computer-supported meeting as already described. The key distinction is that – assuming that the consultant is acting as 'process driver' – he or she will be concentrating on drawing inputs out of the others without being concerned to make more substantive inputs of personal knowledge to the decision process. The benefit of this style of consulting, as compared to consultancy without computer support, is that the clients can see a continually evolving picture on the screen of the decision situation as built up from the various information inputs that they themselves have provided. This enables the clients to make adjustments and corrections at any time, and provides a foundation from which a firmer and more confident client-consultant relationship can be built.

STRAD AS AN INTERACTIVE LEARNING TOOL

In several countries, staff members of schools of management, planning and policy have experimented with the interactive use of STRAD on both undergraduate and postgraduate courses. The challenge is to help students in exploring the realities of strategic decision-making in complex fields where the interests of multiple stakeholders converge and may conflict. Whether working with case studies or with ongoing decision situations, the software has proved a versatile means of introducing students to the general principles and working tools of the strategic choice approach. Also, it has provided significant feedback on ways of improving the software both in terms of its human interface and its range of functions.

THE CHANGING SCENE: ADVANCES IN TECHNOLOGY, EXTENSIONS IN ACCESS

It would have been difficult for either ourselves or others to have started work in developing STRAD as a flexible and interactive tool to support ongoing processes of decision-making earlier than the mid-eighties, when micro-computers were starting to become widely available for individual desktop use. From that time onwards, further waves of techno-logical advance followed in quick succession; advances in hardware capacities, in software design and in human–machine interfaces, and also in communication via local and wide area computer networks. Among the innovations of this period were the development of the first computer-supported *group decision support systems*, in which members of a group of decision-makers are equipped with individual terminals through which to contribute to the build up of a shared view of problem structure, projected onto a wall under the guidance of a facilitator. It was not long before there followed even more dramatic advances in opportunities for communication at a distance, through the rapid spread of access to the Internet, to e-mail and to other new forms of messaging based on mobile telecommunication systems.

The limited scale of investment so far in the development of software to support the strategic choice approach has offered few opportunities to keep pace with these developments; even though it has helped to indicate the wider prospects that these advances in technology, coupled with extensions in access, have been bringing into view.

Shortly after John Friend, as initiator of the STRAD project, reached normal retirement age in 1996, he was to take up a new research and development challenge through a 3-year part-time contract with the Lincoln School of Management, addressed primarily to the extension of participatory planning methods in developing countries.

Through this challenging new assignment, the platform for experimenting with the application of strategic choice methods and the STRAD software was to continue to grow; while, the priority in terms of software development turned to the search for international partners who could bring both experience in relevant fields of application and resources of more professional software development and marketing expertise. In early 2000, an ambitious project proposal was submitted from Lincoln to a new European Commission programme designed to stimulate the development of technologies to support the concept of an *information society*. The proposal brought the Lincoln School together with partners in four other European countries, with the aim of designing an Internet service to support the engagement of citizens in the development of local action plans.

This proposal was to be unsuccessful in the competition for funds in a highly competitive field. Yet the relationships with these partners – who include three of the new contributors to Chapter 13 – have continued to develop. Gradually, negotiations to build an alternative base for the further development of electronic support to processes of strategic choice have been moving in new directions. For further news on these developments, the reader is referred to the relevant section of the companion website, or to the Stradspan website at www.stradspan.com.

IMPLICATIONS OF WIDENING TECHNOLOGY ACCESS FOR PARTICIPATORY DECISION-MAKING

Contrary to what might have been anticipated two or three decades ago, growing experience with STRAD is pointing to the view that experiments in access to flexible decision support software of this kind can be more quickly and successfully designed with people involved in small-scale settings, such as those of local community action or small business development, than with people engaged in the management of larger and more powerful organizations. For those people are likely to have already learned to approach their planning and management responsibilities in other more closely structured ways, designed to fit the particular organisational and budgetary structures through which corporate planning and control functions in those organisations are exercised.

Yet many people who do not work for large organizations are now becoming familiar with the principles and conventions of information and communication technologies through their day-to-day access to the graphical user interface, to the Internet and to cellphone networks, as access to these technologies has become widely diffused to the home, the schoolroom, the community centre and other meeting places within the wider civil society. Members of younger generations repeatedly demonstrate that they can acquire knowledge of these technological capabilities more rapidly and intuitively than members of earlier generations. Whether through immersion in interactive learning programs or in playing computer games, they are acquiring impressive skills of a kind that have not been passed down from earlier generations in the traditional way.

In Chapter 13, several recent experiences are described in introducing strategic choice methods – sometimes with support from the STRAD software – to people who have little or no prior experience of other management methods, in a range of experimental settings in Africa, South America, Italy, the Netherlands and Lincolnshire in England. These accounts give a few indications of the potential that is now emerging for a widely diffused process of experimentation with electronic technologies to support and guide participatory decision processes in such relatively informal settings. Meanwhile, opportunities to support the diffusion of lessons from such experiments are emerging through a range of governmental and inter-governmental investment programmes designed to support capacity-building for sustainable development at grass roots level, both in developing countries and in the more disadvantaged regions of the developed world.

The continuing development of ever-more powerful technologies, in combination with parallel extensions in access, means that new opportunities will continue to emerge for sustained innovation in forms of support for decision-makers who must plan under pressure, both locally and in broader policy settings. Yet it is important that questions of appropriate *balance* between electronic and other forms of technology to support responsible decision-making should be kept under continuing critical review. For deep political issues of access and empowerment will persist, and will have to be confronted in a responsible way, however dramatic the future pace of technological advance may appear.

11   Extensions in process management

Since the first edition of this book went to press, opportunities have arisen to apply the general approach presented here to the management of ambitious projects on an increasingly large scale. Typically, these projects have involved people with many different allegiances and cultural backgrounds coming together to address important issues in which they have a shared concern. The theme of this chapter will be the challenge of adapting the strategic choice approach to extensive projects of this kind, and the further adaptations in technology, organisation, process and products which have been evolving in response.

EXTENSIVE PARTICIPATORY PROJECTS AND THE STRATEGIC CHOICE APPROACH

As mentioned in the preface to this edition, many extensive projects – though by no means all – have been concerned with issues of environmental policy in a national or an international setting. Some of them have brought together participants from different countries of western and eastern Europe, building on the success of the earlier projects in the Netherlands from which several of the illustrations from practice in earlier chapters are drawn.

The emphasis on environmental policy is no accident – for it is this field of policy which, more than any other, reflects the current convergence of two highly significant trends in the modern world of policy formulation, planning and decision-making. These are:

1. *A growing appreciation of the complexity of the issues* – It is becoming more and more clear that the issues we are now facing are often of global significance on a time scale involving generations far into the future – as expressed in the concept of sustainable development. Not only are the issues themselves more complex but, at the same time, they are being seen as increasingly interrelated – to the extent that what could once

be seen as externalities have now to be handled as central concerns.

2. *A growing emphasis on collaborative methods of working* – The wider the set of issues being addressed, the wider the range of interests and organisations that will consider themselves as having a stake in the process – and so the more widely it is now becoming recognised that collaborative as opposed to adversarial styles of working offer the only constructive opportunities for effective progress. There is a widespread understanding that it is only through their involvement in the process that stakeholders will feel the sense of ownership of the results necessary for there to be a high level of commitment to their implementation.

While there is recognised to be still much scope for improvement, the proliferation of projects based on the ideas of consensus-building is increasingly apparent. This has been especially evident in projects where the aim has been to harmonise policies across international boundaries, for example within the European Union.

These two trends have led to three types of changes in the political context within which extensive projects must be planned; and these in turn have called for adaptations in the strategic choice approach. The three main changes are:

1. *Extended numbers of participants* – The wider the set of issues being addressed, the wider the range of interests and organisations that will expect to have a stake in the process – and so the larger the number of people with a claim to be involved. No longer is it sufficient to rely on one or two informal workshops, producing quick results. It has become important that any stakeholder who has the power to make things happen – or conversely to block things happening – should be an active participant.
2. *Extended channels of communication* – The wider the issues, the more attenuated become the channels and procedures of communication which link the participants to their constituents. The more extensive the range of participating organisations, the more complex will become the required procedures of authorisation, resource commitment and control. In particular, those representing governmental organisations will have to assure those to whom they are accountable that they are undertaking a finite project with prescribed forms of outcome.
3. *Extended time-frames* – An important consequence of this is that time scales become extended if lasting progress towards agreement is to be secured. A process has to be designed which may often extend over 1 or 2 years, with successive meetings of many different types, managed together as a series with ample time allowed for maintaining the link between representatives and their constituents.

All these broad trends reflect a growth in the complexity of the organisational and political context within which the search for progress is set. Therefore, they require that greater attention be given to the design of the more political, as opposed to the more technical, aspects of the work. There have been the following consequences for the adaptation of the strategic choice approach:

- in the overall design of the process, considerably greater attention has had to be given to the *design of the work that has to be done in the political arena*, as presented in Figure 89, as against the technical domain;
- an increased emphasis is required on methods designed to *help participants to work with each other*, as much as with the complexities of the issues they are addressing;
- it becomes important to *simplify the analytical methods* used as far as possible, especially where there are differences of culture and mother tongue among the participants;
- concepts relating to the *management of uncertainty may have to be kept in the background* of the work rather than brought to the foreground in the early stages, as they are sometimes seen as threatening and can be stressful until some level of trust has built up;
- it becomes necessary to *reinforce the skills involved in process management*, by introducing other third-party skills from such related fields as mediation and alternative dispute resolution;
- it becomes increasingly difficult for one person to handle effectively the extended facilitation role; so a requirement arises for the *formation of facilitation teams* – often calling for a planned investment in training in facilitation skills;
- it has become necessary to *reconcile the cyclic process with the linear principles of conventional project planning* and to agree a clear series of stages through which progress towards outcomes can be monitored;
- it becomes important to give more explicit attention to the challenge of actively *managing the process within an extended organisational context*, throughout all phases of a project.

For all these reasons, the strategic choice toolbox as presented in earlier chapters has come to be supplemented, in the management of extensive projects, by various further concepts, processes, techniques and methods. Some of these have been borrowed from other toolboxes – with adaptations where appropriate – while others take the form of more direct extensions to the concepts and methods presented in earlier chapters. The main purpose of this chapter is to introduce the extended principles of process management which have evolved as a result of a decade of experience in the management of extensive projects. A few more specific examples will also be given of the more specific adaptations that have been introduced in the technology and the organisation of the strategic choice approach, and in the strategies used to capture both the visible and the invisible products.

A TWIN-TRACK APPROACH

The argument that any process of strategic choice involves a subtle interplay between relatively technical and relatively political types of work was first introduced in the discussion of the basic process diagram of Figure 8, and was developed further in Chapters 4 and 9. This line of argument culminated in the presentation of a general model – Figure 89 – indicating an intricate web of relationships linking a *technical domain*; a *political arena* and a *field of operations*.

To reflect the increased complexity and significance of the political arena in the circumstances of an extensive project, an extended model of the process has now evolved, based on the concept of *a twin-track approach*. This model is based on a recognition of parallel and interdependent streams of work for the technical domain and for the political arena.

These streams have come to be known as the technical and the socio-political work streams. The phrase 'socio -political' is used as a means of reassuring senior civil servants that their role is not being seen as intruding on that of elected politicians. This point can also be reflected by talking of a policy stream rather than a political stream – and this is the term that will be adopted in this chapter.

The two streams of work play complementary roles in the overall process:

1. the work in the *technical stream* involves managing the complexity of the issues, so as to develop confidence in the quality of the results;
2. the work in the *policy stream* involves managing the conflicting positions of those involved, so as to develop commitment to the results.

It is important for the participants to recognise that the distinction is one between types of work rather than between types of roles. Indeed, those in more technical roles often have a significant part to play in the policy as well as the technical work streams and it is helpful to keep them aware of this reality. Likewise, those in policy roles may make contributions to the technical work streams, although pressures on their time will often limit the extent of these.

Most conventional planning projects begin with a series of technical stages leading to the production of a proposal of some sort, for example, a draft plan. Professional norms often create an expectation that this be made as technically perfect as possible, before work begins in a series of political stages aimed at developing commitment to that proposal.

The first diagram of Figure 93 illustrates this relationship – recognising that, for a short while at least, the two types of work may run in parallel, and also that each stage may in practice involve work of a cyclic rather than a strictly linear nature.

It is at the interface between the two types of work that the all-important process of consensus-building takes place. Conventionally, however, the duration of this interface is so short that the opportunities for consensus-building become severely limited. If these opportunities are to be increased, it is important that both types of work should start as early as possible in the life of a project. This means extending the length of the interface, as illustrated in the second diagram of Figure 93.

FIGURE
93

Linking Technical and Political Work

Conventional approach

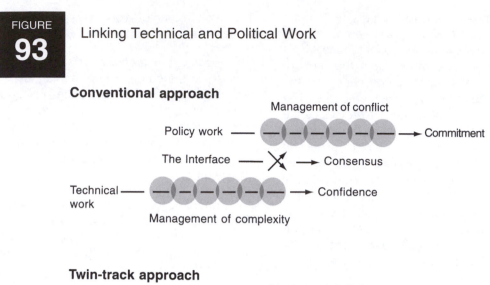

Twin-track approach

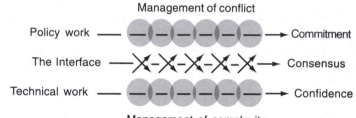

The political – technical U-loop

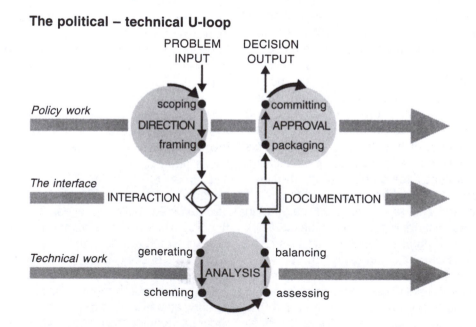

In an extensive project, this can be achieved through structuring the overall project timetable with reference to an agreed schedule of events, each with an emphasis on consensus-building at the policy–technical interface, and each usually involving a substantial number of people. The progress of the overall project can then be managed through commitments on the part of those involved in both work streams to the production of draft documents in preparation for future events.

The policy work and the technical work in combination can be viewed as covering the four modes of work which together form the basic process model of the strategic choice approach – shaping and choosing within the political arena, together with designing and comparing within the technical domain. To further clarify the nature of the work involved in each mode, it has been found helpful to sub-divide these activities further, as follows:

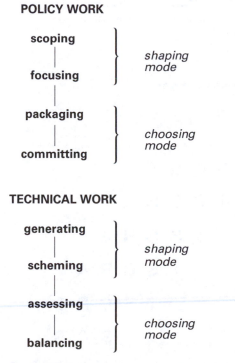

POLICY WORK

scoping

focusing

shaping mode

packaging

committing

choosing mode

TECHNICAL WORK

generating

scheming

shaping mode

assessing

balancing

choosing mode

Several of the terms introduced above reflect the terminology of specific strategic choice concepts introduced in earlier chapters – for example, the terminology of the problem focus, the decision scheme and the commitment package. Some correspondences will also be noticed with the terms used to describe the principal process windows of the STRAD software, as illustrated in Figure 90.

The fundamental relationship between the policy work and the technical work is illustrated in the third diagram of Figure 93. This model has become known as the political–technical U-loop. Recognising that each stage of policy work will rarely in practice follow a linear logic, each policy stage is shown as a cycle, involving inputs not only from previous cycles but also from what is described in Figure 89 as the *field of operations*. The outputs of each policy cycle will then provide inputs to later cycles, together with any agreed policies or actions directed towards the field of operations.

In the diagram, each technical cycle is seen as, in effect, an extension of the middle part of a political cycle. It begins with inputs from the first part of the political cycle, taking the form of agreed directions for the work sometimes expressed in 'terms of reference'. It ends with some form of recommendation or proposal, providing input to the latter part of the political cycle – often taking the form of a draft document.

What is essential is that the two streams of work should not be taken forward in isolation; rather, it is important that the interaction between them should be carefully structured. The principle of the political–technical U-loop, as illustrated in Figure 93, offers an important conceptual reference point in doing this. However, if it is to provide practical guidance over the course of an extensive project, it has first to be adapted to the gradually changing nature of the work carried out at successive stages.

APPLYING THE CONCEPTS TO PROJECT PLANNING

The design of any major project involves planning some progression of activities extending from its beginning to its intended end date, related in some way to the passage of time.

FIGURE
94

Phasing Work in an Extensive Project

Principles of the ISCRA sequence

I = identify issues; S = set structure; C = confirm course;
R = review recommendations; A = approve amendments

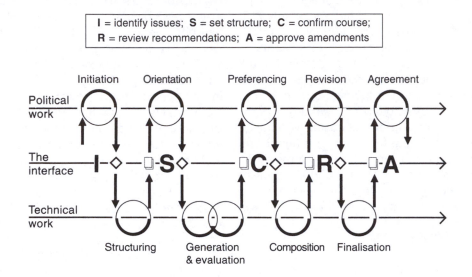

Adapting the ISCRA model for project management

WORK BITES	DOCUMENTS	time dimension → → → → → → → → → → → → → → → → →
Initial focus; aims; organisation; planning	PROJECT PLANNING	I S C R A
Status quo; current action commitments and policies	INFORMATION BASE	I S C R A
Trends; scenarios; problems & opportunities	PROBLEM FOCUS	I S C R A
Criteria; constraints; shortlisted strategies	OPTIONS	I S C R A
Uncertainties; assumptions; selected strategy	OVERALL STRATEGY	I S C R A
Agreed actions; budgets; responsibilities; deadlines	OPERATIONAL INITIATIVES	I S C R A
Research; communication; monitoring; adjustment	ON-GOING MANAGEMENT	I S C R A

The purpose of formalising this is to enable all those involved to keep track of what is going on at any time.

The following set of terms indicates the changing emphasis of both the policy work and the technical work over the course of any extensive project:

	policy work	technical work
1	initiation	structuring
2	orientation	generating
3	preferencing	evaluating
4	revision	composition
5	agreement	finalisation

In practice, it is usual for more than one kind of work to be in progress at any particular time, even though the primary emphasis will tend to shift gradually over the course of a project.

In order to reflect this shift, it has been found helpful to view the progression of a project in terms of a *succession of linked U-loops*, in which the nature of the work to be done at the policy–technical interface changes, as well as the nature of the work within each of the policy and technical streams. This progression is reflected in the first diagram of Figure 94.

In Figure 94 five sorts of activity are identified which, based on experience, are suited to interactive working at the political-technical interface. These are summarised in the acronym **ISCRA**:

I Identifying the Issues
S Setting the Structure
C Confirming the Course
R Reviewing the Recommendations
A Approving any Amendments

It will be noticed in Figure 94 that these five activities do not proceed strictly in step with the five sorts of work in the political arena and the technical domain. In particular, the two closely intertwined technical cycles of generating and evaluating are shown as appearing together between *Setting the Structure* and *Confirming the Course*.

It will also be noticed that the primary inputs to the early stages (I and S) are shown as coming from the political arena, whereas the primary inputs to the later stages (C, R and A) are shown as coming from the technical domain. This change in emphasis recognises that, in an extensive project where there are many diverse interests at stake, value judgements are required in order to identify what are the key issues to be addressed, and thus give direction to the technical work. The contrast here is with more conventional models of planning in which technical issues are regarded as dominant in the early stages.

However, this relationship does not extend throughout the process. Towards the end, those in more technical roles will tend to become more proactive, as it becomes necessary to draw the threads together and prepare documents for the approval of those who carry political accountability for the project.

The most important practical challenge can then be seen as one of designing, over the course of a project, the settings within which the work at the policy–technical interface is to be done. In an extensive project, it has become usual for much of this work to be carried out in the course of relatively large events which are sometimes called *strategic discussions* or *stakeholder dialogue*. These discussions are designed to bring together a considerable number of people in both policy roles and relatively technical roles. Some of the work may, however, be done in smaller sub-group meetings of various kinds. At other times – especially at the beginning or end of a project – it will be appropriate for all the participants to come together for events of a more celebratory nature.

The number of full strategic discussions scheduled over the course of a project will depend on the project context. In a project designed to be completed in a few months there may be relatively few, whereas as many as seven or eight strategic discussions may be scheduled in the case of an international project extending over 2 years or more.

A strategic discussion is usually planned to extend over at least one full day and usually two days, in the course of which various more specific activities – sometimes called 'work bites' – will be scheduled, often in series but sometimes in parallel. Many of these work bites will involve interactive working, but others may involve a more reactive style of work. The overall nature of the work done in a strategic discussion can therefore be described as *inter-reactive* in nature.

As might be expected, the nature of the joint work carried out in such meetings is designed to be different from the nature of the work normally carried out in either the political arena or the technical domain. For there are only certain forms of consensus-building activity that such mixed groups can be expected to undertake. As is also to be expected, the nature of this work will change through time to reflect the changing emphases of the work within both the political arena and the technical domain.

In an extensive project involving many participants, it becomes a practical necessity that most of the primary inputs and outputs take the form of documents of some kind. At some stages, these may be relatively formal papers; at other times, they may be briefer and more informal. This will depend on the overall scale of the project as well as on the progress that has so far been achieved.

THE EXTENDED ISCRA MODEL

In planning major projects, it has become common practice to apply the ISCRA model not just to the project as a whole, conceived as a unitary work programme, but to a set of inter-related *work bites*, each associated with the production of a different type of documentary output. Each document is developed incrementally over the course of the project and becomes a self-contained report on that part of the work – ultimately forming one of the main sections of the overall project document.

A typical set of work bites and their associated documents forms the left hand side of the lower diagram in Figure 94. The names and titles used to identify the work bites are not sacrosanct and, indeed, the whole set, which has been designed to conform to relatively

familiar models of strategic planning, should be adapted to the project in hand.

The ISCRA sequence of activities is then applied to each work bite of the project specific set. This resulting framework is then used for the phased drafting and revision of a series of documents – one for each of the bites. The work in each is usually scheduled to begin at different stages of the project, then to run in parallel with the others to phased completion dates, as shown in the right hand part of the lower diagram in Figure 94. In fact, the work represented in the first few columns and the last few columns is usually undertaken reactively, and only the central columns are used in this way.

It is important to reiterate that this somewhat 'pure' generalised model is intended only as a framework for the design of a process specific to the requirements of each project – depending on such variables as the complexity of the issues, the number of stakeholders and the time available. It is common for documents to be combined and/or some of the steps brought together or extended in time. For example, the Information and Problem Focus documents together can be seen as a *database*; the Options and Overall Strategy documents combine to form a *strategy*, and the Operational Initiatives and On-going Management documents could provide the basic components for an *action plan* (see the illustration from practice in Figure 95).

There are two important advantages in the application of the extended ISCRA model as a general framework for the design of extensive planning projects.

1. Firstly, it provides a practical means of reconciling the principle of cyclic continuity as discussed in Chapter 4 with the expectation of steady and sustained progress which is so vital to most of the participants – and their sponsors – in any project of this nature. For example, opportunities will still remain to review the focus of the project, and to reformulate the options, even when the project is well advanced, as the

participants develop closer mutual under-standing and as they adjust to any important changes in their working environment.

2. Secondly, the extended ISCRA model provides a framework for the design of sufficiently compact 'work bites' even in relatively large strategic discussion meet-ings to be sub-divided in such a way as to give each participant a series of meaningful parts to play, working for much of the time in relatively small sub-groups with defined types of outcome which have a recognis-able role in the overall project design.

EXTENSIONS TO THE PROJECT ORGANISATION

One significant extension to the principles of organisation as discussed in Chapter 9, and illustrated in Figure 84, concerns the overall management of a project.

In an extensive project, it is especially import-ant that there should be a recognised *project leader* who carries continuous responsibility for the overall management of the project, yet who draws authority from an extended *pro-ject group* which includes representation of all the main interests involved. In a typical large environmental project, these will include vari-ous governmental bodies plus a range of organ-isations representing business and community interests.

This project group carries the ultimate responsibility not only for the conduct of the project work itself, but also for the production of a management programme or implementa-tion document through which the work will be carried forward into the field of operations, to influence future decision-making after the pro-ject comes to an end.

In the formation of the project group, it can be important to go through explicit processes of *stakeholder analysis* – preferably extending beyond the kind of brief brainstorming exer-cise which is often considered adequate in a more limited project setting. Various meth-ods of stakeholder analysis are available (GTZ, 1991; Wilcox, 1994) which not only enable lists of stakeholders to be identified, but also help in understanding the positions they might be expected to adopt, the factions or coalitions which might be expected to form, and the pos-sible strategies through which they might be approached when invited to participate in the project work.

It is important too that an extended view be taken of what are referred to in Figure 84 as the *reference* and *representative groupings*. In an extensive project, it has been found use-ful to introduce an extended concept of a *ref-erence network*, emphasising that the task of developing this falls on all those who become directly involved in the project work. For the reference network is intended to tap into the personal networks of all participants, who are encouraged to suggest the names of individu-als whom they consider should be included in the first instance. From this basis the network can be allowed to grow freely, encouraging anyone who shows an interest to join.

Members of this wider network can then be kept in touch with the course of the project work through a periodic project news-letter, and encouraged to contribute by provid-ing inputs of information or opinion through whatever channels are available. In some cir-cumstances it may be appropriate to invite them to particular sessions of the project group – for example in the evening between the two days of a strategic discussion. The membership of this reference network will tend to expand over the course of a project as more and more people find out that the work is in progress – ultimately evolving into an implementation network focused directly on the often complex processes of implementing the agreements reached.

Wherever it is important that the project group should have a larger membership – as is especially the case in international pro-jects – it becomes essential that smaller, more flexible sub-groups be formed to carry out certain aspects of the project group's work at some stages of the process. There is no intention that these groups should take over the responsibilities of the project group – they are merely intended to enable it to work more effectively.

It is usual to view such groups as falling into one or other of two categories – task groups, which are primarily responsible for more technical aspects of the work, and in particular for preparing specific outcomes of this for handling within the project group; and guidance groups, which are responsible for policy aspects and can act as political sounding boards where necessary.

Whereas the task groups will tend to operate in a proactive style, developing proposals for consideration in the full project group, the guidance groups will tend to play a more reactive or responsive role, acting as a sounding board where necessary – typically, during the final stages in the preparation of specific documents.

In an extensive project, as in any other, continuous management through a relatively compact core group between one scheduled event and another is crucial. Typically this group will be enlarged to include at least one process consultant, whose role is to advise the core group on matters of organisation, communication, process management, network development and project methodology. These people will usually be centrally involved also in the strategic discussions and many of the sub-group meetings, acting as facilitators as and when required.

It is also important in some circumstances that the core group includes a *technical support team*, with expert knowledge of the substance of the issues. Its members are likely to be consultants, though this is not necessarily so; they will often have a role in assisting any administrative staff in compiling the documentation necessary to keep the process moving forward, based on the directions indicated by the project group.

EXTENSIONS TO PROCESS MANAGEMENT SKILLS

An important point to recognise, especially for those who are accustomed to the management of more conventional projects, is that the management of extensive participatory projects calls not only for practical project management skills of the kind which are widely recognised as vital to the success of any large and complex project, but also for more subtle skills of *process management*. The more extensive the project in terms of the range of interests involved, the higher will be the premium on skills oriented towards the building of such invisible products as synergy, mutual understanding and commitment, alongside the incremental growth of more visible products.

Furthermore, it is important to recognise that process management in such a context involves much more than the skill of facilitating progress within a single working group – even though this has come to be regarded as the key to success in managing a more intensive 'one-off' strategic choice workshop. Serious attention must also be given to a range of complementary skills, to each of which the strategic choice approach is relevant to a different extent.

These skills cannot be dealt with in detail here, but there follow outline descriptions which are intended to give readers some idea of what is involved and of ways in which their own acquired skills might be extended and improved:

- *Organisational/group development skills* – The concept of the extended 'project organisation' – as expressed in Figures 84 and 85, and further developed in this chapter – provides plenty of scope for creative use of organisational and group design skills. The concept of *dynamic grouping* described in Chapter 9 is highly relevant both at this level and at the level of designing sub-group work within a strategic discussion event.
- *Process design skills* – In the design of strategic discussion events on inter-reactive principles, the concept of flexible scheduling discussed in Chapter 9 plays an important role. The use of 'flexi-time' (time put aside for use when that use becomes more clear) and 'slop' (allowing more time than is technically

necessary for each task) represents a recognition of process uncertainty and can provide vital opportunities for the facilitation team to respond to the needs of the participants as they are expressed.

- *Network management skills* – Recognition of people on the fringe of the regular project organisation, who nevertheless have a serious interest in the subject, can offer the basis for building a broader consensus than would otherwise be possible. The challenge is that, while setting up an extended project network as described earlier is not difficult, without proper maintenance it will just fade away. For this reason members of the network can become the main target audience for regular project newsletters, while innovative thinking in process design can provide occasional opportunities during strategic discussions to obtain input from the wider network. Two-way communication within the network can also be enabled by encouraging written inputs, using methods ranging from simple questionnaires to exercises using the Delphi method (Moore, 1987).
- *Effective negotiation/participation skills* – These skills are sometimes thought of as useful mainly at the point of interaction; but it is now recognised that the way in which any negotiation or interaction is initiated, the amount of effort put into preparation, and the attention paid to follow-up actions can be just as critical, in the context of a wider understanding of process (Hawkins and Hudson, 1986). The concept of strategic choice as a continuous learning process, as presented in earlier chapters, is significant in this respect.
- *Skills in the management of information flows* – The effect of the strategic choice approach here is to introduce new perspectives on the type of information being communicated. Conventional approaches focus on what is known, and there is a strong emphasis on facts. Recognition of uncertainty, as in strategic choice, leads to an emphasis on what is not known and the range of assumptions which may have to

be made. What is more, the focus changes from a concentration on uncertainties of type UE (i.e. data) to a more balanced approach in which peoples' values and intentions become equally important.

- *Project evaluation skills* – The more extensive a project, the more important it becomes to build in explicit methods for keeping track of progress at each stage. For, the more any personal feelings of either satisfaction or dissatisfaction can be shared, the more opportunities will be created for the process manager to make adjustments in the subsequent process, as well as to demonstrate that it is being managed in a truly participatory way. Evaluation exercises may be either at a micro scale – involving quick checks taken during interactive workshops – or at a macro scale where the subject is the whole project and where it is leading. The latter type of evaluation is usually most relevant some way into the project, and can be used to switch the focus of the group to finishing the project as well as to obtain important process-related feedback. This principle applies to both the visible and the invisible products of the process. So far as the visible products are concerned, the division of the work into manageable 'work bites' within parallel streams of work can provide a useful basis for assessing progress. As discussed in Chapter 9, it is not so easy to keep track of the development of invisible products: although they are often made a part of open evaluations within the project group, a more sensitive way is for core group members to check continuously with participants at a personal level.
- *Conflict mediation skills* – So far the principal 'third party' role discussed has been that of facilitator, which may be adopted by an individual or a team. The task is to enable effective utilisation of the time of people with diverse responsibilities and skills, with respect to the prevention of open conflict among the key objectives. However, it is only realistic to expect that unproductive conflict will occur from time to time and, when it

does, it is helpful to have available the mediation skills to manage it. The main difference between mediation and facilitation is that the mediator will spend more time with the conflicting parties separately, helping them come to terms with the needs of the other side – especially with respect to the relationship with their constituents. He or she is also likely to be a little more involved in the substantive content, and the concept of 'options for mutual gain' can play a useful role. The use of a progress package in resolving conflict is also significant here, as conflict is often based on differing opinions about the assumptions to be made. Use of the idea of a contingency plan in case of the assumption being wrong can provide just the breakthrough which is needed.

- *Project planning skills* This can be viewed in terms of process design at the scale of the project as a whole rather than at that of the individual interactive event. The basic strategic choice concept of cyclic continuity is most relevant here, and the ISCRA process provides the framework for putting it into action. The more extensive the project, the more important too that process management should become seen as a team activity; for it can become a heavy load for any individual to carry alone, and the process can be much enriched when each member of a project management team has the opportunity to draw on the experience and resources of others.

CREATING A CONTEXT FOR SUCCESS IN EXTENSIVE PROJECTS

Experience has repeatedly shown that the success of an extensive participatory project does not depend on the quality of its project management alone, even when the importance of good process management is fully recognised and applied.

The experience of ambitious projects that are set up to address complex areas of policy – and, in particular, of environmental policy – has been that a project can only be expected to be fully successful if the conditions for success are in place at the outset. This has proved generally true, but is especially the case where the project has had trans-national sponsorship and the aim has been to work towards harmonisation of policies between different nation states with different languages and cultures.

The effectiveness of such a context has been found to depend critically on the following three conditions:

1. a *significant set of issues* which is agreed to be of sufficient common concern;
2. an *experienced project leader* with a clear understanding of process management issues, as a focus for the project management team;
3. an *internal sponsor* highly placed in the client organisation, with a commitment to seeing the project conducted in an interactive participatory way.

While these aspects are indeed critical, and their absence is likely to make a project extremely difficult – if not impossible, there are others which it may be possible to influence to some extent. These are listed here in an approximate descending order of significance:

- a *long enough project* in terms of the time available for developing the long-term 'added value' represented by the invisible products;
- a *committed project group* which believes in the benefits of the proposed style of working, or is at least willing to suspend its disbelief;
- an *external sponsor* who plays a similar supporting role as the internal sponsor, but from outside the organisation;
- a *non-hostile culture* in the 'client' organisation or organisations, so that the work is not constantly under threat of being sabotaged;
- an *appropriate workplace* which is somewhat larger than normal, with good light, ventilation and uncluttered walls.

The absence of all these characteristics of an appropriate context is likely to make the successful conduct of an extensive participatory project impossible. However we have never experienced such a serious case. The most likely explanation for this is that, in such a situation, this type of project would ever be mooted, let alone get to the stage of serious consideration.

So it is probable that all is not lost. While it may be difficult or impossible to create these conditions if they are not already in place, it may be possible to influence them to some extent. Therefore, in the initial negotiations leading up to the launch of a project, it is vital to discuss explicitly how far such conditions can be fulfilled.

Where any shortfalls exist, it will pay to review ways in which they might be substituted. If this proves impossible, the practical question to be faced is one of how SCA can be adapted to address any of the more negative characteristics that may have been recognised. This is where the process management skills described above, such as those of organisational development, process design and project evaluation, will play a crucial role. Inevitably there will be much uncertainty to be managed, and there is likely to be a case for applying the concept of the progress package to the management of the process itself. It will then be a case of careful negotiation to balance the needs of all the key stakeholders without sacrificing the viability of the approach.

The management of an extended project is a process that offers rich opportunities to many people for many kinds of learning. One of the most important forms of learning concerns the highly complex process of managing the progress of the overall project, linking together the technical and political work by appropriate design of interfaces at every stage of the ISCRA sequence. The more ambitious the project, the more important it becomes that the lessons learnt from it be taken on board in the design of any future projects of similar scope.

ILLUSTRATIONS FROM PRACTICE

Figure 95 on the next page presents an illustration from practice showing interpretations of the ISCRA sequence presented in this chapter. As in the case of the illustrations from practice at the end of Chapters 5 to 8, this figure is accompanied by a commentary to explain more about the context of the European policy projects concerned.

FIGURE

95

Illustrations from practice: working with ISCRA

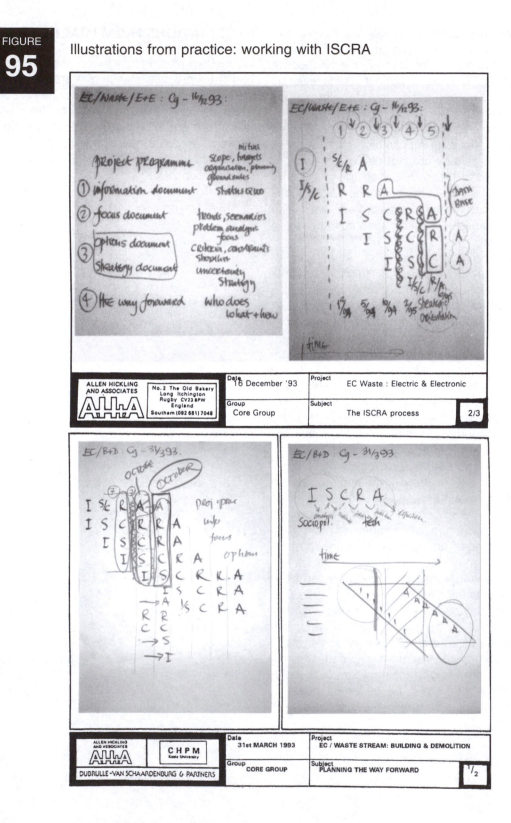

COMMENTARY ON FIGURE 95

These illustrations from practice have been taken from the European Commission's programme to develop implementation plans for the Union's waste management policy. There are examples from two of their six projects, each focused on a different *priority waste stream*.

They are both taken from flip charts that formed parts of the photo-reports of Core Group meetings. They demonstrate clearly the messy process of adaptation that the 'pure' generalised model illustrated in Figure 94 has to be put through. The circumstances of each project can be very different, thus influencing the process management decisions about how the model can best be made to work in each case.

1. The upper example comes out of the project on the management of building and demolition waste, which was carried out in Berlin and Brussels. The flip charts illustrated were drawn up during a session which took place some way into the project, but not yet as far as half way.

   The left hand chart shows how the ISCRA activities have, in some cases, been doubled up to be handled together in one session - while, in others, they have been extended to take place over several sessions. This is quite normal, and reflects how difficult and/or controversial that part of the work is expected to be.

   Also on the left hand chart it can be seen that some of the ISCRA activities have been programmed to end together so that the documents can be more strongly coordinated and released as one. The several vertical areas which have been outlined near the middle of the time scale each represent a programme of work for a strategic discussion.

The right hand flip chart shows at the top the simple ISCRA sequence. Indicated on it are the areas where the participants involved in the policy work stream are expected to be more proactive (i.e. in the early stages), and those areas where the technical work will take over the lead – albeit guided by policy input (i.e. the later stages). Below this is an abstracted version of the ISCRA pattern from the left hand chart. On this are indicated the areas where strategic discussions are less useful (i.e. the triangles to the left and right), and, by deduction, the areas where they are most useful (i.e. in the middle).

2. The lower example comes out of the project on the management of electric and electronic waste, which was carried out in Rome and Brussels. The flip charts illustrated were drawn up during a session which took place very early in the project before it had really got started.

   Here the main concern was to work out how the project could be completed in a much shorter time span than had been the norm up till then. This is reflected in the more vertical shape of the ISCRA pattern, which was achieved by not only doubling up activities, but 'tripling' them up in some cases. Another way to finish more quickly was to reduce the work to be done, and the sacrifice of the on-going management of the plan was considered to be feasible in this case. This is reflected in the fact that there are only six rows as opposed to seven in the other example.

Probably the most important point arising from these examples is the value of the ISCRA model as a structure for communication. It can serve the project management team well in their difficult process discussions, which are necessary when one tries to combine the advantages of cyclic working with the linear constraints of most organisations.

12 Invention, transformation and interpretation

In our early chapters we took care to present our view of the Strategic Choice 'toolbox' as a coherent and balanced whole. Yet we acknowledged from the very first page of our first chapter that it would be too much for us to expect readers to embrace the strategic choice approach (SCA) as a complete new framework for planning or management, without critical comparison with what they have learnt from other sources – including, in the case of more mature decision-makers, their own working experiences as managers or consultants.

So it should be no surprise that many people have taken on our ideas in a selective way. They have imported features of the strategic choice toolbox to their own practices wherever it seems to make sense to them to do so, adapting their language to the situations they meet where they feel it will better serve their own needs and – often crucially – to the needs of the stakeholders they are there to help and to serve. In this kind of process, they have introduced differences of many kinds, as we have ourselves.

ADAPTATIONS IN WORKING METHODS

As described in Chapter 11, many people alongside whom we have worked, especially on relatively extensive projects involving interactive workshop methods, have devised creative ways of combining methods from the strategic choice toolbox with complementary methods from other sources – especially in situations where people have not only to learn ways of handling the complexities of the issues before them, but also to learn ways of working constructively with each other.

In each of the five sections that follow, examples will be given of adaptations to the strategic choice toolbox that tend to arise at successive stages of project work. These can be loosely related to the successive stages in the ISCRA sequence described in Chapter 11;

and also to the strategic choice cycle of Figure 8.

- engaging diverse participants in identifying issues;
- distinguishing different levels of choice;
- extending the areas of agreement;
- agreeing preferred ways forward; and
- developing commitment to action proposals.

The chapter ends with a review of the factors to be considered when customising the approach to different situations, followed by a selection of four further illustrations from practice.

ENGAGING PARTICIPANTS IN IDENTIFYING ISSUES

We have already described, in Chapter 5, a general approach to the shaping of problems through building up a shared list of issues of

FIGURE
96

Setting Levels of Choice

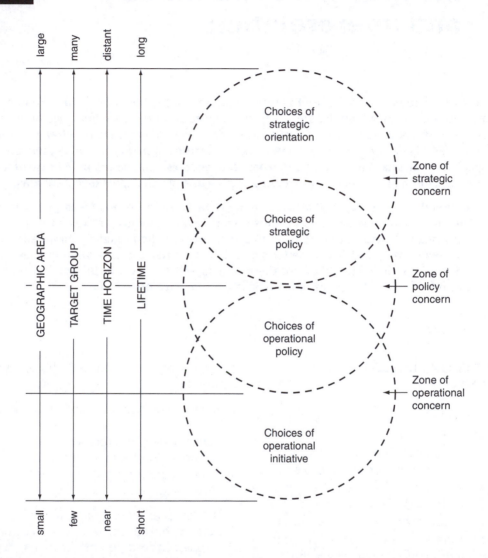

- The terminology used in this diagram is indicative only. In practice the language should be adapted so that the stakeholders can relate to it easily.
- There can be as many levels as necessary for comfortable working – 2 to 5 is the normal range, with 3 or 4 being the most common.
- This is not a process so much as a framework for analysis and communication. It is best to start wherever it is most comfortable, and to keep moving up, down or across according to which is likely to provide the greatest learning experience.

concern – issues which may later become variously reframed as decision areas, comparison areas or uncertainty areas – or in some cases as assumptions or constraints.

When working with diverse participants it is helpful to start building consensus in the group as early as possible in the process. An opportunity for this lies in the generation of a first shared list of issues, as this has been found to provide a non-threatening means of enabling participants to begin working interactively together.

Here it is important that the facilitator should demonstrate both listening skills and questioning skills. For example, it is quite common for the participants to tend, at first, to formulate issues in the form of position statements; this can be seriously counterproductive in the search for consensus. Here the skilled facilitator can demonstrate ways in which these issues can be reformulated in more fundamental terms such as organisational interests or personal needs.

Over time, this process can have the effect of making the contributions of different participants more consistent in their language – with some issues being reframed in terms of broader goals or values, and others in terms of more concrete action possibilities or contingencies. Some examples of relevant questions, sometimes known as 'restructuring heuristics' (Shakun, 1995), are:

- So why should this be a problem?
- What might be the causes of that?
- Why might we want to do that?
- If that is a goal, how might we get there?

Time spent in this kind of discussion can be important in demonstrating to the participants how their own concerns, which may earlier have been expressed in quite diverse ways and at diverse levels, can be gradually reframed in terms of a shared framework of understanding. Once in this form, the issues can be analysed further by clustering similar ones together and, where there are many, establishing the priorities between them so that a

collective approach can be taken in deciding where to begin.

Then, more specific concepts of problem-structuring from the strategic choice toolbox – such as those of the decision area, the decision option, the comparison area and the uncertainty area – can be introduced gradually and selectively, as a means of enabling people to build together on the inputs that they and the other participants have provided.

DIFFERENTIATING LEVELS OF CHOICE

Towards the end of Chapter 6, the notion was introduced that it is sometimes useful to formulate decision areas at different *levels of generality*. This applies particularly in relatively ambitious projects where the participants are responsible not only for exploring relatively specific choices of action, but also broader, more generic policy positions and choices for the longer term.

One of the strengths of the Strategic Choice Approach is that it enables people to break away from more rigid, linear models of planning in which it is supposed that one should begin by setting broad goals and progressively work downwards towards a more specific operational level. Yet, where a need is felt for some kind of differentiation of levels of choice, SCA can be adapted to this by offering a framework for checking the consistency of options in either direction. Only two levels were suggested in the South Side illustration (see Figure 54): one encapsulating more general and long-term issues, and the other specific projects and operations. This distinction corresponds broadly to the familiar differentiation of strategy and tactics in military and business planning.

In some extensive projects, it may be helpful to distinguish more than two levels in addressing the complexity of the issues identified. For example, during a 3-year project concerned with the development of policy options in the preparation of a new generation of structure plans that was being introduced in

FIGURE

97

A Common Grounding Table

Decision Areas	Options	Homogenous Sub-Groups					
		A	**B**	**C**	**D**	**E**	**F**
1	i						
	ii						
	iii						
2	i						
	ii		preferences / choices				
3	i						
	ii						
	iii						
	iv						

This technique can be used with as few as 10 participants but its real value is with 30 or 40. There is no real upper limit, but it must be remembered that the more people are involved the more difficult it becomes to find some common ground with which to start building.

The time necessary depends on the number of participants, but it should be possible to get the main table on the wall in an hour. If it is taking longer than that it is likely that the participants are not ready for it yet. The time required for the subsequent 'give and take' is much more difficult to judge, and can be considerable. However it has to go on until agreement is reached, even if that agreement is to go back and review the formulation of decision areas and options.

The amount of space required also depends to some extent on the number of participants, but also on the scale of the problem. There are no particular spatial requirements, except that the sub-groups should be able to work privately in the first round, if possible.

It is most important that the recording is thoroughly carried out at this stage because it provides the only record of the consensus agreements.

See also the illustration from practice in Figure 99.

- This type of interaction should only be attempted when the group have had the opportunity to establish a reasonable level of trust through working together – for example in agreeing the decision areas and options.
- When the preferences of the homogenous sub-groups have been recorded, and the common ground identified, the process of extending it begins where the disagreement is weakest.
- If such an extension proves difficult, some form of organised reformulation in the light of the 'needs of the other side' is most likely necessary.
- See also the illustration from practice in Figure 99.

England alongside local government reorganisation (Hickling, 1978), many choices arose to do with the choice of *policies* either in relation to specific planning topics or of a more fundamental nature. Because these three zones of concern – strategic, policy and operational – seemed to overlap, a four-level differentiation was identified (see Figure 95):

These levels were described as:

- choices of *strategic orientation*;
- choices of *strategic policy*;
- choices of *operational policy*;
- choices of *operational initiative*.

In any other application the number and the description of levels can be varied according to the range and the complexity of the issues identified. In most extensive projects, experience suggests that a four-level split is usually appropriate.

The definition of the levels of generality should be agreed, at least provisionally, before working across levels can begin. There are three scales that recur: space, population and time, though there can be others that may bear consideration in specific cases. The spatial scale refers to the geographic area relevant to the choices being made, which may vary from a specific site to a wider region or nation state. The population scale refers to the target group for the choices being made – probably human, but not necessarily so. This could be similar to the geographic scale, but is more likely to vary from an individual or small group, through various sectors, to the total population. The time scale is different because there are two aspects that are usually relevant. One is as in the time horizon of the choices being made (when the effects may be experienced), which may vary from tomorrow through next year, to 20 or 50 years from now. The other is as in the life expectancy of the choices being made (the length of time before they should be re-examined), which may be similar to the time horizon, but is most often more short-term.

Any set of levels of choice comprises a framework for problem structuring, and need imply no particular process for working with them. In a hierachy of choice, it is often assumed that one should start at the top and work down; yet it has been found equally revealing to start at the bottom and work up. In the structure plan project (Hickling, 1978), some teams started working at all levels at the same time. In keeping with the cyclic process of strategic choice, we would recommend starting wherever it is most comfortable, and to keep moving up down, or across according to which is likely to provide the greatest learning experience.

FACILITATING EXTENSIONS TO THE COMMON GROUND

Turning to the next stage of ISCRA – confirming concepts – consensus will gradually develop, as the work of a project proceeds, on the nature of the key choices ahead – in strategic choice language, the key decision areas – and also on the range of realistic options available within each, although they may not always be presented as such. An approach can then be introduced which has come to be known as *common grounding*. The purpose of this is first to identify and make visible any common ground which already exists among the various interests represented; then gradually to enlarge this. The experience of effective negotiators (Fisher and Ury, 1981) confirms that this can be a more productive way of working towards agreement than focusing more directly on the differences between the parties.

Common grounding is usually used at some stage well into a project, after a sufficient level of mutual trust has been built up. In any case there will have to have been some activity in developing *options for mutual gain*, leading to some reasonably clear choices to be made and demonstrating that a minimal level of consensus already exists.

This technique requires that the choices faced by the participants should be formulated in the form of decision areas and options as in AIDA, after which homogenous sub-groups of participants (in terms of 'where they are coming from') are formed to decide which of the

FIGURE

98

An Elaborated Progress Package

What *immediate decisions* should we take (which may include to do nothing yet; to undertake direct, partial or holding actions; or to make statements of policy)?	**PROCESS CRITERIA FOR MANAGEMENT OF UNCERTAINTY**	**NOTES ON THE PROCESS CRITERIA**
What *immediate decisions* should we take (which may include to do nothing yet; to undertake direct, partial or holding actions; or to make statements of policy)?	Robustness. Flexibility. Changeability.	Robustness is like 'rugged'. Flexibility refers to keeping future connected options open. Changeability is opposed to 'rigidity'.
What are the *crucial assumptions* entailed (including successful implementation) which, if they turn out to have been wrong, would make the immediate decisions unwise?	Sensitivity.	Sensitivity of the decision to an assumption being wrong is a measure of the degree to which that assumption is 'crucial'.
What *monitoring system* would be sensible to keep track of how the crucial assumptions are standing up over time – probably using indicators?	Cost. Effectiveness.	Cost refers to all types of resource (time; manpower, money, materials). Effectiveness is about the provision of accurate indicative information.
What *contingency plans* will be needed to offset the negative effects of not having got the crucial assumptions right?	Assurance.	Assurance is the level of confidence that all will not be lost when crucial assumptions are wrong.

Where there is no imperative to decide yet, what *deferred decisions* should be identified now (including how long they should be deferred for)?	Opportunity cost Confidence (now and when the time comes to decide).	Opportunity cost is what one misses by not deciding now. Confidence is the increased probability of a good decision later.
Which are the *key uncertainties* (of all three types – UE, UV and UR), which will make these deferred decisions difficult when the time comes?	Sensitivity. Tractability.	Sensitivity of a deferred decision to an uncertainty is a measure of how 'key' that uncertainty is. Tractability is the practical ease or difficulty of reducing an uncertainty.
What *research programme* would it be appropriate to undertake to reduce the key uncertainties before taking the deferred decisions?	Cost. Benefit.	Cost refers to all types of resource (time, manpower, money, materials). Benefit here refers to the expected reduction of uncertainty.

What *performance specifications*, to which deferred decisions and/or contingency plans must conform, can be formulated now to insure a good result?	Consistency. Acceptability.	Consistency relates to statements of policy (see immediate decisions above). Acceptability is for the stakeholders.

- In designing a progress package it will be helpful to first identify: for whom it is being prepared (the decision-taker); what it is aimed to achieve (the strategic orientation); and for how long it should be valid (its expected 'life').
- If alternative progress packages are to be put forward the process criteria are likely to play as important a role in comparing them as the substantive comparison areas - but they may have to be explained first.
- The practical aspects of the commitment (or progress) package in use are described in Chapter 8 – they are also relevant here.

options they would prefer. The output of these groups is then plotted on a simple matrix as shown in Figure 97, and the result then opened for discussion.

Common ground is easily identified where all the sub-groups choose the same option. It is also identified where any option is chosen by no sub-group – so there is common ground that this option is not supported. It is at this stage that it is quite usual for the participants to be surprised to find the extent to which they already agree.

Discussion is then aimed at building on the common ground, so the focus starts where there is least difference in preferences. Typically this will be where only one sub-group is not in agreement. That sub-group is then questioned as follows: 'How would this option, which the others have all chosen, need to be modified to make it acceptable to you?' Frequently the changes needed are quite simple: a slight change of wording, some joint monitoring, or a contingency plan in case of a negative outcome. The modification is then put to the other sub-groups in the form of: 'Can you live with this proposed modification?' When the changes are genuinely small there is rarely a problem, and once again consensus is identified. Where the changes required are more difficult to agree, and where the differences are more evenly split between the sub-groups, there is a clear focus for further work. Here, for example, a decision area can be set aside until later, and another one explored. When only a few decision areas remain which require further work, the experience of working together successfully will often have had the effect of enabling options to be reformulated in a creative way so as to resolve the outstanding difficulties.

Where difficulties prove harder to resolve, one way of proceeding is to invite the participants to join one or other of two competing teams, each with its own appointed 'captain'. Each team is then set the challenge of considering: 'What are the needs of the other side?', and reformulating its preferred option as an option for mutual gain.

At this point, the principles of managing uncertainty covered in earlier chapters become relevant; for they can help people to probe the conflicting assumptions which often underlie apparent disagreements. Inter-group discussion can then help to reduce uncertainty both about the different values in operation, and about the future intentions of relevant parties – leading in many cases to agreement on appropriate exploratory actions or contingency plans.

FRAMING A WAY FORWARD IN THE FACE OF UNCERTAINTY

Chapter 3 concluded with a framework for managing decisions under uncertainty under the name of a *commitment package* (Figure 26). This term has worked well in many different situations, but has been found to be more difficult to use when more people, and thus more different opinions, are involved. It has also been found to need elaboration if it is to be seriously helpful in aiding continuity. As mentioned earlier, we now tend to speak more often about a *progress package*, which addresses some of these issues.

The basic principles are unchanged. However it can often be important to expand the various elements so that they can be addressed more explicitly, and interrelated in a more structured way. One format for doing this is shown in Figure 98. The two main sections remain, but now they are clearly related to either the decisions to be taken now, or those that are to be deferred. The third section is merely included to clarify some of the quality control content which was previously hidden within the cells of the table.

This more explicit structure allows clarification of the role of process criteria for the management of uncertainty. Aspects such as robustness and flexibility can be used more effectively, and others, such as tractability, can be introduced. This is not to say that they should not be handled alongside, and in the same way as, the comparison areas in a regular comparison table if that is more comfortable for the participants, as illustrated in Figure 24.

However it is more usually a case of exploring different aspects of comparison, and interpretation of assessments using substantive comparison areas in the light of uncertainty. This can be especially productive when the level of conflict in the group begins to undermine any progress which is being made towards consensus.

This focus on uncertainty and its management in the form of a progress package is important because it opens the way for the constructive management of conflict. Not only does uncertainty cause conflict – mostly through the parties making different assumptions – but the stresses of conflict can cause uncertainty. These are the classic ingredients of a vicious circle. In an extensive project, if one has the means for effectively managing uncertainty, conflicts can be handled constructively – and their negative symptoms made to disappear.

SECURING COMMITMENT TO ACTION PROPOSALS

At a stage when proposals for action start to be developed in some depth – often through the work of sub-groups charged with generating these within specific policy areas or from the point of view of a specific group of stakeholders – it becomes important to subject these to critical scrutiny, and to encourage constructive amendments or counter-suggestions by members of other sub-groups. At this stage of a major project it has been found helpful to use consistently structured *action forms* with a prescribed sequence of headings such as:

- Description of the action
- Responsibilities
- Funding and Cost/Budget
- Planning (uncertainties, conditions, etc.)
- Crucial assumptions/'Critical success factors'

A structure such as this offers a means of relatively easy access to what can be a considerable amount of detailed information, so that it can be shared among all the members of the wider project group – even in circumstances

where conventionally it might be thought more appropriate to use such concepts explicitly only within the core group. It also provides a way of introducing the set of ideas about the management of uncertainty and the design of commitment (or progress) packages which have been described above, thus releasing the potential for managing conflict which that allows. Some illustrations at the use of action forms in practice are presented in Figure 101 at the end of this Chapter.

One technique which can be used to bring the proposals of the different sub-groups together for display is to create what has become known as an *action gallery* – enabling members of other sub-groups to comment and add any further suggestions of their own. This process can take various forms – including that of the *carousel* described below – all based on the need to allow free interaction between the participants in order to achieve a high measure of pre-coordination, as described in Chapter 9. The principle is that of a picture gallery, in which the action forms are displayed in groupings which may be defined in various ways – for example, according to those with primary responsibility for implementation; according to the relevant issues; or accroding to who is funding it.

OPPORTUNITIES FOR SOCIO-TECHNICAL DESIGN

At all stages of a project, opportunities arise for exercising creativity not only in the methods by which people address the substance of the work, but also in the methods by which they are helped to work with each other. So the challenge can be conceived as one of socio-technical design (Trist and Murray, 1993). The choices open can include: (1) devising completely new methods; (2) adapting and combining established techniques; or (3) making a myriad of spontaneous adjustments as particular challenges present themselves.

- *The Carousel* – An example of the first of these categories of socio-technical design involves a way of structuring interactions between members of different sub-groups which has become known as the *carousel*. This has shown itself to be effective at the stage where sub-groups have been assigned to differentiated but parallel tasks within the context of a strategic discussion event. This approach involves first inviting the sub-groups to work on allotted tasks in different corners of a large room, or a suite of adjoining rooms, using flip charts as a means of recording their progress. Then a schedule is agreed whereby the members of each sub-group visit the territory of each other sub-group in rotation, inspecting the results of their work, commenting spontaneously on what they see, asking questions on anything which appears controversial or unclear, and adding their own ideas and opinions if they wish.

It is essential that one or two members of each 'home' sub-group should stay behind to answer questions, to make notes on the points raised and to report back to the other members of their own sub-group once they have completed their tour and returned to base.

In the second category of socio-technical design, there are four well-established and reasonably well-known methods which have proved to be fully consistent with the strategic choice approach. Either in whole or in part, these form basic tools in the toolboxes of many facilitators. They are:

- *Metaplan* (Schnelle, 1973) – This is a complete approach in its own right, developed by the Quickborn Group in Germany in the early seventies; however two techniques within it have a general application and can be used independently. The first is a form of brain-writing in which the participants write their ideas on small pieces of paper prior to sticking them on the wall for further analysis – usually a form of clustering. The second is the use of small coloured sticky spots as a means of collecting opinions within a group – whether that is a matter of prioritisation in a list of items or an evaluation.

- *Brainstorming* (Rickards, 1974; van Gundy, 1981) – This is probably the best-known technique, although the word is often used with very little understanding of what it actually means. There are many derivative forms, and it is considered to be the fore-runner of most idea-generation methods. Nevertheless, application of the rules of the classical form is still the best way of helping a group to be creative while also maintaining a sense of discipline.

- *Nominal Group Technique* (Moore, 1987) – There are two aspects of this technique (usually abbreviated to NGT), which have proved valuable in association with strategic choice methods. The first is the use of sub-groups working together in the same room, provided that their tasks are kept the same and quite simple. This allows intensive interactive working – even for very short periods of a minute or so, without the waste of time caused by the sub-groups having to change rooms frequently. The second is a simple sequence starting with the generation of ideas (e.g., issues, options or uncertainties) in small groups, leading to the formation of a mutually understood joint list, then discussion of the relative importance of the items on the list – often using the sticky spots technique from Metaplan.

- *Open Space Technology* (Owen, 1985) – This is a way of enabling people in large groups to work effectively together. It was developed about 1985 by an American named Harrison Owen, to enable people to come together, often in large numbers and usually representing enormous diversity, to pool their ideas for creative and collaborative action. The events generally last from one to three days, and can involve 10–1000 or more people.

The secret of Open Space Technology is that it is based on the passion and responsibility of the participants. All that is provided is a structure, a process, and logistic support. Thus after the opening phase, in which the agenda is devised collectively, management and performance of the process is effectively given over to the participants themselves. This includes the means of reporting in a very short space of time.

It is a pre-requisite that the central theme must be of genuine concern to all involved. This provides an essential focus for maintaining the relevance of diverse contributions, and is best formulated with an action orientation

It is in the third area of socio-technical design – that of spontaneous adjustments – that combinations and variations of these techniques are often devised. There are many choices to be made, not only about which techniques to use when, but also about how they are to be introduced. Questions of who does what with whom; the sequence and duration of activities; and adjustments to the physical layout of the room(s) can often be all-important in sustaining the momentum and spirit of participative work.

For example, sub-groups can be formed in different ways – either to be as mixed as possible in their memberships or to be more homogeneous in terms of the interests or disciplines they represent. The tasks assigned to each sub-group may be the same; variations on a theme; or completely different. Also, it is possible to draw on approaches which combine elements of individual, sub-group and plenary work, not only to demonstrate how each participant can make a full contribution from the start, but also to start to build on the contributions of others. These are choices which should not be made lightly because the outcomes can vary according to continually changing circumstances.

CUSTOMISING THE STRATEGIC CHOICE APPROACH

The various concepts, processes, techniques and methods presented in this chapter as extensions and adaptations to the strategic choice approach have been devised in response to the needs of those involved. They cover, between them, all the aspects of the A-TOPP model – Approach : Technology, Organisation, Process and Products – often touching on two or more of these in combination. But they cannot be

used all at the same time, and individually they are often not enough – so they have to be in some way 'orchestrated'. This is a process in which the all-important twin ideas of selectivity and adaptiveness which were introduced in Chapter 9 become a matter of even greater concern.

Although some of the people with whom we have worked have adopted the approach virtually in its entirety, others have seen a case for reshaping it to their own contexts, introducing some of the adaptations described above alongside any other favoured methods with which they personally feel comfortable.

For example, civil servants who adapted the approach in the Waste Directorate of the Dutch Ministry of the Environment in the 1980s were encouraged to merge SCA with some of their own ideas to produce an approach called *Strategie Afvalstoffen (STRAF)*. The phrase translates simply as Waste Strategy – those concerned also being aware that the STRAF abbreviation also means punishment in Dutch! Not long after this Bram Breure, a civil servant who was later to become a private consultant, generalised it to Interactieve Beleidsvorming en Implementatie Systeem (IBIS) – meaning Interactive Policy-Making and Implementation System. Another variant, developed with Hans Knikkink and presented to the World Bank in Washington, was called the Collaborative Action Planning Strategy (CAPS). Some more recent initiatives in interpreting the SCA for particular types of client situation – for instance as Strategic Action Planning (SAP) and Cross-Organisational Learning Approach (COLA) – are described by contributors to Chapter 13.

In most of these cases, the approach as presented clearly has some differences from SCA, and their advocates feel the need to recognise this. In any case, their sense of ownership is increased with the new name that they introduce.

We welcome such continuing exercises in interpretation. For we recognise that we ourselves in the early days did not find it easy to settle on the phrase 'Strategic Choice Approach' to describe our toolkit; and we have since become increasingly aware of how it lends itself to differing interpretations, not all of which reflect the spirit in which it was originally introduced.

One difficulty we have had to face is that the English language phrase 'strategic choice' is itself in common usage, with several subtly different interpretations. We may ourselves choose to interpret the adjective 'strategic' as indicating a (selective) awareness of connections between decision agendas, at whatever level of organisational or inter-organisational choice. However, we should not be surprised when other people relate the adjective to the level of choice to be found in the boardroom of the corporate enterprise. We find also that the three-word phrase 'Strategic Choice Approach' is too long to use frequently in discussion, without shortening them either to just 'Strategic Choice' or an acronym such as 'SCA'. Although the use of 'Strategic Choice' to describe our particular approach tends to be readily accepted by students, we find that it can become more problematic when introduced into communication with managers who will often have their own long-acquired sense of what that phrase implies. So we either become drawn back to the acronym SCA, or start searching for alternative terms.

ADAPTING LANGUAGE TO CONTEXT

So what are the basic needs that have to be satisfied by those who wish to interpret our approach – or indeed any other such approach? We have mentioned 'ownership' from time to time – especially in relation to the products of a project where its value lies in the commitment that comes with it. But the question is more fundamental than that. Yes, having a sense of ownership of the toolbox in use is helpful, and almost certainly reassuring. However the more fundamental need is to feel confident when operating the approach with and on behalf of others – often clients of one sort or another.

This seems to be a key factor that has led people to change the names of particular methods and tools that we have introduced here – including sometimes such basic terms as decision area, comparison area and uncertainty area. We have always encouraged this sort of 'customising' to different situations, recognising that it may be less to do with the confidence of a facilitator – although it can allow them some measure of self-expression – than with the confidence of their clients. If these clients are presented with an approach couched in terms with which they are uncomfortable, the probability of acceptance is likely to be reduced. If on the other hand, after a process of interpretation often involving the clients themselves, more sympathetic terms can be developed, a stronger basis for acceptance can be built.

For example, there are some situations where an emphasis on the management of uncertainty can be resisted as seemingly negative, yet the principle behind it may be more widely acceptable when replaced by more action-directed language. Then we have gradually come to replace the phrase *commitment package* by the more dynamic term *progress package* in most – but not all – contexts. For the focus on commitment may be a welcome one where a group is vested with authority to make decisions; yet where its members are only in a position to make recommendations to others, the emphasis on progress may become a much more acceptable alternative.

Whenever users of our approach have expressed interest in taking it on board as facilitators, we have encouraged them to modify it as they see fit. The hope has always been that, if the modification works, we will find out about it and SCA may evolve accordingly. The development of SCA through this form of action research has been a way of life for us, for what is now many years. Along the way we have been helped wittingly, and sometimes unwittingly, by very many others.

INSIGHTS FROM OTHER LANGUAGES

The experience of seeing our developing vocabulary of strategic choice translated from English into other languages – both European and non-European – has itself been an important learning experience for us. As our experience has grown, we have come to question the value of some of the basic terminology we presented in our first edition – most of it carried forward into the second. So how far should we introduce changes now, in our third edition, based on our experiences in subsequent years?

Frequently, we have found ourselves learning important lessons from translations of our terminology into other languages, which sometimes seem to express the underlying ideas better than our native English. A good example is the translation of *commitment package* as *pacote de compromisos* in both Spanish and Portuguese – conveying a sense of 'promising together' which becomes distorted in English once other less-benign interpretations the English word 'compromise' are introduced.

INVITING VIEWPOINTS FROM OTHERS

In the preceding chapters, we have presented the Strategic Choice Approach as viewed through the eyes and the experiences of the two of us who have played central roles in developing the ideas, and in introducing it to other people, over more than three decades.

In this third edition, we believe that the time has come for us to introduce the voices of some of the many other people with whom we have worked – especially over the years since our second edition was published in 1997 – as they can bring fresh and varied perspectives to bear on present practice and its implications for the decision-making of the future.

So, in the spirit of learning from the experiences of others, and in the wider spirit of action research that we have always embraced, we have invited fifteen short contributions from twenty-one people with whom at least one of us has worked closely, and who seem to us to have important things to say. In doing so, we suggested that they tell us about what they have learnt from their experiences using their own preferred terminology, so that the diversity of interpretations, transformations and translations of the ideas and experiences we have presented here can be more widely shared. These contributions are brought together in Chapter 13.

ILLUSTRATIONS FROM PRACTICE

The final pages of this chapter present four illustrations from practice of the introduction of the methods discussed in this chapter. As in the case of the illustrations from practice at the end of Chapters 5–8, each of Figures 99–102, starting on page 286, is accompanied by a commentary to explain more about the context of the project or projects concerned.

FIGURE
99

Illustrations from Practice: Carousel Techniques in Action

1

2

3

1 Croatia 1997   Exploring organisational futures in post-war Bosnia (Mercy Corps / Scottish European Aid)

2 Botswana 1989   Planning faster availability of land for housing (Ministry of Land and Resources)

3 Latvia 1996   Developing the National Environmental Action Programme (Ministry of Environment and Regional Planning).

COMMENTARY ON FIGURE 99

The basic carousel technique is described in page 286, but there are several variations of it. Together they form a suite of techniques which can be used in various combinations. They provide a means for keeping large amounts of information visible as a basis for structured collaboration between participants.

The Promenade This is a much less structured variation of the carousel. Different tasks are carried out in different parts of a large room – or different rooms which would, however, be ideally inter-connected. For example, there might be several metaplan exercises going on, each concerned with a different subject (various issues, aspects of the work, etc.). The participants move around contributing to the work as and when they are best able and motivated to do so.

The Picture Gallery This is a way of sharing with each other the work done separately, either individually or in sub-groups. It is conducted, as the name implies, rather like an art fair or gallery in a large room with much wall space or screens (separate rooms can be used with some loss of 'flow'). Each of the individuals or groups hangs summaries of the work it has done on the wall – ideally in a form which is easily accessible to others; sometimes in a pre-arranged format. A table, and/or half-circle of chairs, is placed in front of them and this becomes the focus of that group's activities. Participants then walk around learning about the work that has been done. They may suggest new ideas, or alternatives to those already on display. The *Action Gallery* is a special case of this technique.

There is a second phase of this process which is an optional extra – used specially when working with a group of professionals. In this the groups are requested to remove their papers from the wall and to redistribute them according to a completely different classification, such as specific issues, actors, target groups or impact areas. The groups are then re-formed according to the new classification – grouping like specialists together. Their task is

to sort out the new set of ideas or proposals on the wall before them. This can be an ideal starting point for the *Trade Fair* technique.

The Trade Fair This allows free exchange of ideas between groups who will have set themselves up as in the *Picture Gallery*. Participants seek to improve their proposals by negotiating with others to eliminate the three problems which can occur when groups have been working separately:

1. *duplication* in which two (or more) groups propose the same thing – often in different way – a straightforward waste of effort;
2. *contradiction* in which two (or more) groups propose things – often for different purposes – which at best cancel each other out and at worst lead to seriously negative results;
3. *omission* in which two (or more) groups each think that the other is going to propose something – leading to neither of them doing it.

The Guided Tour Sometimes known as the 'travelling plenary' – this is a form of sharing the work done in sub-groups, which is halfway between the *Picture Gallery* and conventional presentations. Starting with a room, or rooms, set up as for a *Picture Gallery, Promenade* or *Carousel*, the groups are shepherded from one group's position to the next. At each position they are given a run-down on what is there. It is very useful when there are many papers to be viewed and moving them around becomes a hassle.

The three photographs in Figure 99 are all of different ways of working with the carousel suite of techniques (although photographs are notoriously uninformative when being used to show process). The top one (1) is a reasonably conventional *Carousel*. As is frequently the case, the rooms are not ideal, but the groups can be seen working in their corners. The middle photograph (2) shows a *Promenade* in progress where the participants are clearly operating in their own style and speed. The bottom example (3) is a much more structured variation which utilises the 'sticky dot' prioritisation system borrowed from the Metaplan technique.

FIGURE 100

Illustrations from Practice: Building Common Ground

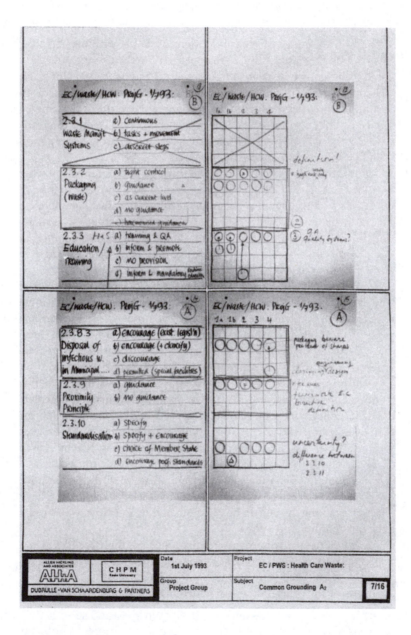

COMMENTARY ON FIGURE 100

The common grounding technique is illustrated in Figure 100 through photographs of some of a set of flip charts from a European Union project concerned with implementation of the European waste management policies – in this case for the priority waste stream for health care waste, carried out in the mid-1990s.

The flip charts to the left show some of the key decision areas and options, as agreed through lengthy dialogue part way through the project. The columns at the right show the preferred options as identified by five sub-groups which, at that stage, were formed to represent different, and relatively homogeneous, sets of interests such as directorates of the European Commission, member states, industry, waste management companies, hospital and other health managers and the environment lobby.

As often happens in such circumstances, the participants were surprised to find the extent to which they already agreed: there were a few decision areas where there was complete agreement, as well as some options which none of the groups had selected. The process of developing common ground then continued by focusing on decision areas where there was a considerable measure of agreement, for example, where there was only one sub-group out of line.

That sub-group was then asked 'In what way would this option, which the other sub-groups have selected, have to be modified to make it acceptable to you?' Often, slight changes were all that was required. Each of the other sub-groups were then asked the classic consensus-building question 'Could you live with that?' If the answer was positive, then the common ground was thereby extended.

Where there was difficulty, the principles of managing uncertainty became helpful in probing the conflicting assumptions that often underlie apparent disagreements. Inter-group discussion then helped to reduce uncertainty both about the different values in operation, and about the future intentions of relevant parties – leading to agreement on appropriate exploratory actions or contingency plans.

Where difficulties proved harder to resolve, only a few decision areas remained which required further work. Here the experience of working together successfully had the effect of enabling options to be reformulated in a creative way so as to resolve the outstanding difficulties.

FIGURE
101

Illustrations from Practice: Use of Action Forms

Form 2 (4.1):

Problēma	Risinājums
Atkritumu ietekme uz vidi	

Rīcība
MK noteikumi par rūpniecisko atkritumu šķirošanu

Atbildīgie *
Darba grupa, kuras sastāvā varētu būt VARAM,
Ekonomikas ministrijas, rūpniecisko uzņēmumu, u.c.
ieinteresēto institūciju pārstāvji

Iespējamie finansēšanas avoti	Aptuvenas izmaksas (Ls)
valsts budžets; ārvalstu donori	~ 1500

Laika grafiks
1.5 gadi

1995 1996 1997 1998 1999 2000 2001 2002

Sagaidāmie rezultāti	Blakusiedarbība
Izstrādāti MK noteikumi, uzņēmumos uzsākta atkritumu šķirošana (vismaz dažos, kur tas ir ekonomiski izdevīgi)	

Piezīmes	Prioritāte
Šobrīd Latvijā nav pieredzes (vai arī tā ir nepietiekoši populārizēta) par rūpniecisko atkritumu šķirošanu, tās tehnoloģiskajiem un ekonomiskajiem rādītājiem	1G

Datums

* Atzīmēt, kur nepieciešams
• Līpdūtājs x Koordinators o Nepieciešams atbalsts

Form 1:

FACILITATION WORKSHEET : Action Planning 2 — AHA
The Strategic Choice Approach
© 1993 Allen Hickling and Associates

Example **ACTION FORM**

STRATEGIC OPTION
Encouragement of prevention

MEASURE
1 *Essential Requirements*
4 *Improvement of Road Surface*

DESCRIPTION OF ACTION
Carry out tests to evaluate on tyre wear, the effect of various surface pavement types (including mixes with rubber binder on rubber aggregates).

RESPONSIBILITIES
IRF could co-ordinate the action managed by road industry with other partners.

X	European Commission
	Member States
✳	Producers
	Industry
X	IRF ....
	Users
	General Public

FUNDING (WHO, HOW, etc)
EZ

COST/BUDGET
to be determined after study

PLANNING (UNCERTAINTIES, CONDITIONS, etc)
Start by 1994, to end by 1997

Time Scale:
1994 1995 1996 1997 1998 1999 2000 2001 2002 2003 2004 2005 2006

CRUCIAL ASSUMPTIONS / 'CRITICAL SUCCESS FACTORS'
- good control of parameters (climate; geometry of roads; type of pavements).
- choice of vehicles

GENERAL NOTES
Paragraphs 'd' and 'g' of measure 4 seem to be non-funded assumptions. We recommend to delete them.

Y. Meunier

Form 3:

Actieprogramma CO_2-technologie

Er zal een actieprogramma worden opgesteld voor de ontwikkeling en demonstratie van
technologieën en in een studie van eventuele stringente CO_2-beperking, invoering hiervan te
kunnen versnellen

ACTOREN	Rijk (VROM/DGM)
	VROM/DGM/LE/KV/dr. L.A. Meyer
	VROM/DGM/LE/KV/dr. L.A. Meyer
	meerdere doelgroepen
	n.v.t.
	EZ; V&W (via WIEK en SKIE)
PLANNING	lopend
	strategienotitie (eind 1995)
	bijdrage aan de Vervolgnota Klimaatbeleid (eind 1995)
	input voor nader onderzoek in de tweede tranche van het NOP-MLK
KENMERKEN	klimaatverandering; milieutechnologie
	voorbeeld zijn op eventuele stringente CO_2-beperking door ontwikkeling van technologie maar ook van andere opties te versnellen en de mogelijke resultaten naar voren te halen in de tijd
	er zal een actieprogramma worden opgesteld om in situatie van stringente CO_2-beperking invoering van maatregelen te kunnen versnellen. Deze maatregelen omvatten technologie, infrastructuur en gebruik van technologie
	kennisvermeerdering, beleidsformulering

CHOOSING

PRACTICE

Theme: The use of action forms in developing draft and final documents (Action Plan).
Project: 1. Action planning for European waste management: used tyres.
2. Preparation of the National Environmental Action Plan for Latvia.
3. Work document for the Netherlands national environmental policy plan.
Context: Various national and international multi-organisational project groups.

COMMENTARY ON FIGURE 101

There are three projects illustrated here. The intention is to reflect different stages of the choosing process and the way concepts were adapted to the situation 'on the ground' for the specific client at the time. Each project will be described in turn, in an order which reflects different stages of development.

1. The first example shows an early attempt to enable a multi-organisational project group, set up in 1993 by of the European Commission, to produce an action plan as part of the Implementation Strategy for the 'Priority Waste Stream' of Used Tyres. This was towards the end of a 30-month project which had demonstrated all the problems of being the first in a series.

    The Project Group had difficulty in adapting to the new style of working, and there had been a long settling in period. The facilitation team were also on a steep learning curve, as they had previously only experienced this kind of working at national level – the increase in scale being not a little challenging. All participants had been asked to fill in forms which would then form the basis of the proposed Action Plan element of a draft strategy. This work was done between strategic meetings and assembled later by a technical support team. As it happened, little more work was done on these forms and they were submitted without the benefit of sustained analysis and comparison.

2. The second example is taken from the work of an inter-governmental project group set up in 1996 by the Ministry for the Environment and Regional Development in Latvia.

While the language here is Latvian, the boxes and their content are similar to those in the first example.

At this early stage in developing an environmental strategy in Latvia, it was decided that this first attempt would be restricted to the Environment Ministry. Accordingly these forms were first filled out by the staff of the regional offices, then brought to an Action Gallery event (see page 290) in Riga, prior to being put through a process of integration to produce a first draft plan. This example shows a format adopted in that second stage of development just after the Action Gallery, after word-processing for presentation purposes.

3. The third example is chosen to demonstrate how an action form can end up by being presented in a published Government document – in this case the so-called Work Document of the second National Environmental Policy Plan for the Netherlands. It is the work of a project group of the Netherlands Directorate General for the Environment in 1994.

    The document contains 125 actions grouped in each case according to the primary actors – described as 'target groups' in the plan (e.g., Agriculture; Industry; Central Government). It also shows the current status of all the actions agreed in the first National Environmental Policy Plan. Although the presentation here is more sophisticated, the various headings are similar to those used in any typical action form. The amount of information under each heading is limited according to the intended readership, but references are provided to enable more detailed information to be located.

First National Environmental Policy Plan for Latvia (NEPP-L)

Autumn 1993

[Various preliminary meetings and arrangements involving senior representatives of Netherlands and Latvian Governments]

Spring 1994

Decision by Latvian Ministry of Environmental Protection and Regional Development to issue National Environmental Policy Plan (NEPP-L)

Setting up of project organization in Latvia, i.e. appointment of NEPP-L project leader, core group and project group.

Drafting of project plan in Latvia.

Meeting in the Netherlands of the Latvian Minister of Environmental Protection and Regional Development with the Dutch Minister of Housing, Spatial Planning and the Environment on the occasion of 1st conference of the International Network of Green Planners.

Meeting in the Netherlands of Director of the Environmental Protection Department, who is the NEPP-L project leader, and Deputy-Director with representatives of Dutch Directorate of International Environmental Affairs and representatives of Directorate of Strategic Planning

Preparation of Ministerial presentations on policy plan by State Minister of Environmental Protection, the NEPP-L project leader and the Dutch for approx. 50 representatives of the Ministry and another 50 key policy-makers in other ministries and institutions.

Visit to Stockholm of a representative of the Dutch Directorate for International Environmental Affairs for meeting with Latvians at Swedish Environmental Protection Agency (EPA).

Involvement of process consultant.

Summer 1994

1st Workshop on policy plan for Latvian project group; approx. 50 people present. The workshop takes 3 days and is organized in a hotel in Jurmala. Facilitation by an external process consultant and Dutch representatives. Dutch representation from Directorates of Strategic Planning and International Environmental Affairs. Representation from the Swedish EPA. Formal reception offered by the State Minister of Environmental Protection. Information on the development of the NEPP-L is presented to the press. Tour through Latvan countryside by some of the Dutch representatives.

Involvement of communication experts from Latvian and Dutch Ministries on policy planning process.

Training of Latvians in workshop facilitation.

2nd workshop on policy plan for Latvian project group; approx. 70 people present. Workshop takes 2 days and is organized in a conference facility in Riga. Facilitation by an external process consultant and Latvian co-facilitators. Dutch representatives from Directorate of Strategic Planning and Department for Information and External Relations. Meeting with State Minister of Environmental Protection and communication experts.

Autumn 1994

Writing of the 1st draft of the policy plan by core group with the assistance of one Dutch representative of the Directorate of Strategic Planning.

Visit to Netherlands by Latvian core-group and communication expert. Discussions on 1st draft of the policy plan at the Directorate of Strategic Planning and with the Dutch informal advisory board for twinning. Discussions on communication strategy for the policy plan. Media training for core-group and communication expert by media consultant.

Redrafting of policy plan.

Further training of Latvians in workshop facilitation.

3rd workshop on the policy plan for Latvian project group. Approx. 70 people present during 2 days. Facilitation by an external process consultant and Latvian co-facilitators. Dutch representation from the Directorate of Strategic Planning and the Directorate of International Environmental Affairs. Discussion with the State Minister of Environmental Protection about the process of accepting the concept NEPP-L by the cabinet of Ministers.

Spring 1995

Redrafting of Policy Plan.

Notification in Inter-Ministerial Meeting of State Secretaries.

Review and comments by other Ministries.

Approval of Policy Plan in Cabinet of Ministers.

Issue of Newsletter

Evaluation of twinning

COMMENTARY ON FIGURE 102

Figure 101 illustrates the importance of investment in creating and maintaining an appropriate context. It does so by summarising all the stages that were involved in the design and management of an important extensive project – in this case, involving assistance to the government of Latvia from the governments of the Netherlands and Sweden in developing its first National Environmental Policy Plan.

This summary – taken from an official project document – begins at the time when it was agreed to set up the project in the spring of 1994, omitting details of various earlier exploratory discussions in 1993. However, the political complexity of the project is well reflected both in the arrangements preceding the series of three workshops held in the summer and autumn of 1994, and in the events leading up to the final adoption of agreed policy proposals. Also, the cross-cultural aspects of the project are reflected in the planned transition from Dutch to Latvian co-facilitators after the first workshop, supported by appropriate training events.

The success of this project was to lead in turn to another in which the focus is on the National Environmental Action Programme. This is an ongoing programme which deals with implementation of the National Environmental Policy Plan, and is reviewed and updated regularly.

Similar projects have been launched in other Baltic and central European states, each of them providing important learning opportunities. The experience of each project has contributed to the design of further extensive projects in response to expressions of interest in other countries, relating to other fields of policy. So the process of development goes on, in pursuit of the 'holy grail' of any learning process – continuous improvement.

13   Learning from others

This chapter enables several other people who have been using the Strategic Choice Approach in their practice to tell us what they have learnt from their experiences. The development of the Strategic Choice Approach has always been based on this style of discovery: action research. As we use the phrase, this means working with practitioners, and together sharing the learning from doing so, then together working out how it can be best codified for the benefit of others.

LEARNING ABOUT PROCESS CHOICES

We have found it helpful to see all decision-making as a learning process. This is in keeping with the cyclic nature of our view of decision-making as developed in Chapters 1 and 4. In this respect the learning model of Kolb (1984), which was being developed in parallel to our work in the early 1970s (Hickling, 1974), offers a valuable point of reference.

Up to this point in this book we have been primarily addressing decision-making as it relates to the substantive problem being worked on. However in our own action research programme, focused as it always has been on the methodology, it has been necessary to concentrate more on the decisions being taken about the process itself. For example: Which mode of work should we move to next? Should we use a cost-effectiveness-based comparison or one based on ends-means? How many decision areas can we address effectively here? Would it be sensible for us to coalesce these decision areas at this stage? What form of progress package is appropriate in this case? What size sub-groups would be sensible for this next part of the work? How are we going to help those stakeholders outside the process to catch up? Such questions relate closely to the areas of concern addressed by Argyris and Schön (1973) in their concept of double loop learning. Although that is concerned more with organisational learning, we see a clear link between their work and ours.

ACTION LEARNING

It seems appropriate here to refer to the ideas of Revans (1983) in his concept of *action learning*, which is based on the value of practitioners learning from each other, and has been a major influence on our decision to add this chapter. The process of Revans, in which small groups form to learn together, clearly has a different focus to ours; yet we see the aims of this chapter as being entirely consistent with the basic notion.

So we asked people with whom we have worked before – though not necessarily on the projects they describe – whether they would like to be involved. Of course there were many more people we could have asked, but there were limits in the extent to which we could add new material in this third edition, so we had to be highly selective. Using criteria such as geographical spread, diversity of problems addressed and relevance to the twenty-first century, we produced a shortlist. We are much encouraged by the 100 per cent response we received.

We challenged our contributors to reflect on their decision-making about process management in practice, so as to identify what they had learnt from their experience, which might be of value to others using the approach. We asked them to select the most significant lessons they had learned, whether positive or negative, and to present them using examples from their experience. We asked them to focus on up to three lessons, and to aim for a target of 1800 words or less, including an introduction and biographical notes.

SELECTIVE READING

We recognise that readers of this chapter may find it more rewarding to begin by selecting those contributions that appear most relevant to their interests, in the spirit of our Quick access guide at the start of this book. So we begin with a listing of all our contributors and the titles of their contributions. We have arranged these in the sequence of their first working contact – ranging from the early 1970s to the early twenty-first century – with either of us, the chapter editors.

Each contribution starts with a short resumé of what is in it, with biographical notes on the contributor(s). So we suggest you pick out first one or two titles which attract you, then turn to the relevant page where you will find the resumé and biographical notes.

LIST OF CONTRIBUTIONS

13.1 Controversy on the Streets: Stakeholder workshops on a choice of carnival route

Jonathan Rosenhead, Department of Operational Research, London School of Economics, UK

13.2 Communicative Learning, Democracy and Effectiveness: Facilitating private – public decision-making in Sweden

Knut Strömberg, Department of Urban Design & Development, Chalmers University, Goteborg, Sweden and *Jaan-Henrik Kain*, Built Environment & Sustainable Development, Chalmers University, Goteborg, Sweden

13.3 Delving into the Toolboxes: National environmental policy-making and strategic choice

Frans Evers, former Director of Strategy, Ministry of Environment, The Netherlands

13.4 Less is More: Controlling decision complexity when using strategic choice

Richard Ormerod, Professor Emeritus, Warwick Business School, Coventry, UK

13.5 Feet on the Ground: Engaging planning students with political realities

Arnold van der Valk, Land-Use Planning Chair, Wageningen University, The Netherlands and *Gerrit J. Carsjens*, Department of Land-Use Planning, Wageningen University, The Netherlands

13.6 Designing Electronic Support: Empowering decision-makers through software for strategic choice

Dave Friend, Software Design Consultant, West Yorkshire, UK

13.7 Neighbourhood Renewal in Rome: Combining strategic choice with other design methods

Alessandro Giangrande, Professor of Planning, Università Roma Tre, Italy
and *Elena Mortola*, Professor of Urban Design, Università Roma Tre, Italy

13.8 Fast Forward with Strategic Choice: Mutual consulting for small enterprise development

Rebecca Herron, Community Operational Research Unit, University of Lincoln, UK
and *Dennis Finlayson*, International Development Consultant, Derbyshire, UK

13.9 The Plutonium Predicament: Managing conflict through strategic action planning

Richard Harris, Independent Process Consultant, East Sussex, UK

13.10 Dealing with the Dumps: Using decision areas and levels in developing national policy for used tyres

Rob Angell, Environmental Policy Consultant and Facilitator, Somerset, UK

13.11 Cross-organisational Learning: Sharing insights from managing major construction projects

Mike Cushman, Department of Information Systems, London School of Economics, UK
and *Alberto Franco*, Warwick Business School, University of Warwick, Coventry, UK

13.12 Capacity Building in Venezuela: Using strategic choice methods with policy-makers and students

Elisenda Vila, Planning Consultant and Professor, Caracas, Venezuela
and *Ana María Benaiges*, Planning Consultant and Professor, Caracas, Venezuela

13.13 Differential Learning: Managing different rates of progress between participants in extensive projects

Brendan Hickling, Independent Facilitator and Mediator, Warwickshire, UK

13.14 Building Commitment in a Rural Community: Use of commitment packages in empowerment through information technology

Jackie Phahlamohlaka, Community Education Project Chair, Mpumalanga, South Africa

13.15 Commitment is the Key: Building inter-agency agreement over the future of an historic estate

Leny Bregman, Environmental Project Manager in Natuurmonumenten, The Netherlands

13.1 Controversy on the Streets

Stakeholder workshops on a choice of carnival route

By Jonathan Rosenhead

This contribution describes the application of the strategic choice approach and related methods in debating the future of the Notting Hill Carnival, a massively popular but risk-prone street festival in West London. A team from the London School of Economics undertook two successive projects in 1998 and 2001, focused on the use of problem structuring methods in the management of complex risk. This involved facilitation of workshops with stakeholder groups whose relationships varied between wariness and antagonism. These groups included local government agencies, emergency services, local residents, transport providers, arts funders and carnivalists. The author reflects on how far the methods helped the stakeholders to make progress.

Jonathan Rosenhead has been on the staff of the London School of Economics since 1967, and was Professor of Operational Research there when these projects took place. His long-standing interests are in problem structuring methods; in supporting the decision-making processes of community groups; in appropriate analytic work in developing countries; and in health service planning and service delivery. His seminal work on robustness analysis in sequential decisions under uncertainty influenced the early development of the strategic choice approach, which he has taught and applied over many years. He has edited a book in which strategic choice is presented alongside other related methods for the interactive structuring of complex problems. (Rosenhead and Mingers, 2001)

THE NOTTING HILL CARNIVAL

Each year the Notting Hill Carnival attracts crowds of up to a million revellers for two days in August to a relatively small area of West London. The first Carnival took place in 1958 as part of the response to riots in which violence was directed against the black immigrant population; then the carnival was small and spontaneous; now it is suffering the problems of success.

This account is of two linked attempts to assist in resolving some of these problems with the chief stakeholders. They were remarkable for the number of these stakeholders, the high political profile of the process, and the prevailing level of tension, conflict and turbulence. Could SCA and related methods really function effectively in this environment?

The Carnival is a unique cultural street festival with its roots in the Caribbean, where it was based on the experience of slavery. The freedom to walk the streets represented symbolically the lifting of that oppression. In Notting Hill the Carnival procession wends its way through the network of streets of that neighbourhood with music and costume bands. There is a wide range of associated activities off the actual route, involving street trading – especially ethnic foods – and static sound systems.

Carnival has often been controversial. At times it has been threatened by significant criminal activity, at others by hostile confrontations with the police. By the late 1990s these had become historical, but the problems of success were evident – a congested circular route with the threat of injuries or death through crushing; the move from a largely ethnic minority base to a mass audience attuned to contemporary commercial culture; the precarious reliance on sponsors for financial viability; and the tension between the desire for a safe carnival with all its disciplines and the symbolic celebration of the spirit of misrule.

THE INITIAL WORKSHOPS

My involvement with Carnival arose initially through a research project funded by the Economic and Social Research Council that I carried out with Tom Horlick-Jones, also associated with LSE though based in Cardiff. That work seemed to have run its course when the issue that we had been dealing with flared up again, and we were again drawn in – this time funded by the BP Complex Risk Programme administered by the Centre for the Analysis of Risk and Regulation at LSE. Both projects were designed to explore the scope for the use of problem structuring methods (PSMs) (Rosenhead and Mingers, 2001) in the management of risk. The work of the first project is described in more detail in Horlick-Jones, Rosenhead, Georgiou, Ravetz and Löfstedt (2001).

Tom supplied the expertise in 'risk' and also in ethnographic methods (Hammersley and Atkinson, 1995). These we used during the 1997 Carnival cycle to gain insights into the inter-organisational dynamics at work.

During the 1998 Carnival cycle we negotiated the participation of the four most significant organisations involved in Carnival in two linked workshops, so moving on from research mode into action research mode. The four

organisations were the Metropolitan Police Service; the Royal Borough of Kensington and Chelsea; the Tenant Management Organisation, representing the residents in social housing in the Carnival area; and the Notting Hill Carnival Trust. Each was represented by its 'top brass' – for example the Commander in charge of policing major events in London and the Leader of the Borough Council – as well as supporting personnel. The aim of the gathering was to do some strategic thinking about the future directions of the Carnival. We were told in advance that we had just the one day. However at the end of the day, the participants spontaneously started talking about the arrangements for a follow-up workshop.

The methods used in these first workshops were not restricted to SCA. In fact, being under extreme time pressure, we started with a simplified version of Soft Systems Methodology, on which we received helpful advice from Peter Checkland.[1] Our purpose was to bring to the surface the different possible objectives that people might have for staging Carnival – important as three of the four organisations would prefer Carnival not to happen! Starting from these possible objectives we elicited modified or new actions that might be relevant to achieving them, and the uncertainties associated with those actions. Following this discussion we prioritised a number of issues for examination in depth.

That was the first workshop. It was in the second workshop one month later – and with a slightly less senior membership – that we employed SCA. We had recorded and transcribed all the discussion at workshop 1, and used cognitive mapping methods to make sense of it. On this basis we had organised the prioritised 'decision areas' into what we thought might be a decision graph representing their interconnections; this was now confirmed by the group. However they selected a subset of three of the decision areas that they

---

1 For an introduction, see Rosenhead and Mingers (2001).

wanted to talk about, none of which were directly linked to any of the others. The result was that each of the areas was discussed separately. Just one of these lent itself to the advantage comparison method of SCA's comparing mode. This was funding. Three new options (in addition to the status quo) were identified. Pair-wise comparison of two of them generated a useful discussion. Then we repeated the exercise, contrasting the status quo with an option of raising money by moving to a non-circular procession routed to pass through an arena with chargeable seating. This time the result was electric. Pooling their expertise, experience and judgement, they came to realise that across a range of criteria (safety, disruption, cultural celebration, promotion of the Carnival arts) the latter option had striking advantages. In a mood of unprecedented enthusiasm and amity, the various representatives took the idea back to their constituencies. Nothing happened.

A LATER INVITATION

Two years passed. The first ever Mayor of Greater London, Ken Livingstone, was elected. Two people were murdered at the August 2000 Carnival. The Mayor took on the issue and set up a Carnival Review Group. The Review staff discovered our report, and the move to a 'linear' route was promptly adopted as a Review Group recommendation. In the summer of 2001 Tom and I were appointed as Advisers to the Group. Mike Cushman became actively involved later.

Our principal responsibility now was to progress agreement on a new route. At our suggestion, a Route Working Party representing stakeholders was convened. Nineteen organisations took part, some of them with more than one representative. With these numbers we had to rethink our intention of using problem structuring methods designed for the dynamics of smaller groups. However our choice of approach was informed by our experience with these methods, including SCA.

The stakeholders were certainly diverse: three boroughs plus the Greater London Assembly, the Association for London Government and the Royal Parks; the Carnival Trust plus two arts funding bodies, three police agencies and three emergency services; three transport organisations; and the Tenant Management Organisation. We had redefined the task of the working party as that of preparing the ground for the selection of a shortlist of routes, to be agreed on by a full conference. This shortlist would then be evaluated by consultants who specialised in space-related technical risk analysis. The Greater London Assembly (in effect the Mayor) would fund this analysis for three routes.

The aim of our process design was to stop the parties, who had very different objectives, from simply disputing the advantages of one route over another, or the need for a change of route at all. To develop a space for discussion and negotiation, we started with abstraction, getting the participants to identify possible generic route shapes. They ended up with seven, from circle, line and horseshoe through to 'tuning fork'. Criteria were elicited and used to reduce the range to the four identified above. So progress was made despite a concerted initial attempt by some members to challenge the approach and the authority of the facilitators.

Ahead of the second meeting of the Working Party, the members generated specific routes, 11 in all. A set of criteria relevant to choice between specific routes was developed, which in turn were condensed into seven clusters – effectively meta-criteria. In heterogeneous break-out groups the routes were rated out of 10 on each criterion.

Looking at the results produced an enlightening discussion. Routes that scored highly on criteria most relevant to the service agencies scored poorly on those of most concern to the Carnival community, and vice versa – so the various parties seemed to gain a better understanding of the logic of each other's positions. Furthermore some routes seemed to be dominated by others on all criteria. However none of the representatives felt they had authority to withdraw them.

The culmination was the tense route evaluation sessions of a two-day conference on October 29–30 with over 50 present. Carnivalists for the first time were there in some numbers. Documentation on the progress made by the working party had been pre-circulated, along with a statistical analysis of the routes by the consultants. Discussion was held in three syndicate groups, this time as homogeneous as possible to promote frank discussion – but with the ground rules that they should each try to produce a shortlist 'balanced' across different types of route. The facilitators ran their three syndicates differently, according to their judgements of their internal dynamics. Each however used methods employing flip charts and 'post-it' notes with an agreed list of evaluative criteria as background.

The Mayor's senior adviser took over the chairing of the final session. That morning he had told me of his strong doubts that agreement would be possible; but I persuaded him to wait and see what the method could deliver. Only one of the groups managed a balanced portfolio of routes. But in plenary discussion movement took place and a consensus began to appear. A larger than intended shortlist was agreed unanimously, and the Mayor's adviser said that money would be found for the additional risk analysis. There was a palpable break in the tension, and fraternisation between members of all the groups.

POSTSCRIPT

Our formal involvement ended there – mission accomplished. We received warm letters of thanks from the Mayor's adviser. And the following year the Carnival route changed, rather timidly, from its previous circle to a horseshoe formation. However that summary of subsequent events misses out much content. In effect between October 2001 and the 2002 Carnival the two principal London boroughs managed to regain control of the agenda from the Mayor. Also, in legal action supported by the main Carnival funders, the Director and most trustees of the Carnival Trust were replaced. This turmoil may in part have militated against more radical route change.

CONCLUDING REFLECTIONS

This was a very rich experience. Most of the lessons relate to multi-organisational engagements. Any conclusions are tentative.

One key question is that of whether SCA and other problem structuring methods can function usefully in an antagonistic environment. The answer in the case of the second engagement seemed to be 'yes – but only just'. It took some facilitators well-toughened in the university of life, and flying by the seat of their pants, to get through to a result.

Politics was of the essence. It was in the room all the time. It has become obvious retrospectively that we only knew a part of what was going on. Better political intelligence would have helped us greatly. We now know that, despite our academic status and independent funding, we were, by some parties for at least some of the time, seen as the Mayor's agents and so not impartial. In a contested environment, the sponsorship of consultants can be crucial.

Carnival is a community-based activity. Carnivalists had day jobs to hold down, and so were under-represented in most of our process, compared with the boroughs and the agencies. We should have been more sensitive to who was not in the workshop.

When powerful decision-makers are not in the room, good results at a workshop may not carry through to implementation. Clearly reserving time at the workshop to devise a plan of action is a good strategy, but may be impracticable when groups are hostile.

Lastly, we found ourselves improvising methods in order to work in larger groups. Recent progress has been made in developing such methods both within the strategic choice tradition, as discussed in Chapter 11 and by later contributors to this chapter (Sections 13.09 and 13.10), and by others (Bunker and Alben, 1997). In the circumstances of the Notting Hill projects, it is very doubtful whether the participants would have accepted more elaborate rules of the game.

REFERENCES

BUNKER BB and ALBEN BT (1997) Large Group Interventions: Engaging the Whole System for Rapid Change. Jossey-Bass

HAMMERSLEY M and ATKINSON P (1995) Ethnography: Principles in Practice (Second Edition). Routledge

HORLICK-JONES T, ROSENHEAD J, GEORGIOU I, RAVETZ J and LÖFSTEDT R (2001) Decision Support for Organisational Risk Management by Problem Structuring. Health Risk and Society, *3* (2), 141–65

ROSENHEAD J and MINGERS J (eds) (2001) Rational Analysis for a Problematic World Revisited: Problem Structuring Methods for Complexity, Uncertainty and Conflict. Wiley

13.2 Communicative Learning, Democracy and Effectiveness

Facilitating private – public decision-making in Sweden

By Knut Strömberg and Jaan-Henrik Kain

Three cases from Sweden, in which public and private interests meet and sometimes conflict, demonstrate the value of moving complex issues from formal arenas for decision-making to informal fora for communication and learning in a wider circle of participants. However, it is vital to link the mutually developed learning experiences back to the formal arenas to inform decision-makers. Lessons from these processes are discussed under three headings: communicative learning, effectiveness and democracy.

Jaan-Henrik Kain is conducting research on trans-disciplinary management of multi-faceted knowledge related to urban development processes. He is a CEI Post Doctoral Fellow at the Department of Built Environment and Sustainable Development at Chalmers University of Technology.

Knut Strömberg has been working with the strategic choice approach (SCA) since the late 1970s. He is using urban design as a tool for social, cultural and economic development and has introduced a profound social science perspective in postgraduate architectural education at Chalmers University of Technology, where he is professor in Urban Design and Development.

BACKGROUND

The public sector's role in urban design and planning has diminished in Sweden as in most European countries during the last 20 years – a transition from formal government to more collaborative forms of governance. This shift is by no means simple to manage and is often criticised for failing in democratic control and for resulting in unsatisfactory mechanisms for change management.

The traditional approach to urban planning, with its formal and sectoral organisations, is not adequate when dealing with non-standard issues going beyond normal agendas and standard procedures. Instead, other approaches are needed to cope with the intra-sectoral and multi-actor decision development needed for new forms of governance.

RESTRUCTURING A MUNICIPAL HOUSING MARKET

During the 1980s, Köping, a Swedish municipality of 24 000 inhabitants, experienced problems with a growing stock of unlet apartments resulting in social and economic segregation. The main explanations were a reduction in jobs, a decrease in population and an increase of single-family housing. Many efforts to solve the problems failed.

An analysis showed that planning procedures followed a narrow sectoral approach based on rigid routines. Although most of the municipal departments were involved, no single department could solve the problem within its own competence. As the situation deteriorated, different administrative agencies blamed one another for the deadlock.

To tackle these problems, SCA was used in dialogue between politicians, administrators, planners and stakeholders external to the politico-administrative organisation. As a result the setting shifted to an informal forum with lateral communication and interactive participation.

This new way of working induced a spirit of collaboration and working groups were set up. By establishing a reference group with representatives from different stakeholders and a steering group of politicians and leading officers, the deadlocked process was reset within new structures (Khatee and Strömberg, 1993).

DEVELOPMENT OF A REGIONAL AGENDA 21

During the 1990s, concerns for sustainable development came to the fore. To establish common ground for future Local Agenda 21 processes, a 3-year Regional Agenda 21 project was initiated by four major public authorities in West Sweden, an area of 700 000 inhabitants.

The project organisation followed standard operating procedures with a political steering group and linear project plan. However, the project got stuck already in the goal formulation phase and the description of the current environmental situation consumed most of the time and money available.

Some participants were disappointed and critical but a new approach was taken when one of the critics was appointed head of the subsequent strategy phase. The task was to make best possible use of the remaining year of the project to regain enthusiasm and trust.

Five strategy groups were formed, of which the interdisciplinary life in the city group was comprised of planners and officials but also of two researchers from Chalmers University, who suggested that an adapted version of SCA should be applied (strömberg, 2001).

IMPLEMENTING LOCAL WASTE MANAGEMENT

In recent years, infrastructure systems have become more and more complex due to a shift from centralised public provision to more decentralised market-driven services. Moreover, different infrastructure systems increasingly tend to overlap and affect each other.

Within such a context, in 2002 the LOCO-MOTIVE project was designed to explore possibilities for integrating operation of a local waste management system with issues, such as social cohesion, management of green space and local economic development in a city district of Göteborg with 14 000 inhabitants.

A cross-sectoral working group of local actors from city district and housing management was set up, while Chalmers provided process facilitation. During the study most SCA modes were worked through. One observation was that the number of theoretically possible decision schemes in a system comprising four different waste streams became very large (2916 schemes), and the process of delimiting the scope of the study thus became an essential issue.

Nonetheless, the use of advantage comparison turned out to provide powerful support for assessment of this complex system. Through a series of consecutive evaluations under diminishing uncertainty, a synthesising assessment across eight comparison areas was achieved (Söderberg and Kain, 2002; Kain, 2003).

LESSONS ABOUT COMMUNICATIVE LEARNING

How did SCA facilitate problem perception and provision of transparent information? In Köping the SCA process generated a shift in problem perception. Moving the problems away from standard agendas and established agencies dramatically revised participant attitudes. This resulted in a complex set of interconnected problems – questioning established rules for taxation, subsidies and structure of decision-making – which engaged political leaders, most departments in the municipality and several stakeholders outside the municipality. Subsequently, incremental decisions by the steering group were developed in collaboration and implemented during the following years. The afflicted housing area was redeveloped from housing only to mixed use.

Also in the 1990s case, work in interdisciplinary constellations revealed complex relationships between different problem areas – such as car emissions, housing market segregation and lack of co-ordinated leadership – and their related decision domains. As an example, out of the dialogue between the different representatives a dramatic shift in problem perception occurred: shifting the focus from over-fertilisation only to the interplay of under-nourishment and over-fertilisation. When the project was formally concluded, it had developed into several informal learning processes comprising numerous organisations and individuals. Although the original problems of the public consortia were not solved, agreement was reached over several more fundamental issues and inter-dependencies.

The stakeholders in the last case repeatedly claimed that the main advantage of SCA was simply the opportunity to work in such a diverse group. Invisible products (cf. Figure 88) such as knowledge exchange and processing, were seen as very productive, generating possibilities for future networking. Consequently, the outcome of the learning process was a close-to-consensus progress package. Learning was so effective that some participants even claimed that this outcome was identical to the opinions they held before entering the process – an argument refuted by our analysis. Another observation was that the arguments underpinning the advantage comparison and the weighting of different evaluation areas remained somewhat obscure – an issue now being studied in ongoing research on complementary multi-criteria approaches at Chalmers Architecture.

LESSONS ABOUT EFFICIENCY

How did SCA influence the consumption of manpower, time and other resources? The 1980s' Köping process went on for 2 years before the housing market turned. It is difficult to evaluate what really influenced the happy ending, but the general feeling in Köping was that the application of SCA made it possible to break a locked situation. One measure of the perceived efficiency is that the municipality later on applied the same approach to other planning sectors.

From the public consortia's perspective, the Agenda 21 work did not reach its anticipated goal: a Regional Agenda 21 Strategy. However, the working group participants were satisfied with the progress and the learning processes. This was also demonstrated by the extensive efforts put in on voluntary basis by individuals, businesses and non-governmental organisations – engagements that lasted long after the formal project was ended.

Yet another measure of process efficiency is whether participants return throughout a series of meetings. In the LOCOMOTIVE case almost all participants were present at all working meetings. Our interpretation is that they judged the time they invested was being matched by achieved results. Even so, some participants argued that SCA 'made simple things complicated' while others saw the procedure as comparatively swift. These different views may be related to differences in problem perception, i.e. how complex is local waste management? It is thus essential that the level of complexity be matched by choice of facilitative approach.

LESSONS ABOUT DEMOCRACY

How did SCA support transparency, manageability and involvement of relevant stakeholders? In Köping, decision-making was moved from established formal arenas, with democratic framing structures for decision-making and access, to temporal informal fora emphasising learning and communication. Since the steering group took decisions in a grey zone between formal and informal structures, questions about democratic control and influence became essential.

Another aspect of this problem is illustrated by the LOCOMOTIVE case where participants were reluctant to acknowledge that others, such as local inhabitants, could not be fully represented by them. In this way, the process grew somewhat isolated from local everyday life. Moreover, in Köping most processes were negatively influenced by hidden power plays among participants resulting from personal antagonism and other forms of complex human relations with little relevance for the issues at hand. Although harming the process these hidden agendas were not discussed openly. Subsequently, a fourth category of uncertainty was introduced, describing in-group power play: intra-organisational uncertainty.

Both the Agenda 21 and the LOCOMOTIVE cases illustrate the essential problem of communicating findings of more or less informal working groups to others, such as politicians active in formal arenas (cf. Brendan Hickling's contribution to this chapter, Section 13.13). The outcome of the processes may hence be understood at two levels. At one level, the invisible results of mutual learning and mutual action-oriented commitment were strongly present. In the LOCOMOTIVE case, the participants were even prepared to embark on co-operative local area management based on their mutual learning. However, at a second level, the informal working forums of both cases had little linkage to formal decision-making arenas. Visible outcomes, such as published reports, were not accommodated at higher municipal levels. As an example, the LOCOMOTIVE report on local waste management received a positive response by the central Recycling Office of Göteborg and was to be brought to the attention of relevant decision-makers for swift processing.

Even so, today – 2 years later – nothing has evolved within the mainstream waste management system in response to the study. The learning effort thus largely remains unrecognised by Göteborg mainstream activities and bodies, and the suggestions of the local stakeholders have been absorbed into the political system without any further reaction. Fortunately, in relation to the Regional Agenda 21, the informal networks have later been involved in problem-solving processes implementing some of the findings.

CONCLUDING REFLECTIONS

In the development of decision-making approaches within the European Union since the Maastricht treaty, with the emphasis on subsidiarity and the current shift from government to governance, we observe that SCA has been well ahead of its time.

The three cases of SCA in Sweden are typical examples of how the planning context has developed during the last three decades, from emergency intra-organisational problem-solving through collective strategic knowledge building to implementation of sustainable development in a complex context of governance with shared power and no one in charge. In all three cases SCA has been robust and adaptable to ever-changing contexts.

Work in political contexts requires special attention to intra-organisational power plays and hidden agendas. The explicit management of such has – at times – been successful in our experience. Separating the roles of process leader and project leader has been important for the management of complex and sometimes conflict-laden problem structuring.

REFERENCES

KAIN, JAAN-HENRIK (2003) Sociotechnical Knowledge: An Operationalised Approach to Localised Infrastructure Planning and Sustainable Urban Development. Department of Built Environment and Sustainable Development Diss. Göteborg: Chalmers University of Technology.

KHAKEE A and STRÖMBERG K (1993) Applying Future Studies and the Strategic Choice Approach in Urban Planning. In: Journal of the Operational Research Society, vol. *44*, No. 3

STRÖMBERG K (2001) Facilitating Collaborative Decision Development in Urban Planning. In: Scandinavian Journal of Architectural Research, 2001: 4

SÖDERBERG H, KAIN J-H (2002) Integrating Knowledge or Aggregating Data – Multi-Criteria Approaches for Sustainable Water and Waste Systems. Proceedings, 3rd International Conference on Decision-Making in Urban and Civil Engineering. London.

13.3 Delving into the Toolboxes

National environmental policy-making and strategic choice

By Frans Evers

In this contribution the author draws on his experience as Deputy Director-General for the Environment in the Dutch government in the early 1980s. The focus is on internal priority setting in the field of environmental policy, which was very poorly developed at that time. Techniques and methods from a number of sources were used in combinations that varied according to the task in hand. They drew selectively from the SCA tool-box, using in particular AIDA and the levels of choice.

Frans Evers is currently Chairman of the Board of the Sustainability Challenge Foundation; Deputy Chairman for the Independent Commission for Environmental Impact Assessment; Adjunct-Professor at Tias Business School; and Senior Fellow at Globus (an inter-faculty institute at Tilburg University). He was Chief Executive of 'Natuurmonumenten' (the Dutch Association for Nature Conservation) from 1996 until 2002; Director-General of the Dutch Public Buildings Agency from 1987 until 1996; and, before 1987, Deputy Director-General for the Environment in the Dutch government (Assistant Deputy Minister in other countries). He has been chairman of several international committees, including the OECD Committee on Environmental Assessment and Development Assistance.

INTRODUCTION

I bumped into Allen Hickling at Schiphol airport sometime in 1980; and I was sceptical when Jan de Koning, the Dutch consultant who introduced us, declared that Allen and his methods could be the answer to many of my problems.

It was the tool-box idea that convinced me though. Being the son of a carpenter, I knew that there is no single way to solve a problem. There is always the combination of man, skill and tools. The inventive, creative carpenter uses his tools very differently from the one that is skilled and experienced, but who lives by tradition. My father used to borrow tools from the blacksmith for jobs that seemed to be impossible. He made his boss rich.

THE SITUATION

As Director for policy and strategy in the Environment Ministry, I was confronted with ambitions to introduce environmental impact assessment, environmental policy planning, risk management-policies (e.g. for the shipping, landing, distribution and storage of LPG) and, last but not least, priority setting within national environmental policies.

Since the department was basically organised by sectors (air pollution, water pollution, radiation, waste, noise, etc.), there was inevitable competition for the scarce resources available. But the ministers, up until then, had refused to embark on the issue of priorities. There was simply no answer to the question whether, for example, the reduction of air pollution had more or less priority than the abatement of noise, which, in the densely populated western part of the country, had attracted major attention from parliament and scientists.

INTRODUCING THE APPROACH

So suddenly there was a workshop to let a few of us know about SCA. Several of the participants recognised that there were possibilities for different areas of concern, and I decided to give the approach a try in the area of internal priority setting. Consequently a proposal for this was launched in spring 1981 with the suggestion to experiment with the AIDA method. Now here is part of the content of the letter I sent to the Director-General (my boss) and my colleague-directors.

In the spring we decided that we can no longer avoid setting priorities for our national environmental policies. It was accepted that, although the final responsibility for making these choices lies with the minister, we are not relieved of the duty to bring forward the necessary data for him to do so wisely. We decided to use a method based on SCA. This means that we do not start from general policy problems and goals, as a top-down approach, but that we focus on the concrete decisions that you expect to be confronted within the coming year. I suggested that after you made your inventory of the fields of decision in your own directorate, we would together look for the relations between the different fields of decision across the whole organisation. We would then be able to identify areas where decisions should be taken together, because there are certain to be choices that exclude each other.

I also suggested looking for possibilities and reasons to cluster certain areas of decision, because I expected that the first inventory of decisions would result

in decisions of different levels. We identified at first three levels, namely strategic, policy and operational decisions.[1] Later we decided in the discussions to add a fourth level, called the normative level of decisions.[2]

This highest level seems to be most relevant for a government organisation, which is related to political goals that are intended to guide decisions outside our organisation. It is clear that it is not easy to do this levelling of decisions right at the beginning on your own. In practice there has to be some overlap, and some civil servants hardly have a clue about this normative level.

Let me be clear: the whole process of priority setting is meant to focus on decisions at the strategic level, but I am quite aware of the fact that limitations at the policy and operational levels can restrict the room for strategic choices.

So far the young director in 1981.

WORKING WITH LEVELS OF CHOICE

The letter not only caused a stir in many civil servants' lives, but it also set us on a difficult and tiresome road of trying to use AIDA to help us find and keep track of the interconnected decision areas. Coincidentally it also forced us to get to grips with the whole idea of strategic planning. It became clear, through use of the various tools from the tool-box, that we had to embark on a discussion with the minister and, indeed, the whole organisation, about the importance of having a strategy for the environment. Otherwise people would continue being too late in dealing with environmental risks. We would continue to be a clean-up organisation,

---

1   See 'AIDA and the Levels of Choice in Structure Plans' by Hickling (1978); and the contribution to this chapter by Angell (Section 13.10).
2   This is the same as strategic orientation in the vocabulary of Hickling (1978) and Chapter 12.

while allowing other ministries and the business community to continue messing around with the environment.

A CHANGE OF DIRECTION

So we embarked on a fascinating trip on which it was not clear what the destination would be. All directors produced their ideas about the connected decision areas within their field of responsibility. As an example, my own in its first draft is presented here (Figure 13.1).

In a huge effort we connected all of them. The result covered a whole wall of my room. Of course we got stuck in such an elaborate effort and had to simplify a lot of things. The most important result was the insight that we could not continue creating solutions in one area while creating new problems in another. At that time we were like many of our colleagues in other countries, shifting waste from the air into the water and from the water into solid waste, and we disposed of the solid waste by creating a soil pollution problem.

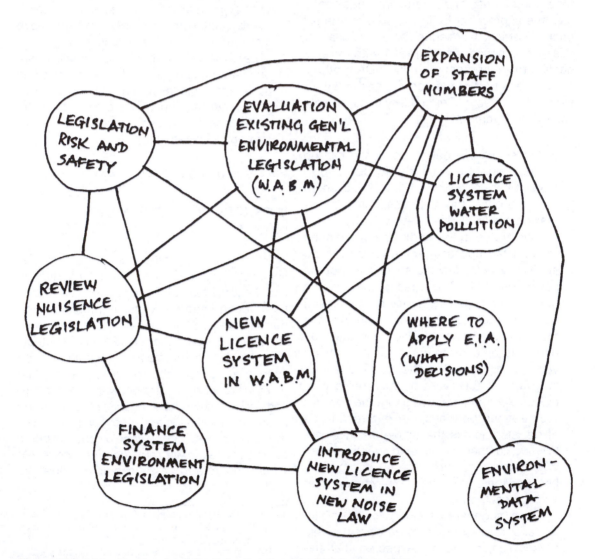

Figure 13.1 Major Decision Areas for Policy Development Directorate in 1981.

THE RELEVANT QUESTIONS

We decided to stop this muddling through and go for a strategic approach. The new minister in 1982, Pieter Winsemius who had a McKinsey background, asked the relevant questions about strategy and priorities after a few months in office. I doubt we would have had any idea how to answer them if we had not done our prior exercises. In finding the relations across the sectors, in creating an atmosphere where levelling of decisions was no longer a threat, we laid the foundations for the guidance position of Dutch environmental policies that lasted until the middle of the nineties.

CONCLUDING REFLECTIONS

We found tools in the toolbox of SCA that we liked and were able to use. But we also used other toolboxes that we borrowed or bought, when we felt that they were better for the job. Consensus building using the mutual gains approach was probably the most important. Professor Lawrence Susskind, the relentless promoter of that approach, became another important advisor. Other tools came from project management as taught by Gerd Wijnen.

13.4 Less is More

Controlling decision complexity when using strategic choice

By Richard Ormerod

In this contribution the author draws on his experience as a consultant helping Severn Trent, a regional water utility in the UK, to develop a customer service strategy. He draws attention to three aspects of the application of the SCA:

1. the need to manage down the complexity of the decisions to be taken;
2. the option of introducing quantitative scoring into the evaluation; and
3. the extension of the progress package to plan a timetable of future decisions.

Richard Ormerod originally became aware of SCA when he read a paper about it in the Journal of the Operational Research Society in the early eighties. He found the categorisation of uncertainty insightful in his then role as a corporate planner in the National Coal Board. However, it was not until the late eighties that he first used SCA as a decision-making aid when working as a management consultant in the PA Consulting Group. On entering academia in the early nineties, as well as teaching SCA and other approaches to postgraduate students, he continued to use SCA in practice as a consultant. He has used SCA on a number of assignments in the retail, mining, water and electricity industries – usually helping clients to develop their information systems strategy, but the projects also involved process, technical and organisational change.

THE SITUATION

Some time before I came on the scene Severn Trent had decided to develop a customer service strategy to address the one area where they performed less well (as measured by the UK water regulator) than other regional water companies.

A core team had drawn up terms of reference for half a dozen or so task forces of senior managers. Each task force was asked to analyse a particular aspect of customer service to develop options and recommendations, and to report back. For example, one task force had examined the nature and organisation of the physical interface with customers and the general public (by letter, telephone and face-to-face). They had addressed issues such as whether customer services should be organised centrally or locally, and whether call handlers should be specialised (billing inquiries only) or deal with several types of query (operational and billing inquiries). The task forces were reporting back their findings. The core team was faced with a wide range of overlapping and conflicting recommendations coming from the different task forces.

THE ASSIGNMENT

It was at this point that they asked me to help them develop a combined coherent strategy for the Board to agree. Time was an issue: an expensive venue had already been booked for a high-profile public launch of the new strategy.

One of the points made in Chapter 5 is that it is advisable to keep the problem focus narrow. I found that this point is key to the success of an SCA intervention. It is my experience that the facilitator must actively manage the complexity of the decisions under consideration if the process is to avoid getting bogged down. The Severn Trent case illustrates the point.

MANAGING COMPLEXITY

In this case it was not difficult to identify lots of decision areas and plenty of options of differing degrees of importance and urgency. Therein lay the problem. To be inclusive everything needed to be acknowledged and made part of the analysis from the start. However, when it came to shaping the decision space the question of complexity had to be addressed or the project would be overwhelmed. For instance, if it is decided to include six decision areas in the problem focus, each with three options, there are potentially 729 decision schemes to be evaluated.

It would take an enormous number of option bars to get the number of schemes down to a manageable level. It is far better to restrict the number of decision areas in the first instance. I persuaded the team to limit themselves to four areas for the first pass while they were getting to understand the approach. They needed the reassurance that the issues parked for the time being would be brought back in a later cycle of the process. If each area has three options this limitation would reduce the maximum number of schemes to 81. In the event they chose four options in one area, two in another and three in the other two (reducing the total number of schemes to 72). Again it pays to struggle to find as many option bars as possible. In this case after identifying

some option bars we were left with about 20 schemes. This was still a lot to understand and evaluate, but it was then manageable. Reducing the number of schemes by limiting the number of areas included in the problem focus, constraining the number of options, and searching out all the option bars is crucial to the success of the evaluation phase.

The decision to restrict the number of decision areas to four in the first instance had been a difficult one. Nevertheless, on returning to the original map of the decision areas it proved fairly simple to consider those decisions that had been left out. Each decision could be considered in the light of the decision schemes favoured by the evaluation. Some options could be barred while others had a particular affinity with one scheme or another. Others still resulted in variants of particular schemes. It seemed easier for participants to handle the complexity this way than to go through the SCA shaping and evaluation again. The three or four remaining schemes were then fully evaluated including a comparison with the way that other regional water companies organised their customer service operations.

QUANTITATIVE SCORING IN EVALUATION

The initial evaluation using a few criteria is another opportunity to manage down the number of schemes, as discussed in Chapter 3. We set the hurdles high so that only a few schemes remained. When it came to the more detailed evaluation, the team wanted to be able to give different weights to the various evaluation criteria. The approach taken was to score each scheme on a scale of 1–5 for each evaluation criterion. Each criterion was then given a weight. An overall score for each scheme was derived by multiplying scores by weights and adding up across the criteria. In doing this, something is lost by turning the evaluation into numbers, but it gave the option of changing the weights to explore the sensitivity to different assumptions.

On another assignment, Sainsbury's, a UK supermarket chain, went a stage further and insisted that all the evaluation scores were translated into monetary terms even though some of the criteria were soft in nature. For many participants this would be a step too far.

EXTENSION OF THE PROGRESS PACKAGE

Finally, when drawing up the progress package the participants decided to go further than distinguishing between decisions now and decisions later. They divided the decisions later into time periods depending on when the results of further explorations would become available. The result was a critical path network of explorations. This provided a basis for setting time limits on explorations and developing a schedule of decision meetings.

Crucially they were able to plan which issues they could reasonably hope to resolve by the time of the launch and those which would be included in the launch as issues that would be explored and resolved in the future. With the launch date rapidly approaching, the realisation that they could present both decisions taken and decisions yet to be taken (depending on further exploration) side by side in the new strategy was a great relief to all concerned.

CONCLUDING REFLECTIONS

In the Severn Trent Water case described above both the introduction of a quantitative method of evaluation and the extension of the progress package using critical path concepts are illustrations of the more general point that it is often desirable to enhance the use of one approach with others – as argued in the previous contribution of Frans Evers. At RTZ (an international mining company) and PowerGen (a UK electricity utility), soft systems methodology (SSM) (Checkland, 1983) was used to generate strategic options while SCA was used to shape and evaluate them. On its own SCA provides little support for creative idea generation, while SSM provides little support for converging on a decision. Combined SCA and SSM can be used to support a strategy development process from idea generation to agreed decisions. It is experiences such as those described above that have led me to appreciate the strength of the SCA framework. All the same I do not to follow it too rigidly. Groups of decision-makers have particular requirements and they appreciate an approach that can be adapted to their circumstances. They like to be in control of the process rather than controlled by it. The consultant/facilitator should have some of the possible variants in mind so as to respond appropriately and confidently as the decision dynamic unfolds and the decision-making requirements become apparent.

REFERENCES

ORMEROD R (1998) Putting Soft OR Methods to Work: Information Systems Strategy Development at Palabora. In: Omega International Journal of Management Sciences 26, 75–98

ORMEROD, R (1999) Putting Soft OR Methods to Work: The Case of the Business Improvement Project at PowerGen. In: European Journal of Operational Research 118, 1–29

PAULEY GS and ORMEROD R (1998) The Evolution of a Performance Measurement Project at RTZ. In: Interfaces 28, 94–118

13.5   Feet on the Ground

Engaging planning students with political realities

By Arnold van der Valk and Gerrit J. Carsjens

The strategic choice approach stands students in planning and management with both feet firmly on the solid ground of day-to-day decision-making. Today planners cannot afford to be called dreamers or ivory tower types. They are supposed to come up with proposals that have a chance of acceptance and of implementation. If not, it reduces the limited supply of public confidence. That is why teaching staff of Wageningen University in the Netherlands includes the philosophy and toolbox of strategic choice in the core curriculum for landscape architecture and spatial planning. Since undergraduate courses in planning methodology are open for students in environmental and social sciences, some 25 engineers graduating at Wageningen University yearly have been exposed to the basics of strategic choice since 1999. In the masters curriculum, 'Planning under Pressure' is used as a textbook by planning students.

Arnold van der Valk has been a full professor in land-use planning at Wageningen University in the Netherlands since 2002. He took a PhD in planning from Amsterdam University with distinction in 1989. He holds an MSc in human geography and an MSc in spatial planning. The emphasis in his scientific work is on planning theory and planning history. His seminal work so far is Rule and Order; Dutch Planning Doctrine in the Twentieth Century, co-authored by Faludi (1994).

Gerrit Jan Carsjens is a senior staff member of the Land Use Planning Group at Wageningen University. His educational work focuses on technical and methodological aspects of land-use planning. This includes working with strategic choice in two strategic planning courses, as described in this contribution. His research focuses at the development of decision-support methods using geographical information systems (GIS). Two main projects are: (1) the FAO project on area-wide integration of crop and livestock activities in Southeast Asia and (2) the integration of environmental aspects into local planning procedures in The Netherlands.

STRATEGIC CHOICE IN A PLANNING CURRICULUM

Strategic choice was introduced by one of the authors who was appointed professor in land-use planning in Wageningen in 1999. He wrote two introductory texts to strategic choice in

the Dutch language for undergraduates. The Dutch texts present elementary information about a decision-oriented view of planning, an overview of strategic choice technology and a glossary both in Dutch and in English. The decision-oriented view of planning was developed by Andreas Faludi and Arnold van der Valk in the 1980s, building on the foundations laid by the pioneers of strategic choice in the preceding decade (Faludi and van der Valk, 1994; Faludi, 2000). This approach sets out to develop a sound scientific foundation for planning rooted into Popperian social philosophy and epistemology. Faludi acknowledges strategic choice as the best application of his interpretation of rational decision-making in practice.

In the Wageningen planning course, the foundations of strategic choice are explained using contemporary examples taken from planning practice. Since jargon has proved to be a major obstacle in the process of teaching strategic choice, staff members have designed role plays, studios and applications based on real-time planning experiences. These situations have been carefully selected and simplified for educational purposes.

Strategic choice basics are taught in an introductory planning course in the second year of the Bachelor's Landscape Architecture and Spatial Planning (in Dutch, BSc landschap, planning en ontwerp). This basic course takes two weeks of part-time classes and exercises. Students participate in a simulated decision-making process about the use of land in a rapidly urbanising region near the city of Rotterdam. The case comes with a lot of substantive information about an anticipated harbour, about the claims of horticulturalists, administrative procedures, the institutional context, and social and economic statistics. Above all the students have to learn about empathy by taking up the role of a stakeholder group or playing the role of a professional. In the role play they are facing the tensions inherent in political power play. They get a first impression of facilitating, mediating and organising participative planning processes.

In the third year, SCA is at the heart of two full grown planning courses that include several weeks of full time exercises. The courses are built upon the foundations of strategic choice as explained in Chapter 1 of this book. The first course is an in-depth planning methodology course, as described below. In the second

course the students are asked to produce a strategic spatial plan for the long term of a complex region in the Netherlands. This second course will be described in more detail in the next section.

The manual for the planning methodology course familiarises the students with the foundations of strategic choice as explained in *Planning under Pressure*. The manual explains the intricacies of choosing strategically, the organisational context, the dilemmas of decision-making and the responses to uncertainty. The emphasis is on the philosophy of strategic choice, perceived as a joint learning process. In this phase of the bachelor, students in planning and architecture are supposed to be familiar with a lot of the conventional expert technology characteristic of routine decision-making.

RESPONSES FROM STUDENTS

In some instances this proved to be an obstacle to the reception of open technology. The good news is that the majority has an open mind for the social conditions that press decision-makers to opt for open technology (see Chapter 4). Group decision techniques are used to sensitise students to an orientation towards participative interaction. The ultimate challenge for most students is the empathy part in the simulation of stakeholder participation. The expert roles, included facilitation, group management, quick and dirty research and chairing negotiations seem to pose much less of a challenge. An explanation for this kind of conventional expert behaviour may be found in the character of the traditional technical training in the first and second year. The emphasis in these 2 years is still very much on traditional learning, i.e. technology for quantitative analysis and cognitive skills for engineers and architects. Traditional engineering competences are still kept in high esteem within Wageningen University, formerly known as Wageningen Agricultural University.

A majority of the students struggle with the strategic choice philosophy as it conflicts with their perception of planning. This holds for social science-oriented students in planning but has even greater relevance for students in engineering disciplines and architecture. Students in their primes tend to equate planning with plan making and design of physical and social constructions. Carefully constructed training exercises contribute to a change in perspective from the dominant blueprint planning philosophy to a decision-oriented process approach.

Our experiences with the application of SCA in academic planning courses show that the proof of the pudding is in the eating. Students cannot grasp the idea of strategic choice by reading a textbook alone. It takes practical training exercises to get students acquainted with these concepts.

The use of the STRAD software is optional in the curriculum. Since planning methodology classes suffer from severe time restrictions, students are warned not to spend too much time in playing around with software. From a software engineering perspective STRAD is obviously still in an experimental phase. Staff and students though praise the STRAD manual as a valuable tool in the course. The software is appreciated by the students for its clarity but too limited in the scope of its applications.

STRAD classes have been replaced recently by group decision sessions. Group decision room (GDR) sessions are limited in the face of high cost. GDR software has proved extremely useful for our students in the shaping mode. Well-prepared group decision sessions save a lot of time and produce more high quality content during brainstorming sessions. Integration of group decision technology with the STRAD software is a must from our perspective.

COMBINING COMPLEMENTARY APPROACHES

The landscape, planning and design curriculum combines a decision-oriented approach and a design-oriented approach to planning. The decision-oriented approach focuses on process management and draws its main sources of inspiration from policy sciences. This approach takes day-to-day decisions and the anticipated consequences as a starting point. It focuses on systematically working towards policy frames and a commitment package. The emphasis is on the 'here and now'. The design-oriented approach emphasises the construction of spatial plans and is built upon traditional architectural design theory. This approach focuses at the construction of alternative futures with the help of creative leaps then taking consecutive steps backward in time in order to arrive at practicable policy guidelines. It encompasses elements of a traditional survey-analysis-plan approach to planning and makes use of prospective scenario techniques. These techniques are indispensable for initiating debate about desirable and probable futures.

The combination of strategic choice technology and prospective scenario techniques has silenced complaints about the neglect of creativity and substance in a decision-oriented approach of planning. For educational purposes it seems highly attractive to develop sophisticated methods for learning, combining the fruits of both perspectives for planners, architects and other professionals-in-training. Friend and Hickling have taken up this challenge under the header 'practicalities' in the technical domain (cf. Figure 89 – strategic choice as a continuous process).

A preference for problem-oriented courses and design studios is an integral part of the Wageningen educational tradition and philosophy. Students are challenged to analyse and solve complex problems taken from practice. Interdisciplinary research and stakeholder participation are necessary ingredients of this approach. In the third year of the bachelor curriculum, students embark upon a realistic regional planning studio. Learning by doing is combined with systematic application of prescriptions taken from the planning methodology classes. Text books provide them with additional information about technology for decision-making. Staff members perform the role of advisers on the job. Core data are taken from a real-time planning process and presented by practicing planners. In the final studio, taking several weeks of full time work, students practise a combination of the decision-oriented approach and the design-oriented approach.

The studio reflects an incremental and cyclical planning process. Students are tempted to produce a proposal for a regional spatial plan. At the heart of this plan is a realistic and reasoned commitment package. In the annexes, students produce a detailed report of the process and the invisible products. Emphasis is laid upon the argumentative part of the work and the role of professionals in planning. Stakeholder participation is simulated in non-regular plenary sessions in the beginning and at the end of the course. Students work under very strict time constraints and are thus confronted with a range of uncertainties.

The design-oriented approach emphasises the use of quantitative analyses i.e. applied soil science, hydrology, landscape ecology, traffic management, land consolidation technology, historical geography, economy, demography, institutional analysis, stakeholder analysis and analysis of cultural values. Future trends are established. Imagery, statistics and maps play a role in visualising alternative futures. Stakeholders and professionals are invited to participate in a process of mapping consequences. This approach diverts attention from seemingly unsolvable conflicts and helps in reframing contested decisions. Playing around with substantive topics takes away some of the stress involved in group processes. The design-oriented element is particularly helpful in scanning distant futures, thus providing eye-openers for politicians and one-issue participants. These results enable students to produce reasoned lists of decisions and uncertainty areas, and discuss priorities.

CONCLUSION

Strategic choice is an indispensable tool for planning education and related fields of professional training. It encompasses a powerful set of ideas and concepts offering help in complex situations of choice under uncertainty. It helps students to develop the facilitation and mediation skills so much needed in modern collaborative planning practice. The open technology leaves scope for add-ons taken from the domain of physical design and planning. These add-ons are used to help students to produce richer arguments by way of combining substantive and procedural knowledge. Combining strategic choice with design-oriented approaches helps in bridging the gap between science and political action.

REFERENCES

FALUDI A (2000) The Performance of Spatial Planning. In: Planning Practice and Research, Vol. *15*, No. 4, pp. 299–318
FALUDI A and VALK AJ van der (1994) Rule and Order; Dutch Planning Doctrine in the Twentieth Century. Dordrecht: Kluwer Academic Publishers

ADDITIONAL INFORMATION

Details on the Wageningen Landscape Architecture and Spatial Planning curriculum can be found on: http://www.wau.nl/rpv

13.6 Designing Electronic Support

Empowering decision-makers through software for strategic choice

By Dave Friend

In this contribution, the architect of the STRAD software for strategic choice draws on his experience in designing and testing marketable prototypes of this package over a 9-year period – starting in the late eighties when the diffusion of access to the fast-developing world of information technology was still in the early stages. He reviews the choices of direction he himself has had to make in the development of this software in the face of changing circumstances and opportunities, and draws some lessons for the design of future electronic support for decision-makers.

Dave Friend is the second son of Mari and John Friend. He was aged 18 when, working with his father, he started developing computer software for strategic choice. At that time, he had become angry about many things he saw in the world around him, and disenchanted with his experiences of the educational system; yet, along with many others of his generation, he was becoming stimulated by the creative potential of the new world of home computing. As a self-taught programmer, he spent 9 years developing successive versions of the STRAD (Strategic Adviser) software, and has since continued to help John Friend in maintaining technical support and upgrade services to users. He lives near Bradford in West Yorkshire and now works as spares supervisor for an international microelectronics corporation.

EARLY WORK ON STRAD

It was in 1987 that I first started work on the development of the STRAD software described in Chapter 10, initially on a four-month trial contract. The personal computer on which I started working was then new on the market but had capacities that would now seem ridiculously limited; it was an Amstrad 1512, with 512 kb of RAM, no hard drive and two 360 kb floppy drives. With some guidance from my father's former colleague John Stringer, I started work using Microsoft Quick-BASIC 3 as a readily available programming language in which a first prototype could be designed.

Then, a few years later, the arrival of more advanced operating systems for IBM-compatible personal computers, with a smarter graphical user interface, allowed further aspects of the Strategic Choice Approach to become more easily incorporated into the design of STRAD. Users now became able to draw decision graphs much as they had previously appeared on flipcharts. They could also interact with software in a more intuitive way, negating the need to learn sequences of keystrokes to navigate around a series of screens.

It was particularly valuable that the Windows interface allowed the results of work from the shaping, designing, comparing and shaping modes to be displayed on screen at the same time. This enabled users to refer back to their earlier work, and to switch from mode to mode, as if they were in a strategic choice workshop with a developing gallery of flipcharts around the walls.

The storage limitations of the desktop computers of that time meant that care always had to be taken not to overload the screen with too many different windows displaying the results of work so far. Yet, with the growing capacities of personal computers, it was to be only a matter of a few more years before these constraints were overcome.

CHALLENGES IN SOFTWARE DESIGN

Throughout the early nineties, the development of STRAD was held back at times by the need to keep up with successive advances in operating systems, and the continuing need to ensure bug-free operation on a range of platforms.

It is easy to concentrate on developing new features, but in doing so one risks the usability of the application. There are many 'what-if' pitfalls to beware of; and I suspect that software that is designed to give flexible support to decision-makers in responding to changing situations will always pose more challenges in this area than most other types of software.

Take this example: A focus of four decision areas may produce a list of 20 possible schemes. The user proceeds to compare options within each decision area and makes an assessment on the combined data that appears. Comparing the relative advantages of these schemes leads the user to exclude some less advantageous schemes and at some stage to adopt a progress package based on these assessments.

After some discussions with colleagues, the user realises that another option is available in one of these decision areas. How is the computer to deal with this kind of scenario? Surely the data requires some review? Should the computer be able to recognise the consequences of this otherwise basic action? Does it simply warn the user, or should it attempt to interlace the new option into the existing choices already made by the user?

SOFTWARE DEVELOPMENT AS A PROCESS OF STRATEGIC CHOICE

I have found that programming the software can itself pose some tricky policy choices and regularly produces areas of uncertainty. For example uncertainty is raised by:

– the range of possible scenarios that users will be able to create under the range of computer platforms available (this could be expressed in SCA terms as UE);

– the effect of a course taken in one area of development on another area of the program (UR);

– policy decisions where it is a matter of debate whether control should lie with the computer or with the user, or indeed whether the user should be given an option either to decide or to trust the computer (UV).

KEEPING PACE WITH FURTHER TECHNOLOGICAL CHANGE

In our small-scale programme to develop software to reflect both the spirit and the practical toolbox of the strategic choice approach, we have had to focus our limited resources on developing a versatile package to meet the needs of individual decision-makers and small informal groups who can meet around a single workstation – a package that could quickly be tested in a range of potential markets. The choices and uncertainties that I have faced in designing the first production versions of the STRAD software can be viewed as a developing story of planning under pressure, in a setting where the technology has been by no means standing still.

Since I started developing STRAD in the late eighties, there have been impressive advances in information and communication technologies on a wide front, as discussed more fully in the later sections of Chapter 10. Among the most important advances in terms of support for decision-making have been not only the technological changes themselves but also the rapid growth in access to new channels of electronic communication. The spread of access to the Internet, e-mail and mobile phone networks has been dramatic in recent years, and the further advances now on the horizon will present not only new opportunities, but tough new choices and new uncertainties for the designers – and the promoters – of future electronic technology for strategic choice.

REFLECTIONS

Many lessons have been learnt from this initial small-scale programme of software development for strategic choice, and some of the wider lessons have already been reported in Chapter 10. I have been able to build some, but as yet by no means all, of these lessons into the design of later editions of the software and its user interface. Meanwhile, some of the lessons have also been absorbed into the wider field of practice on which this third edition builds.

Further development of software support for strategic choice need not result in ever more complicated systems, replacing human interaction, discussion and opinion with rigid and pre-defined computer gimmickry. A more useful way forward is to further develop resources for flexible working around an intuitive interface, which will take the number crunching but not the understanding and control away from the decision-makers.

Several of the other contributors to this chapter report on ways in which they have so far been able to make use of the STRAD software, not only in working on decisions but also in capturing lessons from their experiences. Most of the experiences of software support so far have been at a small and relatively intimate scale of decision-making. So they raise questions of how to reach out towards influencing the choices of other decision-makers, as shown in Figure 31, rather than of co-ordination from some central policy position. In future, continued extensions of access to information and communication technologies, as well as advances in the technologies themselves, will create many opportunities for empowering the decision-makers of the future. As indicated in the previous contribution to this chapter (Section 13.5), they will have an expanding role to play in introducing younger people to all the complexities of real-life planning that they must prepare to meet in their future careers.

13.7　Neighbourhood Renewal in Rome

Combining strategic choice with other design methods

By Alessandro Giangrande and Elena Mortola

The subject of this contribution is a continuous, participatory and incremental procedure which combines three approaches cyclically connected: Visioning, the Strategic Choice Approach and A Pattern Language. In the view of the two authors it helps to strengthen SCA as a planning and design procedure. As members of the team that won a national design competition, the authors utilised it for developing some planning and design proposals for the renewal of Centocelle Vecchia, a sub-urban neighbourhood of Rome that sprang up during the twenties. As a consequence of this success, the municipality of Rome has given the team the task of forming the preliminary plan for the rehabilitation of the neighbourhood. This work is still under way.

Alessandro Giangrande taught Design Methods at the Faculty of Architecture of the University of Rome La Sapienza from 1973 to 1992. Since 1993 he has taught Environmental Analysis and Evaluation at the Faculty of Architecture of University Roma Tre, where he is also the manager of the Information Technology Laboratory for Sustainable Urban Design. During the last 8 years he has been involved in various programmes of community planning and design: in particular he has collaborated with the Municipality of Rome in the establishment of the Neighbourhood Municipal Laboratories, and with the municipality of Quito and the San Francisco University in Ecuador in starting up laboratories for sustainable urban development.

Elena Mortola was professor of Design Methods in the University of Rome La Sapienza between 1983 and 1992. Since 1993 she has taught Computer-Aided Architectural Design at the Faculty of Architecture of University Roma Tre. In association with the European META University network, she directs a master's course on Interactive Sustainable Design and Multimedia. She has been a visiting professor at universities in Scotland, the Netherlands, Ecuador and Mozambique, and has developed methods in the fields of Environmental Impact Assessment, urban design and CAAD.

OUR 'IDEAL' PROCEDURE

In our capacity as teachers in the field of urban design and regeneration, both of us have had opportunities to test over a long period, with our collaborators and students, the effectiveness of the Strategic Choice Approach, especially when linked to complementary design methods of Visioning and A Pattern Language. We have applied this combination to several consulting and research projects, as well as using it extensively in our teaching for first degree courses, master's courses and doctoral theses. In a

Visioning[1] exercise, all the interested parties – such as local authorities and other public bodies, entrepreneurs, professional, cultural and environmental associations and neighbourhood committees – are invited to attend a workshop aimed at developing a participatory scenario.

A participatory scenario is not a picture of the future state of a place, but a tool for identifying problems and exploring possible actions to enable a community to move towards a preferable future. It differs from an expert scenario, where the major focus is on technological and economic forecasting.

In our version of Visioning, the scenario takes the appearance of a 'chronicle from the future'. The participants to the workshop interact under the guidance of facilitators to write a short story set in the distant future, 15 or 20 years later. The participants identify with the protagonists of the story and describe what they see, say or do in order to built up a 'vision', that is a representation of a desired future. Scenario making is the first step of a learning process that continues through the use of SCA. In SCA the interaction takes place in a workshop involving both some regular participants and some ad hoc participants, responsible for specific areas of specialised substantive input. The learning process develops in an adaptive and exploratory fashion, guided by the four working modes of SCA: shaping, designing, comparing and choosing – as shown in Figure 8.

The scenario provides the main input to the workshop. We identify issues as decision areas, options, uncertainty areas or comparison areas, updating this picture – for instance, by opening a new Visioning session – whenever the decision situation changes.

In the designing mode the working group identifies some alternative proposals (options[2])

for each decision area. The options that entail transformations of the physical features of the territory can be more closely defined with the aid of A Pattern Language [3]. This is a language developed by Christopher Alexander and his associates that helps a community to design a set of consistent and effective transformations. Each pattern is an 'archetype' that describes a problem that occurs over and over again in different spatial settings, pointing to possible lines of solution that can be adopted countless times without ever doing it the same way twice. Alexander described 253 patterns that he was able to arrange, starting with the largest, for regions and towns, then working down through neighbourhoods, clusters of building, buildings and rooms, ending finally with details of constructions. New patterns can be created, if necessary, to supply solutions to any problems not considered in this language.

Like SCA, A Pattern Language is an interactive and incremental approach. It is possible to start a process of territorial development or change incrementally through selection and aggregation: each pattern interprets the patterns at the higher scale and is in turn interpreted by the patterns at the lower scale. The rules of the language can help a group to define options within decision areas as patterns, or clusters of patterns, that are compatible and synergetic.

This planning/design process is cyclic. It is not important always to start with Visioning: for some decision areas, options and sources of uncertainty can be identified from the existing decision situation, before developing any scenario. The scenario making can also be interrupted to allow the participants to use A Pattern Language as a diagnostic tool to understand the problems of the area and access some suggestions (patterns) that can help to solve them and so on.

1 See, for instance: Ames SC (1993) A Guide to Community Visioning: Hands-on Information for Local Communities, Oregon Vision Project, American Planning Association (Oregon Chapter), Oregon, Portland.
2 The *options* are the natural consequence of the fact that the *Visioning* procedure usually generates different 'visions' i.e., different solutions to the same problem.

3 Alexander C, Ishikawa S and Silverstein M (1977) Oxford University Press, New York: A Pattern Language. Towns – Buildings – Construction.

THE PROCEDURE APPLIED WITHIN ROME

As members of a team[4] that won the second national competition in Participatory and Communicative Planning[5], the authors applied this procedure to develop some planning and design proposals for the renewal of the neighbourhood of Centocelle Vecchia in Rome. The participation of the inhabitants was managed by way of a laboratorio (workshop) expressly set up by the municipality of Rome for the competition. Through this laboratorio, public meetings were arranged with different groups including local authorities, associations, neighbourhood committees and schoolchildren. As a result, extensive documentation was produced on the problems of the neighbourhood and the wants of the residents. The members of the team made wide use of this documentation, together with other data gathered through special field research, to produce a (simulated) scenario[6].

From this scenario the team developed 21 decision areas, with levels of importance and urgency and a provisional list of options (2–5 for each area). Then they built up a decision graph as an overview of the structure of the problem, and identified several foci with the help of the STRAD software described in Chapter 10.

Within each focus, the choice of a preferred decision scheme was explored using the following six comparison areas:

1. Environmental sustainability
2. Urban sustainability
3. Social and cultural sustainability
4. Economic and financial sustainability

5. Expressed desires of the inhabitants
6. Degree of innovation in solutions.

The first focus includes four decision areas:

1. What interventions for via Tor de' Schiavi?
2. Where to design new pedestrian routes?
3. What traffic improvements in neighbourhood?
4. Where and how to plant new vegetation?

Starting with the preferred scheme for this focus, all options were found impracticable in the immediate future: so they were put in the list of deferred choices of the progress package. In the *explorations now* section, the team put only the exploratory options that they considered appropriate for reducing critical uncertainties. For instance, to realise the preferred option for pedestrian routes, it was important to test whether the owners of the courtyards were willing to transfer to the municipality the ownership of those spaces necessary to complete the network – perhaps in exchange for certain benefits. Similarly, the exploratory options for Tor de' Schiavi were needed to test opposition to the project from residents and tradesmen, including repair garages; and also the possibility of diverting the buses presently using that route.

Meanwhile, the team proceeded to develop more detailed designs for the preferred options in these two decision areas with the aid of A Pattern Language. They wished to test whether the designs, if of sufficient quality, might reduce opposition to the conversion of via Tor de' Schiavi into a pedestrian street; or might induce the owners of the courtyards to grant the spaces needed to build the pedestrian routes. These options are illustrated in Figure 13.2. At first the designers chose the principal patterns, i.e. the patterns that in their opinion should play a major role in implementing the projects. These patterns were *Promenade* (for pedonalizz) and *Children in the city* (for retescuole). Then they used the rules of the

---

4   E. Mortola (team leader), M. Bastiani, G. Cafiero, B. Del Brocco, M. Felici, A. Fortuzzi, A. Giangrande, F. Mecarelli, F. Sartogo, A. Simone and A. Zarfati.

5   The competition had been advertised in 2000 by INU (National Institute of Urbanism of Italy) and WWF (World Wildlife Fund).

6   The rules of the competition prevented the team from keeping continuing contact with the inhabitants of the neighbourhood, so the team was unable to apply the *Visioning* procedure to make a 'true' *participatory scenario*.

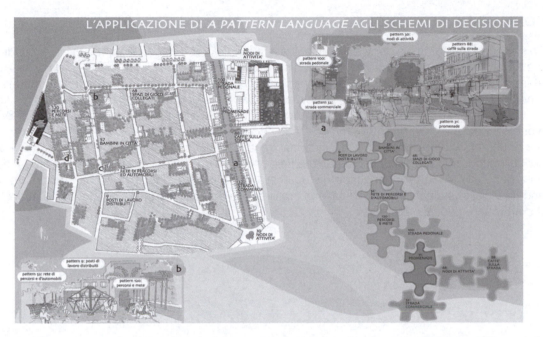

Figure 13.2 Options Retescuole and Pedonalizz Designed with the Aid of A Pattern Language (Artwork by F. Mecarelli).

language to identify both a set of detailed patterns[7] to complete the principal patterns, and the structure of their relationships, visualised in the form of a jigsaw puzzle[8].

Promenade was used to 'create a centre for public life: a place where you can go to see people, and to be seen' and 'encourage the gradual formation of a promenade at the heart of every community, linking the main activity nodes and placed centrally, so that each point in the community is within 10 minute' walk of it'. To complete the pattern the designers made use of *Pedestrian street*, *Shopping street* and *Street cafe*. The project established a strong relationship between *Children in the city* and *Network of paths and cars*.

---

7 The full list of these *patterns* is the following: *Scattered work*, *Activity nodes*, *Shopping street*, *Network of paths and cars*, *Connected play*, *Street cafe*, *Pedestrian street*, *Paths and goals* (see Alexander *et al.*, in ibidem).

8 In this diagram the interlocking pieces represent the *patterns* that realise the two *options* (*retescuole* and *pedonalizz*): the nearer are the pieces, the stronger should be the connection between the corresponding physical spaces and functions in the project.

THE REHABILITATION PLAN

The new procedure was later utilised by the team to draw up a preliminary design for the rehabilitation plan – but, this time, with the direct participation of the inhabitants of Centocelle Vecchia. The working group was now opened up to the residents of the neighbourhood and some representatives of the local government. They were invited to participate in an introductory session of the workshop, in which the proposals were illustrated in some detail, explaining the principles of SCA and the rules of A Pattern Language.

During the sessions that followed, the decision areas and options changed considerably; three new foci were identified and new uncertainty areas emerged through the interaction of the working group with local people. Many people without planning and design expertise expressed their interest in A Pattern Language, and some of them utilised it to represent in greater detail their preferred options.

CONCLUDING REFLECTIONS

This experience confirms our view that, at least in the field of urban design, the cyclic procedure works better than each approach – Visioning, SCA and A Pattern Language – employed as a stand-alone procedure. This is because a participatory scenario helps to identify the aspirations of a whole community, but we need SCA to develop the incremental strategy that helps us to carry it out. Then A Pattern Language enables significant field knowledge to be introduced that SCA alone cannot offer. On the other hand SCA is necessary to establish the connections between the options that entail physical and functional transformations of the territory, and also the non-spatial options such as policy choices in the field of education, social welfare or energy production that, generally, A Pattern Language disregards. Also, the introduction of social, environmental and financial sustainability as comparison areas brings these important future considerations to the attention of local people.

13.8 Fast Forward with Strategic Choice

Mutual consulting for small enterprise development

By Rebecca Herron and Dennis Finlayson

The format of a mutual consulting workshop has recently been found to offer a fast yet effective means of introducing the philosophy and methods of the Strategic Choice Approach to a medium-sized group of experienced decision-makers who have been brought together from different organisational settings through some kind of training or management development programme. For it enables the participants to start interacting with each other quickly in a structured yet informal way, around examples of the decisions and uncertainties that they currently face in their own management roles. The two authors of this contribution draw lessons from the use of this framework when working with owners of small food businesses in the agricultural county of Lincolnshire in eastern England.

Rebecca Herron joined the University of Lincoln in 2000 to direct the Community Operational Research Unit after it moved in 1998 from Northern College in South Yorkshire, where it had been formed 10 years earlier on the initiative of Jonathan Rosenhead while serving as President of the Operational Research Society. Before coming to Lincoln, she worked as planning and development officer for the City of Nottingham Education Department. She holds a doctorate in mathematics and operational research from the University of Leeds.

Dennis Finlayson studied development economics at the University of Southampton then worked on consulting and training contracts in several Asian, African and Latin American countries before coming to the University of Sheffield in 1986 to conduct residential courses for planners and senior administrators from the developing world. Here he met John Friend and started introducing SCA and STRAD as vehicles for enabling the participants to work together on issues facing them in their own development roles. This programme was transferred to the Lincoln School of Management in 1997.

THE FAST PROJECT

In 2000/2001, the authors served as joint co-ordinators of a development project that engaged managers from small and medium-sized enterprises in the agricultural county of Lincolnshire in a programme of learning, reflection and consultancy to strengthen their capacities to adapt to change. This project[1] was supported by the European Social Fund and conducted by a team from the University of Lincoln's Faculty of Business and Management. It enrolled 15 owners and senior managers from local food industries in a series of University-led workshops

---

1 Codenamed FAST, for *Fully Acquainted with Systems Thinking.*

and site-based consulting visits. Different members of staff introduced complementary approaches including Checkland's Soft Systems methodology;[2] Beer's Viable Systems Diagnosis[3] and the Strategic Choice Approach.

THE MUTUAL CONSULTING EXERCISE

After an introductory meeting and overnight stay at a hotel, the programme began with a two-day module to introduce the strategic choice approach as a decision-focused approach to managing complexity, to be followed by further modules that introduced other methods based on systems concepts.

Most of the first day was spent in groups of three, exploring examples of decision problems on each participant's current agenda through a mutual consulting design. This format had already been well received by similar groups, most of which had brought together managers from public sector or voluntary organisations on a management development programme.[4]

Each group started work with a short session in which each participant was asked to offer one example of a difficult current decision problem – in strategic choice terms, a single decision area – that they were prepared to offer for discussion. After a lunch break, there followed a longer and more structured session in which the members of each group rotated through the three roles of problem owner; consultant; and recorder, spending about 30 minutes in each.

The consultant was asked to use a checklist to take the problem owner through a set of

eight questions based on a simplified version of the four modes of strategic choice. Meanwhile the recorder took notes towards building a 'problem profile' to be presented later to members of the other groups. The sequence of questions was as follows:

- Your selected decision problem?
- Who's involved?
- Any related decision problems?
- Options for your selected decision problem? A, B (or C?)
- Advantages to A versus B?
- Uncertainties over preference?
- Explorations to reduce uncertainty?
- Your suggested progress strategy?

Readers of earlier chapters will recognise this sequence as based on a stripped down linear version of the four-mode cycle of the strategic choice approach, as presented in Figure 8, simplified by the requirement to focus on just a single decision area.

THE MUTUAL CONSULTING DAY EVALUATED

We had deliberately chosen the mutual consulting exercise as an early ice breaking activity for several important reasons:

- It requires little complicated background theory;
- It engages all participants and acknowledges the contribution of each (democratisation of the expert);
- It supports different personalities, allowing expression without humiliating the less confident participants;
- It facilitates the speedy identification of major concerns immediately apparent to participants;
- It draws on the business experience of co-participants to cross-examine problematic situations.

This exercise was judged a great success. It served not only to identify business problems but also to act as a social catalyst enabling participants to quickly learn something of the

---

2 See Checkland (1989).
3 Beer (1981).
4 For example a programme on community health services at the University of Leeds; an MBA course at Keele University for health managers from developing countries; and a group of public sector managers attending a residential week for MBA students at Sheffield Business School.

experiences and skills of other members of the network. The process itself created an audible buzz as participants set about their discussions on their favourite topics. The facilitator's role was in this instance mostly one of co-ordination and time-keeping, calling the changes within groups every 30 minutes.

One of the difficulties of discussing live business problems and choices is of course that of trust. How do you discuss the issues of greatest interest to you when potential competitors may be in the room? How much should such a person learn about your personality or response to strategic decisions? Even more basically, how do you avoid embarrassment in expressing your views amongst strangers? These issues had manifested themselves at the launch event of the project prior to the mutual consulting session, with very non-controversial business issues being offered for discussion. However, after the overnight stay in a local hotel the atmosphere softened and one of trust and friendship started to emerge. This had a powerful effect on the subsequent engagement with strategic choice and its software, STRAD.

THE PRESENTATION AND DEMONSTRATION DAY

A week later, all the participants met again to present wall posters of the various problem profiles developed the previous week, in a 'gallery' spread over two walls of the meeting room. They were then asked to use small coloured dots to place votes against those profiles, other than their own, that they were most interested in seeing explored further. By a narrow margin, the most votes went to the profile offered by a sole trader who managed a historic working windmill in a small rural town. This business mills floor in the traditional manner using a wind-powered mill. Not surprisingly much of its business revenue is not from the sale of wholesale flour but from tourism, tearooms and speciality products.

The manager was invited to come to the front of the room to work with John Friend, as organiser of the two-day strategic choice module, acting as facilitator. Another participant volunteered to record the progress made towards building a commitment package using the STRAD software on a laptop computer. The information already displayed in the format of the problem profile was used at a starting point; but it was now possible to work on a focus of a few linked decision areas rather than the single focal decision area required by the problem profiling exercise.

The picture that gradually developed on the screen of the laptop was projected on a wall for all to see. The reliance on a volunteer rather than an expert to operate the keyboard and mouse may have slowed progress somewhat (in that each step in the input of new information had to be spelt out verbally by the lead facilitator – 'now click on X, then type in Y'). However it also made the input process more transparent, as experienced individuals might well be tempted to move through the program too rapidly for those not accustomed to its layout and procedures.

Yet, over the course of little more than an hour, significant progress was made in the shaping, designing and comparing modes, leading into some discussion of the management of uncertainty and the creation of a progress package.

COMPUTER-AIDED FACILITATION REVIEWED

Used in this way, the Strategic Choice Approach was well served by the STRAD software. Instead of a workshop where all participants were already immersed in the problem under consideration, here was a situation where one key decision-maker was surrounded by potential co-facilitators and expert advisers – i.e. the other participants – in addition to the lead facilitator.

This set-up enabled:

- Both broad-brush information and finer detail to be recorded;

- The sole trader as decision-maker to control the development of the SCA model, jointly with the consultant;
- The experience and advice of others to be input at key stages as the decisions were being explored.

An interesting feature of the process was that it enabled the technical detail to be captured through the software whilst the more subtle social aspects were managed through the social interactions of the group. That is, it was not only the model of the decision problem itself that was valuable but the increased understanding gained by the participants through their interaction with each other as the picture gradually built up.

FOLLOW UP THROUGH CONSULTING VISITS

It was valuable that the design of the project enabled the training phase to be followed by a consulting phase in which the training providers visited the participants at their own places of work. John Friend agreed to work with four of the participants – visiting the working windmill twice, and also a partnership making traditional cheeses, a café owner and the manager of a low-price city food shop. Two members of the project steering group, both with extensive knowledge of the food sector, acted as co-consultants on some of these visits.

Whilst the visits had the disadvantage of losing the input from all the other participants that had been possible in the classroom context, it did mean that issues could be explored in more depth. Now it was possible to overcome both the previous time limitations and also the natural reservations that most people have of discussing their most troubling issues in public. Of course, we still do not know what was not being shared with us; but we were now discussing investment decisions and even strategic questions of reorganisation and closure.

CONCLUDING REFLECTIONS

SCA showed once more that it can be a flexible approach, both in the nature of the decisions explored and in the delivery formats and environments used. Its ability to translate quickly from everyday experience was appreciated by the business people participating. While SCA had previously been more widely used in public sector and voluntary fields of decision-making than in the world of business, here was a demonstration that it could also be effective in supporting small businesses where the challenges of development are primarily to do with managing external complexities, rather than with overcoming barriers arising from internal differentiation of roles. Clearly, some difficulties arose from the existence of competitive relations among those present, but these did not jeopardise the success of the exercise. Members of the project steering group also saw a wider potential for use of SCA and STRAD not so much by managers of small businesses themselves as by their business advisers, as a supplement to tools based on financial modelling and other more formal quantitative methods. The second author, from his earlier experience in teaching strategic choice and related methods, saw the mutual consulting workshop as a valuable addition to the SCA toolbox, especially in community development and other relatively open decision settings (Finlayson, 2004).

13.9   The Plutonium Predicament

Managing conflict through strategic action planning

By Richard Harris

This paper is about adapting an SCA tool, the 'Progress Package', to a complex, conflictual and long deadlocked discussion. The process, which became known as 'strategic action planning' (SAP), combines scenario working and strategic planning in addressing a situation of high uncertainty and complexity. The subject was Plutonium (Pu), an important nuclear material, and, more specifically, what to do with the large civil stockpile in the UK that has been built up since the nuclear industry began in the 1940s. This was one of the challenges for the British Nuclear Fuels Ltd (BNFL) 'National Stakeholder Dialogue', a groundbreaking dialogue process independently convened by The Environment Council – an UK charity which aims to enable collaboration and sustainable environmental decision-making.

Richard Harris is an independent facilitator, mediator and process consultant working mainly in environmental conflict management and strategy development. Richard had a first career as a contractor, consultant and local government officer in forestry and arboriculture, working in both Australia and the UK. In 1990 a second career developed with a wider environmental role in local government management. This quickly led to a fascination in the processes by which people can affect the decisions which impact upon their environment, and the growing field of public and stakeholder engagement. In 1998 Richard established his own practice. He took over the facilitation of the BNFL National Stakeholder Dialogue from Allen Hickling in 2001. (See www.the-environment-council.org.uk for all the reports of the dialogue.)

THE CHALLENGE

Plutonium is a thorny subject, not least because of its historic military uses; consequent concerns about proliferation; and perceptions of risk and hazard in nuclear power generation. It is also difficult because of an extensive history of poor relations between the nuclear industry and its critics. This has led to communication, when there is any, being characterised by confrontation.

The project involves up to 120 stakeholder organisations including the industry, departments of central and local government, regulators, trade unions and campaigning (disarmament, environment, transport, etc.) and community groups. The dialogue has been operating since 1998 and seeks to address the long-standing conflicts over nuclear issues whilst informing future policy. Discussions are primarily undertaken in facilitated working groups (12–20 representative stakeholders) and have, not surprisingly, tackled some very challenging subjects.

CONFLICT AND UNCERTAINTY

As with most areas of conflict, the positions adopted by the stakeholders in this case are almost entirely caused by their reaching different sets of assumptions in the face of the same, or similar, uncertainties. These assumptions are typically informed by personal values and beliefs (which tend to be less negotiable), and also by things such as experience and education (which offer more potential flexibility). On a simplistic level these differences result in positional, 'black vs white' arguments about uncertainties such as: whether one option is safer than another, or whether the consequences of an action are likely to be X or Y.

When plutonium management is discussed, it is common for two broad views to emerge. The anti-nuclear view is that it is a dangerous waste and should be immobilised[1] and disposed of without delay. The pro-nuclear lobby considers it a valuable resource which should be reused as a component of fuel for nuclear reactors, thereby realising the energy value for power generation.

So, a key part of the work of the Plutonium Working Group (PuWG) had to include acknowledging and developing a shared understanding of the uncertainties relating to Pu management and perhaps some agreements about how these might be reduced or otherwise managed.

LEARNING AND NEGOTIATION

A significant challenge for the facilitation team lay in developing a process by which a mixed stakeholder group could learn more about the range of strategic options (including their own preferences) and their inherent uncertainties, without resorting to positional, well-rehearsed arguments.

In this it may help to understand that a useful thing to do in deadlocked situations, where the parties seem to have run out of flexibility or room for creativity in their discussions, is to move from a 'negotiating approach', to a 'learning approach'. This is done in the hope that, by enabling the parties to learn more about each others concerns, needs and assumptions, new insights and perspectives on the problem can emerge. The approach we developed became known as SAP.

STRATEGIC ACTION PLANNING (SAP)

The SCA 'Progress Package' provides an excellent framework for strategic planning in the face of uncertainty. So we adapted it for scenario working – an approach which became known as SAP.[2] This would involve the PuWG group in agreeing scenarios which reflected the range of 'possible futures' and then undertaking high level strategic action planning for each, before analysing results and developing recommendations to BNFL. The PuWG worked through four key stages,[3] as follows.

Strategic option selection (Scenarios)

Four scenarios were chosen:

- Two scenarios concerning Pu immobilisation (one in existing plant, one requiring a new immobilisation plant to be built); and
- Two scenarios looking at Pu going into new fuel (one for existing nuclear power stations, one for a new fleet of stations).

Together these provided adequate breadth across the range of 'possible futures' and it was

---

1 Immobilisation involves 'locking up' the Pu in an inert material such as glass (vitrification).

2 Using the term 'strategic action planning' (SAP), to describe the process, clearly appealed to most people. Had we, perhaps more accurately, called it 'strategic options exploration and learning process' few would have supported the approach. As it was, the team had already put much effort into 'selling' 'The Management of Uncertainty' with remarkably little success.

3 The nature of the work was such that it was not quite so linear as this list may suggest; in fact it involved much cyclic working within and between stages.

SCENARIO: USING Pu IN NEW FUEL RODS				
Crucial assumption: Adequate, safe and secure Pu storage will be available over the life time of the fuel manufacture programme				
ISSUE *The heading under which uncertainties arise*	**DECISION** *The current decision*	**EXPLORATIONS** *Required to reduce the uncertainties*	**DEFERRED DECISIONS** *Decisions which can be taken later – usually when the uncertainties have been reduced*	**CONTINGENCY PLANS** *In the event that the assumption turned out to be poor, this activity will be carried out*
		NOW	*LATER*	
Pu STORAGE *(see uncertainties above)*	Continue to use existing stores pending fuel manufacture	By end 2004, assess whether existing storage is safe, safeguarded and structurally sound against risks, now and throughout the envisaged programme	By March 2005, decide how, when and which actions to undertake to ensure that safety, security and safeguards standards are and will continue to be met	In the event that facilities are not adequate in some way – upgrade existing stores or build new stores

Figure 13.3 An Example Showing How an Issue is Managed in an SAP Table.

This is one significant issue within the two scenarios looking at fuel manufacture (i.e. using Pu as a significant component of new fuel rods for nuclear power stations). The time it would take to process all the stored Pu (20 years plus) creates uncertainties relating to the nature and availability of storage facilities, such as: Is current Pu storage capacity adequate? Will it be available over the programme lifetime and will it be able to cope with demand peaks and troughs? Will it continue to be safe and secure over the programme lifetime?

NB This is a simplified extract and some minor changes to the original content have been made to assist the non-technical reader. Each SAP table typically consisted of 6–10 such issue 'rows' most of which were inter-related. For example, the above contingency plan (building new stores) connects with uncertainties under the issue heading 'Regulation' because of secondary uncertainties such as planning requirements and other regulations.

felt that, although there were other possible scenarios, this range should provide adequate learning which could be applied to any other scenario or variant. For each scenario a set of inherent issues and uncertainties were agreed.

Exploring strategic options

The whole group (usually 16–20 in attendance) worked through each scenario, completing a SAP table (see example below) covering all the issues and uncertainties (Figure 13.3). In essence, this involved charting a strategic route, with a focus on short term, robust actions, but mindful of longer-term strategic consequences. It was essential that the group kept together since this was a learning focused process and any sub-group working bought

the risk of the learning being confined to a few.[4] In order to avoid reversion to positions, the group members adopted an attitude that 'this scenario has been chosen for development – the SAP table is being devised to find out what is entailed, not to question its validity (that comes later)'. This drew on the developing trust between group members and provision of a safe working environment (especially through confidentiality and independent facilitation). Without either it would not have worked.

Once a SAP table had been completed for a scenario (typically this took two or three cycles

---

4 See Brendan Hickling's contribution concerning 'differential learning' in Section 13.13 of this chapter.

through the process), all the significant dates were identified and mapped out on a timeline; this gave a graphic view of the strategic option being described. This often revealed critical points in time for example, where a strategic path was weak or vulnerable to early assumptions and decisions turning out to be poor (cf. the contribution from Richard Ormerod in Section 13.4 of this chapter).

Analysis of results

Further analysis involved looking at the results from all the SAPs and timelines together to look for linkages, convergence and divergence. A number of new and significant issues were revealed at this stage, such as: (i) commonality (e.g. where no matter which option was pursued certain areas of research were needed) and (ii) conflict between strategic options (e.g. when adoption of one sub-option might effectively foreclose contingency plans in another).

Crystallising and preparing to share the learning

Effectively, the process now reverted to a negotiating approach, where the common learning was applied as the group set about the task of 'crystallising' what they had learnt into recommendations and conclusions. This resulted in a 'headline' recommendation that a mixed strategy should be developed in the short term to ensure that contingency plans could be well-developed and significant uncertainties could be reduced, through an extensive research programme.

What stood out was the degree to which group members were able to agree. The common ground was extensive (but not complete of course) and exceeded the expectations of many within and outside the group. Clearly, one reason for this was that the SAP work had given each member of the group the opportunity to test the strategic options – both their own preferences as well as options that they would not typically support – in an open, fair and consistent way.

BACK TO THE 'REAL WORLD'

The work was very well received, almost without exception. Many who had not been directly involved in the Working Group reported that they found the content very transparent and easy to understand, and welcomed the clarity about assumptions.

Commonly people expressed surprise at the degree of consensus that the Working Group had developed (only the members will ever really know how hard won that consensus was). One senior civil servant described their report as the 'best analysis of Pu management options that he had seen, and the fact that it was developed by such as wide selection of interests only served to make it more powerful'. The report has been widely distributed in the nuclear industry and government departments. Only time will show its true impact on future policy – but early signs suggest that the key messages are being taken seriously.

CONCLUDING REFLECTIONS

The use of SAP enabled a mixed group of stakeholders to work effectively together on a very difficult issue about which there was a long history of deep-seated conflict. The work was quite time-consuming and at times laborious. However, the results show this to have been a worthwhile investment and commensurate with the complexity and the history of the case. The approach, as briefly described, shows a way forward for both sharing strategic dilemmas and managing strategic decision-making with stakeholders, especially in contentious policy areas.

A number of specific learning points concerning the process are worth highlighting:

- A shift from negotiating toward developing mutual learning can overcome deadlock;
- Uncertainty is a significant source of conflict;
- The language of SCA needs to be adapted for different audiences;
- A 'safe' working environment and independent facilitation are essential;
- Mutual trust, developed with the aid of confidentiality ground rules, is a key to progress;
- Timelines to map strategic options can aid comparison between scenarios.

13.10   Dealing with the Dumps

Using decision areas and levels in developing national policy for used tyres

By Rob Angell

This contribution is focused on the use of Analysis of Interconnected Decision Areas (AIDA) in a project designed to inform UK government policy and general practice by industry and local government over clearing historic used tyre dumps. The work, involving about 150 stakeholders, took place within a stakeholder dialogue process convened by The Environment Council – an UK charity which aims to enable collaboration and sustainable environmental decision-making. Some of the lessons I will draw out of this centre on the use of AIDA and the levels of choice in larger groups; and on getting the concepts across to stakeholders with differing experiences.

Rob Angell has been the lead facilitator and process consultant for a range of clients involving stakeholders in formulating environmental decisions or resolving conflicts. Examples include policy and strategy development for national government and the private sector on waste management; the decommissioning of nuclear power stations; and flood alleviation schemes for the Environment Agency and local government. He has designed and run European wide e-consultations for WWF, and run training courses for the public, private and community sectors on participation, facilitation and sustainable development.

THE PROJECT

The project started in early 2001 when the Environment Agency for England and Wales earmarked tyres as a priority waste stream. The driver was an impending ban on whole tyres going to landfill sites from mid-2003, and shredded tyres from mid-2006. They wanted not only to improve disposal practice and avoid tyre mountains appearing around the country but to increase environmental awareness within the tyre industry. What made this piece of work different was the desire to actively involve stakeholders in deciding how this should be done.

The key stakeholders were the UK government (Department of Trade & Industry); the large tyre manufacturers (such as Michelin); tyre reprocessors and recyclers; the British cement industry (as users of waste tyres as a substitute fuel); English Heritage (as keepers/guardians of land and historic sites); Local government; and the Environment Agency (the main environmental regulator).

THE PROBLEM

Next then, let me describe the problem. For some 30 years there have been large dumps – euphemistically called stockpiles – of old used tyres throughout the UK. A study, carried out as part of this work, listed the locations of 13 stockpiles with 0.5–8 million tyres in each.

These stockpiles have come about in two ways. One is the unscrupulous tyre dealer who pretends to set up a tyre recycling business but just accumulates the tyres and then 'does a runner'. The second is the time that the regulatory system takes in finding out and acting when a registered tyre dealer is acting illegally; and then in pursuing matters through the courts. The end result in both situations is a tyre stockpile.

The dialogue process dates back to July 2001, when I ran the first workshop for a broad range of stakeholders, who agreed that they should 'come up with a recommended approach to clearing the UK's tyre stockpiles'. By mid-2002 they had decided that this work should be done by a working group of about 15 people (on behalf of the 150 stakeholders). Their task became that of developing a generic strategy to guide those who would have to carry out a site clearance; those who would have to co-ordinate a site clearance; and those who were going to provide funding.

THE APPROACH

The working group started by believing that 'there really wasn't anything to it – just secure the funding and clearing the stockpiles would be sorted'.

So, why use AIDA? Well, my rationale was based on this: the stakeholders had a good idea of the underlying issues which have resulted in these stockpiles being untouched for so long, and they seemed eager to delve into each 'problem area'. They were not though considering the interconnectedness of their 'problem areas'; and it was this that I thought was creating the barrier to clearing the stockpiles. The first thing I did was ask them why they were sitting in the room if it was all so easy, and why the stockpiles were still there after 30 years. After kicking around many 'issues', as they saw it, they started to understand there was indeed some complexity to the problem.

It was at this stage that I began to talk to them about thinking of their key issues as areas where decisions would have to be made by anyone wanting to tackle a tyre stockpile. They liked this concept because they saw that if they could work through these decision areas they would be going a long way to having their strategy. After much 'kicking around' we developed an initial set of decision area headings:

- Site after-use
- Location
- Recovery technology
- Partners
- Leadership
- Funding.

Getting to a set of options for each decision area proved a lot more difficult for the group to get to grips with. So, at this stage I introduced them to the concept of levels of choice (cf. Figures 54 and 96). I did this as I sensed that one of the reasons they were finding it difficult to define options was that they were talking at a number of different levels.

It turned out to be a really effective move around the cycle of learning as I could virtually 'see the lights turn on' for a number of the participants. Not only did they really seem to get the concept of levels, but I also felt a change in the group's attitude towards me. They now seemed to trust me as a process person and gave me more 'space' to take them through the AIDA framework.

CYCLIC WORKING

My next move was to help them imagine they had resolved the funding issue and had available as much money as they needed. What would they do to clear the stockpile? I found the discussion within the group fascinating because for some, practicality and immediacy were paramount while for others environmental criteria were more important. There was a further question on funding that the group had to answer: whether solely to satisfy a funder's criterion (such as delivering 'x' number of full time jobs for 'y' period of time), or whether to combine this with their own criteria (such as environmental).

Given that this process was being driven by the UK Environment Agency, the group did accept that environmental legislation was at least the minimum they had to build into their decisions. What this meant in practice was that an option of 'engineered burial' of a stockpile was out of the question (essentially, covering the tyres as they were with inert material and an upper layer of topsoil). Having taken finance as an unlinked decision area I now worked with the group on exploring the linkages between their other decision areas. The result was a reduction in the number of decision areas that they felt they needed to focus on, because it was these that they realised had the strong links between them:

- Leadership
- Funding
- Method of clearance
- Subsequent use of the land.

We spent time working through options for each decision area and working on the uncertainties inherent in these decision areas. I would have liked to have taken the group through the cycle to get to an option tree. However, they were not prepared or interested in doing this as they felt they had got the learning they needed by this stage.

Interestingly, I felt compelled to do an option tree for myself, outside of the group. I really wanted to see if it would bring clarity on what the group should have recommended be done and what they should have recommended be not done. I believe it did.

Nevertheless, the working group were able to draft their recommended strategy for clearing the historic tyre stockpiles in autumn 2003. The paper summarising their work was approved by the main stakeholder group and is available on The Environment Council's website (www.the-environment-council.org.uk).

TWO TYPES OF PARTICIPANT

During the eight months I felt the group unravelled a bit, principally into two segments. One got absorbed in the approach to tackling the issue and became enthusiastic about it, while the other seemed to get almost bored and a bit disconnected. I had to work hard to keep them together.

AIDA is an intense technique that requires close and collaborative thinking. It magnified the gulf between those I call strategic thinkers, and those I call tactical thinkers. The strategists 'got it', the tacticians did not. One notable extreme was the consultants who had been commissioned to carry out the background data research. They simply could not get the reason for approaching the problem in this way at all. They thought that their stockpile survey had come up with the answers and could not understand why the stakeholders did not just see this.

This was highlighted in the extreme when the working group was writing its report. In an early draft, in the section on decision areas, what they meant and why they were important to the recommendations, what the group eventually came up with was left as a 'one liner' – 'to be filled in later'. During one discussion I can recall a participant questioning if they needed to expand on the one line. Thankfully, there was more than one other who replied, before I could, that in fact this was a central part of the group's rationale for what they were saying. It was one of these stakeholders who went on to write this section.

FOR THE FUTURE

Flowing from this is one lesson that was hammered home: that this working group was too big to work through AIDA. It is probably impossible to find a group of 15 people who all happen to be strategic thinkers but, in a smaller group (probably of up to seven), there would have been more time, which would have enabled the strategists and tacticians to learn from each other.

I felt that explaining the concepts in AIDA was a real struggle until I opened a window (the concept of levels of choice) that allowed them to see a different way of thinking and ultimately reporting on their work.

Although you can't push people to do something they don't want to, one thing I could have done was to work through a reduced number of decision areas, to get through (at least as a first pass) this phase quicker. It might have allowed me to get the group to invest some time in an option tree for these elements. Having seen its benefits they might then have had the motivation to cycle back to the other decision areas and on through to a more complete option tree. Indeed, you could argue that the cycle of learning may not be complete without an option tree.

CONCLUDING REFLECTIONS

From a process practitioner's perspective, I found the work completely absorbing because I had to concentrate on the AIDA process as well as helping the group focus on the outcome they had been asked to deliver. However, there were two particularly satisfying parts of this work:

- the participants took on board the concepts of AIDA, notably that interconnectedness between decision areas is important and something you have to work with (and I know that at least one of them has gone on to use them in their work);
- the larger group of stakeholders genuinely appreciated the Working Group's report and the robustness of their work.

13.11 Cross-organisational Learning

Sharing insights from managing major construction projects

By Mike Cushman and Alberto Franco

This contribution reports the main lessons drawn from the experience of developing and applying a strategic choice-based methodology for promoting inter-organisational learning in the construction industry. While the different elements of the resulting methodology reflect those of the traditional SCA, the focus on project review and learning meant that major changes were needed to the original SCA so that participants could engage in reflection and learning rather than in current decision-making.

Mike Cushman is a research fellow at the London School of Economics and Political Science (LSE). Before joining LSE, he worked in community education in inner London for many years, eventually becoming Head of the Lambeth Adult Education Service. He has used problem structuring methods in both his academic research and in his consultancy work. Recent work with strategic choice includes the development of a project review process (with Alberto Franco) and a major review of the provision of Children's Health Services (with Jonathan Rosenhead). He has also worked with John Friend on the development of STRAD.

Alberto Franco is a lecturer in operational research and systems at the University of Warwick. Before moving to the UK from Peru, he worked as a soil mechanics consultant and then as a lecturer in mathematics and operations management. Much of his recent research has focused on exploring how problem structuring methods can assist the development of different types of inter-organisational collaboration. He has held academic posts at the London School of Economics and Political Science, the University of Strathclyde and Kingston University, and conducted research for a number of organisations including Whitbread, Taylor Woodrow, Thames Water and Bombardier.

BACKGROUND

During the mid-1990s, the UK construction industry initiated a move from single-tendered contracts, where the future behaviour of other parties is seen as a marginal consideration, to partnering arrangements, where actions have to be weighed against their effect on future interactions. Partnering was seen as playing a key role in the generation of feedback learning processes, which in turn had been identified as a critical missing process in conventional construction arrangements (Bennett and Jayes, 1998). One way of generating learning in projects is through post-mortems, and indeed construction firms often undertake in-house project reviews. On the other hand, however, there is little tradition of exchanging perceptions with other firms – a lack that has impeded

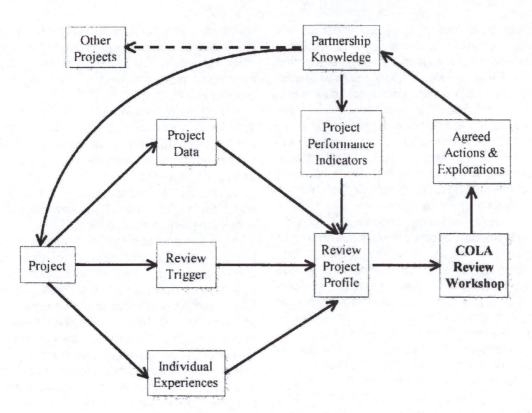

Figure 13.4 The Cross-Organisational Learning Approach (Franco, Cushman and Rosenhead, 2004).

learning throughout the industry (Barlow and Jashapara, 1998).

It was against this background that the authors participated in an action research programme, known as the B-Hive project,[1] and aimed at increasing the value of construction projects. Although both authors were familiar with the Strategic Choice Approach before the project, they had relatively little experience regarding its application in multi-organisational settings. Yet the partnership environment in which the research was developing seemed at the time an appropriate and 'safe' setting for the application of the SCA. That is, there was a setting of multiple stakeholders within

a context of broad agreement which needs to be made operational. Towards the end of the project, strategic choice had become part of a wider framework for cross-organisational learning. The framework, labelled the cross-organisational learning approach or COLA (see Figure 13.4) is aimed at eliciting, reflecting and distributing formal and tacit knowledge within and across partner firms.

THE COLA APPROACH

A key aspect of COLA is a project review workshop which draws significantly on the Strategic Choice Approach (Franco, Cushman and Rosenhead, 2004). One of the main constraints encountered during the research was the lack of time available to conduct one-off project reviews. These had to be carried out

---

1 Engineering and Physical Sciences Research Council and the Department of the Environment Transport and the Regions funded project under the IMI Link/IDAC programme, project no: IMI/c/02/013.

in less than one working day and thus one major innovation and input to the workshop was information collected through a questionnaire. These allowed the facilitators to prepare a list of candidate discussion areas to save time in the workshop. The questionnaire asks participants to rank various aspects of the project and the performance of other firms. These rankings are supplemented by free text comments which usually proved more revealing than the rankings. The questionnaires typically took about 1 hour to complete.

A COLA workshop iterates through four stages: focus, options, plans and commitment, which are derived from strategic choice's shaping, designing, comparing and choosing modes. COLA may make use of some of the distinctive tools of strategic choice, for example decision graphs, or comparative advantage charts. However it is in the emphases of the stages and in the flow of the process between them, rather than in the technology employed within the stages, that the strategic choice influence is most apparent.

During the focus stage, participants identify key opportunities for improvement. However, and this is another departure from traditional strategic choice, they discuss first the project's victories and successes. The discussion is informed by the results of the pre-workshop questionnaire, and the output of this stage is a focus consisting of a set of urgent, important and interconnected opportunities for improvement that is small enough to be manageable during the workshop.

In the options stage, participants are helped to generate options for improvement within the focus chosen in the previous stage. A consideration of the implications of the distinction between single- and double-loop learning (Argyris, 1999) led to another significant change in this stage of the process for later workshops. Options can appear to be self-evidently beneficial, but more deep-seated problems may exist which prevent apparently obvious innovations either being implemented or, if implemented, achieving the inten-

ded improvement. A discussion of possible blockages to action was introduced into this stage, in which discussion was focused on development of initiatives to remove these blockages.

A further constraint at this stage was included in later workshops; actions for debate were limited to those that could preferably be initiated by workshop members or, at minimum, be initiated by their line managers or others that individual workshop members could directly influence. This prevented aspirations masquerading as actions.

The plans and commitment stages closely reflect strategic choice's comparing and choosing modes. The former involves participants in identifying the value criteria needed for the comparison of options for improvement and in evaluating the options against these criteria – though in the process they commonly also uncover uncertainties which stand in the way of identifying a straightforward preferred solution. The latter enables the group to make progress towards agreement in some areas and set up explorations and/or consultations in others (see Agreed Actions and Explorations in Figure 13.4).

LESSONS DRAWN

During the period of the research Whitbread Hotel Company were in the early stages of a partnering arrangement with their service providers for a series of refurbishments of their hotels to meet the standards of their recently acquired Marriott franchise and the construction of new Marriott hotels. Three of the projects completed during the research were the subject of a post-completion review using the COLA workshop. The main lessons drawn from these workshops and others held with Thames Water and Taylor Woodrow are briefly described below.

The use of a pre-workshop questionnaire allowed the intended time saving and compression of the workshop. However, it introduced the risk of a facilitator-imposed agenda and thus it was necessary to explicitly nego-tiate the draft agenda and candidate decision areas with the workshop participants. Members may raise issues in a questionnaire that they would not raise in the workshop and vice versa. Thus the use of the questionnaire, sup-plemented with additional issues identified at the workshop, allows the maximum number of potential issues to be included in the debate.

This pre-description of decision areas is also possible in a conventional SCA workshop, where it is dealing with issues that have already been discussed in a number of fora and the facilitator has access to the records of the previous activities. This allows a fast entry into activities which leads participants to experience progress and build confidence in the benefits of the approach (Cushman and Rosenhead, 2004).

The early consideration of victories and suc-cesses helped to building confidence and avoid a blame environment and a retreat to defens-ive routines. This is particularly relevant to a project review environment where there is a tradition of adversarial relations and lack of trust, but is of wider application. An SCA work-shop will often be held when other approaches have failed and the members bring a his-tory of failure and frustration to the work-shop. Therefore, in order for the workshop to make progress, it is helpful for the facilitator to draw early attention to group successes. While involving representatives of competing interests in the workshop, in the case of COLA different members of a supply chain, may lead to difficulty, it also inhibits loading blame onto others as criticisms must be raised dir-ectly rather than easily passed onto an absent stakeholder.

A focus of concern on blockages to action is an innovation of wider application. In any stra-tegic choice exercise participants may suggest options that may be desired but are not easily attained. A review of possible blockages may cause decision areas to be redrawn to focus attention on necessary actions to achieve a desired state, or options to be discarded as desirable but not attainable in the current exercise. Discussion of blockages may also disclose uncertainties of related areas or uncer-tainties about values.

Similarly the constraint of focusing on actions achievable by the workshop parti-cipants, or at least achievable by people or bodies who may be influenced directly by members of the study group means that that items appearing in the progress package will lead to action rather than failure.

There is one final point of novelty in the application reported here. It can be said that some success has been achieved in apply-ing a strategic choice-based methodology in a process-detached mode of operation (Friend, 1999). This means the use of strategic choice to develop first an idealised state of affairs for the project partners (e.g. a 'zero defects' project) before moving towards the develop-ment of alternative options for action. Strategic choice provided a useful framework for reflec-tion and learning as well as action. Strategic choice can thus form the basis of a methodo-logy to support reflective learning, and the four modes of SCA facilitate learning-based work-shops as well as workshops designed to plan future action.

POSTSCRIPT

Two years after B-Hive, COLA is still used within Whitbread Hotel Company as part of their project review procedures within the part-nership. The COLA processes and tools are now part of the process manual which every project manager should follow, and workshop facilitation is usually undertaken by Whitbread. Whitbread have extended the use of COLA from the Marriott Hotel projects where it was piloted in B-Hive to the much larger pro-gramme of Travel Inn Reservations.

CONCLUDING REFLECTIONS

In conclusion, three main lessons regarding this experience can be summarised as follows:

- Collecting information before a workshop (when possible) leads to a more exhaustive workshop agenda, which can save time and, subject to ratification and amendment by the workshop participants, increase participants' ownership of agenda. This also allows the early identification of potential conflict for which appropriate 'confidence-building' tasks need to be designed and included early in the workshop.
- The explicit elicitation of blockages to action, and identification of activities to overcome them, increases the feasibility of implementation as well as enables the uncovering of uncertainties.
- The use of strategic choice in process-detached (rather than process-engaged) mode is possible and useful.

REFERENCES

ARGYRIS C (1999) On Organizational Learning (Second Edition) Oxford: Blackwell Business

BARLOW J and JASHAPARA A (1998) Organizational Learning and Inter-Firm 'Partnering' in the UK Construction Industry, The Learning Organization, 5 (2), pp. 86–98

BENNETT J and JAYES S (1998) The Seven Pillars of Partnering: A Guide to Second Generation Partnering. London: Thomas Telford Partnering

CUSHMAN M and ROSENHEAD J (2004) Planning in the Face of Politics: Reshaping Children's Health Services in Inner London in Handbook of or/Ms Applications in Health Care (F. Sainfort, M. Brandeau and W. Pierskalla eds) Kluwer, Boston, MA, USA

FRANCO LA, CUSHMAN M and ROSENHEAD J (2004) Project Review and Learning in the Construction Industry: Embedding a Problem Structuring Method within a Partnership Context, European Journal of Operational Research, 152 (3), pp. 586–601

FRIEND J (1999) Process Engagement as a Characteristic of Problem Structuring Methods. Paper presented to the Triennial Conference of the International Federation of Operational Research Societies. Beijing, 16–20 August 1999

13.12   Capacity Building in Venezuela

Using strategic choice methods with policy-makers and students

By Elisenda Vila and Ana María Benaiges

In Venezuela, the Strategic Choice Approach has become increasingly influential in public planning and policy-making since it was introduced in the early 1990s by staff of the Institute of Urbanism in the Central University of Venezuela. It gained added impetus in 1999 when the University's Professor of Planning was appointed as Minister of Planning and Development in the national government. The authors have been involved in applications in the fields of public services management, restructuring of the sugar industry, post-disaster reconstruction and regional economic development. After reviewing the wider background, they review their experience in an application to the management of solid waste on the extensive campus of the Central University. This project influenced management decisions while providing significant learning for the students involved in the work.

Elisenda Vila is a policy adviser to the Venezuelan Ministry of Planning and Development. Through the Venezuelan Institute of Planning IVEPLAN,[1] she runs courses in strategic choice for staff of government institutions including the national oil corporation. In 2002, under contract to IVEPLAN, she translated the second edition of Planning under Pressure into Spanish. After her first degree in architecture and a Master's degree and Doctorate in Urban Planning, she became full Professor at the Institute of Urbanism at the Central University of Venezuela. Here she continues to conduct Master's courses in town planning, policy-making and local action.

Ana María Benaiges is a consultant in planning processes and public services management and a professor at the Institute of Urbanism in the Central University of Venezuela. She graduated in computer science then gained a Master's degree in Urban Transportation Planning. With Victor Poleo, she first applied strategic choice methods to the management of waste in an industrial city in the south of Venezuela. She has since used them in a project on development of the sugar industry for the Ministry of Commerce, and in a review of waste management for the capital city of Caracas.

INTRODUCING NEW APPROACHES TO PLANNING

During the eighties, an informal group of planners in Venezuela, who had become critical of traditional thinking about comprehensive planning, started experimenting with alternatives based on action research principles, including the Strategic Choice Approach. Victor Poleo and members of this group began to

---

1   http://www.iveplan.gov.ve.

introduce courses in these alternative planning methods, first at the Naval Staff College then at the Central University of Venezuela, and to try applying them in practice.

Then, in 1999, one of the leading advocates of this new thinking, Professor Jorge Giordani of the Centre for Development Research at the Central University, was appointed by President Chavez as Minister of Planning and Development in his new national government. Later that year, he invited Jonathan Rosenhead and John Friend to visit Caracas to advise on ways of developing new planning capacities within his Ministry.

Shortly after this invitation, in December 1999, exceptional rains fell on the Avila mountain range separating Caracas from the coast. These rains triggered catastrophic mudslides that engulfed several coastal communities, with heavy loss of life and severe destruction of buildings, infrastructure and livelihoods.

In March and April 2000, representatives of many agencies involved in the response to this disaster were invited to participate in a series of strategic choice workshops addressed towards issues of local and regional reconstruction. John Friend and Jonathan Rosenhead acted as facilitators, with ourselves and other associates acting as co-facilitators and translators. Photographs from one of these workshops appear in Figure 82.

By the time of a further visit by Jonathan Rosenhead and John Friend in 2001, attention had turned to the challenge of developing a legal and policy framework for investment in special economic development zones (ZEDES). These were designed to regenerate employment in rural areas that had become depopulated by a drift of people to the cities in search of jobs.

A PROJECT ON CAMPUS WASTE MANAGEMENT

Meanwhile, on the extensive campus of the Central University of Venezuela, both of us have been involved in the design and management of a participatory project to improve the management of solid waste and thus reduce environmental damage. The site covers 115 ha, within which is contained a range of urban activities equivalent to those of a city of almost 100 000 inhabitants.

The decision-makers in this case included a range of actors both within the University and in other public and private agencies. Also involved in the project were classes of Master's students in urban planning. Not only did they provide a valuable resource for information collection and analysis; at the same time they were able to build an understanding of the complexity of the decisions to be made and of the relationships among the various stakeholders, thus developing their capacities as decision-makers and policy advisers of the future.

The principal agency in the management and supervision of the solid waste services is the university's División de Servicios Generales (DSG), which is responsible for collecting all the non-hazardous waste generated on campus every day through 11 collecting centres, strategically located within the campus. Up to now, the DSG has had no control over the way in which users discard waste at these collecting centres. Inadequacies in the handling of waste could be attributed to lack of container capacity, difficulties in lifting and of course laziness. The disposable bags provided in hallways, on pedestrian routes and on sidewalks are exposed to dogs that rip up the bags and spread the contents. Also the university population tends to discard papers, plastic tumblers and food containers outside the garbage bins, which are sited in open spaces and frequently full. Demolition materials from refurbished buildings are one of the biggest problems because this waste is not taken away by FOSPUCA, the municipal collecting company. For several years, sporadic actions had been taken to deal with the lack of proper and permanent supervision over all the types of waste generated, but with very little success. Then, at the beginning of 1998, a working team was created to improve the university's solid waste management. This brought together the DSG, the university's Institute of Urbanism and its Department of Sanitary Engineering.

The master's students carried out interviews with the various stakeholders to understand their different points of view. The philosophy of SCA was introduced from the outset, so as to approach the problem not in holistic terms but in a selective yet co-ordinated and interactive way.

Our concern was to understand the processes and to identify the possible actions open to the principal stakeholders. Among these were identified the FOSPUCA supervisors, the managers and employees of coffee shops and restaurants, the maintenance chiefs of faculties, the supervisors of green areas, and the student ecological groups.

IDENTIFYING KEY DECISIONS

We experienced some initial difficulties with the students in shaping the dimensions and perceptions of the problem in terms of decision areas. So we tried classifying them by the categories of technical, managerial, political, financial and behavioural. After discussing the links among our initial decision areas, and their degrees of importance, urgency and control, we went on to discuss the choice of a problem focus.

We agreed on two main foci: the one technical/operational, and the other concerned with the behaviours of generators of waste. We decided to study the latter in a separate way, due to its importance and our lack of knowledge in that topic area. The initial focus included the following five decision areas:

1. *COLLECTION?* – how to collect solid waste from the collecting centres? OPTIONS: as now; rent dumper trucks; hire small enterprises.
2. *TRANSFER?* – how to deal with waste not picked up by FOSCUPA? OPTIONS: organise according to type; exclude demolition waste.
3. *TRANSPORT?* – how to pick up waste from producers? OPTIONS: organise waste

transport; DGS collect from each producer; relocate collection centres.
4. *CONSTRWASTE?* – how to manage demolition waste? OPTIONS: DSG in existing role; redesign of contracts.
5. *BEHAVIOUR?* – what to do to change users' behaviour? OPTIONS: UCV campaign in the whole campus; permanent supervision by DSG.

BUILDING A FRAMEWORK OF COMPARISON

A set of four comparison areas was agreed as a basis for evaluating the decision schemes. These were:

1. *COSTS* – associated with each scheme.
2. *CONTROL* – level of control required to guarantee the permanence of the actions.
3. *COMPLEXITY* – could less complex actions be selected to achieve similar expected results?
4. *IMAGE* – impact on the overall image of the university campus.

In addition to these five decision areas and four comparison areas, three further decision areas were introduced later. These concerned the organisation of DSG, the number of collection centres and the composting of green foods. Eight important uncertainty areas were identified, concerned with such matters as danger; legality; payment for service; and the value of a crusher. A first progress package was agreed with the project steering group, including immediate actions in some decision areas. For example:

- **Restructure!** Reorganise and restructure the cleaning section of DSG. The number of workers was increased from 12 to 24 and a supervisor hired for the collection centres.
- **Compost!** Composting of green waste.
- **Supervise!** Supervision of the collection centres and redesign of the collecting system.

- **Contracts!** Remodel building contracts to include demolition waste removal. Exploratory options were agreed to reduce the level of some of the uncertainties that were seen as critical to future decisions. These included:
- **Type UE** – Investigate how dangerous waste is handled now; legality of splitting responsibility from municipal collecting service.
- **Type UR** – How to enforce the remodelled contracts; how to get owners of commercial businesses to pay for waste collection.
- **Type UV** – Would the authorities agree to charge for collecting from businesses; would they agree to pay for a waste crusher.

RESULTS OBTAINED

When these changes were introduced, health and safety and operating conditions improved at the collection centres through the closer supervision from DSG. The accumulation of waste at the centres was cleared through the separation of garbage from cafeterias and faculties, and the relocation of waste containers.

Also, the loading time of the collecting trucks was considerably reduced, demonstrating that, with daily collection and supervision, the number of containers was enough to meet demand. An information system was introduced to monitor waste management inside the campus. Skills were developed within DSG, DIS and IU that enabled them not only to improve daily functioning, but also to commit themselves to continuing research to offer new solutions. Foundations were established to enable the cleaning section of DSG to take on other areas of service identified in the action plan. The project not only contributed to the improved management of waste on the campus site; it also enhanced the environmental and aesthetic rehabilitation of an important national institution, with the capacity to enrich the lives and capacities of future generations of Venezuelan people.

CONCLUSIONS

The example of this project shows how a relatively low-cost application of strategic choice methods can contribute not only to the solution of practical problems of local management, but also to the building of shared knowledge of both problems and methods among managers, university students and their tutors. The commitments to action that resulted were easy to perform and not very expensive, encouraging continuing collaboration among people with different roles and skills.

In Venezuela a wider impetus is now being achieved in introducing flexible methods for structuring complex problems into strategic decision processes, through policy workshops and training programmes involving experienced central policy-makers and managers of institutions, as well as through engaging students in real-time projects at the start of their professional careers. It is hoped that this experience will offer encouragement to innovators in other developing countries who are motivated to construct platforms for the further transformation of traditional planning cultures, at all levels of social organisation from that of local community development to that of national policy.

13.13 Differential Learning

Managing different rates of progress between participants in extensive projects

By Brendan Hickling

This contribution describes a phenomenon we experience on a daily basis in many different ways. The author has named it differential learning, and it occurs where the understanding of an individual or sub-group accelerates away from that of other participants, creating a learning gap. In working with groups in many different contexts he has learnt that it is very important for anyone using the Strategic Choice Approach to be aware of these learning gaps and to be prepared to take steps to mitigate them if serious misunderstandings are to be avoided. Throughout he draws on experience from the BNFL National Stakeholder Dialogue, which is a good case in point because it is an extensive dialogue in which the work is progressed by working groups carrying out in-depth analysis before reporting back their findings to the main project group.

Brendan Hickling is an independent facilitator, mediator and process consultant working in all areas of development in several European countries including the UK. His first exposure to SCA was working with his father (Allen Hickling, co-author of this book) on participative projects and training. More recently he has applied aspects of SCA in helping small to medium-sized organisations cope with growth.

LEARNING AND OWNERSHIP

Our sense of identity as individuals owes a lot to the learning we have accumulated throughout our lives and continue to accumulate with each passing day. As learning is often experienced with associated feelings, such as achievement, loss, relief, frustration, joy and sadness (to name but a few), we are able to see ourselves in what we have learnt and to develop ownership over it. Shared learning gives people a common identity which can bind them together and give them collective ownership over an idea or belief. Little or no shared learning can leave people with the feeling that they do not understand each other or that they have little in common. In the worst case scenarios of strongly opposing learning, such as when two scientific studies appear to give opposite results, people can be set against each other.

Planning is a learning experience which can be shared and therefore owned by as many people who take part in the exercise. The Strategic Choice Approach is at its heart a learning process (cf. Chapter 4). The principles of cyclic learning and working selectively (cf. pp. 21–22) combined with the extensive tool kit provided, enable individuals and groups to make considerable leaps forward in learning in a relatively short time. However there can be a danger in this: in the frequent situation where an individual or sub-group is working on behalf of a larger group or constituency, the sub-group's accelerated learning and ownership of the issues often leaves the others behind. The danger is that, when the sub-group has finished its work, it will not be understood, and further, as they may have developed strong ownership over their ideas, they are very likely to become defensive and closed against any form of criticism.

A startling example of this happened early on in the BNFL National Stakeholder Dialogue (autumn 1999) when a working group (representing the full spectrum of constituencies in the process from environmental groups to industry) had to report on its progress to the main group after six months working on waste management options. They had made good progress and the group had started to develop mutual trust and understanding among themselves, but on the down-side the learning gap between them and the main group had become significant, even although the group's work was still at an early stage.

A progress report was circulated before the main group meeting and the working group was given about an hour to report on progress in the meeting itself. As it turned out this simply was not enough to bridge the learning gap and members of the main group, not really understanding what had been done, started to criticise parts of the report. Some members of the working group took this personally and strongly worded exchanges ensued.

What makes this a particularly interesting example is that the most polarised discussions were between participants who would normally be considered to be on the 'same side' as each other; the differential learning created a perceived shift in loyalties. With some difficulty the facilitators managed to help the stakeholders develop agreement for the working group to continue with its work but it was a close run thing and six months of intensive work was nearly lost. This experience made it clear that a strategy for managing the differential learning was needed if working groups were going to

be an effective tool in this project dealing with very complex and contentious issues.

MANAGING DIFFERENTIAL LEARNING AND SHARING OWNERSHIP

In considering how to manage differential learning, I will focus on the interfaces between the different groups which can exist in an extended project (cf. Figure 84 Organisational Responsibilities in Strategic Choice). Although differential learning does exist in shorter one-off projects, in these circumstances it can usually be managed using workshop facilitation tools which are not the subject of this note.

Exactly how one manages the differential learning in any given project cannot be prescribed. However the over-arching principle is that time must be invested in communication in order to harmonise learning and broaden the ownership base. It can be a considerable challenge for a facilitator to persuade a sub-group, which is making good progress, that it has to stop working on the problem in order to allow sufficient time to consider how they are going to communicate that progress to the others.

I shall now review some of the avenues of communication which can be employed to keep differential learning to a minimum. It is not an either/or list; they should be taken as elements of a multi-level communication strategy.

Newsletters (information giving)

Newsletters are used the world over to keep people informed. Their strength is that they can be used to reach large numbers of people who may be geographically dispersed. Their very great weakness however is that the communication is only one-way. There is no way of knowing what the readers think or even if they have read the newsletter at all. Additionally, as newsletters are by nature very public, they are often inappropriate in contentious issues where it can be very hard to get agreement on what should go in them. In the BNFL National Stakeholder Dialogue it was more than 2 years before a newsletter became feasible.

Newsletters are at their most effective when they are short (easily read) and frequent (providing constant small reminders of what is going on). They can be made slightly more interactive by inviting feedback or even including questionnaires, but there are pitfalls, and the weaknesses mentioned above still apply.

Networking (information giving and gathering, some consultation)

Networking is about taking advantage of the contacts a working group naturally has. Even a small working group has a huge resource of potential feedback, which can be accessed by its members talking to their colleagues and constituents about what they are doing and asking them to do the same with people they meet. Networking is an interactive and responsive way of disseminating information and getting feedback; and it has the added advantage of keeping members of the group in touch with the people and organisations they are suppose to represent. The weakness of networking is that the group's network might not include some key figures and groups; if this is the case then you may need to consider targeted networking.

Targeted networking (consultation)

It is very probable that key opinion leaders and other people or groups of influence are going to be outside of your natural networks and possibly outside the constituencies engaged in the project. Targeted networking is about identifying these people and seeking detailed feedback from them. As with networking this is not about bringing more people into a highly interactive working group; that would defeat the object of having a small group to do the intense analytical work. This is about presenting work in progress and the emerging conclusions, at a time when the overall direction and emphasis can still be influenced.

This kind of communication is the richest and can give the best indication as to whether ongoing work will be understood and accepted. The BNFL National Stakeholder Dialogue used this approach to good effect when key opinion-formers were not directly participating in the process.

Presentation of ideas

When ideas and processes are complex, one must consider carefully how they are presented. There are many ways of presenting information but experience has shown that the very graphic ways of generating and choosing options in the SCA toolkit also work well when it comes to presenting them. The progress package has proved very effective at communicating very complex scenarios and options in the BNFL National Stakeholder Dialogue, especially in the transparent management of uncertainty and exposure of assumptions. (See Richard Harris's contribution for an example, albeit very cut down, of a scenario being presented through the commitment package framework; and also Rob Angell's contribution for an example, from another project, in which the structure of a simple AIDA analysis was used as the basis for presentation.)

Induction meetings

In extensive projects where participation varies over time, considerable disruption is caused by people joining and rejoining the ongoing process afresh. In the BNFL National Stakeholder Dialogue the frustration this caused for the established membership became a serious problem. In the end a ground rule was agreed which stated that newcomers were not permitted to join the dialogue unless they underwent an induction process involving both the facilitation team and participants from all of the key stakeholder groups.

A COMMUNICATION STRATEGY

I have given here some examples of the avenues of communication that can be used and I expect there are many more. However in cases where the work is particularly sensitive a communication strategy is needed to work at multiple levels of participation at the same time. For example: passive information giving, such as newsletters, in parallel with consultative feedback loops to constituencies and opinion leaders, can complement the highly interactive work of a working group. What is certain is that to do nothing to address the potential problems can result in good work being lost simply because it is not understood properly.

CONCLUDING REFLECTIONS

Whenever using the Strategic Choice Approach, but particularly in an extended project where intensive analytical work is carried out by individuals or small groups in isolation from their constituencies, the following is generally true:

Small group learning **without** a communication strategy **leads to** differential learning

Small group learning **with** a communication strategy **leads to** shared learning

The importance of this lies in the different effects of the two:

- The former aggravates misunderstandings between participants and one can expect an ongoing process characterised by disharmony and slow progress;
- The latter provides participants with a sense of ownership of the work which is the essential basis for a broad-based commitment to an agreed way forward.

13.14   Building Commitment in a Rural Community

Use of commitment packages in empowerment through information technology

By Jackie Phahlamohlaka

In community development, it is no simple matter to facilitate a planning process in such a way that the facilitators and the community see it as a learning opportunity. This is especially so if the process includes introducing information and communication technologies; for their adoption and use in such contexts is not yet well-understood. We found that the concept of the commitment package enhances this process of 'learning together' between facilitators and community members. It fits well within an action research framework, enabling both the researcher (facilitator) and the participants (a community) to learn together as they engage in uplifting the lives of the community. The experience reported here involves learning how to improve the lives of a rural community through a local area network (LAN) facility and access to the Internet.

Jackie Phahlamohlaka completed an MSc in Computational and Applied Mathematics at Dalhousie University, Canada in 1991 and a PhD in Informatics from the University of Pretoria in 2003. Before joining the Department of Informatics at the University of Pretoria in 1996, where he is currently a senior lecturer, he served in the strategic planning and statistical services unit in the office of the Premier, Mpumalanga Province. He is a founder member of the Siyabuswa Educational Improvement and Development Trust (SEIDET) and chair of its executive committee. Within the SEIDET context, an opportunity arose in 1998 to apply strategic choice methods alongside John Friend to facilitate a planning workshop as a contribution to the Trust's own evolving planning process.

INTRODUCTION

The aim here is to share with the reader two kinds of situation in which we found helpful either the Strategic Choice Approach, or concepts borrowed from its repertoire. The first occasion is an actual application of SCA in facilitating planning for a rural community education project in South Africa, while the second is an ongoing process of enquiry and further development of the same project, whose design is informed by and accompanied this planning process.

In the language of this book, planning is viewed as a dynamic process of strategic choice, under conditions of uncertainty, resulting in multiple decision outputs. The core concepts of progress package, action scheme, exploratory option and uncertainty area help in organising the decision outputs achieved through the choosing mode. The last two core concepts constitute what we regard as an ongoing process of enquiry. Our experience in using SCA to facilitate a one-day planning workshop for a rural community education project in South Africa partly informed us in the design of an ICT action research study in which we have been actively engaged since the year 2001.

The community education project referred to here is the Siyabuswa Educational Improvement and Development Trust (SEIDET). SEIDET is a community initiated and community based educational project that started in 1991/92, based on the rural town of Siyabuswa in Mpumalanga Province, South Africa.

It started as a supplementary tuition project for high school learners in selected learning areas such as English, Science, Commerce and Mathematics. Over the years, the project has grown from strength to strength. Presently the SEIDET Community Education Centre has two satellites hosted by other institutions at KwaMhlanga (Technikon Pretoria, KwaMhlanga Campus) and Vaalbank (Hlalakahle High School). The main centre in Siyabuswa is a multi-purpose facility providing a variety of educational services and developmental programmes to the local community in association with several other institutions.

AN INITIAL STRATEGY WORKSHOP

On the basis of an annual cycle, SEIDET has developed a process in which the various committees and divisions produce their own plans, and then submit these to the Executive Committee for consolidation into a single organisational plan. Through the writings of Rosenhead (1989) and others, the Executive Committee had become aware of the new generation of participatory problem structuring methods developed by management scientists.

The opportunity to build on this awareness arose when the author was invited by John Friend to visit his University campus in the city of Lincoln, England, in August 1997. A year later, in 1998, John Friend paid an exploratory visit to Zambia and South Africa on behalf of his Centre at Lincoln. SEIDET took the opportunity to invite him, on the final day of his visit, to work alongside the author in facilitating a planning workshop as a contribution to the Trust's own evolving planning process.

A combination of SCA and the nominal group technique was used. Figure 13.5 summarises what the workshop managed to achieve. The positive after effects of the workshop includes an ongoing ICT action research study (Department of Informatics, University of Pretoria). In the next section, I shall focus on the last mentioned after effect, showing how the concept of the commitment package, from the strategic choice repertoire, helped us in designing an ICT action research study at SEIDET.

THE LAN AND INTERNET USE PROJECT

This project is using an action research approach to investigate the community development opportunities brought about by the establishment of a local area network (LAN) and access to the Internet at the community education centre. The purpose of the research is to make a contribution to the further development of the SEIDET project by assisting the Computer Committee of SEIDET to identify the opportunities and possible challenges that may arise from the expanded ICT facilities. In a community-interactive way, the research will then assist the SEIDET community in answering sets of questions while providing the researchers with new perspectives on community development and training.

In the short term, the purpose is to empower the participants and tutors through skills and knowledge acquisition and to assist in structuring the integration of the LAN and Internet technologies with the activities of SEIDET in an efficient way (Phahlamohlaka and Lotriet, 2002).

In the long term, the purpose is to assist the participants in managing and sustaining LAN and Internet-related activities within the context of a rural community education centre.

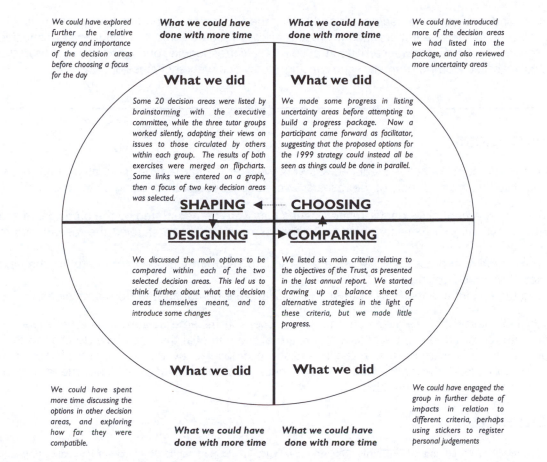

We could have explored further the relative urgency and importance of the decision areas before choosing a focus for the day

What we could have done with more time

What we could have done with more time

We could have introduced more of the decision areas we had listed into the package, and also reviewed more uncertainty areas

What we did

Some 20 decision areas were listed by brainstorming with the executive committee, while the three tutor groups worked silently, adapting their views on issues to those circulated by others within each group. The results of both exercises were merged on flipcharts. Some links were entered on a graph, then a focus of two key decision areas was selected.

What we did

We made some progress in listing uncertainty areas before attempting to build a progress package. Now a participant came forward as facilitator, suggesting that the proposed options for the 1999 strategy could instead all be seen as things could be done in parallel.

SHAPING ◄ ········ **CHOOSING**

DESIGNING ──► **COMPARING**

We discussed the main options to be compared within each of the two selected decision areas. This led us to think further about what the decision areas themselves meant, and to introduce some changes

We listed six main criteria relating to the objectives of the Trust, as presented in the last annual report. We started drawing up a balance sheet of alternative strategies in the light of these criteria, but we made little progress.

What we did

What we did

We could have spent more time discussing the options in other decision areas, and exploring how far they were compatible.

What we could have done with more time

What we could have done with more time

We could have engaged the group in further debate of impacts in relation to different criteria, perhaps using stickers to register personal judgements

Figure 13.5 Overview of Progress in the SEIDET Workshop (Source: Phahlamohlaka and Friend, 2004).

The study seeks to respond to the following set of primary research questions:

- From the perspective of the computer committee (management), what opportunities do these added ICT facilities present?
- What does the computer committee see as new challenges in managing the laboratory brought about by the LAN and access to the Internet?
- What could these developments mean to the local community and to the functioning of SEIDET as a whole?

ACTION RESEARCH WORKSHOPS

In seeking responses to the above questions, eight action research workshops have to date been conducted (March 2001–November 2003). This research – which is continuing – has been designed in accordance with action research principles. It follows a cyclic process of interaction, reflection, action and interpretations between the researchers and the participants. The participants are seven computer committee members of SEIDET. The researchers are two faculty members of the Department of Informatics.

After each session, the participants take the full set of issues raised, the research questions and their new technical skill to the rest of the SEIDET tutors. In the process, the tutors also respond to the issues and questions raised previously while generating new ones.

After a session with the tutors, the participants bring back a new set of responses, issues and questions for negotiation and possible action by the researchers and the process is repeated. The sets of agreed upon action plans are called 'commitment packages', using the SCA term. A commitment package is typically recorded in a tabular format, alongside the corresponding questions and actions of the previous workshop/session.

CONCLUSIONS

The commitment packages produced answers while at the same time generating more questions. The following aspects of the research were experienced as enriching by the researchers:

- The engagement skills on ICT-related issues that were demonstrated by the participants and the questions that were thrown back to the researchers. These enabled the researchers to reflect on the project.
- The negotiation processes that were entered into each time in order to determine the next set of research questions.
- The team spirit and the level of trust that exist and are demonstrated from both sides.

Valuable lessons were also learned in the process. It became evident to us that while the computer committee has become more aware of the potential that they have to change their community, this increased awareness is also accompanied by an awareness of increased responsibility and the critical requirements necessary for further community development through ICT-enabled intervention.

REFERENCES

PHAHLAMOHLAKA LJ and LOTRIET HH (2002) An investigation into community development imperatives brought about by the recent establishment of a local area network and access to the Internet at a rural South African community education centre. Proceedings of the seventh International Working Conference of the International Federation of Information Processing (IFIP) WG 9.4. Bangalore, India, 29–31 May 2002

PHAHLAMOHLAKA LJ and FRIEND J (2004) Community Planning for Rural Education in South Africa. European Journal of Operational Research, *152*, 684–95. Also published online 2003 and is available from Science Direct

13.15   Commitment is the Key

Building inter-agency agreement over the future of an historic estate

By Leny Bregman[1]

When she was appointed Project Leader for the development of the Haarzuilens estate (Figure 13.6), having the Castle (in Dutch Kasteel) De Haar at its centre, the author was faced with many disparate views about its appropriate future use. Plans had already been developed, but no agreement could be reached. She chose to seek consensus over a vision for the estate as it might be 15 years hence, in a two-day multi-agency workshop using the interactive style of the Strategic Choice Approach.

After finishing her study in forestry (1982) Leny Bregman worked as a manager for the Amsterdam Woodland Park Forest. The Park is popular: each year 4.5 million visits are made by 800,000 people of Amsterdam and its outskirts. For the first 7 years she managed the woodland and the visitor's centre. Later on her task was to formulate policies for the Park. She also was responsible for external communication. In 1993 she started working for Natuurmonumenten, the largest non-government organisation for nature conservation in The Netherlands. Her first job was recreation policy. Since 2001 she has been the project leader for the restoration of the Haarzuilens estate.

THE PROJECT

'To each user, be they child or adult, the estate has become their place of many memories – of their first love; a day of roaming about, a childrens' picnic party; or a romantic tour in a horse drawn carriage. They have become aware of the rich history of the region by experiencing the many different aspects of the estate; of nature which has settled there; and of the transformation of the mainly agricultural landscape into an idyllic, green oasis in an otherwise urban area.'

(This is the opening statement of the 2015 vision for the historic Haarzuilens estate, by Bregman and Natuurmonumenten, 10 October 2001.)

In 2000 Natuurmonumenten acquired the Haarzuilens Estate and also became a 50 per cent partner in the Foundation that manages the castle, gardens and grounds (Stichting Kasteel De Haar). The estate comprises 372 ha of agricultural land with 9 farms and 70 buildings in the village of Haarzuilens. Baron Van Zuylen Nijenvelt de Haar previously owned the estate and the castle privately. For a number of years the area had been under some pressure due to a new housing development (called 'Leidsche Rijn') with planning permission for 80 000 new houses to the North West of Utrecht. To provide a recreational zone for the new residents, the central government

---

1 translated from Dutch to English by Martha Vahl, Lincoln

Figure 13.6 Part of the Haarzuilens Estate with the Kasteel de Haar at its Centre, Utrecht, The Netherlands.

had developed a structural development plan (Raamplan) that partly covered the grounds of the Haarzuilens estate. As the Baron and the Province of Utrecht (equivalent to a County Council in the UK) could not agree over the sale of grounds of the estate, this plan failed to be implemented.

Although Natuurmonumenten was critical of the plan's spatial design, it did agree with the principles on which its was based. Usually it acquires land funded by central and local authorities. However, not all the grounds were eligible for such funding. This meant that Natuurmonumenten had to invest a considerable amount of its own capital, even though it was helped by a large donation from 'De Postcodeloterij' (which earns its money through a lottery benefiting charities). The acquisition was justified by the 'nature-near-the-town policy', which Natuurmonumenten had adopted in 1999. Due to unfamiliarity with this policy, and the large sum involved, the acquisition initially could not count on much enthusiasm inside the organisation of Natuurmonumenten.

BEFORE THE WORKSHOP

As the senior officer accountable for the policy document in which the new policy for recreation and for nature-near-the-town had been

laid down, it was obvious that I would experience the acquisition of the Haarzuilens estate as a great idea. This went deeper, however, the moment I heard about the acquisition is engraved in my memory as a 'magic moment'. During this 'magic moment' all the possibilities that the implementation of the new policy would entail leapt to my mind. I saw images of people enjoying a natural landscape. This was a very intense moment. To quote Oliver Sacks: 'Inspiration emerges after intense fascination and concentration, and after a period of distancing oneself. Then suddenly there is the moment of enlightenment, and it becomes clear how things are connected'. (In Psychologie Magazine, March 2002.)

This was what happened to me as well. The only drawback was that I found myself in a situation where very few in the organisation shared my inspiration. On the contrary, people were unsure about the new policy and were criticising the acquisition of the Haarzuilens estate.

In the capacity of project leader I took the initiative to organise an SCA workshop. The aim was to build our team, but also to align the views of those directly involved, both from Natuurmonumenten and the Foundation (Stichting Kasteel De Haar).

While preparing the workshop the Board of Natuurmonumenten introduced additional aims. These included developing a creative vision, co-ordinating the responsibilities of the parties involved and the development of a first action plan. We decided to have a two-day workshop, which would include working in sub-groups, but also a half-day fact-finding and 'acclimatisation' cycle tour across the estate.

A TWO-DAY MULTI-AGENCY WORKSHOP

The workshop started by identifying and naming all the issues. What topics were important? Who were the stakeholders? Next the participants started their cycle tour across the estate. A list of questions was used to explore the surroundings and start the development of a vision. The direct experience of the landscape as well as the opportunity to exchange experiences helped to achieve an open and constructive atmosphere for discussion.

The workshop participants proved able – in a surprisingly short time – to develop four creative visions on the estate, guided by four themes. The visions were:

1. Back to the Middle Ages;
2. Country seat of the twenty-first century;
3. The Utrecht Forest; and
4. Fairytale-Land De Haar.

The following day we were able to get a further handle on the project by mapping the issues already identified as decision areas. In this way it proved possible to increasingly replace most peoples' initial scepticism by trust – in a process of specifying and discussing uncertainties such as: 'Do we have enough money?'; 'Do we have sufficient vision?'; and 'Do we have sufficient experience with large projects?' Elaborating these uncertainties in terms of an SCA progress package: decisions to be made, explorations, deferred decisions, contingency plan (cf. Figure 26), helped to come to terms with the project's complex topic. We concluded that we were dealing with not just one but many interrelated projects, all part of a long-term process. There were issues that required immediate action, but also issues that would not be due for some time. Making this discovery together proved an important breaking point. The insight that we were dealing with many interrelated projects with different time scales helped us realise that we wanted to do too much at the same time. We had to reduce our ambition and divide the work into manageable sub-parts.

AFTER THE WORKSHOP

After the workshop, the learning, which was gained through the creation of the four creative visions, was elaborated to constitute a target vision. This powerful, shared new vision enabled us to inspire and convince other parties. It helped Natuurmonumenten to mobilise a strong lobby so the county authority (the Province of Utrecht) decided to allow for the development of an alternative to the existing structural development plan.

Every phase in a planning process requires internal commitment, but also external interaction with a variety of stakeholders. This interaction has taken, and still takes, much time and energy. In 2002 a first draft design for the alternative structural development plan was produced. It came into being in 2003, in collaboration with the Utrecht Municipality (the City of Utrecht) and the Department of Rural Areas (a regional organisation for plan implementation), under the responsibility of the Land Development Committee (Landinrichtingscommissie). The county authority (Gedeputeerde Staten of Utrecht) is scheduled to discuss the design before the summer of 2004. If it is approved, the implementation is to start in 2005.

EVALUATION OF 'WORKING TOGETHER'

'Natuurmonumenten very much wants to work with others to realise this big project. In the first place this concerns the parties involved in the implementation of the structural development plan Utrecht-West, but also the creative input from farmers, citizens, other folk and entrepreneurs. Naturally, designers and landscape architects are also involved. The varying interplay among Van Zuylen the owner, Cuypers the architect and Copijn the landscape architect at the end of the nineteenth century forms the basis and source of inspiration for today's work.' (This is the concluding statement of the vision of Natuurmonumenten for the Haarzuilens estate by H. Bregman, 10th October 2001.)

The development of the Haarzuilens estate as a 'nature-near-the-town' facility is a long-term process (expected to end in 2013), in which many interrelated projects need to be distinguished and developed in a complex environment of stakeholders from the public as well as the private sector. Since this process will take many years, it will be important periodically to evaluate and adjust the coordination between the projects, while keeping in mind one's own goals. Communication, including lobbying with the various stakeholders, has proved to be an important key towards success and is likely to remain so in the near and distant future.

The current draft design reflects the social and historical aspects of the estate that Natuur-monumenten wishes to retain much better than the original plan. This is in addition to the kind of development of the natural environment it aims to achieve, despite the intensive level of recreation that will develop in the area.

CONCLUDING REFLECTIONS

From this experience I have learned two important lessons, which I would like to pass on to others who might be faced with a similar situation.

- The first is that you do not have to be vastly experienced in SCA to be able to use it. Guidance from experts may indeed be very helpful, maybe even necessary from time to time, but its basis in common sense is its real strength. Combined with the idea that there is no one right way of doing it – there are many good ways – much can be achieved relatively easily.
- The second is that even when SCA plays only a relatively small part in a project, it can be very helpful. In this case the Strategic Choice Approach laid the ground for the team-building that allowed for the development of a powerful target vision. With this vision a strong lobby could be launched to improve on the original structural development plan.

14 The developmental challenge

In this short final chapter, all we wish to do is to draw together some threads from the lessons offered by our contributors to Chapter 13, and from other lessons that the two of us have drawn from our own recent experiences, so as to offer some pointers to further shared progress in the decades ahead. This aim is much the same as that of the closing chapter of our second edition, also called The *Developmental Challenge*; and indeed also the final *Horizons* chapter of our first edition. Yet, in this new twenty-first century edition, a combination of new challenges and new learning points makes it important for us to revisit our earlier speculations about pathways for sustainable future progress.

MAPPING THE CHALLENGES AHEAD

Our final figure – Figure 103 – is a slightly modified version of one that appeared in the closing chapter of our second edition. In it we offer a structured checklist – or what some would term a conceptual map – in which various shared agendas for future development are shown loosely clustered within eight overlapping circles, representing the eight broad spheres of *research*, *education*, *methodology*, *facilitation*, *application*, *communication*, *technology* and *sponsorship*.

The value of any such picture is merely to focus discussion among people who approach these challenges of development from different directions. We have highlighted with bolder outlines the cluster of four spheres that we have positioned in the centre of our map – those of application, facilitation, methodology and communication – because they have long been central to our own primary concerns with action research. Yet several of the contributors to Chapter 13 write from deeper experience in the four important spheres shown in more peripheral positions in Figure 103, concerned with technology, sponsorship, education and research of a more critical academic kind. Here the accent is more on *investment*

in longer-term development of foundations than on impact on pressing decisions. How, we must ask, can the fruits of such investments underpin and complement the learning of those primarily engaged in the management of action research projects?

The thirty-five more specific agendas of development that we show at various positions within the map are again intended to provoke discussion rather than to assert any firm beliefs about their relative significance or positions on the map. What matters is not so much the validity of any such initial picture, as the kind of debate that it can provoke about priorities, linkages, relationships and omissions, as a step towards shared learning by people with different backgrounds of experience and belief.

One brief yet significant opportunity to use the picture presented in Figure 103 as a starting point for this kind of debate arose towards the close of an international working conference held in 1997 at the Lincoln University campus. Here, John Friend had invited twenty consultants, researchers and programme managers from twelve different countries in Europe, Asia, Africa and the Americas to gather for a week, along with staff and postgraduate students of the Lincoln School of Management, to explore ways of

FIGURE
103

Mapping the Developmental Challenge: A Semi-Structured Checklist

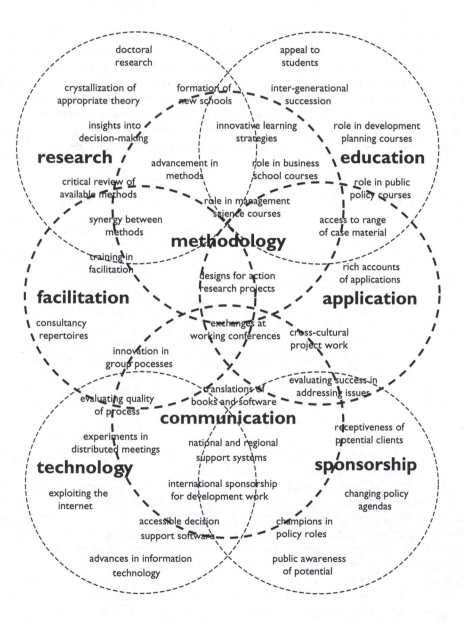

working together in extending the use of the strategic choice approach and related participatory methods in the important cause of building appropriate planning capacities in the developing world.

During a closing session, an enlargement of the map reproduced in Figure 103 was projected on a wall to guide discussion and agreement on priorities for further collaboration. The most immediate priorities that were then agreed included steps to support the six participants from five African countries in coordinating the contributions they might make to that continent's development, supplemented by steps to publish readable accounts of successful applications in developing countries.[1] As a longer-term ambition, a sustained programme of action-oriented research was also proposed over a 5- to 10-year period, to link universities and planning institutions across the world in building a broader momentum of practice-based development of theory and methods on a global scale.

After the participants dispersed, it was not too surprising to those present – most of them well versed in the challenges of planning under pressure – that the initiatives resulting from the conference turned out to be influenced as much by unexpected events – sometimes positively, sometimes negatively – as by the more specific action plan that was agreed among those present. Some promising sponsorship openings were pursued, with modest success; closer working links were forged among the home institutions of several of the participants; strategic choice workshops and demonstrations were arranged in particular developing countries as opportunities arose; and further developments in theory and methods were presented in papers presented at academic conferences or published in journals (see, for example, Finlayson, 2000; Friend, 2001; Phahlamohlaka and Friend, 2004). It is a reflection of the broader products of the conference that several of the contributions to Chapter 13

reflect the links formed through the Lincoln meeting.

DRAWING LESSONS TOGETHER: APPLICATION AND FACILITATION

Because so many of the contributors to Chapter 13 report lessons from their own experiences in facilitating workshops, in very diverse fields of application, it seems relevant to begin drawing together threads by focusing on the central horizontal axis of Figure 103, where the two spheres of *facilitation* and *application* come together.

One striking learning point from several of the applications described in Chapter 13 is that, through various extensions in facilitation and process management methods of the kind described in Chapter 11, the Strategic Choice Approach has shown it can be adapted to support high-level *policy development projects* that bring together stakeholders with widely divergent accountabilities in addressing high-level issues where their positions have long been opposed. This is despite the way in which SCA challenges conventional planning norms, by advocating a selective rather than a comprehensive view of problem scope. Yet recent successes in adapting the Strategic Choice Approach to broader policy agendas by Allen Hickling and his associates, through programmes successively sponsored by the Netherlands government, by international agencies and by the UK Environment Council, have been demonstrating practical ways in which the approach can be adapted to support collaborative work on a broader policy canvas, demonstrating practical ways in which the acknowledged limitations of conventional top-down planning can be overcome.

Meanwhile, other contributors to Chapter 13 describe shorter engagements that have been negotiated in a more opportunistic way around more specific local problems. There will continue to be wide scope for more modest action research engagements of this nature in such fields as participatory community development, small enterprise management and

---

1 It is planned to include some of them in the companion website to this book.

partnership for local action. For here, as much as in broader policy arenas, those in facilitation roles can expect to face challenges of building shared commitment among representatives of stakeholder groups with often deeply conflicting accountabilities. Together, the contributions to Chapter 13 and the illustrations from practice at the end of Chapters 5, 6, 7, 8 and 12 give some flavour of the way in which the variety of applications has continued to increase. We continue to be aware too of applications by other people in other parts of the world. A few of these have been written about in published journals, sometimes with quite specialised readerships. In the list of references will be found English language accounts of applications in Indonesia (van Steenbergen, 1990), in Belize (White, 1994), in Thailand (Kammeier, 1998) and in the favelas of Rio de Janeiro in Brazil (Bredariol and Magrini, 2003). As further new applications are published, it will be possible to keep the list up to date through the *Planning Under Pressure* companion website.

DRAWING LESSONS TOGETHER: METHODOLOGY AND COMMUNICATION

Turning to the vertical axis of the central cluster of spheres in Figure 103, concerned with *methodology* and *communication*, there are other significant learning points to be discussed. In terms of methodology, one significant learning point concerns the importance of learning to *reach out* towards understanding of, and accommodation with, the methods to support decision-making that are already in use by other participants in a planning process. These methods may range from the relatively structured and formal approaches espoused by professionals in many corporate organisations and business consultancies, to the more participatory and informal methods that are increasingly advocated in relatively open fields such as that of local community development.

This is where the challenges of reaching out – of *outreach* – across cultural, linguistic and other divides can become central to the overall communication challenge. It has become evident that not only do those involved in high-level policy development work need tools to enable them to reach out towards greater understanding of the complexities and uncertainties of decision-making faced by those addressing specific problems at a more local level; those local decision-makers themselves also need tools to help them in reaching out towards understanding of the complexities – and the uncertainties – that arise in the often intricate and obscure politics of policy development at the more generic level (Friend, 2001).

FOUNDATIONS FOR FURTHER PROGRESS: SPONSORSHIP AND TECHNOLOGY

Although we believe that the action research focus reflected in the cluster of four spheres in the centre of Figure 103 should continue to be viewed as a leading driver of future progress, we also recognise that developments in the two supporting spheres of *sponsorship* and *technology* shown at the base of Figure 103 can both be viewed as important foundations for sustaining long-term progress.

Investment in sustained *sponsorship* of projects and programmes to support innovation in decision-making will continue to be important if the lessons from future action research engagements are to be fully absorbed and widely shared. It is only realistic to assume that this kind of sponsorship will only be negotiable if future innovators can exercise persuasiveness in attracting support from champions in policy roles, and flexibility in addressing the imperatives of changing policy agendas.

In the story so far of the Strategic Choice Approach, periods of sustained sponsorship over several years have provided foundations for much of the continuing innovation reported both in Chapter 13 and in earlier chapters of this edition. Among the most significant sources of investment have been charitable foundations and government research councils in the earlier years; then departments of the British and Netherlands governments, then directorates of international agencies such as the European Commission and the Organisation for Economic Co-operation and Development. More recently an important role has been played by the UK Environment Council, which is an independent agency drawing wide sponsorship from varied governmental, commercial and voluntary sources to pioneer mediation, training and related services through which to bring together potentially conflicting interests, whether to agree national policy guidelines or to negotiate accommodations on a more local scale.[2]

In reviewing the advancement of *Technology* to support future progress, the most striking change to be acknowledged is the way in which the spectacular recent advances in electronic communication technologies have led to a much higher intensity of global communications through the internet, through e-mail and through mobile communication networks. The rapid diffusion of access to these technologies – from backroom specialists to families and communities, with young people in the vanguard – could scarcely have been imagined even a generation ago.

One consequence of the ever-widening spread of access to communication and information technologies is that computer support to strategic choice has so far found its most promising applications in relatively local applications, rather than in more extensive policy projects. Here is a rich field for experiment in the development of what was described in Chapter 4 as 'open technology' for strategic choice, recognising that there have recently been several other significant innovations in open technology to support dialogue among decision-makers.[3]

2 www.the-environment-council.org.uk.
3 For example, see www.dialoguebydesign.net.

QUESTIONS FOR DEEPER RESEARCH: CONVERGENCE OR DIVERGENCE IN APPROACHES?

Moving to the sphere of research, which we placed in the top-left corner of Figure 103, deeper questions arise about sustaining scientific progress through time. As the approach to which we have given the name *strategic choice* becomes subjected to a variety of interpretations by others, we can ask whether we should expect it to dissolve into some evolving mainstream of knowledge about ways of supporting difficult decisions. Or is there some distinctive core of ideas – or indeed of emergent *theory* – that might be recognised and debated more widely, as a contribution both to decision-making practice and to the growth of human knowledge in a broader sense?

Some pointers towards answers to these questions about distinctiveness can be found by referring back to Chapter 1, where the foundations of the Strategic Choice Approach were discussed. The approach was presented as challenging the four familiar management and planning norms of linearity, objectivity, certainty and comprehensiveness. Instead, a case was made for learning to work with four alternative precepts: those of *cyclicity*, *subjectivity*, *uncertainty* and *selectivity*.

The development of useful theories in management and planning entails striving to draw out common features and differences among specific approaches and methodologies at a more *generic* level, so that they can be subjected to intensive critical debate. In the case of the Strategic Choice Approach, we recognise significant contrasts with some of the other approaches that have emerged in parallel with ours to support difficult decisions – among them those approaches that reflect the more comprehensive perspective that was to emerge from the work of systems scientists in the second half of the twentieth century (Flood and Jackson, 1991).

With its less synoptic emphasis on the making of decisions through time in the face of multiple sources of uncertainty, we can place the Strategic Choice Approach as closer to the recognised world of *decision science* or *decision theory* than to that of systems science. For the origins of SCA lie in opportunities to observe closely, and struggle to understand more clearly, the challenges faced by people attempting to address tough decisions under uncertainty, while working together under insistent yet continually shifting action pressures. Then the more fully developed repertoire of SCA, as discussed in Chapters 5 to 12, has taken shape through wide experiences in active facilitation roles, alongside a growing range of associates and partners in several countries.

THE DEVELOPMENT OF DECISIONS: AN EMERGENT DOMAIN OF THEORY?

As a means of drawing out differences between the approach that we have developed and others based on more synoptic perspectives, the phrase *developmental decision making* was suggested by Friend (1995). He presented the possibility that an awareness of this as an important field of human activity might lead to the recognition of an emergent domain of *developmental decision theory* or *developmental decision science*: a domain within which others in addition to ourselves might be seen as having played a pioneering role.

These phrases were introduced in a speculative vein in the final chapter of our second edition. Since then there has been some debate of alternative phrases that might be less open to misinterpretation – for example a *theory of decision development* or of *decision dynamics*. The important thing is that any such label should convey the richness of the continually shifting relationships among decision problems, and among decision-makers, that marks out the intended field of study, with its implications for planning practice.

Certainly, this kind of language seems to us more apt than any alternative language emphasising systemic relationships in

addressing the social and political as well as the more technical dynamics of the generic field of human activity with which we have been concerned over the last 40 years. We can certainly contend that it was the observable *practices* of developmental decision-making – or of decision development – that have remained our focus ever since our action research began. We can also argue that the methods and process guidelines that we have introduced since then could be described as forming a practical approach to, or methodology for, *developmental decision support*. So could we claim a place among the pioneers of an emergent body of distinctive theory in this hitherto little-explored field?

The purpose of introducing language of this kind is not to add to the range of alternative labels that have already been adopted by others in their interpretations of the particular set of methods that we have been describing as the Strategic Choice Approach. Rather, it is to facilitate constructive debate among proponents, students and users of all the *different* approaches that have been starting to colonise parts of the same emergent field – varying, for example, in their emphasis on the politics of inter-agency negotiation or conflict management. How far, it can be asked, might any of these offer perspectives or insights that can add to what others have done, thereby enriching the wider domain? How far too can they explore in more depth the fundamental differences among different bodies of theory?[4]

We have found that the case for a developmental perspective is especially valuable when working in inter-organisational and other relatively open arenas of decision-making. For in

---

4 For example, it can be hypothesised that one critical difference between the decision orientation and the systems orientation lies in the different concepts of existence of *problems* that is highlighted in Spanish and some other languages by the use of two different verbs 'to be'. The Spanish verb *ser* applies to the *essence* of the subject, whereas the verb *estar* applies to a more transient state of being in some particular *situation*, and is therefore more consistent with a decision orientation than a systems orientation.

such settings it becomes more realistic to treat objectives, purposes and values not so much as foundations to be explored at the outset of a process, but rather as matters to be addressed as and when they emerge, and as relevant to the building of common ground and the sustaining of progress towards agreed decisions. These precepts remain central to our practice and our philosophy. Yet, in the early twenty-first century, we continue to find ourselves engaging with people whose management responsibilities or personal beliefs draw them towards more tightly structured precepts of management and planning, with roots in the more conventional norms of linearity, objectivity, certainty and comprehensiveness – and with little or no recognition of the case for learning to work with more challenging yet rewarding alternatives.

CONNECTING LOCAL AND BROADER PERSPECTIVES ON SUSTAINABLE DEVELOPMENT

One policy field of rising global significance where there is a growing awareness of the case for a developmental approach to decision-making in that of building local capacities for *sustainable development* in more impoverished countries. Another closely related policy field is that of achieving sustainable urban and regional regeneration in older industrial economies. Both fields present similar challenges of learning to link central policy perspectives with the perspectives of disadvantaged local communities, through developing capacities for outreach in both directions. The challenge of helping central policy-makers to learn how to reach out towards clearer appreciation of local concerns is becoming widely recognised (Chambers, 1983; 1997). Less widely recognised, though just as significant, is the reciprocal challenge of developing capacities of outreach from local decision-makers towards central policy sources; so that they can learn to appreciate the uncertainties and the limits of influence, as well as the tangible resources,

which all people with generic policy responsibilities must contend (Friend, 2001).

EMPOWERING FUTURE DECISION-MAKERS

Turning lastly to the sphere of *education*, which we have positioned in the upper-right corner of Figure 103, issues of *inter-generational succession* in sustaining the pace of development have inevitably become of growing significance to both of us, as early pioneers of the Strategic Choice Approach, as we have steadily moved towards retirement age.

One source of potential encouragement lies in the dramatic growth among young people still at school in access to new information and communication technologies (ICT), often leaving those who have grown up with earlier technologies well behind. Many of these young people demonstrate an impressive capacity to put their technological capacities to imaginative use in their leisure pursuits. Yet could these capacities also be harnessed in the cause of facilitating difficult collective decisions, if education and career development channels could be adapted accordingly? What strategies might be devised to steer young people who combine motivations to influence significant decisions with impressive ICT skills towards career paths involving expertise in the facilitation of developmental decision-making, whether close to their own local communities or in wider policy arenas? What is the potential to link such people together in imaginative forms of mutual support networks, reaching across levels of choice and across cultures?

The concept of *empowerment* of people who start from a position of little power to influence the developmental decisions that impinge on their future lives has become a potent driver of policy change in many parts of the world. Yet one lesson from our own recent action research experiences, as well as from the experiences of several of our contributors, is that it is not only members of disadvantaged local communities that tend to feel a lack empowerment in decision-making; so too do many people in central policy roles who struggle to find effective means of exercising greater leverage over intricate local decisions. This explains the concern of many policy-makers and policy advisers with the design of increasingly sophisticated procedures of formal performance measurement and policy evaluation; yet it is apparent that they face serious conceptual and practical difficulties in shaping such procedures in order to engage with complex issues of a more subtle developmental nature.

It will not be enough to pursue new ways forward either solely through high-level policy debates, or solely through debates within local decision networks on issues of more specific local concern. The facilitators of the future will have to be sufficient in number, and widely enough diffused through civil society, to be able to develop and sustain rich connections both between and within levels, and across cultural divides, if the base of shared understanding is to continue to expand.

The interlocking challenges that we have attempted to draw together in Figure 103 can only realistically be addressed through the influence and inspiration of people in many kinds of role – managers, planners, teachers, researchers, students, consultants, political leaders, community entrepreneurs.

Such a diffusion will be important if successive generations of decision-makers and facilitators are to be helped to make imaginative use, selectively and adaptively, of innovative approaches to interactive planning and learning of the kind that we have presented on these pages.

If the dialogue that we have opened up by inviting a number of other people to contribute to this third edition of *Planning Under Pressure* can be sustained into the future through other channels – not least, through the companion website that our publishers have offered – then the dynamics of action research and action learning has the potential to gather momentum in ways that match both the resources for global communication now open to us, and the scale of the global issues calling for collective action.

For the various pointers to more appropriate practice, theory and learning that we have brought together here are built on many peoples' experiences in planning under pressure in many settings and at many levels. The working lives of all these people are finite; yet there can be no respite in the challenges facing them and their successors who will come to share responsibility for the sustainability of life on our troubled planet as this new century unfolds.

Access to further information

MAKING USE OF OUR COMPANION WEBSITE

The second edition of *Planning under Pressure* concluded with a short section entitled *A Guide to Further Reading*, followed by another even shorter section entitled Points of Contact. Inevitably, the information in both these sections showed a tendency to become out of date with the passage of time.

However, In this new twenty-first century edition, we now have a means to surmount this problem, through the resource of a companion website that has been afforded us by our publisher Elsevier. This means that, whenever you call up the address **http://books. elsevier.com/companions/0750663731**, you will be able to find references to further reading and points of contact which we intend to keep continually up to date.

One of our contributors to Chapter 13, Brendan Hickling, has agreed to act as our link with the Elsevier website and as coordinator of whatever new contributions to it may come in from time to time.

Should readers wish to offer any learning points from their own experience that they think might be useful to other readers, they are invited to contact Brendan by e-mail at the address given on the website. Because we cannot predict how many readers will respond in this way, we cannot guarantee that what you say will find a place on the website. However, if you are motivated to write briefly about your experiences and what you have learnt from them, or to send in questions addressed to other readers, please get in touch with Brendan by e-mail. You may, of course, make

reference to other websites where further supporting information will be found.

On the main menu of the website will be found the following options:

- **About the book** – basic information on contents and translations.
- **Action learning forum** – including latest news on applications of Strategic Choice Approach and discussion of learning points.
- **Books** – updated guide to further reading, and additions to the bibliography.
- **Contacts** – latest contact details and news about the two authors, the 21 invited contributors and related institutions - including links to other websites.
- **Learning resources** – this section includes answers and comments relating to the exercises printed at the end of Chapters 2 and 3. It also includes guidance on ways of organising short courses for practitioners, and interactive learning programmes for postgraduate and undergraduate students. It is planned too to include references to other sites from which handouts can be ordered on realistic small group exercises from different fields of planning and management that have been designed by the authors and their associates for courses that they have run in various countries.
- **Software** – latest information on the availability of supporting software.

FURTHER READING: GENERAL

All references to published books and papers that were cited in the lists of references in earlier editions have been retained in the bibliography that follows this section. Most of the publications that are not already cited in earlier chapters will be cited in this guide.

Starting with publications in the English language, earlier accounts of the Strategic Choice Approach will be found in Friend and Jessop (1969, second edition 1977); in Friend, Power and Yewlett (1974); in Hickling (1974) and in Rosenhead and Mingers (eds) (2001) – in which Strategic Choice Approach is presented in two chapters by ourselves together with chapters on other interactive problem-structuring methods. Accounts of relevant early work by colleagues in the Tavistock Institute will be found in Higgin and Jessop (1965), Harary, Jessop, Luckman and Stringer (1965); Crichton (ed.) (1966); Luckman (1967) Stringer (1967) and Morgan (1971).[1]

Later overviews of the work of IOR within the Tavistock Institute will be found in Friend, Norris and Stringer (1988); Friend (1997) and Friend, Bryant, Cunningham and Luckman (1998).

Any future additions to this list will be posted on the companion website.

FURTHER READING: APPLICATIONS

References to early applications of the Strategic Choice Approach will be found in Friend, Wedgwood-Oppenheim et al. (1970); Bunker (1974); Bather, Williams and Sutton (1976); Hickling (1978); Decker et al. (1978); Dekker and Mastop (1979) and van der Graf (1985). Other published applications which we were able to include as references in the second edition included Hickling (1989); van Steenbergen (1990); Ling (1990); Moullin (1991); Thunhurst et al. (1992); Khakee and Stromberg (1993); Swanson (1994) Holt (1994); White (1994); Friend (1994) and Ormerod (1995, 1996a, 1996b).

Not all these sources are easily accessed. Two important additions that we can make to

the list as this edition goes to press – both published in Elsevier journals – include Kammeier (1998) and Bredariol and Magrini (2003), referring to recent applications in Thailand and Brazil respectively. Other published applications are already referenced here in contributions to Chapter 13: Ormerod (1998, 1999); Horlick-Jones, Rosenhead et al. (2001); Kain (2003) and Phahlamohlaka and Friend (2004).

It is planned to extend the list of references to applications further after this edition goes to press, by short direct accounts of applications in the Action Learning Forum section of the website and by additions to the bibliography.

FURTHER READING: LANGUAGES OTHER THAN ENGLISH

An abridged **German** translation of *Local Government and Strategic Choice* was published in 1973 (Friend and Jessop, 1973), while the first edition of *Planning under Pressure* was translated into **Japanese** by Hirotaka Koike et al. (Friend and Hickling, 1991). This was followed by a **Spanish** translation of the second edition, sponsored by IVEPLAN in Venezuela (Friend and Hickling, 2002).

In addition, briefer guides to the Strategic Choice Approach have been published in several other languages. The earlier guides were adapted from an English language handbook by Allen Hickling, first published in Britain (Hickling, 1974) and subsequently in extended form in Canada (Hickling, 1976). The languages involved in these handbooks were **Dutch** (Hickling, Hartman and Meester, 1976); **French** (Hickling, Wilkin and Debreyne, 1980) and **Portuguese** (Hickling, 1985).

Later guides to the approach have been published in **Swedish** (Strömberg, 1986); **Bahasa Indonesia**: (Ismail, Setiabudi and van Steenbergen, 1989); and again Dutch (Hickling and de Jong, 1990). Any future additions to this list will be posted on the companion website.

WIDER READING

Some of the other publications included in the bibliography serve to set the Strategic Choice

---

1 A full set of reports and other documents resulting from the work of IOR and its successor unit the Centre for Organisational and Operational Research has been lodged in the Modern Records Centre at the University of Warwick, along with other OR records co-ordinated by the Archives Committee of the Operational Research Society.

Approach in the context of wider developments in such varied fields as strategic business management, problem structuring methods, urban and regional planning theory, operational research; project management; and participatory community development.

These include such books as Bryant (1989); Eden and Radford (eds)(1990); Ritchie, Taket and Bryant (eds)(1994); Wilcox (1994); Trist, Emery and Murray (eds)(1997); Mingers and Gill (eds)(1997); Wyatt (1999); Salet and Faludi (eds)(2000); Rosenhead and Mingers (eds)(2001); Webb (2003) and Midgley and Ochoa-Arias (eds)(2004).

Between 1977 and 1983, several reports on advances in applications and ideas relating to inter-organisational planning appeared in a series of seven issues of the newsletter *LINKAGE* published through the Tavistock Institute of Human Relations (Friend, Laffin, Norris and Ogden (eds)(1977–83). *LINKAGE* was initially published in association with a research programme on inter-organizational relations supported by a grant from the Social Science Research Council (now ESRC).

The contributions of the work of the 'IOR School' to the development of planning theory are reviewed from both European and North American perspectives in a special issue of the journal *Planning Theory* (Mandelbaum, ed., 2004) (Bryson, Ackerman and Eden, 2004) (Burns, 2004) (Faludi, 2004) (Friend, 2004b) (Needham, 2004).

Bibliography

ACKOFF RL (1970) A Concept of Corporate Planning. New York: Wiley

ACKOFF RL (1974) Redesigning the Future. New York: Wiley

ACLAND AF (1990) A Sudden Outbreak of Common Sense: Managing Conflict through Mediation. London: Hutchinson Business Books

ACLAND AF (1995) Resolving Disputes without Going to Court. London: Business Books

ALEXANDER C, ISHIKAWA S and SILVERSTEIN M (1977) A Pattern Language. Towns – Buildings – Construction; New York: Oxford University Press.

AMES SC (1993) A Guide to Community Visioning: Hands-on Information for Local Communities, Oregon Vision Project, American Planning Association (Oregon Chapter); Oregon, Portland.

ARGYRIS C (1999) On Organizational Learning. Oxford: Blackwell

ARGYRIS C and SCHÖN DA (1973) Organisational Learning: A Theory of Action Perspective. Menlo Park: Addison-Wesley Publishing

ASHBY WR (1956) An introduction to Cybernetics. London: Chapman & Hall

BALBO M (1975) La Pianificazione come Processo di Scelte Strategiche. In: P. Ceccarelli (ed.) Potere e Piani Urbanistica. Milano: Franco Angeli Editore

BARLOW J and JASHAPARA A (1998) Organizational Learning and Inter-Firm 'Partnering' in the UK Construction Industry, The Learning Organization 5 (2), pp. 86–98.

BATHER NJ, WILLIAMS CM and SUTTON A (1976) Strategic Choice in Practice: The West Berkshire Structure Plan Experience. Reading, UK: University of Reading, Geographical Paper No. 50

BATTY SE (1977) Game-Theoretic Approaches to Urban Planning and Design. In: Environment and Planning B 4, 211–39

BEER S (1966) Decision and Control. Chichester: Wiley

BEER S (1981) Brain of the Firm. Chichester: Wiley

BENNETT J and JAYES S (1998) The Seven Pillars of Partnering. A Guide to Second Generation Partnering; London: Thomas Telford Partnering

BENNETT P (1980) Hypergames: Developing a Model of Conflict. In: Futures 12, 489–507

BENNETT P (1985) On Linking Approaches to Decision Aiding: Issues and Prospects. In: Journal of the Operational Research Society 36, 659–69

BENNETT P and HUXHAM CS (1982) Hypergames and What They Do: A 'Soft OR' Approach. In: Journal of the Operational Research Society 33, 41–50

BENNETT P, CROPPER S and HUXHAM C (1989) Modelling Interactive Decisions: The Hypergame Focus. In: Rational Analysis for a Problematic World, ed. J.V. Rosenhead. Chichester: Wiley

BION WR (1961) Experiences in Groups. London: Tavistock Publications

BREDARIOL CS and MAGRINI A (2003) Conflicts in Developing Countries: A Case Study from Rio de Janeiro. In: Environmental Impact Assessment Review 23, 489–513

BREURE A and HICKLING A (1990) Coping with Unconventional Projects: A 'Socio-Technical' Approach. In: Handbook of Management Projects, ed. R. Garies. Vienna: Manz

BRYANT JW (1989) Problem Management. Chichester/ New York: Wiley

BRYANT JW (1993) OR Enactment: The Theatrical Metaphor as an Analytical Framework. In: Journal of the Operational Research Society 44, 551–61

BRYSON JM, ACKERMAN F and EDEN C (2004) Contributions of Planning Under Pressure. In: Planning Theory 3, 3

BUNKER R (1974) Making Decisions in St Albans. In: Built Environment 1974, 316–18

BUNKER BB and ALBEN BT (1997) Large Group Intervention: Engaging the Whole System for Rapid Change. Jossey-Bass

BURNS T (2004) A Practical Theory of Public Planning: The Tavistock Tradition and John Friend's Strategic Choice Approach. In: Planning Theory 3, 3

CARTWRIGHT TJ (1992) STRAD: A New Role for Computers in Planning. In: Computers, Environment and Urban Systems, 16, 77–82

CHAMBERS R (1983) Rural Development: Putting the Last First. Harlow: Longman

CHAMBERS R (1997) Whose Reality Counts? Putting the First Last. London: Intermediate Technology Press

CHECKLAND PB (1981) Systems Thinking, Systems Practice. Chichester: Wiley

CHECKLAND PB (1989) Soft Systems Methodology. In: Rational Analysis for a Problematic World, ed. J.V. Rosenhead. Chichester: Wiley

CHILD J (1972) Organisational Structure, Environment and Performance: The Role of Strategic Choice. In: Sociology 6, 2–22

CLARK AW (1976) Experimenting with Organisational Life: The Action Research Approach. New York: Plenum

CRICHTON (ed.) (1966) Interdependence and Uncertainty: A Study of the Building Industry. London: Tavistock Publications

CUSHMAN M and ROSENHEAD J (2004) 'Planning in the Face of Politics: Reshaping Children's Health Services in Inner London' in Handbook of OR/MS Applications in Health Care (F. Sainfort, M. Brandeau and W. Pierskalla eds) Kluwer, Boston, MA, USA

DALKEY NC (1969) The Delphi Method: An Experimental Study of Group Opinions. Memorandum RM-5888-PR. Santa Monica, Calif: Rand Corporation

DEKKER F and MASTOP P (1979) Strategic Choice: An Application in Dutch Planning Practice. In: Planning Outlook 22, 87–96

DEKKER F et al. (1978) A Multi-Level Application of Strategic Choice at the Sub-Regional Level. In: Town Planning Review 49, 149–62

DELBECQ AL, VAN DE VEN AH and GUSTAFSON DH (1975) Group Techniques for Programme Planning. Glenview, Illinois: Scott Foresman and Company

DELLO P (1985) Strategic Choice and Evaluation: Some Methodological Considerations. In: A. Faludi and Voogd H (eds) Evaluation of Complex Policy Problems. Delft: Delftsche Uitgevers Maatschappi

DOYLE M and STRAUS D (1976) How to Make Meetings Work: Jove

EDEN C (1989) Using Cognitive Mapping for Strategic Options Development and Analysis (SODA). In: Rational Analysis for a Problematic World, ed. I.V. Rosenhead. Chichester: Wiley

EDEN C and ACKERMAN F (1998) Making Strategy: The Journey of Strategic Management. London: Sage

EDEN C and JONES S (1984) Using Repertory Grids for Problem Construction. In: Journal of the Operational Research Society 35, 779–90

EDEN C, JONES S and SIMS D (1983) Messing about in Problems. Oxford: Pergamon

EDEN C, JONES S, SIMS D and SMITHIN T (1981) The Intersubjectivity of Issues and Issues of Intersubjectivity. In: Journal of Management Studies 18, 34–47

EDEN C, WILLIAMS H and SMITHIN T (1986) Synthetic Wisdom: The Design of a Mixed Mode Modelling System for Organisational Decision Making. In: Journal of the Operational Research Society 37, 233–42

EDEN C and RADFORD J (eds) (1990) Tackling Strategic Problems. London: Sage

EMERY FE and TRIST EL (1972) Towards a Social Ecology: Contextual Appreciation of the Future in the Present. London: Plenium

ETZIONI A (1968) The Active Society: A Theory of Societal and Political Processes. New York: The Free Press

FALUDI A (1973) Planning Theory. Oxford: Pergamon

FALUDI A (1984) The Return of Rationality. In: M.J. Breheny and A.J. Hooper (eds) Rationality in Planning. London: Pion Press

FALUDI A (1986) Critical Rationalism and Planning Methodology. London: Pion Press

FALUDI A (1987) A Decision Centred View of Environmental Planning. Oxford: Pergamon

FALUDI A (2000) The Performance of Spatial Planning. In: Planning Practice and Research, Vol. 15, No. 4, pp. 299–318

FALUDI A (2004) The Impact of a Planning Philosophy. In: Planning Theory 3, 3

FALUDI A and MASTOP JM (1982) The IOR School – The Development of a Planning Methodology. In: Environment and Planning B 9, 241–56

FALUDI A and VALK AJ van der (1994) Rule and Order: Dutch Planning Doctrine in the Twentieth Century. Dordrecht: Kluwer Academic Publishers

FERGUSON MJ (1979) A Strategic Choice Approach to Recreation Site Resource acquisition. In: Town Planning Review 50, 325–45

FINLAYSON DE (2000) Internal Legitimacy, Community Development, Action Research and Development Evaluation. In Proceedings of 44th Annual Meeting of the International Society for the Systems Sciences, Toronto.

FINLAYSON DE (2004) Embedding Research and Evaluation in Community Regeneration Projects. In: Proceedings of 48th Annual Conference of the International Society for the Systems Sciences. California

FISHER R and BROWN S (1989) Getting Together: Building a Relationship that Gets to Yes. London: Business Books

FISHER R and URY W (1981) Getting to Yes. London: Hutchinson

FLOOD RL and JACKSON MC (1991) Creative Problem Solving: Total Systems Intervention. Chichester: John Wiley

FLOYD M (1978) Structure Plan Monitoring: Looking to the Future. In: Town Planning Review 49, 476–85

FRANCO LA, CUSHMAN M and ROSENHEAD J (2004) Project Review and Learning in the Construction Industry: Embedding a Problem Structuring Method within a Partnership Context. In: European Journal of Operational Research 152 (3), pp. 586–601

FRIEND JK (1976) Planners, Policies and Organisational Boundaries: Some Recent Developments in Britain. In: Policy and Politics 5, 25–46

FRIEND JK (1977) The Dynamics of Policy Change. In: Long Range Planning 10, 40–7

FRIEND JK (1980) Planning in a Multi-Organisational Context. In: Town Planning Review 51, 261–9

FRIEND JK (1988) Building on Public Sector Wisdom. In: Management Development in the Public Sector: A European Perspective, R. Kakabadse, P. Brovetto and R. Holzer (eds). Aldershot: Avebury

FRIEND JK (1989) Planning as Responsible Scheming. In: Operational Research and the Social Sciences, ed. M.C. Jackson, P. Keys and S.A. Cropper. New York: Plenum

FRIEND JK (1989) The Strategic Choice Approach. In: Rational Analysis for a Problematic World, ed. J.V. Rosenhead. Chichester: Wiley

FRIEND JK (1990) Handling Organizational Complexity in Group Decision Support. In: Tackling Strategic Problems: The Role of Group Decision Support, C.L. Eden and J. Radford (eds). London: Sage

FRIEND JK (1990) Planning Concepts, Planning Contexts. In: Systems Practice 3, 195–206

FRIEND JK (1992) New Directions in Software for Strategic Choice. In: European Journal of Operational Research 61, 154–64

FRIEND JK (1993) Searching for Appropriate Theory and Practice in Multi-Organisational Fields. In: Journal of the Operational Research Society 44, 585–98

FRIEND JK (1993) The Strategic Choice Approach in Environmental Policy Making. In: The Environmental Professional 15, 164–75

FRIEND JK (1993) Planning in the Presence of Uncertainty: Principles and Practice. In: Journal of Infrastructure Planning and Management (Japan), 4761 IV-21, 1–9

FRIEND JK (1994) Community Involvement in Health Strategy in Tower Hamlets. In: Community Works, eds C. Ritchie, A. Taket, J. Bryant. Birmingham: Operational Research Society

FRIEND JK (1995) Supporting Developmental Decision Processes: The Evolution of an OR Approach. In: International Transactions in Operational Research 2, 225–32

FRIEND JK (1996) Strategy on the Run: Decision Support for Hard-Pressed Managers. In: IT Support in the Productive Workplace, ed. J. Chapman. Cheltenham: Stanley Thornes

FRIEND JK (1997) Connective Planning: from Practice to Theory and Back. In: The Social Engagement of Social Science. Volume III: the Socio-Ecological Perspective, eds E.L. Trist, F. Emery and H. Murray. Philadelphia: The University of Pennsylvania Press

FRIEND JK (1998) Operational Choices and Strategic Spatial Planning. In The Revival of Strategic Spatial Planning, eds W. Salet and A. Faludi. Amsterdam: Royal Netherlands Academy of Arts & Sciences

FRIEND JK (1999) Process Engagement as a Characteristic of Problem Structuring Methods. Paper presented to the triennial conference of the International Federation of Operational Research Societies, Beijing, August 1999. (Journal of the Operational Research Society 56, forthcoming)

FRIEND JK (2001) Engaging with Transient Complexity in Development Projects. In: Understanding Complexity. Kluwer/Plenum, London for International Society for the Systems Sciences

FRIEND JK (2004a) Perspectives of Engagement in Community Operational Research. In: Community Operational Research: OR and Systems Thinking for Community Development, eds G.R. Midgley and A.E. Ochoa-Arias. New York: Kluwer/Plenum

FRIEND JK (2004b) A Future for the Non-Academic Planning Theorist? In: Planning Theory 3, 3

FRIEND JK and HUNTER JMH (1970) Multi-Organisational Decision Processes in the Planned Expansion of Towns. In: Environment and Planning 2, 33–52

FRIEND JK and JESSOP WN (1971) Hvad er Planlaegning. In: BYPLAN 23, 134–40

FRIEND JK and JESSOP WN (1973) Entscheidungsstrategie in Stadtplanung und Verwaltung. German translation by Zwirner WGO. Dusseldorf: Bertelsmann

FRIEND JK and JESSOP WN (1977) Local Government and Strategic Choice: An Operational Research Approach to the Processes of Public Planning (Second Edition). Oxford: Pergamon [First Edition (1969) – London: Tavistock Publications]

FRIEND JK and HICKLING A (1991) The Strategic Choice Approach. Japanese translation of Planning under Pressure by H. Koike et al. Tokyo: Gihodo

FRIEND JK, POWER JM and YEWLETT CJL (1974) Public Planning: The Inter-Corporate Dimension. London: Tavistock Publications. Reprinted (2001) in the International Behavioural and Social Science Library, Routledge

FRIEND JK, LAFFIN MJ and NORRIS ME (1981) Competition in Public Policy: The Structure Plan as Arena. In: Public Administration 59, 441–63

FRIEND JK, NORRIS ME and STRINGER J (1988) The Institute for Operational Research: An Initiative to Extend the Scope of OR. In: Journal of the Operational Research Society 39, 705–13

FRIEND JK, BRYANT DT, CUNNINGHAM JB and LUCKMAN J (1998) Negotiated Project Engagements: Learning from Experience. In: Human Relations 51, 1509–42

FRIEND JK, WEDGWOOD, OPPENHEIM F et al. (1970) The LOGIMP Experiment: A Collaborative Exercise in the Application of a New Approach to Local Planning Problems. London: Centre for Environmental Studies (refer to Tavistock Institute of Human Relations)

GIANDRANDE A and MORTOLA E (1996) L'ipertesto per l-applcazione de Strategic Choice a Venezia. In: La Qualita dell'ambiente (ed. Mortola). Milano: Francoangeli

GLASER B and STRAUSS AL (1967) The Discovery of Grounded Theory. Chicago: Aldine

GTZ (1991) Methods and Instruments for Project Planning and Implementation. Eschborn: Geselischaft fr Technische Zusammenarbeit

GUPTA SK and ROSENHEAD J (1968) Robustness in Sequential Investment Decisions. In: Management Science 15, 13–18

HALL P (1980) Great Planning Disasters. London: Weidenfeld & Nicholson

HAMMERSLEY M and ATKINSON P (1995) Ethnography: Principles in Practice, 2nd edition. Routledge

375

HARARY F, JESSOP WN, LUCKMAN J and STRINGER S (1965) Analysis of Interconnected Decision Areas: An Algorithm for Prohect Development. In: Nature 206, 118

HART DA, HICKLING DA, NORRIS ME and SKELCHER CK (1980) Regional Planning Methodology. London: Tavistock Institute of Human Relations. Internal Paper 2T/436

HAWKINS L and HUDSON M (1986) Effective Negotiation. Melbourne: Information Australia

HICKLING A (1974) Managing Decisions: The Strategic Choice Approach. Rugby: Mantec (refer to Tavistock Institute of Human Relations, London)

HICKLING A (1976) Aids to Strategic Choice (Second Edition). Vancouver: University of British Colombia, Centre for Continuing Education

HICKLING A (1978) AIDA and the Levels of Choice in Structure Plans. In: Town Planning Review 49, 459–75

HICKLING A (1979) Aids to Strategic Choice Revisited. London: Tavistock Institute of Human Relations. Internal Paper 2T/226

HICKLING A (1981) Abordagerm da Escolha Estrategica. Sao Paulo: Fundacao do Desenvolvimento Administrativo

HICKLING A (1982) Beyond a Linear Iterative Process. In: B. Evans, J. Powell and R. Ralbot (eds) Changing Design. Chichester: Wiley

HICKLING A (1985) Evaluation is a Five Finger Exercise. In: A. Faludi and H. Voogd (eds) Evaluation of Complex Policy Problems. Delft: Delftsche Uitgevers Maatschappij

HICKLING A (1989) Gambling with Frozen Fire? In: Rational Analysis for a Problematic World, ed. J.V. Rosenhead, Chichester/New York: Wiley, pp. 159–92

HICKLING A (1990) Decision Spaces. In: Tackling Strategic Problems, C. Eden and J. Radford. eds London: Sage

HICKLING A and DE JONG A (1990) Mens en Beleid. Leiden/Antwerpen: Stenfert Kroese Uitgevers

HICKLING A, HARTMAN R and MEESTER JG (1976) Werken met Strategische Keuze. Alpen aan den Rijn: Samson Uitgeverij

HICKLING A, WILKIN L and DEBREYNE F (1980) Technologie de la Decision Complexe: Des Aides pour l'Elaboration des Choix Strategiques. Bruxelles: Universite Libre de Bruxelles, Centre E Bernheim pour l'Etude des Affaires

HIGGIN G and JESSOP WN (1965) Communications in the Building Industry: The Report of a Pilot Study. London: Tavistock Publications

HILL M (1968) A Goals–Achievement Matrix for Evaluating Alternative Plans. In: Journal of the American Institute of Planners 34, 19–28

HILL M (1985) Decision-Making Contexts and Strategies for Evaluation. In: A. Faludi and H. Voogd (eds) Evaluation of Complex Policy Problems. Delft: Delftsche Uitgevers Maatschappij

HOLT J (1994) Disarming Defences. In: OR Insight 7 (4), 19–26. Birmingham: Operational Research Society

HORLICK-JONES T, ROSENHEAD J, GEORGIOU I, RAVETZ J and LÖFSTEDT R (2001) Decision Support for Organisational Risk Management by Problem Structuring. Health Risk and Society 3 (2), 141–65

HOWARD N (1971) Paradoxes of Rationality: The Theory of Metagames. London: MIT Press

HOWARD N (1989) The Manager as Politician and General: the Metagame Approach to Analysing Cooperation and Conflict. In: Rational Analysis for a Problematic World, ed. J.V. Rosenhead. Chichester: Wiley

HUXHAM C (ed.) (1996) Creating Collaborative Advantage. London: Sage

ISMAEL M, SETIABUDI T and VAN STEENBERGEN F (1989) Modul Pendekatan Pilihan Strategis (in Bahasa Indonesia). Aceh: Bappeda Provinsi Daerah Istimewa Aceh

JACKSON MC (1992) Systems Methodology for the Management Sciences. New York: Plenum

JAGO L and NORRIS M (1981) Training in interOrganisational Working: An Experimental Course. In: Linkage six. London: Tavistock Institute of Human Relations

JAGO L et al. (1983) Strategies for Working between Organisations: A Training Experience Reviewed. In: Linkage seven. London: Tavistock Institute of Human Relations

JONES S and EDEN C (1980) OR in the Community. In: Journal of the Operational Research Society 32, 335–45

KAIN JH (2003) Sociotechnical Knowledge. An Operationalised Approach to Localised Infrastructure Planning and Sustainable Urban Development. Chambers University of Technology, Göteborg

KAMMEIER HD (1998) A Computer-aided Strategic Approach to Decision-making in Urban Planning: An Exploratory Case Study in Thailand. In: Cities 15 (2) pp. 105–19

KELLY GA (1955) The Psychology of Personal Constructs. New York: Norton

KELLY GA (1972) A Theory of Personality. New York: Norton

KHAKEE A and STROMBERG K (1993) Applying Futures Studies and the Strategic Choice Approach in Urban Planning. In: Journal of the Operational Research Society 44 (3), 213–24

KOLB DA (1984) Experiential Learning. New Jersey: Prentice-Hall

KRAVATZKY AJ (1995) Hiview and Equity: Decision Analysis for Environmental Management. In: PARKS. The International journal for Protected Area Managers 5 (1), 32–45

LEITH M (1997) The CLGI Guide to Large Group Interventions. Amsterdam: The Centre for Large Group Interventions

LICHFIELD N (1966) Cost-Benefit Analysis in Town Planning. A Case Study: Swanley. In: Urban Studies 3, 215–49

LICHFIELD N (1985) From Impact Assessment to Impact Evaluation. In: Evaluation of Complex Policy Problems. Delft: Delftsche Uitgevers Maatschappij

LICHFIELD N, KETTLE P and WHITBREAD M (1975) Evaluation in the Planning Process. Oxford: Pergamon

LINDBLOM CE (1965) The Intelligence of Democracy: Decision Making through Mutual Agreement. New York: Free Press, London: Collier-MacMillan

LING M (1990) Making Sense of Planning Evaluations: A Critique of Some Methods. In: Planning and Development (Hong Kong), 6 (1), 14–20

LUCKMAN J (1967) An Approach to the Management of Design. In: Operational Research Quarterly 18, 345–58

MANDELBAUM S (ed.) (2004) A Symposium on the Work of John Friend. In: Planning Theory 3, 3

MASON RD and MITROFF II (1981) Challenging Strategic Planning Assumptions. New York: Wiley

MIDGLEY GR and OCHOA-ARIAS AE (eds) (2004) Community Operational Research: OR and Systems Thinking for Community Development. New York: Kluwer/Plenum

MILLER EJ and RICE AK (1967) Systems of Organization. London: Tavistock Publications

MINGERS J and GILL A (eds) (1997) Multimethodology. Chichester: Wiley

MOCKLER RJ and DOLOGITE DG (1991) Using Computer Software to Improve Group Decision-Making. In: Long Range Planning 24, 4447

MOORE CM (1987) Group Techniques for Idea Building. London: Sage

MORGAN JR (1971) AIDA – A Technique for the Management of Design. IOR Monograph No. 2. London: Tavistock Institute of Human Relations

MORTOLA E (ed.) (1996) La Qualita dell'ambiente. Milano: Francoangeli

MOULLIN M (1991) Getting Planners to take Notice. In: OR Insight 4 (1), 25–9. Birmingham: Operational Research Society

NEEDHAM B (2004) John Friend: Advising and Theorising. In: Planning Theory 3, 3

NEUMANN JE, HOLTI R and STANDING H (1995) Change Everything at Once! Didcot: Management Books 2000

NORRIS ME (1985) Operational Research and the Social Sciences: Review of Local Government and Strategic Choice. In: Journal of the Operational Research Society 36, 870–2

NUNAMAKER JF, DENNIS AR, VALACIO JS, VOGEL DR and GEORGE JF (1991) Electronic Meeting Systems to Support Group Work. Communications of the ACM 34 (7), 40–61

OPEN SYSTEMS GROUP (1981) Systems Behaviour (Third Edition). London: Harper & Row

OPENSHAW S and WHITEHEAD P (1986) The Decision Optimising Technique: History, Development and Progress Towards a Future Machine Based Planning System. In: K.G. Willis (ed.) Contemporary Issues in Town Planning. Aldershot: Gower

ORMEROD R (1983) Corporate Planning and its use of OR in the NCB: A Personal View. In: Journal of the Operational Research Society 34, 461–7

ORMEROD R (1995) Putting Soft OR Methods to Work: Information Systems Strategy Development at Sainsbury's. In: Journal of the Operational Research Society 46, 277–93

ORMEROD R (1996a) Information Systems Strategy Development at Sainsbury's Supermarkets using 'Soft' OR. In: Interfaces 26, 102–30

ORMEROD R (1996b) Putting Soft OR Methods to Work: Information Systems Strategy Development at Richards Bay. In: Journal of the Operational Research Society 47, 1083–97

ORMEROD R (1998) Putting Soft OR Methods to Work: Information Systems Strategy Development at Palabora. In: Omega International Journal of Management Sciences 26, 75–98

ORMEROD R (1999) Putting Soft OR Methods to Work: The Case of the Business Improvement Project at PowerGen. In: European Journal of Operational Research 118, 1–29.

OWEN HH (1992) Open Space Technology – A User's Guide, Cabin John, MD: Abbot Publishing

PAULEY GS and ORMEROD R (1998) The Evolution of a Performance Measurement Project at RTZ. In: Interfaces 28, 94–118

PHAHLAMOHLAKA LJ and FRIEND JK (2004) Community Planning for Rural Education in South Africa. In: European Journal of Operational Research 152, 684–95

PHAHLAMOHLAKA LJ and LOTRIET HH (2002) An investigation into community development imperatives brought about by the recent establishment of a local area network and access to the Internet at a rural South African community education centre. Proceedings of the seventh International Working Conference of the International Federation of Information Processing (IFIP) WG 9.4: Bangalore, India, 29–31 May 2002

PHILLIPS LD (1982) Requisite Decision Modelling. In: Journal of the Operational Research Society 33, 303–12

PHILLIPS LD (1990) Decision Analysis for Group Decision Support. In: Tackling strategic problems: the Role of Group Decision Support, C. Eden and J. Radford (eds). London: Sage

RAIFFA H (1968) Decision Analysis. Reading. Mass: Addison-Wesley

REVANS RW (1983) The ABC of Action Learning. Bromley: Chartwell-Bratt

RICE AK (1965) Learning for Leadership – Inter-Personal and Inter-Group Relations. London: Tavistock Publications

RICKARDS T (1974) Problem Solving through Creative Analysis. Epping: Gower Press

RITCHIE C, TAKET A and BRYANT J (1994) Community Works: 26 Case Studies of Community OR in Action. Birmingham: Operational Research Society

ROBINSON I (ed.) (1972) Decision-Making in Urban Planning: An Introduction to New Methodologies. London: Sage

ROSENHEAD JV (1978) An Education in Robustness. In: Journal of the Operational Research Society *29*, 105–11

ROSENHEAD JV (1980) Planning under Uncertainty: II A Methodology for Robustness Analysis. In: Journal of the Operational Research Society *31*, 33–42

ROSENHEAD JV (ed.) (1989) Rational Analysis for a Problematic World. Chichester/New York: Wiley

ROSENHEAD JV and MINGERS J (ed.) (2001) Rational Analysis for a Problematic World Revisited. Chichester/New York: Wiley

SAATY T (1980) The Analytical Hierarchy Process. New York: McGraw-Hill

SAGAR T (1993) Paradigms for Planning: a Rationality-Based Classification. In: Planning Theory *9*, 79–118

SCHARPF FW (1972) Komplexitat als Schranke der Politischen Planung. Politische Innovation und Gesellschafliche Wandel: Politische Vierteljahresschrift

SCHNELLE E (1973) Metaplan: Op Zoek naar Doelstellingen Leerproces an Medewerkers Betrokken. Amersfoort: DHV

SCHON DA (1971) Beyond the Stable State: Public and Private Learning in Changing Society. London: Temple Smith

SHAKUN MF (1995) Restructuring a Negotiation with Evolutionary Systems Design. In: Negotiation Journal *11* (2), 145–50

SÖDERBERG H and KAIN J-H (2002) Integrating Knowledge or Aggregating Data – Multi-Criteria Approaches for Sustainable Water and Waste Systems. Proceedings of 3rd International Conference on Decision-Making in Urban and Civil Engineering, London

STRINGER J (1967) Operational Research for Multi-Organisations. In: Operational Research Quarterly *18*, 105–20

STRÖMBERG K (1986) Planera met Onsakerheter! (in Swedish) Stockholm: Byggforskningsradet

STRÖMBERG K (2001) Facilitating Collaborative Decision Development in Urban Planning. Scandinavian Journal of Architectural Research *4*

SUSSKIND A and CRUIKSHANK J (1987) Breaking the Impasse: Consensus Approaches to Resolving Public Disputes. New York: Basic Books

SUTTON A and WILKIN L (eds) (1986) Related Socio-Technical Approaches to the Management of Uncertainty. Dordrecht: Martinus Nijhoff

SWANSON J (1994) Sending out the Right Packages. In: The Surveyor (UK), 18 August

TAKET AR and WHITE LA (2000) Partnership and Participation: Decision-Making in the Multiagency Setting. Chichester: Wiley

THUNHURST C, RITCHIE C, FRIEND JK and BOOKER P (1992) Housing in the Dearne Valley: Doing Community OR with the Thurnscoe Tenants Housing Co-operative. Part I – the Involvement of the Community OR Unit. In: Journal of the Operational Research Society *43*, 81–94

TRIST EL, HIGGIN GW, MURRAY H and POLLOCK AB (1963) Organizational Choice. London: Tavistock

TRIST EL and MURRAY H (eds) (1990) The Social Engagement of Social Science. Volume I: The Socio-Psychological Perspective. London: Free Association Books

TRIST EL and MURRAY H (eds) (1993) The Social Engagement of Social Science. Volume II: The Socio-Technical Perspective. Philadelphia: The University of Pennsylvania Press

TRIST EL, EMERY, F and MURRAY H (eds) (1997) The Social Engagement of Social Science. Volume III: the Socio-Ecological Perspective. Philadelphia: The University of Pennsylvania Press

URY W (1991) Getting Past No: Negotiating with Difficult People. London: Business Books

VAN AKEN JE (2004) Management Research based on the Paradigm of the Design Sciences: the Quest for Field-tested and Grounded Technological Rules. In: Journal of Management Studies *41–2*, 219–46

VAN DE GRAAF R (1985) Strategic Choice in LPG Policy. In: A. Faludi and H. Voogd (eds) Evaluation of Complex Policy Problems. Delft: Delftsche Uitgeres Maatschappi

VAN GUNDY AB (1981) Techniques of Structured Problem Solving. New York: Van Nostrand Reinhold

VAN STEENBERGEN F (1990) The Strategic Choice Approach in Regional Development Planning. In: Third World Planning Review *12* (3), 301–04

VICKERS G (1965) The Art of Judgement. London: Chapman & Hall

VOGEL DR (1993) Electronic Meeting Support. In: The Environmental Professional *15*, 198–206

WATSON SR and BUEDE DM (1987) Decision Synthesis. Cambridge: Cambridge University Press

WEBB A (2003) The Project Manager's Guide to Handling Risk. Aldershot: Gower

WEDGWOOD-OPPENHEIM F (1972) Planning Under Uncertainty. In: Local Government Studies *2*, 53–65

WHITE L (1994) Development Options for a Rural Community in Belize – Alternative Development and Operational Research. In: International Transactions in Operational Research *1* (4), 453–62

WILCOX D (1994) The Guide to Effective Participation. Brighton: Partnership Books

WORLD BANK (1996) The World Bank Participation Sourcebook. Washington DC: The World Bank

WYATT R (1999) Computer-Aided Policymaking: Lessons from Strategic Planning Software. London: E & FN Spon

Index